GEORGE WASHINGTON'S OPPONENTS

British Generals and Admirals in the American Revolution

Books by George Athan Billias

INTERPRETATIONS OF AMERICAN HISTORY:
PATTERNS AND PERSPECTIVES, *Co-editor*.

THE AMERICAN REVOLUTION:
HOW REVOLUTIONARY WAS IT?, *Editor*.

LAW AND AUTHORITY IN COLONIAL AMERICA,
Editor.

GEORGE WASHINGTON'S GENERALS, *Editor*.

GENERAL JOHN GLOVER AND HIS MARBLEHEAD
MARINERS.

MASSACHUSETTS LAND BANKERS OF 1740.

GEORGE WASHINGTON'S OPPONENTS

British Generals and Admirals in the
American Revolution

Edited by

GEORGE ATHAN BILLIAS

CLARK UNIVERSITY

WILLIAM MORROW AND COMPANY, INC.

NEW YORK　1969

Grateful acknowledgment is made to:

Alfred A. Knopf, Inc. for permission to reprint the maps entitled "The Theater of War in New York and New Jersey," "The Northern Theater of War," and "The Campaign of 1781" from *Portrait of a General* by William B. Willcox, © copyright 1962, 1964 by William B. Willcox.

Harper & Row, Publishers, Incorporated, for permission to reprint the map entitled "Campaigns in New York State" from *The American Revolution 1775-1783* by John Richard Alden (Harper & Row, 1954).

The Macmillan Company for permission to reprint the map entitled "Seat of War in the Southern States 1775-1781" from *The War of the Revolution* by Christopher Ward.

Longmans, Green & Co. Limited for permission to reprint the map entitled "The Caribbean and Central America" from *War for America 1775-1783* by Piers Mackesy.

Library of Congress Catalog Card Number 69-11350

To Herbert J. Bass: sound scholar, gifted teacher, and gentle friend.

Contents

Illustrations appear between pages 78–79.

Preface

THIS BOOK is a collection of interpretive essays covering some of the most important generals and admirals who served on the British side during the American War of Independence. One purpose of the volume is to present the findings of recent scholarship. Few reliable biographies about such men were available before the 1940's. Since that time, however, two definitive studies have appeared—John R. Alden's account of General Thomas Gage and William B. Willcox's Bancroft Prize-winning work on General Henry Clinton. Piers Mackesy's book, *The War for America, 1775–1783*, moreover, devoted much attention to an analysis of the character and capabilities of numerous high-ranking officers. British cabinet members as well as commanders in the field have been subjected to closer scrutiny in the last few years. Recent writings on the leaders in London—Bradley D. Bargar's study of William Legge, Earl of Dartmouth, as American secretary; Gerald S. Brown's monograph on Lord George Germain as American secretary from 1775 to 1778; Alan Valentine's biographies of Lords North and Germain; and George Martelli's life of John Montagu, Earl of Sandwich, as first lord of the Admiralty—have told us more about the war effort mounted by the mother country. Much of this latest scholarship on Britain's statesmen was revisionist in nature and has necessitated a reevaluation of her military leaders.

A second aim of this book is to view the Revolutionary War in a broader perspective than has been done in the past. The authors have tried at times to remove military history from the narrow confines of battles and campaigns, and to discuss the war instead in terms of the complex problems of strategy, logistics, and civil-military relations facing the British. In this same vein, the writers have often explored the degree to which military decisions for the North American theater of operations were dictated by political considerations.

This book, conceived as a companion volume to *George Washington's Generals,* admittedly has certain inherent limitations in its organization. Because of restrictions of space, only a few of the major British generals and admirals are discussed; the editor alone bears the responsibility for the selection. The essays, moreover, concentrate solely upon an officer's military career during the Revolutionary War in the American theater of operations. Thus, Admiral Howe's triumphs in European waters in 1782 and the careers of General Cornwallis and Admiral Hood in subsequent wars are not dealt with. Also, primary attention is focused upon naval affairs in the North Atlantic; very little has been said about important campaigns in Caribbean waters. Finally, there is some unavoidable repetition in these essays because many of the generals and admirals under discussion participated in the same military operation.

The contributors to this volume are all scholars who have written previously in the area of military history. Although they may disagree in many of their judgments, as editor I have let their conclusions stand unchanged in the best interests of scholarship.

I should like to express my thanks to many individuals who gave me a helping hand. To my contributors, I am obligated for their part in this book. My major thanks in this regard must be reserved for Professor William B. Willcox of the University of Michigan, who not only contributed two selections but kindly consented to review and comment on the other essays. To my fellow historians—Dean Milton M. Klein of the State University of New York at Fredonia, Dr. Clifford K. Shipton, former Director of the American Antiquarian Society, and Professor Gerald N. Grob of Clark University—I am indebted for reading parts of the manuscript. To my graduate students—Lawrence Kazura and Mrs. Barbara Rosenkrantz—I am grateful for certain insights into the character of General Burgoyne. And to my wife, Joyce Baldwin Billias, I am beholden once again; she helped me on this book, provided inspiration during the task, and, as always, contributed to my happiness.

The book is dedicated to an old friend, Herbert J. Bass, whose personal and professional qualities I have admired for many years.

G.A.B.

Introduction

To WHAT extent did the quality of British military leadership affect the outcome of the Revolutionary War in America? The war was *lost*, some scholars insist, because British commanders on land and sea were guilty of incompetent leadership—bungling their assignments, resorting to outmoded strategy and tactics, and demonstrating a lack of desire for an all-out victory on many occasions. The war was *won*, other historians argue, because Washington and his colleagues exercised superior generalship—adopting sounder strategy, applying shrewder tactics, and motivating their men with a greater desire to win. Almost two centuries have passed since the fighting began, but the debate regarding the relative importance of British military leadership goes on.

The answer may be supplied, in part, by studying those generals and admirals who conducted operations in North America. Of course, such an answer can only be a partial one. Viewed in the broadest possible setting, it is clear that the outcome of this war was profoundly influenced by nonmilitary factors—diplomatic, economic, and constitutional considerations—over which these men had no control. Even if the conflict is evaluated strictly in military terms, any judgment on the performance of British commanders is complicated by other circumstances. The Revolutionary War was only one part of a world-wide struggle in which Britain was involved from 1775 to 1783. The depth of that involvement is sometimes overlooked: hostilities with France, Spain, and Holland as well as America; threats of invasion of England itself; struggles to maintain control of the seas and the Channel; attacks upon Canada, the West Indies, and Gibraltar; the war in India; and popular unrest in Ireland and other parts of the realm. It was little wonder, then, that the Ministry relegated the war in America to a position of secondary importance at certain stages. The demands of the army and navy in this theater of operations often had to be balanced against those needs in other parts of the globe; and not infrequently the requests of British commanders in America for men and materials were given a lower priority. Finally, many of the major strategic decisions were made by cabinet ministers in London rather than by men in the field.

The assessment of any British general or admiral must take into account the period of the war during which he was in command. For this purpose, the Revolutionary War may be conveniently divided into two phases—the periods before and after France's entry into the war. In the first phase—the colonial phase from 1775 to 1778—Britain faced two major problems: the military struggle with the American colonies abroad and the political struggle at home. Despite her military and naval supremacy throughout the first phase, Britain's commanders were unable to deal a decisive blow in America. Political divisions on the domestic scene between those who backed a policy of coercion toward the American colonies and those who favored a policy of conciliation also made it more difficult to carry on the war. During the second phase—the international phase from 1778 to 1783—Britain's problems grew even more acute. Military leaders now could count on a stronger united front in the homeland because France and Spain, her traditional foes, had come into the war. But Britain was forced to cope with this coalition of enemies on the continent and to fight a global war. From 1778 on, British armies and fleets in the American theater had to conduct their operations under the constant threat of enemy sea power. Between the first and second phases, the character of the war was completely altered.

When fighting first broke out, British commanders in America appeared to possess an overwhelming military superiority. All the advantages, it seemed, were on their side. They could depend upon a professional army—a well-equipped, experienced, and disciplined force; a navy that outnumbered American ships of war by one hundred to one; financial resources which would permit the hiring of foreign troops to supplement the regular army; the cooperation of American loyalists who formed a significant portion of the colonial populace; and a bureaucracy in Britain to provide a system of command.

But as the war wore on, many disadvantages became apparent and certain advantages decreased or disappeared. Two of the most decisive disadvantages were geographical in nature—the vastness of America and the width of the Atlantic. Invading British armies found it impossible to conquer or occupy the far reaches of the North American continent. The three-thousand-mile supply line from Britain to America proved cumbersome and costly. Another disadvantage was the military assistance America increasingly received from her ally, France. Many of Britain's earlier advantages, moreover, were sharply diminished with the passage of time. The army was undermanned and given greater responsibilities as the war spread to other parts of the world. The navy—Britain's most powerful military machine— was forced to stretch its resources thin, as France, Spain, and Holland sent out hostile fleets to attack the home island and parts of the empire. The system of public finance was found to be weak and Britain soon faced a mounting war debt. Proper strategic management of the war became impossible, in part, because lines of communication were slow and undependable. And British generals proved reluctant or unable to mobilize the loyalists into an effective fighting force. Viewing the many obstacles the British had to overcome, certain historians have concluded that the surprising thing about the Revolutionary War is not that the Americans won, but that they did not win more easily.

The first British military man to grapple with the problem of rebellion was Thomas Gage—commander-in-chief of the army in America in 1775. Gage was more than a military figure, however; he played a dual role as a kind of proconsul as well as general. Both in his capacity as imperial statesman and commander-in-chief, he appears to have lacked the perception necessary to cope with the crisis facing him. Despite almost two decades of service in America, he completely misjudged the temper of the people. From the point of view of the British government, he was an alarmist about the large number of troops that would be needed for coercion and his warnings were ignored. His judgment on matters of military strategy was likewise faulty. He believed that Boston was the major source of unrest; if the city could be isolated and subdued the discontent would lessen. Only after the march on Concord and the battle of Bunker Hill did he begin to show a growing awareness of the complexities involved in dealing with the uprising.

Sir William Howe—who replaced Gage in the fall of 1775—was, perhaps, the British commander-in-chief who had the best chance of crushing the rebellion. In 1776 the mother country mounted a war effort of unprecedented proportions; Howe could count upon a 34,000-man army—the greatest expeditionary force ever assembled by Britain to that time—and the support of a vast naval armada—one of the largest fleet of warships ever seen in North American waters. A methodical and experienced soldier, he proceeded to show his superiority as a tactician over Washington by defeating the American general in battles at Brooklyn, Brandywine, and Germantown. But Howe had fatal flaws as a field commander. His strategy was not based upon any clear-cut conception of how the war might be won; he preferred a war of posts and maneuver rather than a ruthless and single-minded pursuit of the Continental army. Howe clung stubbornly to conventional eighteenth-century methods of warfare and tended to maneuver for position, to occupy strategic points, and to avoid battles except when success was certain. Above all, he was ultracautious and argued that the British army in America was a national resource to be hoarded and kept intact at almost all costs rather than risked in aggressive engagements.

Howe's successor, Sir Henry Clinton, proved something of a paradox as commander-in-chief during his four years from 1778 to 1782. While serving as Howe's subordinate from 1776 to 1778, Clinton showed great promise in his sure grasp of strategy, penchant for sound planning, and competence in field operations. Once he became commander-in-chief, however, he grew as cautious and hesitant as Howe. Much of his time was spent in drafting plans that were rarely carried out. His inability to cooperate with his colleagues—both generals and admirals—produced what has been called a paralysis of command: he and Cornwallis were temperamentally unsuited to work with one another and each tended to frustrate the other's plans; and Clinton's incapacity to collaborate with Admiral Arbuthnot made it impossible to conduct joint operations against Newport in the summer of 1780. There may well be, as his biographer has suggested, a psychological explanation for Clinton's behavior—a pathological incapacity on his part to use or share authority. Although Clinton succeeded in winning the greatest single British victory of the war—the capture of General Benjamin Lincoln's army at Charleston in 1780—it was his ironic fate also to be in over-all command of the British forces in America when Cornwallis met defeat at Yorktown.

The last commander-in-chief in America during the war—Sir Guy Carleton—was, in many ways, the most controversial. Serving as governor of Quebec at the outbreak of the war, Carleton helped to shape the future course of the conflict by keeping Canada loyal during the American invasion in 1775–76. But he has been both praised and criticized for the proclamation issued early in 1776 in which he offered to pardon Americans taken as prisoners. Carleton was seeking, no doubt, to counter the growing movement toward independence with a policy of kindness and conciliation. Historians have also taken sides on the dispute between Lord George Germain—secretary of state for the American colonies—and Carleton regarding the latter's failure to pursue more aggressively the Americans retreating from Canada during the summer and fall of 1776. When Carleton was appointed to succeed Clinton in 1782, it was too late to change the outcome of the conflict on the continent; having lost two armies at Saratoga and Yorktown the British had given up hope of recovering America by military means.

Of all the British generals who held high command, none has been ridiculed more than John Burgoyne. Pictured by some historians as a playboy who drank and danced his way to defeat, Burgoyne was actually a hard-driving, courageous commander consumed with ambition for fame, high rank, and honor. Burgoyne had more ability than most scholars credit him with; he was a superb leader of men, recognized the role of ideology in the Revolutionary War, and proved flexible enough to adapt his tactics to American conditions. But he was also hasty and seemed devoid of a sound sense of strategy. He should not bear the entire blame for the disaster which befell him at Saratoga in 1777—it should be shared with Germain and Howe—but Burgoyne's bold attempt to fight his way to Albany more or less on his own was reckless and unrealistic. Hoping to gain great glory by reaching his objective, he never seems to have given thought to the questions of broad strategy he would face after arriving at Albany—exploiting his victory, supplying his army, and dealing with Gates' force. When he lost his gamble, Burgoyne changed the course of history; the loss of his army was destined to bring France into the war.

Lord Cornwallis, like Burgoyne, showed more boldness than most British generals. Serving as Howe's subordinate in the north during the early years of the war, he proved to be aggressive, resourceful, and capable in a series of important battles. As a commander in the field, he courted danger but was as decisive as he was daring. After a brief leave of absence, he returned to America in 1778 to become Clinton's second in command. When personal differences arose between the two men, they were compounded by the fact that Cornwallis held a dormant commission as commander-in-chief in the event of Clinton's resignation or death.

Cornwallis, placed in command of a British army in the summer of 1780, set out to secure the southern colonies for the mother country and to exploit the imagined strength of the loyalists in that region. Although his force of 2,200 men was outnumbered by almost 3,000 Americans facing him at Camden,

South Carolina, in August, 1780, he inflicted a crushing defeat upon Horatio Gates' army. After much maneuvering, during which his subordinates suffered defeats at King's Mountain and Cowpens, Cornwallis met the Continental army led by General Nathanael Greene at Guilford Court House, North Carolina, in March, 1781. In a bloody battle in which he was once again outnumbered, Cornwallis won the field. But he did so at a tremendous cost—nearly one-fourth of his small army. The anticipated uprising of large loyalist forces in the Carolinas had failed to occur and Cornwallis found his victories to be barren ones because of the surprising resilience of the American forces. He thereupon made a fateful decision to march his army to Virginia to join the British troops already stationed there. Trapped at Yorktown by superior French and American forces on land and sea, Cornwallis surrendered his army on October 19, 1781, ending the last major land campaign on the North American continent.

At the same time that Britain sought to subjugate America with land armies, she also employed her mightiest military weapon—the navy. Undisputed control in North American waters for the first three years of the conflict presented her with an opportunity to win the war primarily by the application of sea power. By strangling American trade with a tight blockade clamped upon colonial seaports, it is conceivable that Britain could have brought about the collapse of the rebellion before France entered the war. Such a solution, of course, would have been predicated upon two conditions: a clear understanding of the problem on the part of the British Ministry so that a major strategic decision would have been made to concentrate upon a full-scale effort to impose a close blockade; and a solid commitment of ships and other resources required to exploit to the fullest this form of naval warfare. Throughout the first phase of the war, neither of these conditions was met.

The Ministry was guilty of muddled thinking in framing its broad strategy of war from 1775 to 1778. Although cabinet members dimly perceived the possibilities of applying sea power and subordinated military operations on land to the needs of a blockade up to 1777, they never saw the problem with sufficient clarity to adopt such a strategy of naval warfare as a clear-cut policy. Too often, British strategy and planning constituted a series of *ad hoc* responses to meet particular military situations in America or to cope with domestic political considerations in England. As a result, the British never undertook a consistent policy to station fleets in America with systematic plans for blockading all major colonial ports, attacking American privateers and commercial vessels, and destroying dock facilities with periodic raids.

The resources of the Royal Navy, it is true, were rather limited at the outbreak of the Revolutionary War. After Britain's victory over France in the Seven Years' War, the navy entered upon a period of decline as the service reverted to peacetime footing. Ships were decommissioned, junior officers discharged in droves, and naval recruits sharply cut in numbers. Between the two wars, the navy continued to decline both in strength and efficiency. The result was that when fighting began in 1775, Admiral Samuel Graves—commander-in-chief on the North American station—did not have enough ships on hand to cow the colonists. But even when more ships and sailors were sent to America in the next two years, the idea of exerting pressure at sea by a tight blockade was never fully exploited. Inhibited by the Ministry which failed to think through clearly the problem of an over-all war strategy, limited in the number of ships and men that could be raised and deployed in the American theater of operations, saddled with the burden of supporting the army in major land operations, and commanded by admirals who would not or could not adopt a vigorous policy, the navy was never able to impose a really successful blockade during the first phase of the war.

While the British navy was undergoing a decline after the Seven Years' War, the French navy was being rebuilt and improved. By the time of the Revolutionary War, France possessed a naval force that could challenge Britain's supremacy of the seas. The initiative in naval warfare in North America after 1778, therefore, frequently passed over to the French.

Whether or not the British had sufficient ships to impose a close blockade on the French fleet in European waters in 1778 is a matter of controversy among historians. At any rate, developments in the next two years diminished the possibility of employing such a strategy. By 1780 two other principal naval powers—Spain and Holland—were at war with Britain. When a coalition of neutral countries hostile to Britain—the League of Armed Neutrality—was formed in 1780, the presence of yet another potential enemy force restricted even further the efforts of the Royal Navy. The British Ministry during these years found itself incapable of matching the size of the naval forces France and Spain sent into the English Channel or countering all of the enemy fleets that appeared in the Caribbean and Mediterranean. French squadrons often sailed unopposed in American waters where the Royal Navy lost its superiority at least once a year from 1778 to 1781. Under these conditions, the capture of a beleaguered British army—such as that which occurred at Yorktown—became almost inevitable.

Although the surrender of Cornwallis' army practically ended the fighting in North America, the war continued elsewhere. Throughout 1781 the British had suffered a series of setbacks in the Caribbean as Tobago, St. Kitts, Nevis and Montserrat fell to the enemy. Having lost the war on the continent, they appeared to be well on their way to losing it in the West Indies. But in a brilliant naval victory near Martinique in April, 1782, Admirals Rodney and Hood helped to restore the balance. This triumph went far toward retrieving the British position in the West Indies and was, in fact, the last major battle in the waters of the New World.

Of the naval leaders appointed to the post of commander-in-chief on the North American station, Admiral Richard Howe, named in February, 1776, was perhaps the first to possess the necessary resources to conduct meaningful operations against the colonists. The Admiralty ordered him to prosecute the war vigorously with the 73 warships and 13,000 seamen that were to be under his command. He was authorized to deal with the Americans only in the event of a surrender, but after he joined his brother—General William Howe—at New York in July, 1776, he set about to promote a reconciliation instead.

The admiral appeared determined to use the olive branch as well as the sword. He first approached the Continental Congress to discuss a peace proposal in September, 1776—after the American defeat on Long Island. When Congress indicated its unwillingness to negotiate, Howe, with his brother, issued a proclamation in November appealing to the people to lay down their arms. Throughout the second half of 1776, he apparently adopted a deliberate policy toward the Americans: to make a show of strength, to exert limited use of force, and then to make repeated overtures of peace. But General Washington's victories at Trenton and Princeton around the end of the year revived America's expectations of victory and dashed Howe's hopes for reconciliation.

Howe's naval policy underwent several changes in the course of 1777 and 1778. Seeing little prospect of negotiating a peace and having little taste for exerting overwhelming military force, he adopted halfhearted measures in 1777. Although Howe applied a blockade, he never fully exploited its possibilities. Firstly, he was unwilling to carry the war into colonial ports where American shipping might be more easily destroyed. Secondly, he committed much of his force to supporting the army in land operations and thereby limited the number of vessels available for blockade duty. Once the French entered the war, however, Howe's attitude altered completely. He showed great gallantry in preparing to fight d'Estaing's superior fleet at New York and off Newport in the summer of 1778—even though these impending battles never took place. After conducting a successful defensive naval strategy, Howe returned to England in September, 1778.

Howe's successors proved to be either mediocrities or incompetents. The Royal Navy was in the doldrums by the time of the Revolutionary War because it lacked great leaders as well as sound ships. Many gifted admirals who served in the Seven Years' War had died or retired, and some senior British officers still on active service refused to accept command in America for political reasons. Lord Sandwich—first lord of the Admiralty—had few outstanding men to choose from and those he picked often proved to be singularly bad selections. General Henry Clinton aptly characterized his naval colleagues as a pack of "old women."

Three of the long list of admirals who followed Howe in North America—James Gambier, Marriot Arbuthnot, and Thomas Graves—illustrate how poor naval leadership was throughout most of the war. Although not all were appointed to the position of commander-in-chief, delays in naming and replacing admirals to that post frequently enabled subordinates to assume responsibility on the station. Gambier—who held command during part of the winter and spring of 1778–79— was probably the sorriest of the lot. Timid and indecisive, Gambier found himself in a position that called for qualities of leadership he did not possess; he returned to England without accomplishing a great deal. Arbuthnot, on the other hand, worsened the friction already existing between the two services to a point where it was impossible for the army and navy to cooperate on joint operations during 1780. Matters became so bad that Clinton sent an ultimatum to the Ministry declaring that either he or his colleague must go. As a result, Arbuthnot was recalled. Thomas Graves, an uninspired tactician, fought an undramatic but crucial battle with the French fleet under Admiral de Grasse off the Virginia Capes in September, 1781. When the British fleet was driven off and the French were left in command of the sea near Yorktown, the fate of Cornwallis' army was sealed.

The admirals who served mostly in West Indies waters—in contrast to many who held command off the coast of North America—were often competent, if not talented, men. Sir George Rodney, one of the more able and energetic officers, had had a highly successful career in the Seven Years' War before being offered command of the fleet on the Leeward Islands station late in 1779. It is possible that Rodney missed his first opportunity to defeat the French fleet in February, 1781, because part of his squadron was engaged in gathering booty from St. Eustatius—the rich island in the Dutch West Indies. But he gained a decisive victory over de Grasse in the battle of the Saints off Martinique on April 12, 1782. Partly owing to luck, he was at considerably greater strength than his opponent and made the most of his advantage. Certain of his contemporaries and some historians argued, however, that Rodney might have exploited his advantage even more.

Sir Samuel Hood, who worked mainly with Rodney in the West Indies, was a brilliant officer; but the full range of his capabilities may never be known because he was a subordinate so much of the time. His ability to anticipate enemy intentions, to analyze strategic situations, and to make moves with decisiveness marked him as a man of great potential. But the fortunes of war never favored him with an outstanding victory. The final outcome of two engagements in which he was involved—the battles of the Virginia Capes and of the Saints—might well have been different if he had been in full command.

Although the Royal Navy had at least three outstanding admirals in the Revolutionary War—Howe, Rodney, and Hood—the service failed to produce final victory as it had in the past. Why? In part, because naval commanders in America had to cope with many complex problems not of their own making. The government's neglect of the navy between two wars resulted in too few ships and too few seamen to carry out too many missions. The Ministry's failure to plan decisively for the American theater during the first phase of the war left admirals in a quandary as to what strategy they should follow. Once France entered the war, demands for naval resources from other theaters of war resulted in a lower priority as North America was downgraded to a subordinate theater. The Ministry's failure in 1778 to blockade the home ports of France—though it is by no means certain that Britain had the necessary naval superiority to employ such a strategy in that year or thereafter—exposed British naval commanders to an annual foray of French fleets in American waters and enabled French commanders to seize the initiative quite often. But British admirals must also share much of the blame for the war's outcome. They evaded for the most part the hard thinking that was required to formulate a successful naval strategy and merely drifted instead into a course of action that led to a series of expedient but haphazard moves. Some admirals, like Howe, adopted halfhearted measures and refused to prosecute the war vigorously. Friction between the services also blunted the effective use of the naval arm at times. And in certain situations—such as the battle of the Virginia Capes—British commanders showed themselves unwilling to take risks against an equal or slightly superior French fleet at the crucial moment. In short, the admirals failed to make the most of the means at their disposal—particularly during the first phase of the war.

This last comment applies to British generals as well as admirals—but to a lesser degree. The chances of winning the war by waging land campaigns were slimmer than those of ending the conflict by a strategy of naval warfare during the first few years. But opportunities did present themselves to generals to put down the rebellion—to Gage at Bunker Hill in 1775; to Howe on Long Island in 1776; and to Howe and Burgoyne along the Hudson River Valley in 1777, if they had coordinated their campaigns. Why did these men fail? The generals, like the admirals, faced problems over which they had no control: the British government's failure to frame a consistent war strategy and to adhere to it; the Ministry's refusal to recognize that even more troops were required to conquer an entire continent; and Britain's system of command which was so complicated and inefficient as to create misunderstandings between the leaders in London and the men in the field.

British generals, nevertheless, must bear part of the blame, even when allowances are made for such matters. In carrying out their campaigns, many of them tended to be too traditional and to cling too closely to the military orthodoxies of the day. Howe after the battle of Long Island in 1776, for example, was more interested in maneuvering into position to occupy New York City than in capturing Washington's army. Waging warfare along conventional eighteenth-century lines which called for the conservation of forces, battlefield commanders were often too cautious in committing their troops in aggressive engagements or campaigns. Two generals—Burgoyne and Cornwallis—went to the other extreme, on occasion, and ran bold risks; but they gambled with their armies on unlikely objectives and lost. Although commanders in the field were granted considerable latitude by Germain in conducting operations, none of them produced a battle plan which would have assured Britain of total victory. There was no military genius in their midst—no Marlborough or Wellington—who could come up with a successful strategy before 1778; a strategy to suppress a colonial rebellion in a vast country where a people, not a professional army, was under arms.

To return, then, to the original question: to what extent did the quality of British military leadership affect the outcome of the Revolutionary War in America? From this brief survey of generals and admirals which has concentrated perforce upon their errors in strategy and tactics, it might be tempting to conclude that the war's outcome was determined primarily by British mistakes. But such a view runs the risk of giving rise to a new myth: that between bungling British commanders and foreign aid from France, the American army had little or nothing to do with the winning of the war, and that the non-military and quasi-military factors mentioned in this introduction were of small consequence.

The fact of the matter is, British miscalculations alone would not necessarily have led to defeat: the American high command had to capitalize on these mistakes if they were to have any meaning. Much more important than British blunders themselves was the ability of the Americans to exploit these errors—especially during the first phase of the war. However much Howe erred in separating his army from that of Burgoyne in

1777, for example, it would have come to nothing unless American commanders perceived this flaw in strategy and acted upon it. By taking advantage of such mistakes, the American army was able to survive and to gain time—time to develop from an amateur into a professional fighting force, and to secure the foreign aid from France which brought final victory. By preventing the British from winning the war before 1778, the Americans made possible ultimate military success, and, in this sense, the Revolutionary War may be called an American victory rather than a British defeat.

GEORGE ATHAN BILLIAS

Clark University

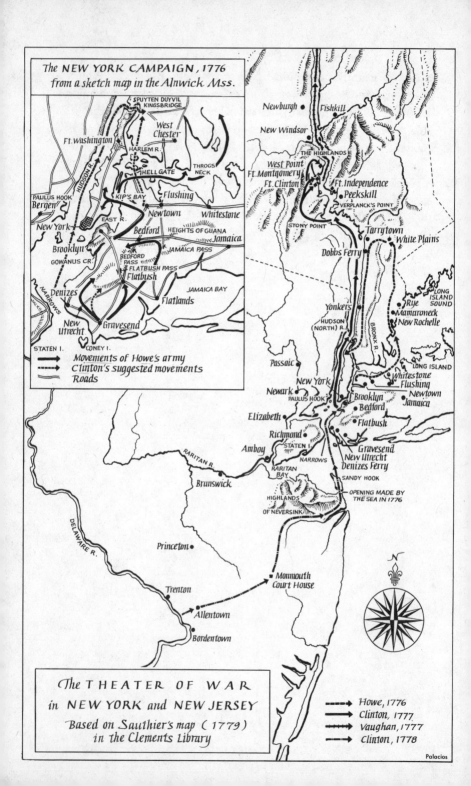

The NEW YORK CAMPAIGN, 1776
from a sketch map in the Alnwick Mss.

SPUYTEN DUYVIL
KINGSBRIDGE
WEST CHESTER
Ft. Washington
HARLEM R.
THROGS NECK
HELL GATE
PAULUS HOOK
Bergen
HUDSON R.
KIP'S BAY
Flushing
New York
EAST R.
Newtown
Whitestone
Brooklyn
Bedford
HEIGHTS OF GUANA
Jamaica
GOWANUS CR.
JAMAICA PASS
BEDFORD PASS
FLATBUSH PASS
Flatbush
JAMAICA BAY
Denizes
NARROWS
Flatlands
New Utrecht
Gravesend
STATEN I.
CONEY I.

Movements of Howe's army
Clinton's suggested movements
Roads

Newburgh   Fishkill
New Windsor
THE HIGHLANDS
West Point
Ft. Montgomery
Ft. Clinton   Ft. Independence
                   Peekskill
                   VERPLANCK'S POINT
STONY POINT
Tarrytown
                   White Plains
Dobbs Ferry

Yonkers
HUDSON
(NORTH) R.
BRONX R.
                   LONG ISLAND SOUND
                   Rye
                   Mamaroneck
                   New Rochelle
Passaic
                   LONG ISLAND
                   Whitestone
New York   Flushing
Newark   Newtown
PAULUS HOOK   Jamaica
Elizabeth   Brooklyn
                   Bedford
Richmond   Flatbush
                   Gravesend
Amboy   STATEN I. New Utrecht
         NARROWS   Denizes Ferry
RARITAN R.   SANDY HOOK
Brunswick
RARITAN BAY
                   OPENING MADE BY
HIGHLANDS   THE SEA IN 1776
OF NEVERSINK
DELAWARE R.

Princeton

Trenton   Monmouth
                   Court House
Allentown
Bordentown

N

The THEATER OF WAR
in NEW YORK and NEW JERSEY
Based on Sauthier's map (1779)
in the Clements Library

- - - → Howe, 1776
——→ Clinton, 1777
+++→ Vaughan, 1777
···→ Clinton, 1778

Palacios

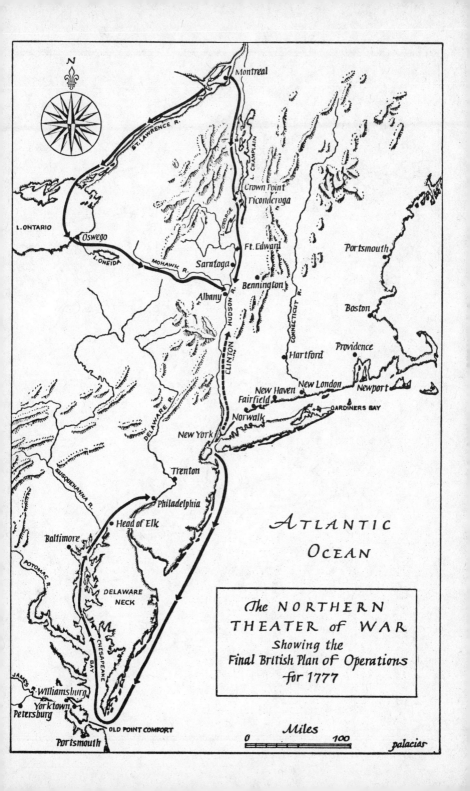

The NORTHERN THEATER of WAR
Showing the Final British Plan of Operations for 1777

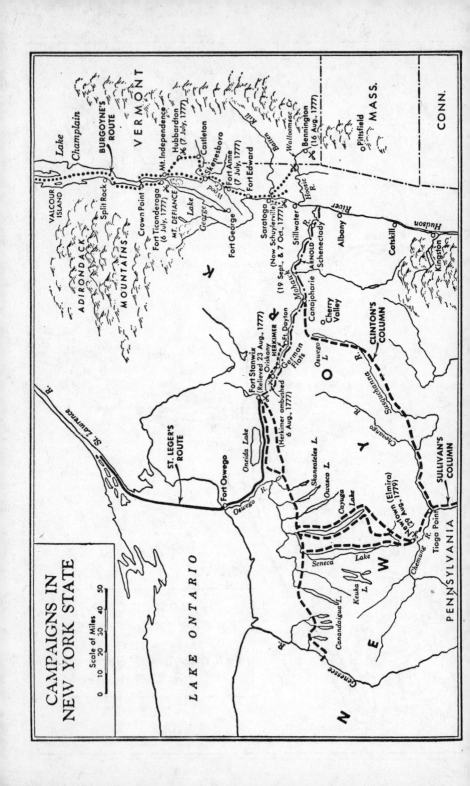

CAMPAIGNS IN
NEW YORK STATE

Scale of Miles
0 10 20 30 40 50

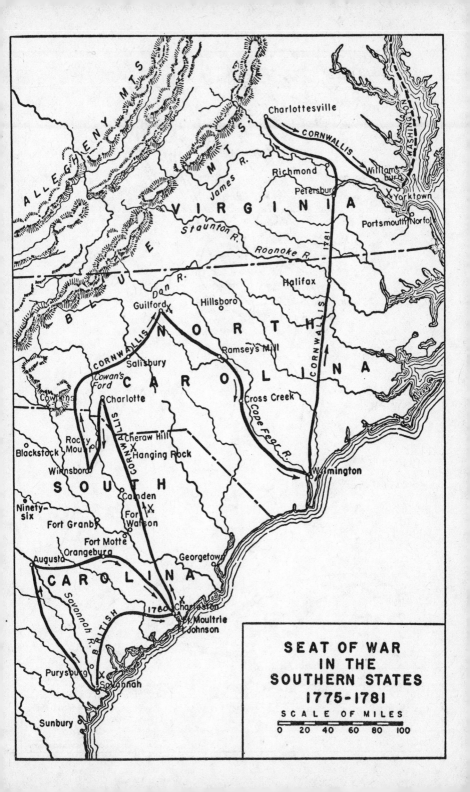

SEAT OF WAR
IN THE
SOUTHERN STATES
1775-1781

SCALE OF MILES

0   20   40   60   80   100

The CAMPAIGN of 1781

palacios

Miles

0   300

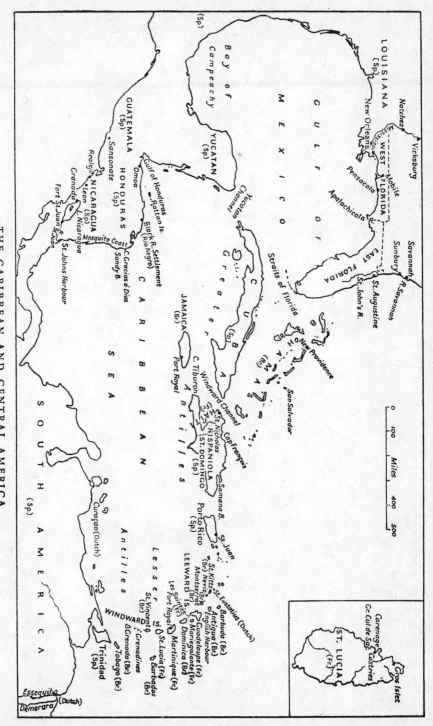

THE CARIBBEAN AND CENTRAL AMERICA

GEORGE WASHINGTON'S OPPONENTS

British Generals and Admirals in the American Revolution

Thomas Gage:

WEAK LINK OF EMPIRE

JOHN SHY

University of Michigan

THOMAS GAGE, as commander-in-chief of the British army in North America in 1775, was trapped by historical forces he could neither control nor avoid. But his frantic efforts to elude the trap, if unsuccessful, were not inconsequential. He could not have prevented the American Revolution, but he could, and did, give its beginning a particular shape. The Revolutionary War began on land, under ambiguous circumstances, at the heart of rebel strength, in an area that could only be a dead end for British strategy, and with a series of humiliating setbacks for His Majesty's arms. In the years that followed, British policy could never quite shake free of this bad beginning—never again was the range of strategic and political choice as wide as it had been in 1775. There were others who must share the blame with Gage, but he more than anyone else might have made a different beginning. His personality and previous military experience suggest why he did not.

Thomas Gage was the second son of a noble family known primarily for its lack of distinction and its reluctance to give up Catholicism. His father, the first Viscount Gage, pursued an erratic course in British politics. Thomas' mother had a reputation for sexual promiscuity, while his brother's outstanding trait seems to have been absent-mindedness. His sister married into

a Catholic family, and both of his parents, after living as nominal Anglicans, appear to have returned to the Catholic Church at
the end of their lives. Great wealth entered the family only when
Thomas' brother, who was the eldest, married a Jewish heiress.
But long before that event, Thomas had to find his own way.

The Church, the law, the army—these were the paths open to
younger sons of nobility in eighteenth-century England, and so,
after eight years at Westminster School, young Thomas set out
on a military career. In getting a commission, he naturally had
the help of his brother William, the future Lord Gage, who just
as naturally would soon enter the House of Commons from the
borough of Seaford, Sussex, one of whose seats was in the Gage
family pocket. For fifteen years, Gage's military career was not
unusual in any way: service in Flanders against the French, in
North Britain against the Jacobites; a captain at twenty-three,
a lieutenant colonel at just past thirty, both ranks acquired of
course by the purchase of a vacant commission. As an officer
with good "connexions," however, he was expected to serve some
time at headquarters: "For a man who intends to be military
nothing so pretty as an aide de camp in service with an intelligent general," was the advice of Jeffrey Amherst, later conqueror of Canada, to his younger brother.[1] Accordingly Gage
served on the staff—in "the family" was the phrase—of the
Earl of Albemarle, father of his school friends at Westminster,
the Keppels.

In 1755, he told an historian many years later, some American
land speculators, among them George Washington, interrupted
the typical pattern of Gage's military career, and incidentally
started a world war.[2] But the British government at the time
decided that the troubles of the governor of Virginia and his
land-hungry cronies were caused by French aggression in the
Ohio Valley. Neither version was more than half true. The
cabinet nevertheless took drastic action: it ordered British regulars to defend American territory and colonists, something
rarely done in the past. The 44th, Gage's regiment, and the 48th,
both stationed in Ireland, received orders to embark for Alex-

andria, Virginia, under the command of Major General Edward
Braddock, who carried a commission as commander-in-chief for
North America.

"My honest friend Gage is to be of the Ohio party," wrote
James Wolfe when he heard the news of Braddock's expedition.
It is interesting to learn that Wolfe, already known in the army
as an exceptionally zealous and able officer, thought well of
Gage.[3] But the Braddock campaign against the French at the
forks of the Ohio turned into a disaster. Crippled at the start
by problems of supply, Braddock lost the advantage that either
a rapid march or methodical approach might have offered. When,
after more than two hundred miles of marching, his column
ran into ambush almost within sight of its objective, the French
had had ample time to bring up reinforcements. The British
force, on the other hand, was hungry and its march formation
cluttered with wagons, cattle, and pack horses. Only a 300-man
advance party was in position to prevent surprise and to protect
the main body while it deployed, but the advance party failed.
It collapsed at first contact, transmitted its panic to the entire
force, and its commander, Lieutenant Colonel Thomas Gage,
could do nothing to stop the ensuing rout.

Modern historians have criticized Gage on several grounds—
failing to occupy the high ground near the line of march, leaving
behind a pair of light cannon that might have turned the tide,
even fleeing the battlefield—but all such criticism is captious,
and some is merely uninformed, for no one criticized him at the
time.[4] The French force, though outnumbered by the whole
British column, simply overwhelmed the advance party. Surprise,
fear, inexperience in forest warfare, and a faulty tactical arrangement of the main body did the rest. It was not a battle,
but a massacre.

Gage "distinguish'd himself by Encouraging the men as much
as he Could," according to an anonymous eyewitness, and had
"several narrow escapes."[5] But if he had minor wounds to prove
his bravery, and in justice deserved little blame for the debacle,
Gage had shown no special talent for leadership in combat. His

own account of the battle puts all blame on the rank and file, which he certainly knew was an exaggeration. He had hardly reported the death of his colonel before he was asking for promotion to the vacancy. His assertion that he was the senior lieutenant colonel on the field, and that Braddock, "had he lived a few days longer," would have given him the regiment, hit a sour note even for the eighteenth century.[6] He did not get the colonelcy.

With Braddock's defeat, the British government found that the small expedition was becoming a full-scale war, and Thomas Gage found that his military education in America was going to last more than a season. New commanders with new regiments came over with new plans; Gage and the 44th moved north toward Canada in keeping with those plans. British North America spent all of 1756 trying to reorganize its military effort, and Gage soon learned how low regular troops could sink under the primitive conditions of the frontier: he had seen a mutinous detachment of the 51st "in a filthy condition covered with vermin, . . . legs mortified thro dirt cold and want of change." [7] His own regiment was not much better: "The [44th] Regt is in Rags," wrote Lord Loudoun, the new commander-in-chief, but added that "they look like Soldiers" because "Lt Col Gage is a good Officer and keeps up Discipline Strictly." [8] In 1757, he was a member of the amphibious expedition that never quite reached its objective—the fortress of Louisbourg on Cape Breton Island. He did, however, manage to avoid the epidemic of backbiting and recriminations that infected the officer corps after the abortive campaign that summer which saw the fall of Fort William Henry and the slaughter of some of its garrison by Indians.

During the following winter, Gage moved toward the colonelcy that had eluded him in 1755. All British officers with experience in America recognized the value of provincial rangers, armed woodsmen who were somewhat more dependable than Indians and more skillful than either British regulars or American militia in the techniques of forest warfare. Rangers were vital elements in gathering intelligence and in screening the army when it was in camp or on the move. But rangers were expensive because of their high rate of pay, they were unmilitary in dress and deportment, and, during the illness of their leader Robert Rogers, they had become unruly, even mutinous. Gage apparently saw his chance, and offered to raise a regiment of light infantry that could, in time, obviate the need for rangers.

It was a good idea, and often has been noted as a landmark in the history of the British army. There is little to suggest, however, that Gage was leading his British comrades toward a full acceptance of the lessons of Braddock's defeat. Gage raised his light infantry regiment, the 80th, and it served in 1758 along-side rangers and Indians in the unsuccessful campaign against Ticonderoga. But Gage himself, for some reason, hardly appears in the record. The 80th was parceled out among the three bri-gades of regulars, while Gage was an acting brigadier general and became second in command after the death of Lord Howe. But Gage seems to have done nothing to help the unfortunate General Abercromby avoid or retrieve his errors of judgment, which included a frontal attack without artillery support on a strongly fortified position. It is difficult to resist an impression that Gage had finally got his regiment, and was content. He improved his situation still more when at the end of the summer he hurried away from the sick and defeated army to marry Margaret Kemble, daughter of a wealthy New Jersey family.

His position as brigadier general became permanent in 1759, and that year he got his first independent command. Amherst, Abercromby's successor, sent Gage to take over the siege of Fort Niagara. Once the fort had fallen, Gage was to move against the French post of La Galette at the head of the St. Law-rence. While Wolfe attacked Quebec, and Amherst led his army down Lake Champlain toward Montreal, Gage was expected to exert pressure on Canada from the West. As in 1755, Gage, if he did not fail, at best failed to succeed.

He had excuses: the failure of the quartermaster at Albany to support him properly, the unexpected size of the French garrison at La Galette, and the attrition of his own force. But Amherst and especially Wolfe badly needed a diversionary attack, even if it were repulsed, and the commander-in-chief refused to accept the excuses. Gage had not carried out his orders, and "may not have such an opportunity [again] as long as he lives," was Amherst's judgment. "They have found out difficulties where there are none." [9] In the final campaign of the war on the continent in 1760, when Amherst accepted the surrender of Canada, he had Brigadier General Gage bringing up the rear.

Perhaps the rear was the right place for a general officer whose record indicated that running a regiment—making men look like soldiers and keeping strict discipline, as Loudoun had put it—was about the ceiling of his military abilities. In the rear he could keep the supplies moving forward and the reserve forces in good order, ready for the commander's call. In the rear he could avoid the need to make quick decisions under pressure. There were some, though, who thought that Gage was not inept as a commander, only unlucky. Dr. Richard Huck, a highly intelligent surgeon on the headquarters staff, believed that Gage had received impossible orders and then been blamed when he could not execute them. "Gage is certainly none of the Sons of Fortune," Huck wrote to his old chief, Loudoun, and his epigram seems an apt description of Gage's entire wartime record, from Braddock's field to Bunker Hill. But even Huck reported that, according to French prisoners, the situation in Canada had been so desperate that two or three more days of pressure on La Galette would have brought collapse, and the doctor conceded that Gage perhaps had too much "Nonchalance" for his own good. [10]

In reviewing Gage's early military career in America, the record that he would carry into the opening battles of the Revolution, one is struck by how little combat experience he had had in six years. Twice he had been involved in an approach march through broken, unfriendly country: once with Braddock in 1755, and again near Ticonderoga in 1758. On both occasions he had seen a British army surprised. The result in 1755 had been panic and slaughter; in 1758, confusion, disorganization, and moderately heavy casualities. He had also taken part in an unsuccessful infantry assault on an entrenched position, at Ticonderoga in 1758, at a cost to the attackers of one quarter of their force. The following year at Niagara, just a few weeks before he arrived to take command of the siege, a relief column of French regulars had smashed itself against an entrenched position in a small-scale repetition of the Ticonderoga attack; Gage must have seen the ground and heard the action described in detail.[11] Two surprise marches, two bloody infantry assaults—these made up his personal fund of tactical experience in American warfare before 1775.

The war ended for Gage in 1760. He did not go campaigning in the West Indies during 1761–62; instead, he served as military governor of Montreal, where combat experience was less important than some other qualities like intelligence, patience, honesty, and tact. Gage was a good governor, and became popular among people who had recently been his enemies. The "nonchalance" of which Dr. Huck had complained was an asset under peacetime conditions; a relaxed, understanding approach was what postwar Canada required.

But Montreal was cold and primitive, and, when peace came early in 1763, there was little to keep him there, or anywhere else for that matter, on active service. He held the rank of major general, and had become colonel of a senior regiment that would not be disbanded, as was the 80th, in the peacetime reduction of the army. Further promotion seemed unlikely. Few colonels actually served with their regiments, but merely enjoyed the honor and the emoluments. Gage could have done likewise, pleading perhaps that the climate of Canada was ruining his health, and have retired to Sussex or even New Jersey.

The Indian uprising of 1763 changed all such thoughts, which clearly Gage had been entertaining. The commander-in-chief, Sir Jeffrey Amherst, had grossly underestimated the Indian problem after the war. For years the Indians had complained of traders who cheated them with rum and short weights, but now, with countervailing French power eliminated, they increasingly feared Anglo-American migration onto their hunting grounds. The war had taught Amherst to have utter contempt for Indians; he refused to listen to the pleas of Sir William Johnson, the Indian superintendent, and instead cut off their supply of ammunition and relied on small garrisons of regulars scattered through the West to hold them down by force. It was a stupid policy. The Indian uprising had been brewing for several years and may have been unavoidable, but when it broke out Amherst seemed the obvious culprit and was recalled. Thomas Gage took his place.

As the new commander-in-chief moved into his headquarters at New York, he faced two related problems: pacifying the northern Indian tribes, and managing a peacetime army scattered over a half-continent. For the first task he had the plans already developed by Amherst, the reinforcement by provincial troops which had been requested, and two able and experienced subordinates—John Bradstreet and Henry Bouquet. Bradstreet and Bouquet, with mixed forces of British regulars and American volunteers, moved westward from Albany and Pittsburgh, respectively, against little resistance. Gage, as he had been instructed, left the negotiation of peace to Sir William Johnson, whose stock with the British government had risen upon the fall of Amherst. The campaign of 1764 was arduous, but it was almost bloodless because the Indians had failed to destroy the garrisons at Detroit, Niagara, and Fort Pitt in 1763, and their small resources were nearly exhausted. Gage was able to put down the uprising more easily than expected.

The Indian problem did not disappear, however, with the end of the uprising. In fact, preventing another costly Indian war became more than ever a major concern to those responsible for British colonial policy, and the regular garrison in America figured prominently in their plans.

Prior to the French and Indian War, Britain had kept few regular troops in the colonies: several regiments to watch over a hostile population in Nova Scotia, and several more to curb slave insurrections in the West Indies. But, with the exception of a few undermanned companies in New York and South Carolina, the mainland colonies were completely dependent on their own militia for defense.[12] This arrangement seemed to break down in 1755, and Braddock's defeat brought thousands of regulars to America. At the end of the war it was decided to keep fifteen regiments on the mainland—three in Nova Scotia, four in Canada, four in Florida and along the Gulf coast, and the remaining four dispersed among the middle Atlantic seaboard, the Great Lakes, the Carolina and Georgia backcountry, and the Illinois side of the Mississippi. Gage was to command this army of about six thousand men, stretched across a thousand miles of wilderness.

The presence of a regular garrison led directly to the British attempt to raise a revenue in the colonies, but even now the mission of this military force is not altogether clear. Defense, properly speaking, was not a major consideration. The French population of Canada, and the relative emptiness of Florida and the trans-Appalachian region, demanded a garrison for those areas. It was hoped that military posts in the backcountry could keep frontiersmen off Indian lands and bring some order to the fur trade, thus allaying the grievances that had led to the Indian uprising of 1763. New York City, New Jersey, and Philadelphia were convenient places for the rest and recuperation of units en route to other stations; these units would also be available, if needed, to act against smugglers. Finally, there was a vaguely expressed fear that troops might be useful to keep unruly Americans "in due subordination." No one, on the other hand, thought that a few thousand regulars could protect the whole frontier from another Indian attack, and everyone knew that sea power was the principal defense against France or Spain.[13]

Specifically, Gage was told to conciliate the Indians by:

1. "Restraining all unjust Settlement, and fraudulent Purchase of their Lands,

and

2. "Suppressing all unfair Practices in the free and open Trade to
   be carried on with them at the several [military] Posts,"
and to assist the customs officers in

3. "The effectual Suppression of Contraband Trade in America." [14]

Privately Gage was warned of the general opinion within the government "that the Indians have of late Years been too much neglected, and that the . . . present Hostilities, have been in great Measure owing to an apparent Contempt of their Consequence." [15] The message was unmistakable.

What thus appears on the surface to be a reasonable attempt to improve the administration of the empire soon gave rise to a set of complicated, interlocking problems that were difficult even to state clearly, much less solve. Gage himself was one of the sponsors of the new plan to placate the Indians through protection of their lands and regulation of the fur trade, but he gradually came to understand that enormous obstacles stood in the way. Frontier settlers and fur traders easily avoided the few small garrisons in the back country, and when Gage tried to restrict their movements he often found himself caught between rival pressure groups. His legal authority against civilians was virtually nil, and colonial governors hesitated to cooperate with the army against their own subjects, especially when they were associated with land companies or commercial firms. Army post commanders themselves could not be relied upon to refuse bribes or to refrain from abusing Indians, nor could their behavior be controlled or checked easily when they were hundreds of miles from headquarters. Although the British government continued to fear the financial and political cost of another Indian war, Gage and a few well-informed officials in London were beginning to realize that the army could do little to prevent it.

By the end of 1765, civil disorders along the seaboard seemed to pose a more pressing problem for the army than the danger of Indian uprisings on the frontier. During the riots over the Stamp Act in the autumn, no governor dared to call for military assistance, apparently because the troops nearby were too few to be employed effectively against the mobs in Boston, New York,

Philadelphia, and Charleston. Gage began moving troops eastward, but was abruptly stopped when the Rockingham government decided to repeal the Stamp Act at the end of the year. Obviously the mission of the army in America was changing, but no one in an official position dared to articulate the change.

Confusion on the British political scene exacerbated the situation, making it difficult to adopt or pursue any coherent policy for the colonies or for the army in America. This confusion was only incidentally a result of trouble over American affairs. It was caused primarily by the successive political impact of the great but unorthodox war leader, William Pitt, of a new young king, George III, who was equally unorthodox in his view of politics, and by the collapse of a coalition that had ruled England for most of the century. The resultant bitterness among political leaders, coupled with severe economic distress in the postwar period, produced an instability at the cabinet level that is reminiscent of the Fourth French Republic.

From the American point of view, a "hard" Grenville Ministry was succeeded in 1765 by a "soft" Rockingham government, which in turn was followed in 1766 by a coalition with Pitt at its head. Nominally "soft," this coalition steadily hardened in its approach to the American problem, becoming the "hardest" of them all when reorganized by Lord North in 1770. But Gage's immediate superior was the secretary of state for the southern department, and the succession of men in that office did not quite conform to the general pattern of political change. The Earl of Shelburne, who served from 1766 to early 1768, was believed to be liberal in his approach to American grievances; the Earl of Hillsborough, who took the new office of secretary of state for the American colonies and served until mid-1772, was notoriously conservative. But Hillsborough was followed by the pious Earl of Dartmouth, North's step-brother, a man thought to be even more sympathetic than Shelburne toward America. More important than any of these dubious labels was the fact that, for a variety of reasons, no colonial secretary after the war held a strong position either in the cabinet or in the House of Commons. Under these circumstances, American questions were buffeted by the rapidly shifting wind of politics. No question was more exposed to those winds than that of the colonial army, which was draining over £400,000 from the Treasury every year.

Gage responded to this instability with caution. During the past decade, British governments had dealt harshly with military commanders who had made mistakes: Admiral Byng had been shot, the Duke of Cumberland disgraced, three commanders in America sacked in three years, Lord George Germain (who would direct the war against the colonies after 1775) court-martialed, and Amherst recalled. When Shelburne asked Gage for his opinion on desirable policies for the Indians, the unsettled West, and the American army, Gage sent back a long report full of information, but almost devoid of opinions that might later be used against him if things went badly. He knew that the historic antipathy in Britain toward a standing army would encourage a shaky government to make him the scapegoat if his advice turned out wrong.

Gage had opinions, however, and the men closest to him played on those opinions, drawing him toward a more active role in colonial affairs. A hint of what was in his mind came during the war when he wrote to his brother of the need to change the constitutions of Pennsylvania and Maryland. Sir William Johnson won Gage's official support for the plan to regulate the fur trade. And Lieutenant Colonel James Robertson, Gage's principal staff officer and a Scot whose view of American disorder was unusually narrow, persuaded him in early 1765 to propose an Act of Parliament that would legalize the quartering of soldiers in private houses. The Ministry, under pressure from the agents in London of the colonial governments, revised the bill to allow quartering only in vacant buildings and existing barracks, though at colonial expense. Even as modified, the Quartering Act was a chronic source of trouble between Britain and her colonies.

More than anyone else, the secretary at war, Lord Barrington, worked on and with Gage to help shape American policy. The office of secretary at war was a secondary administrative post that constitutionally had nothing to do with either policy-making or the American colonies. Yet Barrington, who was at once a political hack and a charmingly honest fish in a sea of courtly hypocrisy, enjoyed the personal confidence of the king, serving him in the War Office from 1765 to 1778. Barrington had given up higher political ambitions, and the security of his position was due to a genuine zeal for the welfare of the army. Frequent visits to the royal closet on minor matters of military business gave Barrington an access to the king that even cabinet officers must have envied. It also gave Gage, one of Barrington's oldest friends, a line to the center of power if he cared or dared to use it.

In 1766, Barrington drafted a memorandum in which he proposed withdrawal of the army from the western posts and the middle Atlantic seaboard, and its concentration in Canada, Nova Scotia, and Florida. The West was to become a vast Indian reservation—"a desert," Barrington ignorantly called it—where no white settlement would be permitted to stir up another war. Withdrawal of troops from the West would facilitate their removal from the East, where there would no longer be any need for the Quartering Act. He appealed to the king and the army staff with the argument that a concentrated army would be better disciplined and better trained; he appealed to the cabinet with the prospect of eliminating the heavy cost of supplying troops in many remote garrisons. A few regiments, he suggested, might even be brought back to the British Isles.

Barrington showed his memorandum to Shelburne and Pitt (newly created Earl of Chatham), and sent a copy to Gage. At first Barrington thought that Chatham and Shelburne liked the plan, but he soon learned that his proposal to make the West "a desert" was drawing serious opposition to the plan as a whole. All those with an interest in western colonization or land speculation, including the postmaster general for America, Benjamin Franklin, were lobbying against it. General Amherst, who had returned to a position of influence on colonial and military ques-

tions when the Chatham government came to power, criticized
Barrington's suggestion that small garrisons in the West (where
Amherst had first put them) were useless against Indian uprisings. Amherst had never really understood what had gone wrong
in 1763, and he never would, but his opinion carried weight.
Shelburne vacillated. Chatham, meanwhile, fell ill and lost his
effectiveness as a political leader. Thus, when the question of the
cost of keeping the army in the American West came before the
House of Commons, the leaderless cabinet divided. Parliament
thereupon passed a new set of measures to raise a revenue in
America—the Townshend Acts of 1767.

Barrington had expected that at least Gage would support
him. For the most part, Gage did. But he objected to one key
feature of Barrington's plan—the proposal to remove troops
from the seaboard. Barrington had argued that troops in the
colonial port cities were of little use, because by law only a civil
magistrate could employ them against a mob, and few magistrates, however loyal they might be to the Crown, had shown
themselves willing to take this extreme step. Withdrawal of
troops would remove an irritant and serve as a conciliatory gesture, Barrington reasoned, but they could quickly return from
their bases to the North and South in case of a real rebellion.
Gage disagreed. With more troops on the spot, he reasoned,
magistrates would act more vigorously. Halifax, Quebec, Montreal, and St. Augustine were too far away for prompt action in
the event of serious trouble. It is possible, and what is known
of Mrs. Gage makes it rather likely, that Gage also did not want
to move his headquarters away from the temperate, civilized at-
mosphere of New York City; he had already served one bleak
tour in Canada, and had read enough dispatches relating the
horrors of Florida to know what awaited the Gages at St. Augustine. Barrington deferred to firsthand knowledge of his friend
Gage for the time being, but the secretary at war never gave
up the hope of removing all regular soldiers from those colonies
that had resisted taxation.

Whatever their disagreement over deployment of troops in the

East, Gage and Barrington were as one on the need to get as many troops as possible out of the West—the soldiers stationed there were expensive, of no apparent use, and suffering from poor morale and inadequate supervision. The two men also agreed that the government ought to take a firm line toward American disorder. Both were ready to make minor gestures of conciliation, but they were unwilling to compromise on the basic issues of taxation, sovereignty, and obedience to law. In a fascinating private exchange of letters over the years, they alternately prayed for the government to stand firm and condemned its pusillanimity when it did not. In 1768, when another old friend of theirs, the Earl of Hillsborough, became secretary of state for the American colonies, their prayers and complaints stood in a fair way to be answered.

Hillsborough began by blocking Shelburne's plan for three new colonies in the West, and then gave Gage permission to reduce some of the western garrisons. Barrington was disappointed that withdrawal was only partial—troops remained in Illinois and at Fort Pitt for the time being, and there was no sign of the three Great Lakes posts (Niagara, Detroit, and Michilimackinac) being given up. But Hillsborough as secretary of state would suffer the political consequences in case his orders and an Indian war happened to coincide, and so he was moving cautiously. Hillsborough was aware that he had already incurred the enmity of influential Englishmen and Americans who were interested in western colonization by his resistance to their plans; they would not miss a chance to attack him if he made a mistake. He next used a minor fracas at Boston in March, 1768, as an excuse to order a regiment there, where troops had not been since the Seven Years' War. But before Gage received the letter, a real mob had run the customs officials out of town when they tried to seize John Hancock's sloop *Liberty* for smuggling, and Hillsborough told Gage to rush more troops to Boston.

Gage himself, confident as never before in the support of his two colleagues, dropped the mask of caution. "Quash this Spirit at a Blow," he wrote privately to Barrington, "without too much

regard to the Expence and it will prove oeconomy in the End."
Later, in an official dispatch to Hillsborough, he stepped well
outside the limits of his military duties: "I know of nothing
that can so effectually quell the Spirit of Sedition . . . as Speedy,
vigorous, and unanimous Measures taken in England to suppress it." Earlier he had warned Barrington: "If the Principles
of Moderation and Forbearance are again Adopted . . . there
will be an End to these Provinces as British Colonies." [16] For
once even the Parliamentary Opposition, frightened by a series
of riots in London and throughout the country during the year,
seemed ready to acquiesce in "vigorous measures." By November,
four regiments and part of a fifth had assembled at Boston; the
crisis had come.

But nothing happened. Boston leaders kept the town quiet
while the troops landed, and subsequent reports received in
England, including one from Gage, who had paid a visit to
Boston, suggested to the government that the *Liberty* riot might
have been provoked and then exaggerated by royal officials in
Boston. At home, the government found itself deeply involved
in another crisis, unrelated to America, over the election of the
radical leader, John Wilkes, to the House of Commons. The
Opposition was taking heart, and the Ministry was losing its
zeal for a crackdown at this time in Massachusetts. Only Hillsborough continued the fight, pushing for a set of meaures similar to those adopted five years later. He would have altered the
Massachusetts charter, bringing the province more directly
under royal control, and military enforcement was implicit in
such a step. But even the king had lost interest by February,
1769, and Parliament disposed of the matter by passing eight
fiery, ineffectual resolutions.

Gage thus had almost a third of his army in Boston to no
apparent purpose. During the year that followed, he had a
chance to learn a little more about the dynamics of a revolution.
Bostonians found ways to harass the customs officers and the
troops without breaking any laws. Magistrates, who were as
afraid of not being supported by a fickle Ministry as they were

of retaliation from their neighbors, refused to call for military aid. Gage, when he saw that troops were worse than useless, wanted to use the discretion Hillsborough had given him to withdraw them, but the Massachusetts governor, fearful of agreeing to any step that might be wrong, demurred. Two regiments remained in Boston during the next winter, 1769–70. With no one—the Ministry, the governor, or Gage—able to make a decision, and with Bostonians growing in their determination to get soldiers out of their town, it was only a matter of time before an incident like the "Massacre" of March 5, 1770, took place. Under the direct threat of a massive uprising in the countryside on March 6, one regiment departed and the other moved to Castle Island in the harbor.

Gage, Barrington, and Hillsborough were sobered if not discouraged. Yet the experience left their belief unshaken that something drastic would have to be done about Boston; if anything, their belief was strengthened, because they could charge past failures to weakness in the government. Never in the next few years do they seem to have considered seriously whether military coercion was really feasible.

Gage had his hands full during 1771–72 merely administering an army that was slowly deteriorating under the pressure of its American environment. Though regiments rotated across the Atlantic every four years or so, the chronic shortage of recruits forced Gage to permit men who wanted to stay in the colonies for some reason to transfer out of departing regiments. There proved to be hundreds of such men. Likewise, those officers most willing to remain at their posts in the colonies were the ones who had acquired American wives or American land or both, like Gage. The army gradually became a domesticated core of aging officers and men who were themselves virtually Americans, joined by a growing proportion of raw young subalterns (many of them sons of officers) and recruits (some illegally enlisted in America itself).

Away from the middle Atlantic coast, living conditions were unusually bad, even for an eighteenth-century army, and they were not getting any better. Gage had won respect from the government for his honesty and ability to cut costs, but human misery paid the price for part of his reputation. Being stationed at a post like Niagara was unpleasant to begin with, but it became unbearable when the roof was leaking, the bedding was filthy and falling apart, and the commander-in-chief asked for further information before agreeing to any expenditures. In the 1760's Gage had emphasized tactical training—marksmanship, for example—but little was heard of training in the early 1770's; sheer survival was task enough.

In 1772, Hillsborough fell from power when he refused to agree to a new colony in the Ohio Valley. Many speculators had merged to form this "Vandalia" project, as it was called, and they had managed to purchase a good deal of support even within the Privy Council. The whole affair was "an Infamous Jobb in every part of it," according to an undersecretary of state in a letter to Hillsborough's successor.[17] Gage was convinced that a western colony would mean an expensive and distracting war with the Indians, and he took up the fight that Hillsborough had lost. Barrington was now showing the king parts of his private correspondence with Gage, and the two friends worked together to delay royal approval of Vandalia until Gage could come home on leave. When he arrived in the summer of 1773, he succeeded in quietly getting the colony quashed, despite the powerful interests behind it.[18]

It is difficult to assess Gage's position with the government accurately at this crucial point in his career. His ability to block the Vandalia scheme suggests that he stood well with the king himself. But close association with the deposed Hillsborough and the fairly unpopular Barrington did not help him in the cabinet. Gage wrote in late 1773 from London to an old comrade, Lieutenant Colonel James Abercromby, who in turn reported as follows: "I am told General Gage is to go back to America. It seems they have offered him nothing on this side, and paid him but little attention." [19] It appears that Gage was seeking a better or an easier office—a major governorship or a sinecure. The adjutant general, Edward Harvey, added another dimension to Abercromby's report: "Gage is come Home, it was thought not to Return, but the whisper now is, that M-d-m [Mrs. Gage] likes her Native Country better than Britain." There is evidence that the government had considered, even before he returned to England, replacing both Gage as commander-in-chief and Thomas Hutchinson as governor of Massachusetts with a single officer—Robert Monckton, a British general who had won great popularity in America during the last war.[20]

There is no clue as to whether the government was dissatisfied with Gage, or Gage had given the government some hint of being dissatisfied with his job. Despite his harsh private views on American resistance to British policy, Gage had been able to maintain an image of moderation within the colonies. Perhaps the strain of dissimulating toward Americans, of managing an army stretched over unmanageable distances, and of dealing with an erratic government, were proving too much for him. Five years before, an officer visiting headquarters, in writing to his commander in Florida, noted that Gage was so affected by his failure to get a clear statement of military policy from the government that "he is not the same Man he was when you left [New] York."[21] A reasonable guess is that Gage was indeed sick of his job, had thought seriously of giving it up, but changed his mind when Margaret Kemble Gage began longing for what they had left behind in New York and New Jersey.

Whatever the truth about Gage's motives and position, his situation changed abruptly in early 1774 when news of the destruction of the tea in Boston harbor reached London. Within a week Gage had had an interview with George III, and the king's report to Lord North is worth quoting at length:

Since You left me this day, I have seen Lieutenant General Gage, who came to express his readiness though so lately come from America to return at a day's notice if the conduct of the Colonies should induce the directing coercive measures, his language was very consonant to his Character of an honest determined Man; he says they will be Lyons, whilst we are Lambs but if we take the resolute part they will undoubtedly prove very meek; he thinks the four Regiments intended to Relieve as many Regiments in America if sent to Boston are sufficient to prevent any disturbance; I wish You would see him and hear his ideas as to the mode of compelling Boston to submit to whatever may be thought necessary.[22]

Years later, in reply to the question of an historian, Gage recollected that he had said something quite different:

The General [Gage referring to himself] not long from his command by leave, and still holding it, made no objection to return to his duty, but was averse to taking the Government of the Massachusetts Bay. He desired at length that a much larger force than four weak regiments might be sent out, and the Town of Boston declared in rebellion, without which his hands would be tied up.[23]

About the same time, James Paterson, who had been a colonel in 1775 and became a major general in the American war, told Frederick Haldimand, who had been one of Gage's brigadier generals, that "he was present when the general told the King (speaking of Boston) that he had sufficient troops to bring these people to reason." [24] The presumption must be that Gage, who had been gradually becoming more outspoken in his opinions on America, made promises to the king that both men would live to regret.

For Gage, regret may have begun as soon as he stepped out of the royal closet. He had promised to ram the policy of the government down American throats before he (or anyone else) even knew what that policy would be. Anxiously he sought to strengthen his legal position by asking the cabinet if he could use troops against civilian disorder. As commander-in-chief, he had no power to do so, and when made governor, he was constitutionally required to seek the advice of his Council. The cabinet, with some equivocation, said that he could.[25]

So far as is known, Gage played no part in drafting those "Coercive Acts" of the spring of 1774, which closed the port of Boston, made the Council of Massachusetts appointive, and curbed the power of town meetings. He certainly had a hand in new laws for the trial of accused persons outside the province, and for the quartering of soldiers wherever they were needed; both were intended to prevent some of the problems the army had had previously with juries and quarters in Boston. It is also likely that he supported the Quebec Act, which among other things provided for a clear legal authority in the trans-Appalachian West.

When Gage had departed New York in 1773, the mayor and Council had tendered him the freedom of the city and a flowery address. When he returned to America a year later, Boston welcomed him with dignity and even a touch of warmth. As one intelligent Bostonian reported, Gage was proclaimed governor "amid the acclamations of the people. He express'd himself as sensible of the unwelcome errand he came upon, but as a servant of the Crown, he was obliged to see the [Port] Act put in execution: but would do all in his power to serve us." At an "elegant entertainment" afterward at Faneuil Hall, Gage toasted the prosperity of Boston.[26] Since he had intervened to prevent bloodshed during the Stamp Act riots at New York in 1765, Gage had been surprisingly popular in the colonies. He had run his army with evident care and common sense, avoiding disputes whenever possible, and he had behaved himself with tact and sobriety. Late in 1774, Dr. Joseph Warren, a leader of the Boston radicals, still considered Gage as "a man of honest, upright principles" who would work for "a just and honourable settlement."[27] Americans looked to him as their last hope for some reasonable solution of the tea controversy, while his own government believed that he was the man who could bring Boston to its knees without a civil war. He could not possibly satisfy both at once, and he was doomed to satisfy neither.

His first dispatches home were fairly optimistic. With the help of the navy, he had closed Boston port, and had shifted the capital to Salem. There was little that rebellious spirits could do about a blockade, and they were less daring as regiment after regiment moved into Massachusetts. But with the announcement of the Massachusetts Government Act, which virtually annulled the charter of the province, effective August 1, the situation began to change. On September 7, the British government heard from Gage that trouble was likely; by October 1 it was learned that trouble had occurred—the new Crown-appointed members of the Council had been terrorized into resignation, courts had been closed by mobs in the interior of the province, and "Civil Government is near its End . . . Conciliating, Moderation, Reasoning is over, Nothing can be done but by forceable Means." Gage complained that his troops were too few, and he promised to "avoid any bloody Crisis as long as possible" while "His Majesty will in the mean Time Judge what is best to be done." [28] The government, believing that it had already decided "what is best to be done" when it sent Gage to Boston, was apparently thunderstruck; it took sixteen days to write an answer to his letter.

Even more incredible, Gage did not send off his next dispatch for another three weeks. As autumn storms lengthened the time-distance between Boston and London, the government heard nothing from him until November 18. Throughout this seven-week interval Gage's stock had been dropping; it dropped lower still when the government read his next bundle of dispatches. He reported that all the northern colonies were supporting Boston to a degree "beyond the Conception of most People, and foreseen by none. The Disease was believed to have been confined to the Town of Boston . . . But now it's so universal there is no knowing where to apply a Remedy." Only the conquest of New England would be effective. To accomplish this end, he proposed, in a private and round-about way, suspending the Coercive Acts, withdrawing all troops, blockading the coast, and returning only after a much larger army, including German mercenaries, had been raised. From that time on, the government stopped listening to Thomas Gage.[29]

Gage seems not to have realized what was happening to his reputation at home. Toward the end of October he was reading warm praise in a private letter from Secretary of State Dartmouth for his prudent conduct under "the nice and delicate circumstances" which existed in Massachusetts.[30] But that letter had crossed those dispatches of his own that would cause his supporters in the government to lose faith in him. As early as September they had been irritated by the infrequency of his letters and their lack of detailed information. By December, both of the undersecretaries of state for the colonies, men who had supported the hard Hillsborough line toward colonial disorder, were writing to Dartmouth of Gage's "timidity and weakness," and the "Inactivity and Irresolution of his Conduct," which "astonished and alarmed" everyone because it seemed "devoid of both sense and spirit." [31] Even his friend, the tactful and cautious ex-governor of Massachusetts, Thomas Hutchinson, warned him that his proposal to suspend the Acts and to raise German mercenaries had not been well received.[32] Only Barrington continued to write encouragingly.

The government went on listening to messages from America, if not to those of Gage. When he had decided in late August that the next move was up to the king and his ministers, he had withdrawn himself and his army to the Boston peninsula and had begun buttoning up for the winter. Boston had a population of less than 20,000 and it was now occupied by over 3,000 officers and men who had come to police the whole province. Little imagination is required to see what was likely to happen. The townspeople were angry and afraid, the army—especially its officer corps—was bored and humiliated, and everyone was tense and crowded. Gage, as governor, was determined to prevent trouble. If trouble came despite his efforts, he was determined that he, his army, and the home government would not be caught on the wrong side of any dispute or incident. He negotiated an agreement with a committee of the town in which he promised to keep his troops on a tight rein and to listen sympathetically to all complaints concerning their behavior. He kept his promise to Boston, but it cost him the morale of his men and confidence of his officers.

Not all the officers attacked Gage; there were a few who understood his predicament. But there were many more who sent home disparaging comments about their general. Young John Barker of the 4th Foot, for example, was an immature officer who might have criticized any commander under whom he served, but Barker's complaints of "Tommy" who favored the Yankees over his own soldiers were the sort of news from Boston that had made Gage's timidity a subject of coffee-house gossip in London by the end of the year.[33] Far more weighty with the government, however, was a letter like the one from Lieutenant Colonel James Abercromby, a respected officer who had served with Gage during the last war and who had been sent to Boston especially to serve on his staff. Soon after Gage withdrew to the Boston peninsula, Abercromby wrote that "he likes his Colonel [that is, Gage] as a gentleman, but would never employ him on a forlorn hope." [34] Even Bostonians knew that his army was calling Gage *"Old Woman."* [35]

In eighteenth-century England, where a small aristocracy both ruled the country and officered the army, such complaints struck resonant chords. For those at the highest levels of government, policy and honor were becoming hopelessly confused with one another. The honor of the army, virtually penned up inside Boston by fear of a rabble that had proved its cowardice and indiscipline during the last war, was at issue; thus, by extension, the honor of the king (commander-in-chief of the army), of the nobility (whose sons led it), and even of the "nation" (which the army represented in the eyes of the world), were involved. Though the Boston crisis required the most careful calculations of power and interest, the king seemed more upset by the shameful rate of desertion from his regiments in Boston than by the prospect of war; reportedly he wept on General William Howe's shoulder when they heard how fast soldiers were running off into the Massachusetts countryside. By the end of 1774, there was no more calculating of the evidence at Whitehall, Westminster, or St. James. The king had told Lord North, "Blows must decide"; the government had ceased to think—it was merely reacting.[36]

Only a few men in the government had both the knowledge

and the self-control to realize that Gage was right, however unpleasant the realization might be. Barrington and the adjutant general, Edward Harvey, believed him when he said that Americans would fight rather than submit. They understood also how nearly impossible it would be for Britain to carry on a land war across an ocean against an armed population. Both men thought that pacification had to be achieved by naval blockade. At Boston itself, Frederick Haldimand, a capable Swiss officer and a veteran of the last war in America who had served as Gage's second in command, was not impressed by those who dismissed the colonial militia as a rabble in arms. "The Americans," Haldimand noted, "would be less dangerous if they had a regular army." [37] A later generation of Americans, learning lessons of their own about revolutionary wars, can readily understand what Haldimand meant.

But the government had already made up its mind. Gage would have to be superseded, though the king was unwilling to recall him in disgrace. General William Howe would go out to Boston, nominally as second in command, but all would understand that Howe was to be the "acting officer." [38] Howe would take with him as lieutenants Henry Clinton and John Burgoyne. While Howe, Clinton, and Burgoyne were gathering together their baggage and the reinforcements they would take with them, Gage himself should do something to salvage the situation. Dartmouth accordingly signed a long, secret letter which first rejected Gage's appreciation of the situation and his proposals for action, and then ordered him to go out into the countryside and arrest the leaders of the Massachusetts Provincial Congress. In case there was any doubt about what the government expected of him, Barrington also wrote to say that he was organizing a hospital for the army in America "on a large scale." [39]

The actions at Lexington and Concord, like that at Bunker Hill, have been exhaustively studied, but they raise more questions about Gage than have ever been answered. He had known in February that spring would bring some positive order from the government, and that the order would probably mean war. Through an excellent spy system, he also knew what was going on in the countryside, that the Americans were training troops and gathering supplies at Concord, Worcester, and elsewhere. By early April, he had begun to get unofficial news of the measures adopted by the British government. At the same time, one of his spies informed him that the Provincial Congress had been greatly alarmed by the recent march of a brigade of British regulars out of Boston. A committee of the Congress had reported its opinion "that should any body of troops, with Artillery and Baggage, march out of Boston, the Country should instantly be alarmed and called together to oppose their March, to the last extremity." Towns around Boston had petitioned Congress to the same effect. Gage had seen the militia rise on several previous false alarms, and he had no reason to think these words were an empty threat.[40]

Gage had already started preparations for an offensive move into the countryside when he received the secret orders from Dartmouth on April 14. The Massachusetts leaders were as well informed about his preparations as he was about their activities, so there was little mystery on either side. More obscure is the question of why Gage organized the expedition as he did. He must have known that the colonists would resist if he marched to destroy their munitions or arrest their leaders, yet his plans suggest that he counted on avoiding hostilities. He knew the sort of broken terrain his troops would be marching through, and he could not have forgotten the difficulties it posed for a column of regulars, but there is no hint that he was seriously concerned about tactical problems. He sent an improvised brigade made up of 21 grenadier and light infantry companies—the elite troops drawn from each regiment, about 800 men. Every man carried one day's ration but no knapsack. No artillery or baggage accompanied the column. Its commander was the senior field officer on duty, "a very fat heavy Man," seconded by a major of Marines. One can only guess that Gage hoped to make up in speed of movement what such a force lacked in weight and cohesion. Its mission was to destroy the American supplies at Concord and return to Boston, 32 miles round trip.

There was a brief skirmish at Lexington, ten miles out, a fight at Concord, and a running battle all the way home in which the British suffered over 250 casualties. In what seems to have been an afterthought, Gage ordered a brigade to set out with two light artillery pieces ten hours later in support of the first column. The grenadiers and light infantry probably would have been wiped out except for meeting this relief force with its cannon near Lexington on the journey back. Numerous details of the whole operation—its conception, the security measures surrounding it, and its execution—indicate that either Gage did not really believe the militia would fight (which would have contradicted what he had been telling the government), or he did not do even a routinely competent job of planning and supervision. As far as the historian can tell, he had learned nothing from the last war about ambush and tactical marches in America.

Although Gage was henceforth literally besieged in Boston by thousands of New England militia, he obviously continued to hope that Lexington and Concord were not the beginning of a civil war but only an incident that might somehow be smoothed over. He disarmed the people of Boston, and severely restricted civilian movement over Boston neck, but he did not declare martial law. There was talk, at least, of conciliatory measures in both London and Philadelphia, and Gage did not want to jeopardize even a slim chance for peace. Admiral Samuel Graves, who commanded the small fleet in Boston harbor, wanted Gage to seize and fortify Charlestown and Dorchester peninsulas which, like Boston, commanded part of the harbor from their heights and were connected to the mainland by narrow, easily defended causeways. But Gage refused. He was convinced that his army of 4,000 effectives was too weak. Moreover, he was unwilling to begin offensive operations before all political remedies were exhausted. Nor did Graves himself employ the navy on offensive missions. In the end, both men suffered from criticism for their inactivity.

With the arrival of Howe, Clinton, and Burgoyne in late May, Gage, though still commander-in-chief, all but disappears in a fog of collective responsibility. How he finally came to declare martial law on June 12 is unknown, but it is certain that Burgoyne wrote the bombastic proclamation. In a leisurely manner, the generals began to plot how they might pursue Graves' sound proposal to occupy Charlestown and Dorchester, clearly a necessity if Boston were to remain tenable. But they do not seem to have spent much time discussing broader questions of strategy, such as why an army should be in Boston at all. Gage had asked for help from Governor Guy Carleton of Canada, and he had authorized Lieutenant Colonel Allen Maclean to raise a corps of Scottish Highland immigrants in the Carolina back country; otherwise the commander-in-chief waited for reinforcements, further orders, and the next American move.

That move came, of course, with the appearance of fortifications one morning in mid-June on a spur of Bunker's Hill, on Charlestown peninsula. General Clinton wanted to cut off the American forces by landing behind them on Charlestown Neck, but his colleagues decided that the militia should be taught a different kind of lesson. Some insight into the mind of the British council of war, which decided to make a frontal assault, can be gained from a letter written by Burgoyne two months after the ensuing battle:

> I believe in most states of the world as well as in our own, the respect, and control, and subordination of government . . . depends in a great measure upon the idea that trained troops are invincible against any numbers or any position of undisciplined rabble; and this idea was a little in suspense since the 19th of April.[41]

In short, the attack at Bunker Hill, which cost the British over 1,000 casualties, was to be understood on psychological rather than tactical grounds.

Once again, as at Lexington and Concord, neither the plan nor its execution does Gage any credit, though not all the blame can justly be laid to him alone. But, as at Lexington and Concord, he seems to have learned nothing from his own previous military experience. The unsuccessful assaults at Ticonderoga in 1758 and at Niagara in 1759 were basically similar to the situation at Bunker Hill in 1775, with one exception: at Bunker Hill the *militia* stood behind the fieldworks. Gage apparently thought that the one difference made all the difference, for his post-mortem lament to Barrington shows that he finally understood:

> These People Shew a Spirit and Conduct against us, they never shewed against the French, and every body had Judged of them from their former Appearance, and behaviour . . . which has led many into great mistakes.

And, at last, he had begun to grasp the strategic problem as well:

> We are here, to use a common expression, taking the Bull by the horns, Attacking the Enemy in their Strong parts, I wish this Cursed place was burned . . . its the worst place to act Offensively from, or defencively. I think if this Army was in New York, that we should find many friends, and be able to raise Forces in that Province on the side of Government.[42]

Boston was a trap; New York was the key. But by then everyone saw it (Howe had seen it as early as June 12), and it was too late to move the army until 1776. Gage could only wait gracefully for his recall, which arrived in September.

Thomas Gage lived 12 more years, to the age of 67, never doing or saying anything to attract special notice. He made few excuses and blamed no colleagues, which is remarkable among disgraced leaders in any age. Equally remarkable was the agreement among his contemporaries in their estimate of him. Burgoyne had begun a tortuous description of his chief with the following words:

> I have a most sincere value for his private character which is replete with virtues and with talents. That it is not of a cast for the situation in which he is placed I allow; and hence many, tho' far from all, of our misfortunes.

Major James Wemyss, on the other hand, wrote incautiously, but he said the same thing about Gage:

> Of moderate abilities, but altogether deficient in military knowledge. Timid and undecided in every path of duty, was unfit to command at a time of resistance, and approaching Rebellion to the Mother Country.

Almost every other estimate of Gage points in the same direction: pleasant, honest, sober; a little dull; cautious, even timid at times; no talent at all for making war.[43]

Despite his comparatively simple personality, and the contemporary consensus about him, it is difficult to reach a satisfactory judgment on Gage's role in the outbreak of the American Revolution. Without the revolution smoldering beneath him, he would have been the ideal peacetime military administrator. Before 1774, he was generally liked and respected, both by his troops and by the colonists. He had gone far to keep the army, as such, from being an important grievance to Americans. Unlike some other British officials in the colonies, Gage never played with a high hand, nor was there ever a sign of scandal in his conduct of business. Finally, he was tied to America by marriage, property, and length of service on this side of the Atlantic.

His administrative record is balanced by his combat record. Americans could count themselves fortunate to have been opposed in the beginning by a general with so little ability as a fighter. Perhaps, as has been said about other British leaders in the Revolutionary War, he had no heart for the fight against fellow Englishmen. Or perhaps, as Dr. Huck had said, Gage was unlucky—"none of the Sons of Fortune." But chance ought to have given even an unlucky man, provided he had a modicum of skill, some small success in the course of two years.

Gage the military administrator and Gage the combat leader were, however, incidental to his third role—Gage the imperial statesman.[44] Nothing in his commission as commander-in-chief required that he play such a role, and a great deal in his personality indicated that he would not, but circumstances thrust him into the part. His particular interest in finding a policy for the trans-Appalachian West, and his strong personal ties to Barrington and Hillsborough, tended to erode his self-protective reserve. The king's special concern with the army offered Gage a better chance to be heard, and the coincidence of his presence in London with the Boston Tea Party brought all circumstances to a focus. Gage encouraged the king and his government to make him the last major link between Britain and America.

Unfortunately, Gage was a weak link: his understanding of the situation in the colonies was surprisingly feeble. There were those who thought that Gage, despite almost twenty years' service in America, had permitted a few personal associates to insulate him against the facts of colonial life. Whatever the explanation, his poor understanding of the problem was responsible for the government's resting its policy on a false premise: that the main obstacle to the use of military force in America was legal, not practical; that Britain actually could coerce the colonists whenever it decided to pass the necessary laws. The ministers managed to slight the fact that Americans, unlike Englishmen or Irishmen or Scots, were armed. In playing his political role, Gage did not remind them early or forcibly enough to make them reconsider. Only at the end did he himself see the great difficulty of coercing thousands of armed men, and even then, through another kind of weakness, he failed to make himself heard.

This other weakness, weakness of temperament rather than of understanding, led him to support a second false premise of British policy: that Boston was the source of revolutionary infection, and that Boston could be isolated. He must have known better as early as 1769, when New York and South Carolina gave Massachusetts vigorous support against military occupation. But he also must have been temperamentally unable to tell Barrington, or Hillsborough, or the king, anything except what they wanted to hear and he wanted to believe—until it was too late.

The obverse effect of temperamental weakness was the kindly

face he presented to the colonists themselves. Even as he arrived at Boston to enforce the Coercive Acts, he exuded easygoing charm and gave Americans a feeling that he, and the government he represented, would never push matters to civil war. A Boston radical read the smiling face and solicitous manner as weakness in the man and in the government behind him. It is only fair to admit that Gage was indeed unlucky, that he was caught up by forces no one could direct or deflect. But it is also fair to conclude that he was a modest force in his own right, and that his impact served to increase miscalculation by both sides.

FOOTNOTES

1. Quoted in John C. Long, *Lord Jeffrey Amherst, a Soldier of the King* (New York, 1933), p. 41. The information on Gage's family and early life comes from John R. Alden, *General Gage in America* (Baton Rouge, 1948), a sound study that is the only full biography of Gage.

2. Massachusetts Historical Society, *Collections*, 4th series, IV (Boston, 1858), pp. 369–70, in reply to the queries of the historian George Chalmers.

3. October 17, 1754, quoted in Robert Wright, *The Life of Major-General James Wolfe* (London, 1864), p. 293.

4. And it was not for lack of contemporary criticism of the conduct of the campaign in general, because invective flew after the battle. The principal sources are Winthrop Sargent, ed., *The History of an Expedition Against Fort DuQuesne in 1755* (Memoirs of the Historical Society of Pennsylvania, vol. V, Philadelphia, 1855); Stanley M. Pargellis, ed., *Military Affairs in North America, 1748–1765: Selected Documents from the Cumberland Papers in Windsor Castle* (New York, 1936), pp. 77–132, hereafter *Military Affairs;* and Charles Hamilton, ed., *Braddock's Defeat* (Norman, Oklahoma, 1959). A case of modern, uninformed criticism is in the editorial note by Hamilton, pp. xvi–xvii, which is not supported by any contemporary account. The most interesting analysis is by Pargellis, "Braddock's Defeat," *American Historical Review*, XLI (1936), pp. 253–69, though I cannot agree with all of his opinions, and the fullest account is in Lee McCardell, *Ill-*

Starred General: Braddock of the Coldstream Guards (Pittsburgh, 1958).

5. July 25, 1755, Pargellis, *Military Affairs*, p. 117.

6. Gage to the Earl of Albemarle, July 24, 1755, in Thomas Keppel, *The Life of Augustus, Viscount Keppel* (London, 1842), I, pp. 213–18.

7. Gage to Major Craven, June 19, 1759 (copy), LO 6114, Loudoun Papers, Henry L. Huntington Library and Art Gallery, San Marino, California, hereafter Huntington Library.

8. To the Duke of Cumberland, October 2, 1756, Pargellis, *Military Affairs*, p. 235.

9. J. Clarence Webster, ed., *The Journal of Jeffrey Amherst* (Toronto, 1931), p. 171.

10. Huck to Loudoun, December 3, 1759, LO 6153, Loudoun Papers, Huntington Library. Huck may have been grinding some ax in this letter for Loudoun's benefit, but I doubt it.

11. The fullest account of these battles is in Lawrence H. Gipson, *The Great War for the Empire: the Victorious Years, 1758–1760* (*The British Empire Before the American Revolution*, vol. X; New York, 1949).

12. The introduction to Stanley M. Pargellis, *Lord Loudoun in North America* (New Haven, 1933), is an excellent discussion of defense policy before 1755.

13. A good discussion of the rationale for an American garrison is in Bernhard Knollenberg, *Origin of the American Revolution: 1759–1766* (New York, 1960), pp. 27–28, 87–98, though he is wrong in his contention that the Indian problem had little to do with the decision.

14. Secretary of State Halifax to Amherst (received by Gage), October 11, 1763, Clarence E. Carter, ed., *The Correspondence of General Thomas Gage . . . 1763–1775* (New Haven, 1931–33), II, pp. 2–3, hereafter *Gage Correspondence*.

15. Halifax to Gage, "Private," January 14, 1764, *ibid.*, p. 10.

16. Gage to Barrington, June 28, 1768, "Private," *Gage Correspondence*, II, pp. 479–80; Gage to Hillsborough, September 26, 1768, *ibid.*, I, p. 197.

17. John Pownall to the Earl of Dartmouth, September 22, 1773, Dartmouth Papers, I (2), nr. 882, William Salt Library, Stafford, England, hereafter Salt Library.

18. Alden, *Gage*, p. 149; and John Armstrong to George Washington, December 24, 1773, Stanislaus M. Hamilton, ed., *Letters to Wash-*

ington and Accompanying Papers (Boston and New York, 1898–1902), IV, pp. 290–91.

19. Abercromby to Loudoun, December 2, 1773, LO 6447, Loudoun Papers, Huntington Library; Harvey to Governor Johnstone of Minorca, September 21, 1773, War Office Papers 3/23, pp. 126–27, British Public Record Office, London. I have repunctuated and expanded abbreviations in these sentences for clarity.

20. James Grant to [James Wemyss], June 14, 1773, Wedderburn Papers, I, p. 38. William L. Clements Library, Ann Arbor, Michigan, hereafter Clements Library.

21. Captain J. Marsh to Brigadier Haldimand, January 22, 1768, British Museum Additional Manuscripts 21728, London.

22. King to North, February 4, 1774, Sir John W. Fortescue, ed., *The Correspondence of King George the Third* (London, 1927–28), III, nr. 1379, hereafter *Correspondence of George III.*

23. Massachusetts Historical Society *Collections,* 4th series, IV (Boston, 1858), p. 371, in reply to the queries of the historian George Chalmers.

24. "Private Diary of Gen. Haldimand," Douglas Brymner, *Report on Canadian Archives, 1889* (Ottawa, 1890), p. 129.

25. Cabinet minutes, April 7, 1774, Dartmouth Papers, II, p. 883, Salt Library.

26. John Andrews to William Barrell, May 18, 1774, Massachusetts Historical Society, *Proceedings,* VIII (Boston, 1866), p. 328.

27. Warren to Josiah Quincy, Jr., November 21, 1774, Josiah Quincy, *Memoir of the Life of Josiah Quincy, Junior* (Boston, 1875), pp. 178–79.

28. Gage to Dartmouth, September 2, 1774, *Gage Correspondence*, I, p. 371. I have rearranged the order of sentences slightly.

29. Gage to Dartmouth, September 25, 1774, two letters, one of them private, *ibid.,* pp. 275–77. His specific proposals were made in a private letter to Thomas Hutchinson, which he asked Dartmouth to peruse.

30. Dartmouth to Gage, "Private," August 23, 1774, *ibid.,* II, pp. 171–72. Gage received the letter October 28.

31. William Knox to John Pownall, September 13, 1774, Knox Papers, II, nr. 17, Clements Library; Knox to Dartmouth, November 15, 1774, and Pownall to Dartmouth, December [16], 1774, Dartmouth Papers, II, nrs. 994 and 1022, Salt Library.

32. Hutchinson to Gage, November 19, 1774, Gage Papers, Clements Library.

33. Barker's diary is printed in the *Atlantic Monthly,* XXXIX (1877), pp. 389–401, 544–54.

34. Peter O. Hutchinson, ed., *The Diary and Letters of . . . Thomas Hutchinson* (Boston, 1883–86), I, p. 232.

35. John Andrews to William Barrell, March 18, 1775, Massachusetts Historical Society, *Proceedings,* VIII (Boston, 1866), p. 401.

36. Horace Walpole, *Journal of the Reign of George the Third,* ed. John Doran (London, 1859), p. 445; King to North, *Correspondence of George III,* III, nr. 1556.

37. Quoted in Allen French, "General Haldimand in Boston," Massachusetts Historical Society, *Proceedings,* LXVI (Boston, 1942), p. 91.

38. Major Philip Skene to Lord North, January 23, 1775, Dartmouth Papers, II, nr. 1116, Salt Library.

39. Dartmouth to Gage, "Secret," January 27, 1775, *Gage Correspondence,* II, pp. 179–83. The circumstances surrounding this letter are discussed in John R. Alden, "Why the March to Concord?" *American Historical Review,* XLIX (1944), pp. 446–54. Barrington's private letter, February 3, 1775, is in the Gage Papers, Clements Library.

40. "Intelligence" received April 3, 1775, Gage Papers, Clements Library.

41. Burgoyne to Lord George Germain, August 20, 1775, Germain Papers, Clements Library.

42. Gage to Barrington, "Private," June 26, 1775, *Gage Correspondence,* II, pp. 686–87. I do not agree with Alden, *Gage,* p. 254, that Gage understood the importance of New York *before* the battle of Bunker Hill.

43. Burgoyne to Lord George Germain, August 20, 1775, Germain Papers, Clements Library; Wemyss quoted in Allen French, *The Day of Lexington and Concord* (Boston, 1925), p. 61.

44. I am indebted to Professor Howard H. Peckham, director of the Clements Library, where he has lived many years with Gage, for the suggestion that Gage's crucial role was political.

BIBLIOGRAPHY

Alden, John R. *General Gage in America: Being Principally a History of His Role in the American Revolution.* Baton Rouge, 1948. This is the only biography. The present essay is indebted to its scholarship, but does not completely share its sympathy with the subject.

Carter, Clarence E. (ed.). *The Correspondence of General Thomas*

Gage. 2 vols. New Haven, 1931–33. Basic published sources for Gage's career.

Donoughue, Bernard. *British Politics and the American Revolution: The Path to War, 1773–1775.* London, 1964. An excellent, thorough study, accurately described by its title.

French, Allen. *The First Year of the American Revolution.* Boston and New York, 1934. An outstanding work of scholarship and historical understanding that was the last of a series of works by the author on 1775.

Gipson, Lawrence H. *The British Empire Before the American Revolution.* 13 vols. to date. Caldwell, Idaho, and New York, 1936—. A monument of historiography that provides detailed accounts of the campaigns, 1755–60, and of problems of the empire after the war.

Ketchum, Richard M. *The Battle for Bunker Hill.* Garden City, 1962. A reliable, well-written narrative that owes a great deal to French's work.

Knollenberg, Bernhard. *The Origin of the American Revolution: 1759–1766.* New York, 1960. An argumentative, thoroughly researched book that has some provocative things to say about the army.

Pargellis, Stanley M. *Lord Loudoun in America.* New Haven, 1933. Provides an understanding account of British defense problems to 1757 and of the army that Gage would soon command.

Tourtellot, Arthur B. *William Diamond's Drum.* New York, 1959. Republished in paperback as *Lexington and Concord,* it is, like Ketchum, an excellent popularization that draws heavily on French.

Sir William Howe:

CONVENTIONAL STRATEGIST

———•◆•———

MALDWYN A. JONES

University of Manchester, England

SIR WILLIAM HOWE, one of the Revolution's most controversial military figures, remains so down to this day. He was, perhaps, the only British commander-in-chief with a real chance to crush the American rebellion. Why did he fail to do so? Why did he let slip a succession of seemingly easy opportunities to destroy Washington's army? Was he more concerned with reconciliation than with reconquest? Did his political responsibilities as peacemaker interfere with his military obligations as general? These questions, raised by his contemporaries, have divided historians ever since and make the problem of evaluating Howe's record a perplexing one.

It is not difficult to see why Howe's lack of success chagrined and disquieted the loyal subjects of George III. During the first three years of the war Britain mounted a truly prodigious effort on both land and sea. Howe was provided with a military force which seemed more than adequate to restore royal authority in the colonies. It represented the greatest army Britain had ever sent overseas and was infinitely superior to anything that the Americans could put in the field. The British fleet enjoyed complete mastery of the sea and kept lines of communication open at all times. Yet in three successive campaigns this formidable military machine failed either to inflict a decisive defeat on the

Continental army or to recover more than a tiny portion of enemy territory. Small wonder, then, that in the dark days after Saratoga, Englishmen confessed they were at a loss to understand how "such an army, so well appointed, served by so large a train of artillery, and attended by so numerous a fleet, could fail of success against a divided people, destitute of Officers, Soldiers, Magazines, fortified towns, ships of war, or any apparent resources." [1]

Many Englishmen, feeling that the Saratoga defeat was a national humiliation, eagerly cast about for a scapegoat. Some blamed Burgoyne, others Lord George Germain, but a considerable number placed the responsibility squarely on Howe's shoulders. The same was true of American loyalists. "It is a unanimous sentiment here," wrote a disgruntled New Yorker in December, 1777, "that our misfortunes this campaign have arisen, not so much from the genius and valour of the rebels, as from the misconduct of a certain person." [2] Howe, the writer went on, had made many mistakes in earlier campaigns, but these seemed trivial compared to the "gross and mortifying blunders" committed in 1777. Either the general had never looked at a map of America or, if he had done so, he had not understood it. Otherwise, how could he have chosen the campaign in Pennsylvania while Burgoyne was attempting to link up with him on the Hudson? By making Philadelphia his main objective in 1777, Howe had abandoned Burgoyne to his fate.

After Howe's recall in the spring of 1778 such indictments against him lengthened steadily. He returned to London to face criticism, not merely for his supposed miscalculation in the Saratoga campaign but for his entire conduct during his three years in America. In Parliament and the press he was accused, among other things, of having conducted the war with no clear appreciation of strategic realities; of having moved his army backward and forward to no apparent purpose, "as if valour consisted in a military jig"; of having shown undue tenderness to the rebels; and of having failed to make proper use of the loyalists.[3] Besides having abandoned Burgoyne, he had failed to take advantage of his opportunities to smash Washington's army. Even the Americans, declared Howe's critics, recognized that their salvation was due to his excessive caution and procrastination. To many it seemed that Howe had prolonged the war deliberately, either for his own financial advantage, or because he was "wedded to a system of politics that favoured the rebellion." [4]

Howe resented such attacks all the more keenly because Lord North's government made little effort to defend him. Indeed, many believed that the more pungent criticisms of the general were inspired by a member of the government, Lord George Germain.[5] To vindicate himself Howe in 1779 demanded a parliamentary inquiry into his conduct of the war. He seized the opportunity not only to answer his critics but to bring charges of his own. He claimed that to have pursued Washington with greater vigor would have exposed his army to grave dangers; that the loyalists, being a minority in America, would not have aided his cause greatly; and that the government had failed to send him the reinforcements required for the task at hand.[6]

The inquiry led nowhere. Producing nothing but a flood of charges and countercharges, it became little more than a verbal duel between Howe and Germain. Each man claimed he was making no allegations against the other, but was concerned only with defending his honor. The fact of the matter was that the investigation became enmeshed in a factional struggle between the administration and those opposition critics like Fox and Barré who opposed the war. With the entry of Spain into the conflict, the inquiry petered out in June, 1779, and the committee never even rendered a report.

Thus Howe's generalship remained an enigma for historians to puzzle over. Scholars have been no more able to agree on a solution than the inquiry of 1779. Some have attributed Howe's lack of success simply to incompetence—to that "monotonous mediocrity" about which his subordinate, Charles Stedman, complained in his early history of the war.[7] According to such historians, Howe was by nature slow, unimaginative and excessively cautious.[8] Others have suggested that indolence and self-indulgence left him disinclined for active military operations.[9] Still others have endorsed the contemporary charge that Howe's failure resulted from his sympathy with the American cause.[10]

But Howe has not gone undefended. Some scholars have asserted that Sir William had real grounds for complaining that he was not adequately supported by George III's ministers, especially Lord George Germain.[11] Howe's champions have also stressed the difficulties of his task.[12] Indeed, certain historians have argued that, in the long run, Howe's generalship was of little consequence in deciding the outcome of the Revolution. The scales were heavily weighted against Great Britain from the start, they claim, and there was little hope of holding the populous and distant American colonies. Howe's inadequacy amounted, therefore, to no more than that he failed to achieve the impossible.[13]

There are grounds, however, for believing that George III and Germain may have been right—at least until Saratoga—in their conviction that the rebellion could be subdued by force of arms. The triumph of independence movements is not inevitable, as subsequent events in American history were to show. Between 1861 and 1865 the Southern Confederacy was to learn that an embryonic nation could be destroyed on the battlefield. That the Confederacy was finally obliged to surrender to superior force suggests that a similar outcome might not have been impossible during the Revolutionary struggle nearly ninety years earlier. If British commanders had waged war on the colonists as remorselessly as Grant and Sherman did on the Confederates, or if Washington's army had been as decisively defeated in 1776 or 1777 as Lee's was in 1865, patriot morale in all probability would have been shattered as completely as the final campaigns of the Civil War demoralized the South.

If this assumption is correct, then Howe's military failures were neither unimportant nor irrelevant. Howe was the key figure in the first crucial stages of the Revolutionary War, while it was still a domestic rebellion and before France intervened and changed the character of the contest. For the first three years, Britain was spared those distractions that later made it necessary to deploy her strength against other foes and in distant parts of the world. General Howe thus had advantages denied to his successors. That he failed to capitalize on them, that in so doing he allowed the rebellion precious time to take root, was probably the decisive factor in the outcome of the struggle.

Howe was born in 1729, the third son of the second Viscount Howe and of his wife, Mary Sophia, the daughter of Baroness Kielmansegge, who had been a mistress of George I. All three Howe brothers were destined for prominent careers in military service—a fact their enemies often attributed, perhaps unfairly, to the family connection with the house of Hanover. Certainly William's early career showed no evidence of royal favor. In 1746, at the age of seventeen, he joined the army as a cornet in the light dragoons of the Duke of Cumberland. Promoted to lieutenant the following year, he served in Flanders in 1747–48 with the British force sent to oppose Marshal Saxe. After the war he served for several years in the 20th Foot with James Wolfe, with whom he became close friends.

Howe's acquaintance with America did not begin with the Revolution. During the French and Indian War he spent several years in the colonies, and served under Wolfe in the conquest of Canada. At the siege of Louisbourg in 1758 he commanded a regiment and won Wolfe's warm commendation. The following year he distinguished himself by leading the light infantry who first scaled the Heights of Abraham and thereby facilitated the capture of Quebec. In 1760 he commanded a brigade in the Montreal expedition. Returning to Europe, Howe took part in the siege of Belle Isle off the French coast, and then served as adjutant general of the army which captured Havana from Spain in 1762.

By the close of the war Howe had compiled a splendid record and his star was clearly in the ascendant. He added further to his reputation in the early 1770's by introducing a new system of light drill in the army. With the idea of increasing infantry mobility Howe, now a major general, organized lightly equipped companies drawn from the line regiments and trained them to move rapidly. The innovation was an instant success and led to light companies being introduced into all line regiments.

In the period between the two wars opportunities for active service were scarce, and Howe's only military employment was in the purely nominal position of governor of the Isle of Wight. He followed also a political career and represented the town of Nottingham in the House of Commons, being first elected in 1758 to succeed his brother George, who had been killed at Ticonderoga. There was nothing unusual about military men serving in Parliament at that time. In the general election of 1761 no fewer than sixty-four army officers were elected.[14] Besides Howe they included two other men who were to hold important commands during the Revolutionary War—John Burgoyne and Charles Cornwallis. But, unlike Burgoyne, Howe was not an active politician. He entered politics no doubt because, as Lord Chesterfield remarked in 1741, it "was the known way to military preferment." [15] At all events Howe apparently played no part in the prolonged controversy over colonial taxation prior to the war.

There is every indication, however, that Howe held the Americans in high regard. In part this stemmed from his service in America. But even more it sprang from the friendly relationship that had developed between his brother George and the colonists. George Howe—the third Viscount Howe—had been one of the few British officers to welcome personal contact with Americans, and during the French and Indian War had gained the affection of the colonial troops who had served under him. When he fell at Ticonderoga there was genuine grief in the colonies, and the Massachusetts Assembly erected a monument in his honor in Westminster Abbey. The surviving Howe brothers appreciated this gesture and it created for them a sentimental attachment to Americans that they found difficult to break.

When a policy of coercion against Massachusetts was adopted by Parliament, General Howe opposed it. During the winter of 1774–75 he informed his Nottingham constituents that he would not accept an American command, if it were offered him.[16] But in February, 1775, he changed his mind. Among his Nottingham constituents were many who were notoriously pro-American, and one was so disturbed that he wrote to Howe asking for an explanation.

Howe's reply was not entirely convincing. He was going to America, he declared, because he had been ordered to do so. Refusal would have meant that he would incur "the odious name of backwardness to serve my country in distress." "A man's private feelings," he added, "ought to give way to the service of the public at all times." [17] This view was not shared by other prominent military men who faced the same dilemma. General Amherst and Admiral Keppel, for example, both refused to command against the Americans, while other officers resigned their commissions rather than take part in a war they found distasteful. Howe evidently had fewer scruples about serving against the colonists. If he had felt an initial twinge of conscience about the matter, he was not prepared to sacrifice his military career to his feelings. Indeed, if Burgoyne is to be believed, Howe actively sought the chief command in America.

Troyer Anderson, Howe's most ardent advocate in modern times, argues that there was no inconsistency in the general's behavior at this time. Howe, he says, believed his task would be primarily one of negotiation, and his willingness to serve in the colonies did not imply that he was willing to wage war on the Americans.[18] While it is true that Howe and his brother Richard, Admiral Lord Howe, were subsequently appointed in 1776 to a commission empowering them to negotiate with the rebels, there is no evidence that they thought their mandate was political rather than military. Along with most other Englishmen, General Howe believed that the great bulk of the colonists were still loyal to George III and that the insurgents, being an insignificant minority, would not present a serious military problem.

Although he may have hoped for some formula to remove colonial grievances, he seems to have gone to America prepared to use force to restore the authority of the Crown.

Certainly it was Howe's qualities as a soldier which weighed most with the Ministry in deciding to send him to America. Major Philip Skene in reporting to Lord North in January, 1775, that Howe was prepared to serve under Gage, declared that he had served with Howe in many difficult situations and had found him to be "unsurpassed in activity, bravery and experience, and beloved by the troops." [19] Germain, a few months later, gave the Ministry's reasons for choosing Howe. No one, wrote the American secretary in June, 1775,[20] understood the peculiarities of American campaigning better than Howe, who in the French and Indian War "Had command of the light troops and . . . will, I am persuaded, teach the present army to be as formidable as that he formerly acted with." Germain went on to say that the conduct of the coming war required "more than common ability [for] the distance from the seat of Government necessarily [left] much to the discretion and resources of the general." General Gage, for all his good qualities, found himself "in a situation of too great importance for his talents," and rarely ventured to take a single step beyond the letter of his instructions. Dissatisfied with Gage, Germain believed that in Howe he had a general not only experienced in tactics but capable of acting on his own initiative.

Despite the misgivings about Gage, he remained for the moment as commander-in-chief. But to rouse him into taking more vigorous action Howe and two other major generals, Clinton and Burgoyne, were sent to Boston in the spring of 1775. Within a few days of their arrival on May 25, Gage decided to take the offensive and occupy the Charlestown peninsula. Forestalled in this intention by the American militia, Gage instructed Howe to make a landing at the tip of the peninsula and to lead an assault on the American entrenchments. In the ensuing battle—known to posterity as Bunker Hill—the Americans were ultimately driven from the peninsula, but at a terrible cost. Over one thousand of Howe's men, 40 per cent of his entire force, were either killed or wounded. In his own words, it was a "success . . . too dearly bought." [21]

Howe has often been blamed for Bunker Hill. But in two important respects he does not deserve censure. The decision to concentrate upon a frontal assault—rather than land in the American rear at Charlestown Neck—was one in which Howe probably concurred, but final responsibility rested with Gage, who was the ranking officer. Secondly, there seems to be little substance in the charge that Howe failed to pursue the Americans during their retreat to the mainland. His force suffered so heavily in gaining the peninsula that it was in no condition to take up further pursuit.

Yet Howe cannot be excused altogether. Defective as the British plan was, it might have been executed without such heavy losses by a more energetic and resourceful general. For the attackers, speed of movement was essential because the Americans were using every moment to strengthen their defenses. But Howe saw no need for haste. Confident that the rebel militia would scatter before an assault by regulars, he wasted precious time and did not land his men on the peninsula until the afternoon.[22] He erred also in ordering an advance in line instead of in column—a decision which exposed a better target to the defenders. Observers agreed that Howe behaved with exemplary courage on the battlefield and rallied his men at a critical point of the attack.[23] But his tactics, resulting from what one of his subordinates termed his "absurd and destructive confidence," contributed not a little to the slaughter.[24]

Whether Howe's experience at Bunker Hill colored his subsequent generalship has been much debated. It may well have. His account of that "unhappy day," as he called it, spoke of his horror at losing so many brave men.[25] The battle left a deep impression and for the remainder of the war he shrank from frontal assaults whenever possible.

After succeeding Gage as commander-in-chief, Howe received orders in early November, 1775, to abandon Boston and move the army to New York. But owing to the lateness of the season and to lack of transports, Howe decided instead to spend the winter in Boston. There he remained until March 17, 1776, when Washington's seizure of Dorchester Heights made the city untenable. Howe thereupon withdrew his army to Halifax.

Howe's inactivity during the siege of Boston is difficult to understand. His own explanation, which his modern defenders have endorsed, was that nothing decisive could be accomplished in Boston. The Americans outnumbered him and were strongly fortified; any attempt to storm their lines might have led to another Bunker Hill. He complained also that his army lacked the supplies and transport necessary for offensive operations.[26] The most that could have been attempted, according to his apologists, was a large-scale raid, but even that might have ended as disastrously as the Concord expedition. Far better, therefore, to wait until 1776 when reinforcements would arrive and New York would offer a more promising base of operations.[27]

There is no denying that Howe had serious problems during the winter of 1775–76. But that does not excuse him, for his opponent was, perhaps, even worse off. The Continental army was disorganized and undisciplined, and desperately short of powder and artillery. Worst of all, it threatened to disband itself, when enlistments expired on the last day of 1775.[28] Washington, driven to despair by "such a dearth of public spirit, and such want of virtue" as he saw around him, was apprehensive lest the British take advantage of his difficulties and attack him. "Our situation," he wrote in November, "is truly alarming; and of this General Howe is well apprized, it being the common topic of conversation . . . [in] Boston. . . ." [29] That this critical period passed without any offensive action by the British was an immense relief to Washington. But at the same time, he was puzzled. "Search the vast volumes of history through," he wrote in January, 1776, "and I must question whether a case similar to ours is to be found; to wit, to maintain a post against the flower of the British troops for six months together . . . and at the end of them to have one army disbanded and another to raise within the same distance of a reinforced enemy." [30]

Washington's astonishment is understandable. Even if Howe
was incapable of carrying out a major offensive, he should have
made harassing attacks upon the besiegers, if only to retain the
initiative. That he failed to do so has sometimes been attributed
to the attachment he formed for Mrs. Joshua Loring, and to his
love of gambling. But Howe's dissipation was probably more
a result than a cause of his military inactivity. His disinclination
to set his troops in motion at this time in reality can be traced
to another source, namely, the limitations imposed by his military education. Like most soldiers reared in the formalized military tradition of the eighteenth century, Howe closed his mind
to the possibility of winter campaigns. With the first frosts, he
put aside all thoughts of soldiering until spring. The fact that
the Americans did not share this attitude was shown when
Arnold assaulted the fortress of Quebec in a blinding snowstorm
in December, 1775. It was to be demonstrated still more strikingly a year later by Washington's daring riposte at Trenton.
But Howe proved incapable of learning anything from the
Americans. Hence he remained passive during the winters of
1776 and 1777, hibernating snugly in New York and Philadelphia respectively, and ignoring the existence of Washington's
shivering army barely a day's march away.

Howe revealed his true character in his first few months as
commander-in-chief. His flair for improvisation—demonstrated
earlier in his organization of the light infantry—gave way to a
timid adherence to accepted practices. The boldness he had
shown on the Heights of Abraham and at Bunker Hill were
replaced by a policy of caution. Howe's frame of mind boded
ill for Britain's hopes of reconquering America; once the chief
responsibility was his, Howe became oppressed by the magnitude
of his task and had doubts about his ability to carry it to a
successful conclusion. The American army, he informed Dartmouth in January, 1776, was not "by any means to be despised,
having in it many European soldiers, and all or most of the
young men of spirit in the country." To defeat the Americans
large reinforcements would be required. If these were not forth-

coming, Howe concluded, it might be "better policy to withdraw entirely from the delinquent provinces, and leave the colonists to war with each other for sovereignty." [31]

For a man newly appointed to put down the rebellion, this was an astonishing statement. On the strength of a single encounter with the rebels, and six months before the Declaration of Independence, Howe was prepared to contemplate a complete withdrawal from America. Nothing could better illustrate his bankruptcy of mind than this gloomy prognostication. Howe seems to have expected the mere presence of a sizable British force in America to bring about a collapse of the rebellion. When that hope was shattered, he was no longer sure how to proceed. He could have understood much better a purely military problem, but a situation in which he had both to conquer and to pacify appears to have made him uncertain what measure of coercion was to be used. It is true that there were occasional moments when his confidence returned, as in April, 1776, when he wrote to Germain of his hopes of bringing Washington to a decisive action at New York, an action "than which nothing is more to be desired or sought by us, as the most effective means to terminate this expensive war." [32] But such optimism was short-lived. As the war dragged on, his doubts multiplied. Small wonder that his operations, instead of reflecting a sense of urgency, were characterized by hesitancy and delay.

Howe's decision, on abandoning Boston in March, 1776, to go to Halifax instead of New York was a correct one. He had little alternative. The reinforcements promised him had not yet arrived and his army was in no condition to attack New York. The winter in Boston proved to be a trying one and the troops required a period of rest and reorganization. Howe in particular wanted an opportunity to exercise them in line—"a very material part of discipline," as he later remarked, "in which we were defective until that time." [33]

Nor was the delay in opening the 1776 campaign entirely Howe's fault. His timetable, already disarranged by his forced withdrawal from Boston, was thrown further into disarray by the difficulty of obtaining supplies at Halifax and by Germain's instructions to postpone the expedition against New York until reinforcements had arrived from England. But even after landing on Staten Island in early July, Howe waited nearly two months before moving against the Americans on Long Island.

Howe's dilatoriness has been explained by his alleged desire to attempt a reconciliation before resorting to further bloodshed. But his peacemaking efforts in July do not appear to have interfered much with his military plans. The determining factor was Howe's unwillingness to begin operations until he received reinforcements from England and from the expedition against South Carolina. The last of these reinforcements did not reach him until mid-August, a circumstance to which he later pointed as proof that he could not possibly have started his campaign earlier.[34]

The validity of his argument depends on whether Germain's instructions to await reinforcements before commencing operations were so binding as to deprive Howe of freedom of action. The inescapable conclusion is that they were not. The Ministry had given Howe full discretionary powers to crush the rebellion and, in view of his distance from London, did not expect him to carry out particular instructions if local circumstances or his own judgment suggested otherwise.[35] Proof that Howe understood the situation perfectly lies in his earlier decision to remain in Boston during the winter of 1775–76 despite instructions to the contrary.

Howe's failure to attack sooner in New York was a serious mistake. Even without the expected reinforcements, he enjoyed a substantial margin of superiority over Washington. Had he attacked at once he might have captured New York City with even less difficulty than he subsequently experienced. While he delayed, the Americans improved their defenses: fortifications were strengthened, arms and ammunition poured in, and Washington imposed some semblance of discipline on his army.[36] Washington's force, moreover, was joined by local militia, and by the time Howe belatedly began operations he was facing the largest number of Americans to be gathered in one army during the entire war.

The weather provided Howe with another excuse for doing little that summer. During the Parliamentary inquiry of 1779, Howe reported that "from the violent heat of the weather, little active service could have been done, and . . . such service would probably have been attended with much sickness to the troops." [37] Having earlier rejected American winters as too cold for campaigning, Howe now complained the summers were too hot. Here was additional proof of his tendency to exaggerate his difficulties and his readiness to submit to circumstances.

Slow though he was to begin operations, Howe could exhibit considerable skill in planning and executing military maneuvers of a conventional and uncomplicated nature. His handling of the battle of Long Island showed him at his best. Landing his army in the vicinity of the Narrows under the cover of the fleet, Howe exposed the American left by a flanking march which, timed to the minute, resulted in the rout of the enemy. This victory, greeted in Britain as a sure sign that the rebellion would shortly be over, raised Howe's reputation to its peak. Germain paid Howe a high compliment by describing the battle as "the first Military Operation with which no fault could be found in the planning of it, nor in the Conduct of any Officers to whom you entrusted the Command." [38] George III rewarded Howe by conferring a knighthood upon him and showed concern that the general was too fond of exposing himself to fire. He ought to consider, the king told Germain, "how much the Publick would suffer by the loss of a General, who had gained the Affection of his Troops, and the Confidence of the Country." [39]

Yet Long Island was not the complete British victory it might have been. Had Howe taken the advice of Clinton and others to continue the pursuit and storm the American entrenchments, there is little doubt that the entire American force on Long Island would have been annihilated. But he halted the attack short of the American lines, observing that "the Troops had for that day done handsomely enough." [40]

Howe was bitterly assailed for this decision during the Parliamentary inquiry. His critics fastened upon his own admission, made within a week of the battle, that "had the Troops been permitted to go on . . . they would have carried the Redoubts." [41] Confronted with this statement three years later, Howe swallowed his words and claimed that storming would not have produced the destruction of the rebel army. [42]

It is, of course, true that only half the American army of 20,000 was stationed on Long Island. But to have destroyed or captured this substantial force personally led by Washington would have dealt the Americans an irreparable blow. Had such a stroke been followed by a prompt landing on the northern part of Manhattan, the war would no doubt have been over.

Howe's defense of his conduct at Long Island goes far to explain his failures in the Revolutionary War. It provides also a revealing comment upon the military system that produced him. He declared in 1779:

> The most essential duty I had to perform was not wantonly to commit his majesty's troops where the object was inadequate. I knew well that any considerable loss sustained by the army could not speedily, nor easily, be repaired. In this instance . . . to have permitted the attack in question would have been inconsiderate, and even criminal. The loss of 1000 or perhaps 1500 British troops, in carrying those lines, would have been but ill repaid by double that number of the enemy, even could it have been supposed they would have suffered in this proportion. [43]

Howe's sentiments were characteristic of British—indeed of European—military thought in the eighteenth century. The army was recognized as the product of a great national effort. It took several years of intensive training to instruct soldiers in the complicated maneuvers required in the warfare of the period. It took equally long to amass the necessary weapons and equipment. The cost of raising and maintaining military forces imposed such a severe strain on the limited resources of the government that the army came to be regarded as a species of national wealth. It had to be husbanded accordingly. To lose an army in battle was an almost irretrievable disaster; for this reason it was more important for a general to preserve his own force than to defeat that of the enemy.[44]

The precepts on which Howe's military education were based posed a serious handicap in a war which, by its very nature, required bold offensive action if it were to be won. It is true that some of Howe's subordinates, notably Clinton, who had received the same education, urged a bolder course on Howe at Long Island. But these generals did so knowing that Howe, and not they, would bear ultimate responsiblity for the army's safety. It was significant that once Clinton became commander-in-chief, he became as cautious as Howe.[45] The truth was that Howe's military upbringing made it difficult for him to act otherwise than he did. If that consideration is given due weight, the allegation that Sir William, out of sympathy for the Americans, deliberately withheld the *coup de grâce* at Long Island so as to permit the enemy to retire in safety to Manhattan, can be seen for the absurdity it is.

Howe's critics can nevertheless be pardoned for continuing to suspect his intentions. His dawdling in the weeks after the battle of Long Island seemed to suggest that he was not serious about his efforts to end the rebellion. Having bestirred himself sufficiently to take possession of New York on September 15, he left Washington undisturbed on Harlem Heights for nearly a month. Despite the fact that the American army was again on the verge of dissolution and was too weak to attack him, Sir William went to elaborate lengths to fortify his newly won base. Indeed, he had already concluded that there was "not the smallest prospect of finishing the contest this campaign," and had turned his thoughts to 1777.[46]

There was no justification for so gloomy a view. The military situation still offered Howe splendid opportunities for striking a decisive blow. As long as Washington remained at Harlem Heights, the American army was in a highly precarious position: British landings in Westchester, if followed up quickly, could sever his lines of retreat to the mainland. But Howe's amphibious operations against Westchester, tardily begun on October 12, aimed not at trapping Washington but only at maneuvering him out of Manhattan Island. After landing his troops behind the American lines at Throg's Neck in the East River, Howe remained inactive for several days. According to his own account, he was anxious to secure his supply lines before penetrating inland. To have struck out at once from Throg's Neck, he claimed later, would have been "an imprudent measure, as it could not have been executed without much unnecessary risk." [47]

Yet if Howe had acted promptly to seize the exit from the Neck, and had then moved inland, Washington could not have escaped encirclement. As it was, Sir William's hesitation permitted the patriot army to slip away to White Plains. Though he achieved his object of forcing the Americans out of their entrenchments, Howe failed to take full advantage of the situation.[48]

At White Plains, Howe repeated his performance at the Battle of Long Island. Having carried an American outpost on Chatterton Hill, he declined a further assault on the enemy lines. Thus, in the eyes of many observers, he let slip one more opportunity of inflicting mortal injury. As at Long Island, he excused himself by claiming there was no reason to suppose that the forcing of the lines would have led to the destruction of the enemy: Washington, he said, would simply have withdrawn to another defensive position.[49]

The final phase of the 1776 campaign virtually settled the outcome of the war. The reduction of Fort Washington in mid-November presented Howe with a fresh and unexpected opportunity. The way was open for an advance into New Jersey and, if vigorously pursued, this might have carried the British into Philadelphia. Washington's army, weakened by desertion and dispirited by defeat, could not have halted a British offensive.

Indeed, Howe might have intercepted the American army as it straggled across the Delaware.

Yet this opportunity too was squandered. Howe's rigidity of mind prevented him from seeing how vital a rapid advance on Philadelphia was at this stage. In light of the changed situation, he might have recast his strategy. He had planned, as a preliminary to the 1777 campaign, to send an expedition to take Newport, Rhode Island. But once there was a prospect of annihilating Washington's army in New Jersey and of capturing Philadelphia, Newport ceased to have strategic significance. Clinton, who had been named to command the Newport expedition, quickly grasped that what was needed was a concentration of force to the south. He proposed that the troops intended for Newport should be landed instead on the New Jersey shore to cooperate with Cornwallis, who was in pursuit of Washington. As another alternative, Clinton urged that they be transported by sea to the Delaware to chase Congress out of Philadelphia.[50] But Howe rejected both suggestions. He insisted on sending the expedition to Newport as planned.

The decision was a grievous mistake. But it was not necessarily a fatal one; Cornwallis still had twice as many troops as Washington. At the time the American army retreated across the Delaware, its situation was desperate. "With a little enterprise and industry," Washington wrote later, it would have been a simple matter for the British "to dissipate the remaining force which still kept alive our expiring opposition." [51]

But enterprise and industry were qualities Sir William Howe lacked most. Even with so rich a prize within his grasp he made no attempt to hasten the pace of pursuit. He ordered Cornwallis not to go beyond New Brunswick until reinforcements arrived, and when the Americans retreated across the Delaware he called off the pursuit for lack of boats with which to cross the river.

His action was a characteristic one—an expression of the caution which had now become second nature. Had Howe been determined to continue as far as Philadelphia, the river barrier at the Delaware might have been surmounted. He could either have built boats from the lumber that lay near at hand or brought small craft down from New York. But Howe felt the campaign had gone on long enough.[52] At the end of November, he decided to defer further operations until spring and went into winter quarters.

The consequences of his decision were not long in coming. Taking swift advantage of the unexpected respite, Washington revived American hopes with two stunning victories at Trenton and Princeton. Howe had been aware of the risk involved in extending his outposts to Trenton. But he believed the disposition of his troops was justified by the need to give protection to the New Jersey loyalists and the fact that the American army appeared too weak to strike a counterblow.[53] In fact, Howe was less to blame for the Trenton setback than his subordinates who failed to erect redoubts as he had ordered. But the fact remains that had the pursuit across New Jersey been conducted with greater vigor, Washington would have had neither the strength nor the opportunity to counterattack.

The 1776 campaign, in retrospect, proved to be the turning point of the war. No other British general was presented with such a succession of opportunities for ending the struggle as Howe had in the summer and fall of that year. Time and again sluggishness and timidity prevented him from taking chances. When Howe turned his back on the Delaware, he decided the fate of the Revolution.

British strategy in the campaign of 1777 was equally defective. It was aimed at the conquest of territory instead of the destruction of Washington's army. Moreover, the moves of the British armies were ill-planned. Howe's invasion of Pennsylvania and Burgoyne's descent from Canada were conceived as two entirely separate operations and no attempt was made to coordinate them. It was little wonder that British arms met with disaster at Saratoga.

Howe cannot bear the entire blame for the Saratoga defeat. He had nothing to do with the planning of the Canadian expedition; it was worked out in London by Burgoyne and Germain. Nor was it Howe's responsibility to coordinate his own offensive with that of Burgoyne. The trouble here was a faulty command structure. It had been decided early in the war to have two independent commands in North America, one under Howe for the American colonies, the other under Carleton for Canada. The relationship between the two theaters was never defined, so that each commander was dependent for information upon the other and upon what he learned from Germain. If anyone was responsible for coordination, it was Germain.

During the planning of the 1777 campaign, however, Germain failed to discharge this responsibility. It was not that he neglected to inform Howe of Burgoyne's movements; the old story of a forgotten dispatch, unsent through Lord George's indolence, need no longer be taken seriously.[54] It was rather that Germain failed to insist upon Howe's completing operations in Pennsylvania in time to return to the support of Burgoyne. Indeed, the need for such a precaution did not occur to Germain until it was too late.

Thus when Howe left New York for the Chesapeake, his mind was focused almost entirely upon reaching Philadelphia. He was aware of the impending invasion from Canada, but he had no reason to suppose that a northward advance in strength up the Hudson was expected of him. Nor did Burgoyne count upon such a move. He was confident when he set out from Canada that he could reach Albany without Howe's help. It was only after his surrender that Burgoyne complained of lack of cooperation.

These facts, however, do not absolve Howe altogether of blame for Saratoga. His critics may have been wrong when they accused him of willfully sacrificing Burgoyne. But what he did was almost as bad. By moving away from the strategic center, he deprived himself of the opportunity of influencing events. To embark on a seaborne invasion of Pennsylvania without making clear provision for a junction with Burgoyne was to act as though the Canadian command did not exist.

Howe's part in the chain of events that led to Saratoga reveals his limitations as a strategist. Between November, 1776, and April, 1777, Howe sent Germain three separate plans that varied greatly. The first envisaged an attack on Boston from Rhode Island by one army and an advance up the Hudson by another. Within a month of sending this plan to London, and prior to his receiving a reply, he drew up a second one that was radically different. This proposal envisaged a double offensive against Philadelphia: the main force to proceed overland across New Jersey and a smaller contingent to go by sea. No sooner had Germain given his approval to this second scheme than Howe produced a third—the one he actually put into practice. The advance across New Jersey was abandoned and the entire army was to be taken to Philadelphia by sea instead.[55]

Whatever the respective merits of these plans considered individually, the fact that they succeeded each other so rapidly is a commentary on the shallowness of Howe's strategic thinking. No general with a clear appreciation of the task confronting him could have shifted so abruptly from one set of strategic ideas to another. Indeed, it was irresponsible on Howe's part to bombard Germain with a succession of divergent proposals over so short a period of time. When every packet from New York carried fresh proposals from the commander-in-chief, the American secretary could hardly be expected to coordinate operations effectively.

During Parliament's inquiry Howe spent a good deal of time defending his decision to campaign in Pennsylvania instead of going up the Hudson to assist Burgoyne. He produced plausible arguments. The Canadian army, he asserted, was thought to be fully capable of looking after itself. Had he gone up the Hudson, he would have been accused of wasting the campaign and of attempting to steal some of Burgoyne's thunder. In any event an attack on Philadelphia was, in his opinion, the most effectual diversion that could be made to help Burgoyne. Washington was obliged to defend the American capital and this precluded his marching up to the Hudson. Moreover, an attack on Philadelphia was the best way of bringing Washington to battle.[56]

But Howe's arguments had serious weaknesses. It was only

after the Saratoga surrender that he began to think of the Pennsylvania campaign as a diversionary move in Burgoyne's favor. Nor could he have been certain at the time that Washington would decide to defend Philadelphia in preference to marching northward. Indeed, during the six weeks he spent on the voyage to the Chesapeake, Howe was out of touch with Washington's army and was powerless to influence its movements. Had the American commander been better equipped to exploit his advantage of interior lines, he might have intervened decisively against Burgoyne during Howe's absence at sea and then have marched south with his army and that of Gates in time to repulse the British invasion of Pennsylvania.[57]

Howe's fundamental error was not that he chose to invade Pennsylvania, but rather that he failed to do so overland. Had he advanced on his objective across New Jersey, as the second of his plans proposed, he would have been justified in his claim that he was helping Burgoyne. He would also have been in position to double back instantly if Washington had threatened either New York City or Burgoyne's army. When asked during Parliament's inquiry why he had not proceeded overland, Howe could only offer the same puerile excuse he had used to explain his failure to capture Philadelphia in 1776: he lacked "sufficient means" to cross so large a river as the Delaware and therefore "judged the difficulties and the risk too great." [58]

Howe conducted the whole campaign of 1777 with all the deliberation for which he was now notorious. He began the year by neglecting to take advantage of Washington's weakness at Morristown. After the American army had doubled its size during the spring, Howe wasted precious time in a series of half-hearted attempts to induce Washington to do battle.[59] Thus the summer was far advanced before the Pennsylvania expedition even got under way. Keeping his troops on board transports for two weeks in New York harbor, Howe finally set sail for Philadelphia on July 23.

His progress by sea was painfully slow. The armada first of all put in at Delaware Bay, probably to allow Howe to find out whether Washington had moved toward Albany. Learning that he had not, and finding the Delaware heavily fortified, Howe abandoned his plans for a landing and put out to sea again. Owing to contrary winds three more weeks elapsed before he sailed into the Chesapeake and disembarked his army at Head of Elk. Defeating Washington at the Battle of Brandywine on September 11, Howe tarried another two weeks before occupying Philadelphia. It thus took him more than two months to reach an objective only one hundred miles away from his New York base.

At Brandywine, Howe repeated the tactics he had employed so successfully at Long Island. Once more he skillfully executed a flanking movement which obliged the American army to retreat in disorder. However, he again halted the attack at a time when, had he pressed on, he might have turned the American retreat into a rout.

Sir William fought his last major battle when Washington's surprise attack caught him off guard at Germantown in early October. Contrary to his usual policy, Howe relaxed his vigilance once Philadelphia was captured and failed to order entrenchments built. He felt that to do so might be taken by Washington as a sign of weakness. When the battle began the British were in danger of defeat, but the American attack miscarried and Washington's men finally retired in confusion.

Germantown destroyed what little remained of Howe's military reputation. It did not add much to Washington's either. In fact, the inadequacies of the rival commanders were such that neither seemed capable of winning a decisive victory. An anonymous correspondent of a London newspaper aptly summed up the battle in these words: "Any other General in the world than General Howe would have beaten General Washington, and any other General in the world than General Washington would have beaten General Howe." [60]

Soon after hearing the news of Saratoga, Howe requested that he be allowed to resign his command. He gave two reasons for stepping down: the government had failed to support him adequately, and his recommendations had been consistently ignored. But Howe had other motives for resigning. He correctly anticipated that he would be blamed for Burgoyne's defeat and he was anxious to return to London so as to answer his critics. After spending a final winter of inactivity in Philadelphia, Howe learned his resignation had been accepted and he was free to go home. On the eve of his departure a mock tournament, known as the Mischianza, was staged in his honor. It was described by one eyewitness as "the most splendid entertainment . . . ever given by an army to their General," [61] and this absurd spectacle demonstrated, if nothing else, that Sir William had not lost the regard of his officers.

Howe sailed from Philadelphia for England on May 25, 1778, three years to the day since his arrival in Boston aboard the *Cerberus.* The years had been ones of frustration, disappointment and lost opportunities. To the very end Howe believed that the fault did not lie with him. But some contemporaries disagreed. In the papers of Sir Henry Clinton is the following anonymous and acid comment:

> Had Sir William fortified the hills around Boston he could not have been disgracefully driven from it; had he pursued his victory at Long Island he had ended the rebellion; had he landed above the lines at New York not a man could have escaped him; had he cooperated with the Northern Army he had saved it, or had he gone to Philadelphia by land he had ruined Mr. Washington and his forces; but, as he did none of these things, had he gone to the D . . . l before he was sent to America, it had been the saving of infamy to himself and indelible dishonour to his country.[62]

The inconclusiveness of Parliament's inquiry left Howe a haunted and an aggrieved man. His critics shared his feelings of dissatisfaction, and they kept up their pamphlet attacks upon him for more than a year. The most bitter and persistent of his adversaries was the loyalist refugee, Joseph Galloway, whose attacks stung Howe in 1780 into publishing a lengthy rejoinder.[63]

About this same time, Howe suffered a political setback when he lost the seat in Parliament he had occupied for more than twenty years. His Nottingham constituents were deeply divided by the American war. The noncomformist members of the corporation were strongly pro-American; their opponents were no less anxious to stamp out the rebellion. Howe's participation in the war cost him the support of both groups, and he was defeated in the general election of 1780.[64]

But Sir William's military career had not yet run its course. Although rejected by the electorate and unpopular with the Ministry, Howe still managed to retain the favor of George III. When North was replaced by Rockingham in 1782, Howe was made lieutenant general of ordinance. Had the Nootka Sound dispute with Spain in 1789 led to war, he would have commanded the so-called "Spanish armament." By the time war broke out with France in 1793, he was considered for active service abroad, but remained at home to command first the northern, and then the eastern, military districts of England. It was not until 1803 that he finally retired from the army. In 1799, on the death of his brother Richard, he became Viscount Howe. He had been appointed governor of Berwick-on-Tweed in 1795, and in 1805 he became governor of Plymouth, where he died nine years later at the age of eighty-five.

The crushing of the American rebellion was a task bristling with difficulty. But it was not an impossible one for a country with such a preponderance of military force as Great Britain possessed. How it could be achieved was to be demonstrated a century later when the British faced a similar problem in South Africa. Just as the Boers were first crushed and then persuaded to accept the continuance of British rule, so might a defeated America have been brought, at least for the time being, to abandon its aspirations to independence. But the first requirement was military victory and this a gifted soldier might have won. Contrary to what has often been asserted, the cards were not stacked against the British from the start; the trouble was that they were dealt to a general who was not qualified to play an admittedly difficult hand.

Sir William Howe's deficiencies as a general are obvious enough. His movements were incredibly slow and ponderous; his tactics were timorous, unimaginative, and predictable; and his strategy was based on no clear conception of how the war was to be won. His plans, accordingly, lacked not only inspiration but even coherence.

But Howe's failings, though easy enough to catalog, are difficult to account for. To some contemporaries, the explanation lay in his weaknesses of character. Charles Lee, who spent several months in Sir William's company in 1777 as a prisoner of war, subsequently painted this unflattering picture of his host.

> He is naturally good-humour'd, and complacent, but illiterate and indolent to the last degree, unless as an executive Soldier, in which capacity He is all fire and activity, brave and cool as Julius Caesar. His understanding is . . . rather good than otherwise, but was totally confounded and stupefy'd by the immensity of the task impos'd upon him. He shut his eyes, fought his battles, drank his bottle, had his little Whore, advised with his Counsellors, receiv'd his orders from North and Germain . . . took Galloway's advice, shut his eyes [and] fought again. . . .[65]

This portrait of Howe contains some element of truth. There can be no doubt that he had an easygoing, even a lethargic, disposition. But he was neither a fool nor a libertine. An experienced and competent soldier, he had no need to lean on others for advice; indeed, it might have been better for him if he had done so. Fond though he was of pleasure, he does not appear to have pursued it to the neglect of his duties.

But if Lee was wrong perhaps in suggesting that Howe's moral shortcomings were responsible for his lack of military success, he was surely right to depict him as a man of average abilities placed in a situation which called for something more. This assessment was confirmed by one of Howe's subordinate officers, Allen Maclean, who wrote in 1777:

It would not be unjust to say that General Howe is a very honest man, and I believe a very disinterested one. Brave he certainly is and would make a very good executive officer under another's command, but he is not by any means equal to C. in C. . . .[66]

To the embittered group of loyalist refugees who spent the war years in England and became some of Howe's sternest critics, the issue was not Sir William's alleged incompetence but his reluctance to exploit his victories. It seemed to them that after each of the major battles of 1776–77—Long Island, White Plains, Brandywine and Germantown—Howe could have destroyed the Continental army if he had wanted to.[67] Howe, in Galloway's words, "succeeded as far as he chose"; but because of Sir William's delusion that the empire might be saved by conciliation, he had chosen to prolong the war.

These unsubstantiated charges are almost certainly false. Sympathetic though Howe may have been to the rebels at the outset, his sense of duty as a soldier and his loyalty to the Crown would have precluded his showing them undue tenderness. One must accept his statement that he never permitted the hope of reconciliation to color his military thinking.

That Howe failed to strike relentlessly and unremittingly at Washington's army was a consequence of the philosophy of war he had imbibed during his military education. In the course of the inquiry in 1779, he summed up that philosophy in one tortuous but revealing sentence:

As my opinion has always been, that the defeat of the rebel regular army is the surest road to peace, I invariably pursued the most probable means of forcing its Commander to action under circumstances the least hazardous to the royal army; for even a victory, attended by a heavy loss of men on our part, would have given a fatal check to the progress of the war, and might have proved irreparable.[68]

In short, Howe would seek a battle only when he could be sure that the engagement would leave his army virtually intact. This was because the army was, in Howe's own words, "the stock upon which the national force in America must in future be grafted." [69] Given such an attitude, the wonder is not that Howe so rarely took the initiative against Washington, but that he took it at all.

There is some reason, therefore, to doubt Howe's assertion that he always considered the Continental army to be his primary objective. Many of his strategic dispositions were directed, not toward bringing Washington to battle, but toward occupying territory. His strategic planning was based on the assumption that the civilian population could be cowed into submission by an overwhelming display of force.

This assumption was most clearly demonstrated in Howe's original plan for 1777—a plan he abandoned when the large reinforcements he required for its execution were not forthcoming. It called for 10,000 men to operate against Boston, and 10,000 more to move up the Hudson to facilitate Burgoyne's approach. Washington's army, meanwhile, was to be held in check by an additional force of 8,000 men which was to make feints against Philadelphia. In the fall there was to be an advance into Pennsylvania, followed by winter operations in Virginia, the Carolinas, and Georgia. These operations, Howe wrote in November, 1776, "would strike such terror through the country that little resistance would be made to the progress of His Majesty's arms." [70] The main function of the British army, as Howe conceived it, was to make a demonstration over a wide area in order to encourage the loyalists and to persuade the rebels of the futility of further resistance. Washington's army entered hardly at all into these calculations: it was simply to be prevented from interfering with the triumphant march of the British.[71]

There was nothing eccentric or sinister in such an approach. It was all of a piece with Howe's conventional military ideas. In proposing to march his soldiers through the length and breadth of the colonies in preference to attacking the Continental army, Howe was simply conforming to the widely held belief that campaigns were not necessarily won by fighting battles. "Battles," wrote one of his contemporaries, "have ever been the last resource of good Generals. . . . The fighting of a battle only because the enemy is near, or from having no other plan of offence, is a direful way of making war." [72] The proper method of proceeding was to maneuver for position, to occupy strategic points, to avoid engagements except when success was certain, and above all to preserve the army intact.

This method was appropriate enough for the limited wars of eighteenth-century Europe, but it was useless in the struggle for America. The Revolutionary War was not a war about territorial boundaries or dynastic rivalries; it was a war of ideology, and could be won by Britain only by a decisive victory on the battlefield. Even if Howe had come to recognize the need for this kind of warfare, he would have been inhibited by his professional training from practicing it as commander-in-chief. It was one thing for Howe as a young colonel to lead a daring exploit to the top of the Heights of Abraham; it was quite another for him as a middle-aged general to risk losing the only army his country could raise. Faced with a situation that demanded boldness, ruthlessness, and imagination, Howe could only take refuge in a military orthodoxy that was irrelevant to his needs.

FOOTNOTES

1. [Anon.], *A View of the Evidence relative to the Conduct of the American War.* . . , 2nd ed. (London, 1779), p. 127.

2. *Ibid.*, p. 86.

3. *Ibid.*, pp. 7, 138.

4. *Ibid.*, p. 129.

5. Worthington C. Ford, "Parliament and the Howes," Massachusetts Historical Society, *Proceedings*, XLIV (November, 1910), pp. 120–43.

6. *The Narrative of Lieut. Gen. Sir William Howe . . . relative to his Conduct . . . in North America*, 2nd ed. (London, 1780).

7. Charles Stedman, *The History of the origin, progress and termination of the American war* (London, 1794), I, p. 398.

8. John R. Alden, *The American Revolution, 1775–1783* (New York and London, 1954), p. 127.

9. Charles F. Adams, "Cavalry in the War of Independence," Massa-

chusetts Historical Society, *Proceedings,* XLIII (April–June, 1910), p. 580.

10. Bellamy Partridge has alleged—though without producing any evidence to substantiate the charge—that Howe's failure on several occasions to press home his advantage against the enemy was directly attributed to his friendly feelings toward the Americans and to his hopes for a reconciliation. See Partridge, *Sir Billy Howe* (London and New York, 1933), pp. 98–99, 101–03, 148–51, 168, 241–42.

11. The famous historian of the British army, Sir John W. Fortescue, who was always ready to blame politicians rather than generals, exculpated Howe on these grounds. See John W. Fortescue, *A History of the British Army,* 13 vols. (London, 1899–1930), III, pp. 174–75, 204, 208, 397–98.

12. Howe's most persuasive modern advocate has been Troyer S. Anderson. In *The Command of the Howe Brothers during the American Revolution* (New York and London, 1936), Anderson noted that Howe had to act as military commander and as peacemaker simultaneously; that he was beset by immense logistical problems because all supplies had to be sent from England; that he had to conduct operations over vast distances; and that he found fewer loyalists prepared to make personal sacrifices for George III than ministers in England believed. According to Anderson, Howe's caution and avoidance of risks were due to the precariousness of his position. Because British losses could not speedily be replaced, Howe felt bound to conduct operations with prudence in order to minimize the chances of a serious defeat.

13. This argument was, in effect, that of Fox, Burke, and Chatham, who believed from the first that the colonies could not be recovered by force. The same thesis appears in the works of Whig historians, notably in George O. Trevelyan's *History of the American Revolution,* 2 vols. (London, 1899–1903).

14. Lewis B. Namier, *The Structure of Politics at the Accession of George III* (London, 1929), pp. 32–33.

15. Quoted in *ibid.,* p. 31.

16. Anderson, *op. cit.,* p. 48.

17. *Ibid.,* p. 49.

18. *Ibid.,* p. 50.

19. Skene to North, January 23, 1775, Historical Manuscripts Commission, *Dartmouth MSS.,* II, p. 262.

20. Germain to Suffolk, June 16 or 17, 1775, Historical Manuscripts Commission, *Stopford-Sackville MSS.,* II, p. 2.

21. John W. Fortescue, ed., *Correspondence of King George III*, 6 vols. (London, 1927–28), III, pp. 220–24.

22. Alden, *The American Revolution*, pp. 38–39. For a detailed account of the battle, see Allen French, *The First Year of the American Revolution*, (Boston, 1934), pp. 211–67.

23. Sydney G. Fisher, *The Struggle for American Independence*, 2 vols. (Philadelphia and London, 1908), I, pp. 337–39.

24. *Detail and Conduct of the American War*, p. 13, quoted in Henry S. Commager and Richard B. Morris, eds., *The Spirit of 'Seventy-Six* (Indianapolis and New York, 1958), I, p. 135.

25. Fortescue, *Correspondence of King George III*, III, p. 220–24.

26. Anderson, *op. cit.*, pp. 108 ff.

27. *Ibid.*, pp. 88–90, 97.

28. John C. Miller, *The Triumph of Freedom, 1775–1783* (Boston, 1948), pp. 80–84.

29. Washington to the President of Congress, November 28, 1775, John C. Fitzpatrick, ed., *The Writings of George Washington* (Washington, D.C., 1931–1944), IV, p. 122.

30. Washington to Joseph Reed, January 4, 1776, *ibid.*, IV, p. 211.

31. Howe to Dartmouth, January 16, 1776, C.O. 5/94, pp. 65–74, quoted in Anderson, *op. cit.*, p. 117.

32. Howe to Germain, April 25, 1776, C.O. 5/93, pp. 277–84, quoted in Anderson, *op. cit.*, p. 121.

33. Howe, *Narrative*, p. 4.

34. *Ibid.*, pp. 47–48.

35. Eric Robson, *The American Revolution, 1763–1783* (London, 1955), p. 140. Howe later admitted that he had had a free hand, and made no complaint of interference from London. See Howe, *Narrative*, p. 46.

36. Fisher, *op. cit.*, I, pp. 484, 490–91.

37. Howe, *Narrative*, p. 4.

38. Quoted in Miller, *op. cit.*, p. 125 fn.

39. *Ibid.*

40. *Ibid.*, p. 124.

41. Quoted in *ibid.*, p. 124.

42. Howe, *Narrative*, pp. 4–5.

43. *Ibid.*, p. 5.

44. Eric Robson, "The Armed Forces and the Art of War," in J. O. Lindsay, ed., *The New Cambridge Modern History*, VII, pp. 163 ff.

45. William B. Willcox, *Portrait of a General: Sir Henry Clinton in the War of Independence* (New York, 1964), pp. 494–96.

46. Quoted in Fisher, *op. cit.*, I, p. 522.

47. Howe, *Narrative*, p. 6.
48. Fisher, *op. cit.*, I, pp. 524–25.
49. Howe, *Narrative*, pp. 6–7.
50. William B. Willcox, ed., *The American Rebellion: Sir Henry Clinton's Narrative of his Campaigns, 1775–1782* (New Haven, 1954), pp. xxiii, 55.
51. Circular to the States, October 18, 1780, Fitzpatrick, *Writings of Washington*, XX, p. 206.
52. Fisher, *op. cit.*, I, pp. 537–38.
53. Howe, *Narrative*, pp. 7–9.
54. Willcox, *Portrait of a General*, pp. 143 ff; Anderson, *op. cit.*, pp. 213 ff; Piers Mackesy, *The War for America, 1775–1783* (London and Cambridge, Mass., 1964), pp. 117–18.
55. Anderson, *op. cit.*, pp. 214–22; Howe, *Narrative*, pp. 9–13.
56. Howe, *Narrative*, pp. 16–21.
57. Charles Francis Adams, Jr., "The Campaign of 1777," in Massachusetts Historical Society, *Proceedings*, XLIV (October, 1910), p. 30.
58. Howe, *Narrative*, p. 16.
59. Fisher, *op. cit.*, II, pp. 11–13.
60. *The Gentleman's Magazine*, XLVIII (August, 1778), p. 368, quoted in Martin Kallich and Andrew MacLeish, *The American Revolution Through British Eyes* (Evanston, Illinois, and New York, 1962), p. 113.
61. *Annual Register for 1778*, pp. 267–70, quoted in Commager and Morris, *op. cit.*, I, pp. 657–60.
62. Quoted in Alan Valentine, *Lord George Germain* (Oxford, 1962), pp. 259–60.
63. Worthington C. Ford, "Parliament and the Howes," Massachusetts Historical Society, *Proceedings*, XLIV (November, 1910), pp. 120–43.
64. Ian Christie, *The End of North's Ministry* (London, 1958), p. 145.
65. Lee to Benjamin Rush, June 4, 1778, *Lee Papers, Collections of the New York Historical Society for the Year 1872*, p. 398.
66. Allen Maclean to Alexander Cummings, February 19, 1777, quoted in E. Stuart Wortley, *A Prime Minister and his Son* (London, 1925), pp. 105–06.
67. William H. Nelson, *The American Tory* (Oxford, 1961), pp. 134 ff.
68. Howe, *Narrative*, p. 19.
69. Quoted in Robson, *op. cit.*, p. 109.

70. Howe to Germain, November 30, 1776, *C.O.* 5/93, quoted in Anderson, *op. cit.*, pp. 214–15.
71. Anderson, *op. cit.*, p. 215.
72. Major Thomas Bell, *A Short Essay on Military First Principles* (London, 1770), quoted in Robson, *The American Revolution, 1763–1783*, p. 99.

BIBLIOGRAPHY

Alden, John R. *The American Revolution, 1775–1783.* New York, 1954. Concludes that Howe lacked ability and being unimaginative merely followed traditional British military practices and procedures.

Anderson, Troyer S. *Command of the Howe Brothers during the American Revolution.* New York, 1936. The most recent reliable study of the Howe brothers, and concentrating more on the general than the admiral. Anderson is sympathetic to General Howe, claiming that his dilemma arose from the fact that he had to function as a military commander and as peacemaker at one and the same time.

Brown, Gerald S. *The American Secretary: The Colonial Policy of Lord George Germain, 1775–1778.* Ann Arbor, 1963. Casts new light on the relationship between General Howe and Lord Germain. The book dismisses the idea of a "pigeon-holed dispatch" which Germain reputedly failed to send that would have ordered Howe to lead his army up the Hudson.

Fisher, Sydney G. *The Struggle for American Independence.* 2 vols. Philadelphia and London, 1908. A diatribe against Howe, suggesting that the Whig general may have wished to deprive the Ministry and Burgoyne of a victory at Saratoga.

Ford, Worthington C. "Parliament and the Howes," Massachusetts Historical Society, *Proceedings*, XLIV (October, 1910), pp. 120–143. Serves as the best guide to the materials in the confrontation between General Howe and Parliamentary leaders.

Fortescue, Hon. John W. *A History of the British Army.* 13 vols. in 20. London, 1899–1930. Tends to excuse General Howe and to place the blame for Britain's defeat on the Parliamentary leaders.

Howe, Sir William. *The Narrative of Lt. Gen. Sir William Howe in a Committee of the House of Commons on 29th April 1779, Relative to His Conduct During His Late Command of the King's Troops in North America, to Which Are Added Some Observations upon a Pamphlet Entitled Letters to a Nobleman.* London, 1780. This is Howe's own defense of his conduct.

Partridge, Bellamy. *Sir Billy Howe*. London, 1932. A popularized biography that is often unreliable and undocumented.

Mackesy, Piers. *The War for America, 1775–1783*. Cambridge, Mass., 1964. Tends to be very critical of Howe's generalship.

Robson, Eric. *The American Revolution, 1763–1783*. London, 1955. A perceptive evaluation of General Howe, showing that he adapted well to American conditions in his use of tactics but often showed a lack of imagination.

Willcox, William B. *Portrait of a General: Sir Henry Clinton in the War of Independence*. New York, 1964. Demonstrates that Howe was often unwilling to accept sound suggestions on strategy from his subordinate, General Clinton.

Sir Henry Clinton:

PARALYSIS OF COMMAND

———•·•———

WILLIAM B. WILLCOX
University of Michigan

SIR HENRY CLINTON stands out in a number of ways from his military and naval colleagues in the War of Independence. He served longer than any of them, for two and a half years as second in command to Howe and for four years as commander-in-chief; between 1775 and 1782 his tour of duty was interrupted only once, by a two-month leave in England. He alone, among the officers of high rank, wrote a full account of his campaigns; he spent years in compiling it, and it was virtually ready for the publisher by the time he died in 1795. He also left behind him an enormous mass of official and private papers, in which he reveals himself more fully in his own words than almost any other general of the eighteenth century.[1] He was not a winning person; his friends were few and his enemies legion. Neither was he a great general. He was a better one than most of his critics averred, and would have been better still if his talents had had free scope; but he was the victim of both external circumstances and his own inner uncertainties. He did not fail sensationally, like Burgoyne and Cornwallis, or put his hand on victory and let it slip through his fingers, like Howe in 1776. His failure was slower and more subtle, and punctuated by successes; but in the end it was just as important in determining the outcome of the war.

Clinton was an aristocrat by birth and a New Yorker by up-bringing. He was the first cousin, protégé, and for a time the heir presumptive of the second Duke of Newcastle-under-Lyme, who came as near to being a political nonentity as a duke could in an age when title and influence went hand in hand. Clinton's father and the duke's uncle was Admiral George Clinton, the governor of New York during King George's War. The admiral was a fussy and ineffectual man, who received his governorship largely because he was incompetent to command a fleet; he had, however, like most of his aristocratic contemporaries, great skill in finding and pulling every string that might lead to a lucrative plum. Young Henry stayed with his father in America, mostly on Manhattan, until 1749, when at the age of nineteen he left for England. His connections there brought him promotion in the army; and during the Seven Years' War he was sent to Germany, became an aide-de-camp to Prince Charles of Bruns-wick, and made a name for himself by his gallantry in action. When he was ordered to Boston to strengthen the hand of Gen-eral Gage in 1775, in company with William Howe and Bur-goyne, Clinton was a middle-aged major general of forty-five, who had never had a command and had not seen active service for many years.

On the voyage to Massachusetts he was thrown (literally as well as figuratively, for the weather was rough) with Howe and Burgoyne, and their acquaintance slowly ripened. They were an interesting trio, destined to be closely linked for the next two years but far apart in character and background. Burgoyne was eight years older than Clinton, Howe one year; their seniority in the army, however, was determined by the dates of their pro-motions, and here the order was Howe first, then Clinton, then Burgoyne. Clinton differed markedly from both his shipmates. He lacked their self-assurance and the ease of manner that at-tracted friends; for he was, as he said of himself at the time, "a shy bitch." He did not have their natural gift for command and was never, as they were, popular with the army. But he had compensating advantages. His mind was keen and worked smoothly, with none of Howe's intellectual torpor; and his judgment was not warped, like Burgoyne's, by a gambler's recklessness. As a planner he was superior to them both. If generalship had involved no more than planning, he would have been the outstanding member of what Gentleman Johnny, with his taste for the orotund phrase, called their "triumvirate of reputation."

The professional backgrounds of the three during the Seven Years' War were as diverse as their personalities. Howe's principal service had been in America under Wolfe. Burgoyne, whose military career had been delayed by a runaway marriage, had redeemed himself late in the war by a distinguished record against the Spaniards in Portugal. Only Clinton, of the three, had served in the German campaigns; and the veterans of that hard school tended to look down upon officers who had had their military education anywhere else. Clinton rarely mentioned his training, but colleagues who did not share it either sensed in him or imputed to him a superiority that annoyed them. Although he would never have been popular at headquarters in any case, because he lacked the gift of popularity, it seems to have been this antipathy to the German school that at critical moments tipped the scales against him.

The three generals, when they landed at Boston in May, found everything at sixes and sevens. Lexington and Concord had brought on an investment of the city, and the garrison was in a state of nerves bordering on panic; "the rebels are seen in the air carrying cannon and mortars on their shoulders." If General Gage had been going to start a war, Clinton complained, he should have started it by striking a first blow, at Concord, that was sudden and severe. "Alas, it was the last—but to us!" [2] The three newcomers agreed that the British position had to be enlarged; and Clinton was particularly active in reconnoitering the enemy defenses, forming ideas for attack, and then pushing them at Gage. But, before any plan could be acted upon, the Americans suddenly occupied and fortified Charlestown Neck;

and the attempt to dislodge them brought on the battle of Bunker Hill.

The problem that faced Gage was simple. The Americans on the neck, which communicated with the mainland by a narrow isthmus, could readily be attacked from the bay; if they were thus taken in the rear, their fortifications would be useless and their retreat would be cut off. Clinton proposed that the main army should attack their front, while he landed with a detachment near the isthmus. The importance of his landing might have seemed self-evident; it would have unhinged the whole enemy position. But the commander-in-chief ignored him. "Mr. Gage," he commented later, ". . . would not take any opinion of others, particularly of a man bred up in the German school, which that of America affects to despise." [3] Howe consequently led the direct frontal assault, unsupported on the isthmus, and lost almost half his force in casualties.

This was Clinton's initiation to his role as a subordinate, and it was a foretaste of much that was to come. He had presented an eminently sensible idea, which promised to secure possession of the neck at minimum cost *and*, in the process, to surround and destroy the enemy; this would have been the kind of blow that Gage had failed to strike at Concord. Clinton may have been tactless in approaching his chief, although on that point there is no direct evidence. In any case his plan was turned down out of hand, and for an alternative that was patently inferior on its merits and that proved to be disastrous in its result. The episode is puzzling.

The next phase of Clinton's career was significant for the future in a different way. In the autumn he became second to Howe, who took the command on Gage's recall; and in the following January the new commander-in-chief detached him on an expedition to the southern colonies. The government planned to send a large reinforcement from Britain to meet the expedition in early spring at the Cape Fear River, in North Carolina, to raise the loyalists of the south and permit them to reestablish royal authority; command would be shared by Clinton and the naval commandant of the reinforcements, Sir Peter Parker. In March, Clinton reached the Cape Fear, where he waited idly for two months while his small force almost starved. In early May, Parker arrived at last, and after considerable discussion he and Clinton decided to attack Sullivan's Island, which guarded the entrance to the port of Charleston. The general landed his troops on an island adjacent to Sullivan's, thinking that they could wade to it across a small inlet—which turned out to be seven feet deep. The army was helpless to co-operate with the navy. Parker eventually went ahead on his own, bombarded the fort on Sullivan's, and was ignominiously repulsed. The two commanders thereupon threw in the sponge and sailed for the north.

This fiasco reveals Clinton at his rock-bottom worst. He had no valid reason for attacking Sullivan's in the first place, because he could never have held it if he had captured it. His landing, based on no reconnaissance worth the name, brought his troops to the wrong island and turned them into mere spectators. This was bad enough; what was worse, in its implications for the years ahead, was that he made no real effort to collaborate with Parker. The two services went their separate ways, and for months afterward the two chiefs quarreled about what had happened. They might have agreed to share the blame and keep quiet; instead each tried to fix responsibility on the other, and Clinton was far the more pertinacious of the two. In the process of wrangling he acquired an ineradicable sense of grievance. It spilled over onto the new secretary of state for the American colonies, Lord George Germain, who he believed was supporting Parker against the army; and the principal purpose of Clinton's returning to England in the following year was to secure redress from the minister.

But a great deal happened between grievance and redress. At the end of July, 1776, the battered expedition from South Carolina joined General Howe and his brother, Lord Howe, for the opening of the New York campaign; and Clinton resumed his former position of second in command. He also resumed his habit of offering advice, with which he bombarded his chief throughout the campaign. Only one of his suggestions was accepted, the design for the battle of Long Island. Headquarters grumbled and sniffed at this plan "as savoring too much of the German school," but finally, reluctantly, decided to try it.[4] Clinton used his favorite maneuver, envelopment, by leading the main attack in a wide circuit around the Americans' left wing, so that he was behind their center before the real fighting began. The result was the most brilliant tactical triumph that the British scored in the field during the war.

Triumph might have been expected to give weight to Clinton's future suggestions, but it did nothing of the sort. In the rest of the campaign he argued over and over again for using other forms of envelopment to destroy Washington's army—enveloping Manhattan while the Americans were still on it, by way of the Hudson or the East River to the Harlem; enveloping their army later as it retreated across New Jersey, either by seizing Philadelphia in its rear or attacking its flank from the Jersey coast. All these plans were turned down. Instead Howe, in slow and stately fashion, maneuvered the enemy out of Manhattan to White Plains, out of White Plains to the New Jersey side of the Hudson, out of New Jersey into Pennsylvania; and there the campaign ended. It had produced great but not decisive gains. Washington's army was still in existence and, as he soon proved, capable of striking back.

Clinton and his chief had contrasting views of what the operations around New York ought to achieve, and the contrast reveals their different styles of generalship. Howe's focus was territory, Manhattan and its environs; and he used military means to clear the enemy out of that area at the smallest possible cost to himself in killed and wounded. This was a policy of minimum risk, which by precluding the chance of heavy losses precluded the hope of a quick decision. Clinton's focus was the enemy army. He wanted to encompass its destruction, not merely drive it back; and for that purpose he wanted to exploit to the full the mobility that the British derived from controlling

THOMAS GAGE

From an engraving by Rogers.
Courtesy of William L. Clements Library, University of Michigan.

SIR WILLIAM HOWE

Engraving by Ritchie.
Courtesy of William L. Clements Library, University of Michigan.

SIR HENRY CLINTON

Engraving by Ritchie.
Courtesy of William L. Clements Library, University of Michigan.

SIR GUY CARLETON

Engraving by Ritchie.
Courtesy of William L. Clements Library, University of Michigan.

JOHN BURGOYNE

Photograph of painting.
Courtesy of National Portrait Gallery, London.

CHARLES LORD CORNWALLIS

From the painting by John Singleton Copley.
Courtesy of National Maritime Museum, Greenwich, England.

RICHARD LORD HOWE

Bartolozzi after Northcote. Courtesy of National Maritime Museum, Greenwich, England.

THOMAS GRAVES

By Hodges after Rising. Courtesy of National Maritime Museum, Greenwich, England.

MARRIOT ARBUTHNOT

SIR SAMUEL HOOD

inting by Mosiner. Courtesy of National Maritime Museum, Greenwich, England.

SIR GEORGE RODNEY

the water. All his plans for envelopment, except the one that was adopted on Long Island, involved the fleet; and the amphibious operations that he proposed may have been as unwelcome to Lord Howe as to his brother.[5] In any case they were never tried. Washington extricated himself from the trap into which he had blundered, and at the turn of the year the battles of Trenton and Princeton showed how far his army was from being defeated.

By then Clinton was far away. In the late autumn of 1776 he had occupied Rhode Island, which Lord Howe wanted as a naval base and his brother, now Sir William, was determined to give him; and in the following January Clinton secured permission to go home on leave. He hoped to stay there. He was still nursing his grievance against Germain over Sullivan's Island, and the recent campaign had confirmed his resolve never again to serve under Howe. A knighthood, however, solaced the grievance and weakened the resolve. Clinton was also given to understand that he might have command of the invasion from Canada that Burgoyne had mapped out and that was then in preparation; but this suggestion, much as it appealed to him, he turned down out of deference to Burgoyne. Germain promised to support, the king refused to let Clinton resign, and his friends persuaded him that all might yet be well. In early May, 1777, the newly dubbed and still reluctant Sir Henry sailed from Plymouth to resume his post.

He arrived in July, to find that Howe was about to take his army by sea against Philadelphia, so that the commander-in-chief could be of no help to the invasion from the north, and that Clinton was to be left as garrison commander at New York. Sir Henry was appalled. In his opinion the southern move would imperil Manhattan, Burgoyne's Canadian army, and the whole war effort. The New York garrison would be condemned to what Clinton called "a damned starved defensive"; and Howe's approaching Philadelphia from the south, by way of the Delaware or Chesapeake, would permit Washington to abandon Pennsylvania and bring the whole weight of his army against Manhattan. Burgoyne's troops, once they reached the upper Hudson and lost their supply lines to Canada, would have to depend on river communication with New York, which could not be secured unless Howe's entire force were on hand to break through the barrier of forts that the Americans had erected in the Highlands near West Point. The move to Pennsylvania would jeopardize the war effort by making a quick, decisive victory impossible. Philadelphia was not important enough for the Americans so that Washington would be forced to fight for it; this was one of the few points on which Clinton and Howe agreed. Once the British occupied the city, furthermore, most of their army would be pinned down in garrison duty, and could not return to win the war on the Hudson. The only way to win, Sir Henry argued, was to move northward from New York at once and in full force. If Howe and Burgoyne cooperated in the neighborhood of the Highlands, they might draw the Americans into battle and destroy them, or cut off New England from the middle colonies. In either way the rebellion might be crushed before winter set in.

The logic of this argument was unanswerable, and Howe made no real attempt to answer it. For weeks the two generals talked at cross purposes, until at last they decided that "by some cursed fatality we could never draw together." [6] The trouble, however, was not in their stars but in their characters. Under his genial surface Howe was as stubborn as a mule (*entêté*, Gage had called him); in a less genial way so was Clinton. Almost from the start of their service together Sir William had been exposed to an unrelenting flow of advice from his junior. It had sometimes in the past turned out to be sounder than his own opinion, and he seems to have wondered at moments whether it could be in this case. But he could scarcely derogate from his position by saying so. He was too deeply committed to Pennsylvania to let himself be overruled by a subordinate, no matter how good the logic. The government had approved his plan, he said; he could not change it now even if he would. On July 23 he sailed for the south.

By the end of the summer Burgoyne was clearly in trouble.

Although Clinton did not know where Washington's troops were (Howe had not bothered to tell him that they had been committed to the defense of Philadelphia), he decided that the crisis in the north justified some risk to Manhattan; and in early October he moved against the Highlands. It was the nearest approach to a gamble that he ever made, and his reasons for making it were cogent. He had no hope of opening the Hudson and keeping it open with his small force; his aims were less ambitious and more realistic—to take pressure off Burgoyne and to demonstrate to Howe that the barrier could be broken. Sir Henry carried out the attack in masterly fashion, and within three days had captured the two key forts and possessed the Highlands. At that moment came word from Burgoyne that he was in desperate straits, and Clinton responded at once by detaching half his force up river on an equally desperate attempt at rescue. On the day that his ships reached their farthest point, some forty-five miles below Albany, Burgoyne surrendered. Sir Henry had done what he could by speed and skill, and in the process had won a neat little victory. But its fruits, like the larger fruits of Howe's Pennsylvania campaign, were lost at Saratoga.

That blow shattered the government's plans for winning the war, and forced a drastic review of strategy. As autumn wore on into winter in London, the news from Paris grew more and more ominous; and it was clear to the Ministry that Britain, if France intervened, could not go on fighting as she had. It was much less clear to Howe in Philadelphia. All he proposed was opening an offensive in the south, for which he would need ten thousand more troops, or sitting still for a year to see what happened— suggestions that were scarcely calculated to galvanize an apprehensive government. After prolonged debate the cabinet decided that Sir William must go, and then tackled the question of who should succeed him. Lord Amherst declined. Sir Guy Carleton detested Germain and vice versa; they could not serve together, and jettisoning the minister was too high a price to pay for finding a commander-in-chief. Someone, in a moment of madness, suggested Prince Ferdinand of Brunswick, Frederick the Great's chief lieutenant in the Seven Years' War. The list of those who deserved sober consideration, however, was extremely small; and Clinton was at the head of it. Lord North distrusted him, because of his constant complaints and attempts to resign; but the administration had no feasible alternative. On February 4, *faute de mieux*, Sir Henry was appointed.

The circumstances of his receiving the command influenced his tenure of it. He had no firm backing in the political world of London. Newcastle, his only patron, was singularly ineffective; Sir Henry's friends in the House of Commons were few and far between, and such support as he had from leaders of the Opposition was for their purposes rather than his. The king kept sending him kind messages, but did not have the partiality for him that he had shown earlier for Burgoyne and showed later for Cornwallis. The prime minister looked on him askance. Lord Sandwich, as spokesman for the navy, was cool toward a man as talented as Clinton in quarreling with naval officers; and Germain, after the Sullivan's Island affair, could not be expected to be his wholehearted champion. Sir Henry's position in America was no stronger than at home. He lacked Burgoyne's and Corwallis' magnetism, and the geniality that made Howe popular. Perhaps inevitably, after his long dissension with Sir William, Clinton had disparaging critics even among his own entourage; and his capacity for feuding increased their numbers. Within a year of taking the command he was aware that "I am hated— nay, detested—in this army." [7]

Success was his only way to gain support from the government and the army, but here two major factors militated against him. One was the gulf that developed between Britain's military ambition and her attenuated resources for waging war in America. She refused to do what Adam Smith, in concluding *The Wealth of Nations* in 1776, had warned that she might have to do, "accommodate her views and designs to the real mediocrity of her circumstances"; instead she reached for conquests that were beyond her grasp. The other factor was Clinton's inability to cooperate with the colleagues to whom he was yoked. The pattern of conduct that he had first revealed on Sullivan's Island became more pronounced as his responsibilities increased, until in the last year and a half of campaigning his friction with the two men on whom he chiefly depended for success brought about a slow but inexorable paralysis of command.

Sir Henry was promoted at a moment when the government was ready, if need be, to surrender the whole area of rebellion. His instructions in March, 1778, ordered him to evacuate Philadelphia and authorized him, in an emergency, to abandon New York and Rhode Island as well and fall back on Halifax, Nova Scotia. Simultaneously the Carlisle Peace Commission was sent to offer the colonies the substance of independence without the name, and to keep open the possibility that even the name might be formally recognized.[8] Whitehall, in short, was ready to conclude the American war on almost any terms it could get, including military withdrawal and political capitulation on every point worth fighting for.

The reason for this retreat is obvious. French intervention shifted the focus of the struggle from the American theater to the West Indies, which for Britain had far more economic importance than the mainland. The only hope of success in the West Indies lay in withdrawing troops from Clinton, because no other forces were available; he would therefore have to retrench if he did not evacuate. Retrenchment, furthermore, was required by the altered naval situation. French sea power, once it was thrown into the scales, jeopardized British supply lines to America and lateral communications along the coast. To mitigate the danger from this new quarter Sir Henry's army, spread out from the Delaware to Narragansett Bay, had to be consolidated. He was consequently ordered to begin his command by abandoning Pennsylvania, and simultaneously to detach roughly one-third of his troops to the Caribbean; and for the next four years he never was given more than driblets of reinforcements.[9] He complained that he was being willfully neglected, which was a half-truth. The neglect was not willful, but it was only too real.

He was forced to pull in his horns at just the moment when the Americans were extending theirs. The French alliance was an enormous stimulus to their self-confidence—a much greater one, in fact, than was justified by anything that France did for them until the summer of Yorktown. They had other reasons for believing in themselves. They had survived the loss of New York, Newport, and Philadelphia; their cause had proved to have no geographical center without which they could not exist. Their militia had stood up to the redcoats and Germans in the wilderness around Saratoga, where for the first time European regulars had blundered their way to disaster. Washington had learned to be a general since the dark days of 1776, and his prestige had grown accordingly; during the recent winter at Valley Forge, furthermore, he had fashioned an army that was more effective than anything Howe had met, as Clinton soon discovered at Monmouth Court House. Thus Sir Henry had a depleted force with which to meet opponents who were stronger than before, and the Royal Navy could no longer guarantee his communications and supplies.

The British government under these circumstances might have been expected to follow a consistently defensive policy in America. But it did not. Once Clinton and Lord Howe had succeeded, by the skin of their teeth, in holding out against d'Estaing in the campaign of 1778, Whitehall began to recover from the shock of French intervention and to forget how narrowly defeat had been averted. The mood in official circles became more cheerful, and Germain reverted to the old idea of a move against South Carolina. His reason was an unconquerable hope that somewhere, if only the British could find them, were thousands upon thousands of loyalists ready to rise en masse as soon as the king's troops appeared, and to take over their own defense while the regulars passed on to new conquests. If the hope were well founded, even Clinton's small army could produce great results. The experiment had already been made in Rhode Island, on the upper Hudson, around New York, in New Jersey and Pennsylvania; everywhere it had failed. But the minister was an incor-

rigible optimist, whose power of wishful thinking drew strength
from any one—hopeful exiles in London, colonial governors—
who told him what he wanted to hear. He urged Clinton on to
the south. In the autumn of 1779, Sir Henry fell in with the
idea. His detachments had already safeguarded Florida and secured Georgia; he had just failed, in the summer of 1779, to
achieve anything decisive in the north against Washington, and
may have been eager for new fields to conquer. On the day after
Christmas he and Admiral Arbuthnot, his new naval colleague,
sailed for South Carolina.

In the spring of 1780, Clinton invested Charleston, using just
the kind of envelopment that he had urged upon Howe at New
York, and captured the city and the American army of over
5,000 men that defended it. This was the most resounding British
victory of the war. It was also the most dangerous. Sir Henry
now had two bases, New York and Charleston, that depended
upon Britain for their supplies and were in communication with
each other across hundreds of miles of water. He had committed
himself to dispersing his exiguous forces along the seaboard, and
soon had to disperse them even further by establishing a post on
the Chesapeake. Command of the sea was more vital than ever,
and he quickly discovered that it was more precarious than ever;
for a French fleet and army established a base on the New England coast. His whole position was endangered, but by then he
could not turn back from the road on which he had started.

Why Clinton started on it, apparently with little thought for
the risks that might be involved, is hard to understand. No one
in the army recognized more clearly than he did the overriding
importance of sea power, or was more realistic about its effects
upon land operations. He knew that the navy gave British troops
their mobility, what Washington called their "canvas wings."
Sir Henry also knew that their mobility on land was limited
because they were tethered to the coast, from which alone they
could be supplied. Their existence depended on naval predominance, and in full knowledge of this fact the commander-in-
chief moved to South Carolina.

If he did not weigh at the start the risks he was running, he soon became aware of them. His awareness is revealed not only in his reiterated pleas to the government, from the fall of Charleston to the eve of Yorktown, for an adequate supporting fleet, but also in his idea of the way in which the southern campaign would develop. When he returned to New York in June, 1780, and left that campaign to Earl Cornwallis, his second in command, Clinton expected the earl to extend his conquests methodically northward, keeping in touch with the sea, holding onto gains already made, and above all never endangering the safety of his base at Charleston. Sir Henry meanwhile would detach troops from New York to establish a post on the Chesapeake, partly to assist the earl's operations to the southward, partly to provide a base for the navy, and partly to furnish the loyalists of the area with a secure refuge. Once North Carolina was firmly in Cornwallis' hands and he was able to send part of his troops to Virginia, Clinton hoped to cooperate with him in a two-pronged attack on Pennsylvania, from the upper Chesapeake and from New York. This was the design for a war of attrition, and it had much to be said for it.

One of its major virtues was that it would utilize the loyalists in the only way that Sir Henry considered feasible. Cornwallis, to judge by his subsequent conduct, shared Germain's illusion that loyalists with any initiative could stand by themselves without support from the regulars. Clinton disagreed. Throughout the war he frequently expressed his conviction that the loyalists could be expected to lend their assistance only when they were assured of lasting protection. Once they were led to declare themselves by the appearance of British troops, those troops had to remain. Too often the military had departed, leaving the civilians to their fate and thereby discouraging others from following their example. Such a betrayal, to Clinton's mind, was stupid as well as immoral, because it cut off the roots of loyalist support. If, on the other hand, the friends of Britain felt themselves secure, they would in time be extremely useful, as militia for home defense and for guarding supply lines; and the regulars would then be released to continue their advance. But the process could not be hurried and, once begun, should never be reversed.

Clinton's plan for the south was designed to do two things: to give the loyalists the maximum chance to show what they could do, and to make the maximum use of the regulars at his command. If reinforcements came from England—always a large *if*—they would help to accelerate the advance, but it would not depend upon them. Extending conquest northward through the Carolina lowlands would keep the army in touch with the sea, so that the navy could safeguard supplies and, if worst came to worst, could evacuate the troops. This strategy was unlikely to yield quick or dramatic results. But it might yield significant ones, always provided that Cornwallis would collaborate and that Whitehall would be patient.

At this stage of the war Clinton was a gradualist. Although he never entirely lost hope of drawing the enemy into one final, decisive battle, he did not put much stock in the possibility; the days when he had been intent on a bold envelopment, a blow at the heart, were over. Part of the reason was in him: he became more cautious as soon as he had sole responsibility. Another part of the reason was in his circumstances: he did not have the means to strike at the enemy's heart. His only chance was to build up his position cumulatively, step by step, until it became so strong that the Americans either lost the will to continue the conflict, or grew desperate enough to fight him on terms of his own choosing.

Before the British had more than begun this gradual build-up in the south, however, they were confronted by a situation in the north that required a quite different strategy. A substantial French armament suddenly materialized, in the form of a fleet under the Chevalier de Ternay and an army under the Comte de Rochambeau; this force was bound for Rhode Island, from which the British garrison had been withdrawn in the previous year. When the enemy landed there in July, 1780, they posed a threat that could not be countered by slow and systematic advance, but only by fast action. The crisis demanded an energy and resolution that Clinton no longer possessed. He had once known how to cope with a sudden demand on him, as in the Highlands in 1777; and before that he had often urged on Gage and Howe the daring course that his intelligence told him was the right one. Now, when his intelligence told him the same thing, he did not respond.

Why he did not is a matter of speculation. He was coming to distrust his naval colleague, Admiral Arbuthnot; but that in itself is an inadequate explanation. Sir Henry could have done far more than he did—could have gone to the fleet that was cruising off Rhode Island, could have observed the enemy position for himself, could have tried to persuade his colleague to take some kind of action. Instead he allowed the precious weeks to pass in letter-writing, as if his will to act had drained away. He became a spectator, as he had during his first independent command four years before in South Carolina. "This business . . . does not crush me," he had written then, "but [is] rather too much merely to steady me." [10] In the summer of 1780 he again was not crushed, but neither was he steady enough to push through to his objective.

When he and Arbuthnot failed to dislodge the French that summer, they imperiled British operations in the south. De Ternay's squadron, which was thenceforth blockaded in Narragansett Bay, might at any time break through the blockade, disrupt communications, and even join the Americans to attack and destroy a British army that depended on the sea. The threat of such an attack increased as Cornwallis moved northward, within closer range of Rhode Island and of Washington's forces. The situation, therefore, required the British army and navy to work hand in glove with each other; yet by the end of the summer of 1780 cooperation between them was out of the question. Clinton detested Arbuthnot too much to have any dealings with him, and could never predict what his colleague would do on his own. Either the admiral must be removed, Sir Henry told the government, or he himself would resign.

The situation also required the two army chiefs to work in

close harmony, and whether they could do so remained to be seen. During the siege of Charleston, Clinton had come to distrust Cornwallis, who held a dormant commission to succeed him and was quite ready to do so. For a time during the siege the earl, supposing that Whitehall would grant one of his chief's periodic demands to resign, had behaved almost as if the command were already his. Sir Henry was profoundly ambivalent about wanting to be recalled, but not at all so about Cornwallis' eagerness to fill his shoes, or about the army's patent delight at the prospect. The earl's conduct was intolerable to his chief, who concluded that the man was a Machiavellian schemer. Sir Henry, when he was forced to return to New York and leave his subordinate to an autonomous command in the south, carried with him distrust and suspicion; and absence did not make his heart grow fonder.

The two men had more than personal reasons for friction; they were poles apart in their views of the war. Cornwallis either never understood or chose to ignore his chief's ideas, and Clinton took less pains than he should have to make them clear. The earl was a man of action. He wanted victories, not a slow, methodical advance up the coast; and he was convinced that the only way to solidify his hold on South Carolina was to destroy the American forces between him and the Chesapeake. He was so intent upon the enemy that he paid scant attention to the other two factors in his situation, of which Clinton was intensely aware—the need to bring out the loyalists and the need to keep in touch with the navy. These two factors were interrelated: an army out of communication with the sea was chronically short of supplies; it could not remain stationary long enough to encourage the loyalists to show themselves, but had to move on in search of food. The earl rejected the invasion route along the coast that Clinton had suggested, as too fever-ridden to be safe for his troops, and chose to advance by way of the North Carolina piedmont. There, far from the sea, he found neither supplies nor loyalists, but only the elusive army of Nathanael Greene.

Cornwallis retreated once from North Carolina, after a detachment was wiped out at King's Mountain, but was back by the beginning of 1781. After a second detachment was defeated at Cowpens he refused to retreat again; he threw caution to the winds, destroyed most of his baggage, and advanced. Greene was more than a match for him, and gained even in defeat. At Guilford Court House, in March, Cornwallis won "that sort of victory which ruins an army." [11] All the battle netted him was casualties, and he was by now as short of men as he was of supplies. With the wreck of his force he retreated to Wilmington, on the Cape Fear, and there pondered where he would go next.

Clinton meanwhile was totally ignorant of what was happening, for his subordinate sent him no word. All he knew was that the earl had requested a post on the Chesapeake, which was thoroughly in accord with his own ideas. In December, 1780, Sir Henry had sent an expedition under his new American brigadier general, Benedict Arnold, to seize Portsmouth, Virginia; and in the following March Major General William Phillips superseded Arnold and brought substantial reinforcements. In April, Cornwallis informed headquarters that he was at Wilmington. A month later, before Sir Henry could communicate with him, came the staggering news that the earl had marched to the Chesapeake and joined Phillips' army. He had thereby ruined Clinton's whole concept of the southern campaign.

Cornwallis had begun to undermine this concept months before in North Carolina, by his fast-moving invasion that gained nothing solid. He had lost all chance of loyalist support, and therefore of progressive occupation; but he had at least kept his army between the enemy and his base. Now he had thrown away even that advantage. Once he was on the Chesapeake he was out of touch with South Carolina, which Greene was free to attack and did. The whole position that the British had built up in the south during the past year began to crumble. Cornwallis believed, for reasons he never explained, that Virginia must immediately become the focus of the war; to make it so he was willing to imperil Charleston and, if necessary, to abandon New York.

To Clinton this idea was midsummer madness. He knew that

tidewater Virginia, which was as fever-ridden as the Carolina coast, was a death trap for an army during the hot months; in May, General Phillips had died of fever. The Chesapeake, furthermore, was wide open to an enemy fleet; if the British lost command of the bay for even forty-eight hours, Clinton remarked, their operations would be crippled. These two dangers, from climate and from French sea power, made Sir Henry adamant against a large-scale summer campaign on the shores of the Chesapeake.

When Cornwallis brought his army there, he converted Virginia into a major theater of war against the wishes of his chief, but not against the wishes of the government. Germain had long been harping on the importance of the bay, and had recently made clear that he and the earl thought alike, whatever Clinton might think. The commander-in-chief's caution was no longer popular in Whitehall, where his energetic subordinate looked like the coming man; and the minister took no pains to conceal this change of attitude. He hoped to jolt Clinton into greater activity, or into resigning; but he misjudged his man. Sir Henry still expected, so he said, to resign at any moment unless a new naval chief were appointed; and he jumped to the conclusion that Cornwallis had come north in expectation of taking over the command. But giving it to him was another matter. His unauthorized move to Virginia, which in his chief's eyes amounted to insubordination, was one that Clinton expected the government to support. Germain and Cornwallis were in league to oust him, Sir Henry concluded; and his reaction was defiant. He refused to budge.

His obvious alternative to resigning was to bring Cornwallis to heel. This he might have done in either of two ways. He might have gone to Virginia to assess the situation, and then decided for himself and forced the earl's compliance; or he might have sent explicit orders from New York. He did neither. He thought of visiting the Chesapeake, but decided against it on the implausible ground that New York would not be safe in his absence; and during the whole summer he sent Cornwallis only one categorical order. For the rest he sent him suggestions and requests, interlarded with criticism of his previous conduct, almost as if he had no more control over the earl than over the navy. This bifurcation of authority within the army had the effect, which Clinton might have anticipated, of ruining his plans.

He knew what he wanted. The navy was eager for a base on the Chesapeake, and neither Arnold nor Phillips had found a suitable one; Cornwallis must locate the best available site and fortify it promptly. For this purpose he could not conceivably need his entire complement, Sir Henry believed, and would be able to return a substantial proportion to New York. It would be welcome there. The French and Americans were known to be planning a concentration of forces, backed by de Grasse's fleet from the West Indies; and Clinton was convinced that their objective was Manhattan. If he could draw reinforcements from the Chesapeake, he would both decrease the dangerous commitment there that Cornwallis had forced upon him, and strengthen his own defenses against the siege that he expected.

For months he tried, with no success whatever, to get Cornwallis to detach some troops. His first request arrived in late June when the earl was approaching Yorktown, which he had finally decided was the best base he could find. He misinterpreted the request as a demand that took precedence over establishing a base at all; he did not, he protested, have enough men to do both. In high dudgeon he marched to Portsmouth to embark the regiments asked for, and prepared to abandon the Chesapeake entirely. Clinton was aghast; he wanted the base even more than the reinforcements. For once he sent an explicit order—to return to Yorktown, fortify it, and keep whatever men were needed. He went on trying to get some of them, but he had vitiated his own efforts by permitting Cornwallis to retain such force as he thought necessary. Not a man was sent.

The long-run effect of this imbroglio was disastrous. The earl wasted a month in marching to Portsmouth and then back again, so that he did not start fortifying his position at Yorktown and Gloucester until the beginning of August. When he was besieged there in late September, consequently, his works were incomplete; and he could not hold out in them long enough for the attempted rescue from New York.[12] Far more important, by retaining his entire force he preserved the Chesapeake as the focus of the war. He had hoped to concentrate enough troops there for final victory; instead he kept enough for final defeat.

He cannot be blamed for keeping them, because he was authorized to do so if they were needed for establishing a base, and he was the proper judge of need. Whether Clinton was to blame for insisting on a base is another question. The insistence stemmed from his plans for the future. He had long intended to make the Chesapeake a major theater as soon as the Carolinas were subdued; he still intended, after Cornwallis reached the bay, to conduct important operations there in the autumn. Those operations would depend on water-borne supplies and therefore on naval control, for which the prerequisite, as the navy kept pointing out, was a safe anchorage for ships of the line. But was the need for such a base immediate and important enough to justify risking troops in the sickly season, especially when de Grasse was expected on the coast? This question Clinton and Admiral Graves, who replaced Arbuthnot in early July, never seem to have considered, any more than they did the risk in again attacking Rhode Island.[13] Throughout the summer they remained consistently blind to what might happen, in Virginia or in Narragansett Bay, if the French West Indian fleet gained even a temporary predominance.

But, whatever Clinton's share of responsibility for the ensuing disaster, Cornwallis' share was greater. After failing to establish control of North Carolina the earl moved to Virginia entirely on his own responsibility, and once he arrived there he wasted precious time; even when he did belatedly start to fortify his position he showed little sense of urgency. When the French fleet arrived he did nothing, but waited passively for the trap to close upon him. He shifted the focus of the war to the Chesapeake on his own initiative, in short, and then the initiative evaporated.

His shortcomings are worth emphasis because Clinton was subsequently saddled with all the blame. Cornwallis went home months before Sir Henry did, and arrived when North's government was on its last legs and desperately hunting for scapegoats. The earl was not an attractive one, partly because he had powerful connections and was on hand to use them, and partly because he had a warm welcome at court. His simple explanation of the surrender, that he had been ordered to hold his post at all cost and had been promised succor that did not come, gained wide credence; it put the whole onus on Clinton, and there it remained. The earl went on to a new and more successful career in India. Sir Henry, forced into retirement, did not receive even the routine honors that were usually accorded to commanders-in-chief when they were laid on what he called "the shelf of oblivion." Posterity benefited from his bitter sense of injustice, which turned him to compiling the record of his services that was to be his *Apologia pro Bello Suo*. But writing did not expunge his bitterness or clear his name.

Injustice was done him, for in considerable measure he was the victim of circumstance. He came to the command at a time when British resources in America were at their lowest ebb, and he never thereafter received a fraction of the support that his predecessor had had. His first campaign began with a retreat and ended with a defensive at New York and Rhode Island, in which he and Lord Howe preserved everything that the government had hoped they would and more than it had feared they might. His second campaign, in 1779, came to nothing because the meager reinforcements on which he had counted did not arrive in time. His third, in South Carolina, was the only one that developed according to plan; and it was a complete success. The surrender of Charleston in May, 1780, was the zenith of his career; thereafter his fortunes declined. The decline was only in part his fault. To work hand in glove with Arbuthnot would have taxed the patient finesse of a Marlborough; and even the great duke, if he had been in Clinton's place, could scarcely have worked hand in glove with Cornwallis, who was not only hundreds of miles away in the Carolinas but was touchy, headstrong, and egged on by his own government. No one in North America, in the summer of 1781, could have influenced the series of miscalculations in the Caribbean that left Admiral Graves so much inferior to de Grasse; and no general could have prevented Graves' subsequent defeat. Yorktown was not the product of any one man's incompetence, but the collapse of a slipshod system.

Although Clinton as commander-in-chief was the victim of that system, he might have used it to better effect than he did. If he lacked the force for sensational achievements, he also failed, except in the Charleston campaign, to obtain maximum results with the force that he had. "Generals gain at least as much honor by their able management of small armies," Germain told him in 1779, "as when they act with a superiority that commands success." [14] A generation later, in the early phase of the Peninsular War, Wellington demonstrated the truth of this comment; but Clinton was no Wellington. In three summers, from 1779 to 1781, Sir Henry had opportunities to gain honor by able management. In every case he *planned*, laboriously, meticulously, almost lovingly, and then fell back upon inaction. Of course he had reasons not to act; any general has. But the ones that he gave are not sufficient to explain his passivity.

Take for example his failure to attack the French on Rhode Island in 1780, and grant him his point that Arbuthnot was an infuriatingly inert colleague. Clinton ought to have known him well enough to realize that the one way *not* to get a decision out of him was by badgering from a distance, "amusing me with his situation," as the admiral put it, ". . . and aide-de-camps dancing backwards and forwards." [15] The old man was easily confused, and confusion bred annoyance. In trying to reach him through formal letters and dancing aides-de-camp Sir Henry was ensuring failure. But he preferred those methods to direct involvement, to using his own eyes and tongue, and never tried until too late to meet the admiral in the flesh.

This shying away from personal confrontation is typical of Clinton. At Sullivan's Island he and Sir Peter Parker almost never met, but carried on their business—as they later carried on their quarrel—by letter. As second in command, Clinton's peculiar relationship with Howe permitted him many face-to-face discussions with his chief, some of them extremely heated; yet even to Howe, on Long Island, he submitted his battle plan in writing and through an intermediary. As commander-in-chief Sir Henry was even more averse to disagreeable meetings. In the summer of 1781 he should have gone to the Chesapeake, as he should have gone to Rhode Island the summer before, to feel out the situation for himself; but again he fell back on letters. Even if he had been a forthright and pellucid correspondent, he would have had trouble in concerting plans in that way; and he was far from pellucid. His letter-writing style was formal, involved, and sometimes ambiguous, as he discovered in asking Cornwallis for reinforcements. Clinton knew that the earl had misread him (intentionally, he suspected), and the knowledge gave him all the more incentive for an interview, which he evaded on a flimsy excuse. The reason for these repeated evasions seems to have been in the character of the man.

Sir Henry, the "shy bitch," insulated himself from the men around him. He was able to be surprisingly open with a few, usually his juniors; but sooner or later he quarreled with most of them. Among the senior officers in America he had only one lasting friend, General Phillips. All the others he kept at a distance, and they did not know what he was thinking; "the commander-in-chief lives so retired that his secrets seldom take air." [16] His colleagues reacted by calling him proud, but pride and diffidence are two sides of the same coin. He was not enough at ease with himself to be at ease with his peers. He did not like to confront them, particularly one of them, like Arbuthnot or Cornwallis, in whom he sensed hostility yet with whom he had to work. The reason may have been that he did not trust his assertiveness in the give and take of conversation, and preferred a letter because he could fashion it to his purposes without interruption. He needed to impose order upon his dealings with his colleagues, according to this hypothesis, and found the written word more orderly than the spoken. "The tongue can no man tame."

A similar hypothesis may explain his passion for planning. He almost never relied upon the inspiration of the moment, but was continually drawing up on paper his ideas of what he could or should do. He had a sound analytic intelligence; and the ideas, when written down, looked good. Yet he seems to have cared more about formulating a plan than about implementing it, as if the plan itself met his problem without any need for acting. In his last two years at headquarters the hours that he spent at his desk writing, often far into the night, must have greatly exceeded the hours that he spent in the field. Burning the midnight oil, or rather the midnight candle, apparently gave him a sense of ordering, regulating, and somehow mastering whatever difficulty he had to face. A case in point is his design for attacking Rhode Island in the summer of 1781. He spared no effort to work out the plan in detail—forges for heating shot, ammunition for the cannon that he expected to capture from the French—and made no commensurate effort to see that it was carried out. He knew that time was short, because de Grasse might appear at any moment; yet when Admiral Graves postponed all action for weeks Clinton did not lift a finger to dissuade him.[17] The plan existed; by existing, his conduct implies, it took care of the matter.

Such an implication would of course have infuriated him; but he did realize that his plans were seldom executed, and that he was consequently blamed for inaction. He wanted to avoid the blame by finding explanations outside himself, as any man would; his need to find them was abnormally intense, however, because he would not admit to any slight share of responsibility. Others were blameworthy, not he; hence his almost incredible proclivity for quarrels and accusations. Before he was through he had a long list of the guilty men and the charges against them. Germain had not supported him properly and had interfered with his plans for the Chesapeake. Sandwich had neglected the American station. Parker had caused the failure at Sullivan's Island, Arbuthnot at Rhode Island, Rodney and above all Cornwallis at Yorktown. None of these men was completely innocent, but that is not why Clinton went on accusing them for the rest of his life. They turned his bitter criticism outward, away from himself.

Where and to what extent was he open to criticism? Little can be said against him as a military thinker, for here he was at his best; his ideas were not brilliant, but they were eminently sound. He understood the relationship of geography and sea power to all land operations, and he had a realistic view of the loyalists and of how they could and could not be utilized. He frequently showed his strategic acumen. In 1776 he contended that Washington's army was the focal point of the rebellion, and in 1777 that the Highlands, not Pennsylvania, were the key to the war; he cannot be proved right in either contention, but he had a better argument for both than Howe had for his strategy. As a leader of troops in the field Sir Henry won more praise than censure. He showed his skill in planning and executing the battle of Long Island, in attacking the Highland forts, in his retreat across New Jersey in 1778, and at Charleston two years later. On the other side of the ledger was one lamentable failure, at Sullivan's Island, but this was the exception. When he acted, by and large, he acted successfully. He almost never showed the boldness that elicits, if successful, wild acclaim from the public and from historians; but boldness in itself is no military virtue. Burgoyne displayed it after Bennington in marching to Saratoga, Cornwallis after Guilford in marching to the Chesapeake. Clinton's record is better, not worse, because it contains no such resolute blunder.

The principal charges against him arise from his inaction at moments when he himself recognized the opportunity to act. All those moments were after he became commander-in-chief.

Only one was when he was virtually his own master, in the wasted summer of 1779; the others were when he was trying to concert action with Arbuthnot or Graves or Cornwallis. With those colleagues his task was not easy, but even with them a more determined and self-confident man might have had some degree of success. Sir Henry had none. From the fall of Charleston to the fall of Yorktown he moved from one frustration to another; he watched, as if in a paralysis of will, as his plans were vitiated and his power to command evaporated, until in the final weeks before the catastrophe he was reduced to being what he had been years before at Sullivan's Island, a spectator of the navy's failure.

The end of a man's career has an element of pathos, especially when he does not know that the end is at hand. Four days before he sailed, as he thought, to gamble his army and his life on rescuing Cornwallis at Yorktown, Sir Henry wrote to say good-by to his sisters-in-law, the only family that he had; and his letter was at moments unconsciously symbolic. He had settled his affairs, paid his servants, and made his will, he told them; for "I guard as much as possible against everything." The time had come to close; "I have got to the end of my paper, my candle, and my eyes. I therefore, dearest sisters, take my leave, and after two hours' midnight writing . . . go to rest." [18]

FOOTNOTES

1. His memoirs remained unpublished until I edited them a decade ago (*The American Rebellion: Sir Henry Clinton's Narrative of His Campaigns, 1775–1782, with an Appendix of Original Documents;* Yale historical publications, manuscripts and edited texts, XXI; New Haven, 1954). His papers, which fill almost 300 volumes in the Clements Library of the University of Michigan, are the principal source of my biography, *Portrait of a General: Sir Henry Clinton in the War of Independence,* New York, 1964. Most of what follows is drawn from this study, and the footnote citations below refer to the biography.
2. *Ibid.,* p. 45.

3. *Ibid.*, p. 48.

4. *Ibid.*, p. 105.

5. The navy certainly scotched one of them. In September, just before the landing on Manhattan, Clinton suggested that he should take a detachment by the East River to the mouth of the Harlem, to cut off the enemy's retreat. This scheme was turned down because it would have brought the troop-laden boats nearer to the tide rips of Hell Gate than the naval officers thought safe. *Ibid.*, p. 109.

6. *Ibid.*, p. 160.

7. *Ibid.*, p. 279.

8. Mackesy strongly implies that the British government would have conceded independence if the war could have been ended on that basis (Piers Mackesy, *The War for America, 1775–1783*; Cambridge, Mass., 1964; pp. 187–89). I contend that the king would not agree to this final concession (Willcox, *op. cit.*, pp. 219–20). If the Americans demanded it—in fact they refused to negotiate at all —the commissioners were instructed to refer the demand back to London, which does not mean that it would have been accepted there. The king, I believe, did not intend to go beyond the terms authorized by Parliament; in case they were rejected, he seems to have envisaged military evacuation of the colonies and a continued naval war against their commerce. See his correspondence cited in Mackesy and, for the attitude of the government when the Commission left England, Charles R. Ritcheson, *British Politics and the American Revolution* (Norman, Okla., 1954), pp. 266–67.

9. In the four years after Saratoga the army at New York, by Sir Henry's computation, received 4,700 men as reinforcements from home, and lost 19,200: 6,000 in Burgoyne's surrender and 13,200 in detachments to Canada, Florida, Georgia, and the West Indies. The total depletion was therefore 14,500. Clinton memorandum filed at the end of September, 1781, Clinton Papers, Clements Library.

10. Willcox, *op. cit.*, p. 68. For the unsuccessful attempt on Rhode Island, and the resultant breakdown of collaboration between the two services, see *ibid.*, pp. 323–337.

11. The remark of General Phillips, Willcox, *op. cit.*, p. 384.

12. *Ibid.*, p. 426.

13. *Ibid.*, pp. 419–420.

14. *Ibid.*, p. 316.

15. *Ibid.*, p. 335.

16. Chief Justice William Smith in 1779, Historical Manuscripts Commission, *Fifteenth Report* (London, 1897), App., pt. VI, p. 432.

17. Willcox, *op. cit.*, p. 423. Even this brief survey of Sir Henry's char-

acter is enough, I hope, to make clear that he showed strong neurotic tendencies. These I have examined with a psychotherapist, and our tentative conclusions are embodied in the final chapter of *Portrait of a General*.

18. To Elizabeth and Martha Carter, October 15, 1781, Clinton Papers, Clements Library.

BIBLIOGRAPHY

Clinton, Henry. *The American Rebellion: Sir Henry Clinton's Narrative of His Campaigns, 1775–1782, with an Appendix of Original Documents,* William B. Willcox, ed., Yale historical publications, manuscripts and edited texts, XXI. New Haven, 1954. Sir Henry's apologia, for all its bias, is invaluable for understanding his role in the war; and he also goes into considerable detail about campaigns, during his command-in-chief, in which he was not a participant. With a few exceptions he is scrupulously accurate in citing evidence and in imputing to himself the views that he actually held at the time. Most of the exceptions are pointed out in the editorial notes, and the few that I have found since are mentioned in my biography.

Mackesy, Piers. *The War for America, 1775–1783.* Cambridge, Mass., 1964. See comment in the bibliography of "Arbuthnot, Gambier, and Graves: 'Old Women' of the Navy."

Stevens, Benjamin F., ed. *The Campaign in Virginia, 1781: an Exact Reprint of Six Rare Pamphlets on the Clinton-Cornwallis Controversy.* 2 vols., London, 1888. The standard source for the British side of the military campaign after the fall of Charleston. It contains chronological correspondence, primarily between Clinton and Cornwallis, and the dreary polemics of the pamphlet war that broke out between them after Yorktown.

Stuart-Wortley, the Hon. Mrs. E. *A Prime Minister and His Son, from the Correspondence of the 3rd Earl of Bute and of Lt.-General the Hon. Sir Charles Stuart, K. B.* London, 1925. Young Stuart was for a short time one of Clinton's confidants at headquarters in New York, and his letters are filled with comments—largely uncharitable —on the commander-in-chief and his entourage. Neither his views nor his facts are reliable, but they make good reading. Although he had an annoyingly high opinion of himself, his subsequent career bore it out.

Van Doren, Carl. *Secret History of the American Revolution.* New York, 1941. The focus of the book is the Arnold conspiracy; but it also contains a great deal of information, drawn largely from the Clinton Papers, on Sir Henry's negotiations with other Americans and the workings of the British intelligence system in general.

Ward, Christopher. *The War of the Revolution,* John R. Alden, ed. 2 vols., New York, 1952. The fullest modern account of military operations in the war, with much less attention to the naval side. Thickets of detail often obstruct the narrative, and emphasis is badly apportioned between minor and major campaigns. The work is, nevertheless, the most authoritative in the field.

Willcox, William B. *Portrait of a General: Sir Henry Clinton in the War of Independence.* New York, 1964. See comment in the bibliography of "Arbuthnot, Gambier, and Graves: 'Old Women' of the Navy."

Sir Guy Carleton:

SOLDIER-STATESMAN

PAUL H. SMITH

University of Florida

GUY CARLETON, governor and captain-general of Quebec at the outbreak of the American rebellion, was the only one of George Washington's high-ranking opponents whose official career in America successfully survived the War of Independence. Applauded for his defense of Quebec against American attack in 1775–76, but passed over for John Burgoyne when command of the 1777 "northern" invasion was assigned, Carleton resigned in pique prior to the debacle at Saratoga and escaped virtually unscathed from the recriminations that followed that event. Hopelessly at odds with Lord George Germain, the secretary of state for American affairs, he then spent more than three quiet years in England until the collapse of North's administration brought the more pacific Rockingham Ministry to power in the spring of 1782. When Carleton returned to America, it was as commander-in-chief to negotiate the reconciliation of the colonies. Though disappointed in that enterprise, he managed the subsequent British evacuation from the now independent United States with great competence and compassionately directed the flight of thousands of loyalists to their new homes in Canada. After a second interlude in England, he capped his distinguished career with a second term as governor of Canada—from 1786 to 1796—during the formative period of the second British Empire when difficult adjustments were required because of the sudden intrusion of exiled loyalists upon the dominant French-Canadian society. Thus, Carleton's career in North America was a dual one as soldier and statesman.

As an imperial statesman, Guy Carleton (Sir Guy after 1776, and finally Lord Dorchester after 1786) has an undeniable claim to eminence. But his career as a military commander during the War of Independence is curiously ambiguous. Though a soldier by profession, and the senior officer in America after Gage returned to England in November, 1775, he never commanded a sizable army in a significant or major battle. His military reputation rests almost entirely upon two modest—though meaningful—achievements: the repulse of an American force which attacked the formidable walled city of Quebec on December 31, 1775, and the defeat on Lake Champlain of a small enemy flotilla commanded by Benedict Arnold in October, 1776. Upon several other important occasions his conduct was equivocal at best. He responded ineffectively to the initial enemy thrusts into Canada in 1775, losing control of the approaches to the St. Lawrence Valley, and, when the tide turned after massive British reinforcements arrived in the spring of 1776, thrice permitted a weak and disorganized enemy to escape his superior army. The contrast between his reputation as a soldier-statesman and his actual achievements in the field is striking. The disparity suggests that his military career has not attracted the critical attention that has been focused upon his fellow British generals.

The little that is known of the early life of this puzzling man is quickly told. He was born in 1724, of Scotch-Irish stock, the third son of Christopher Carleton, a landowner of County Down, Ireland. When Guy was fourteen his father died, and his mother, of County Donegal, married a second time. His stepfather, the Reverend Thomas Skelton, apparently arranged for Guy's education and had an important share in molding Carleton's character; but Skelton's influence can only be surmised. Commissioned an ensign in 1742, the young officer advanced slowly for a decade, and then attained the rank of lieutenant colonel after the outbreak of the Seven Years' War. Apparently befriended by James Wolfe, who was three years his junior, new vistas opened to Carleton as Wolfe secured for him an appointment as quartermaster general to the army charged with the capture of Quebec in 1759. Before the war was over, Carleton saw action in Canada, in Europe, and against the Spanish at Havana. In the course of combat, he was wounded three times. Little more than this is known of Carleton until he was appointed lieutenant governor of Quebec in 1766, for upon his own instructions Carleton's widow faithfully burned the entire collection of his personal papers after his death in 1808.[1]

Carleton's return to Quebec in September, 1766, as successor to Governor James Murray launched him on a long career closely bound up with the future of British rule in North America. He inherited from Murray a difficult situation that put his talents as a statesman to a stern test—his lot being to fit an old French and Catholic colony into an English and Protestant empire. Though many officials believed that Canada could be treated like any other British colony, Carleton boldly attacked that widely held assumption. "This country must, to the end of time, be peopled by the Canadian race, who have already taken such firm root, and got to so great a height, that any new stock transplanted will be totally hid and imperceptible amongst them, except in the towns of Quebec and Montreal." In seeking to give substance to this insight, Carleton led officials in London to accept the assumptions that were woven into the Quebec Act in 1774. From these assumptions there developed the finest flower of the empire—the concept of a larger "British" liberty of non-English people to retain their own distinctive character.

It was quite another matter, however, to nurse such a policy to fruition because there were elements in Canada inimical to it. Before he completed his first administration in 1778 (he was formally promoted to the governorship in January, 1768), the ties of empire were strained to near the breaking point. Carleton was limited from the outset by the conditions prevailing in the colony at the time it passed to the British and by the policies and experiences of his predecessor. Although it was imperative that the Canadians not remain a sullen and hostile people, the small yet important English-speaking mercantile minority that settled in the towns of Quebec and Montreal after the British occupied Canada had interests which conflicted with the vast majority of persons of another race, language, and religion. To administer a government satisfactory to all these groups would have confounded Solomon. Nor was it likely that Britain could extend justice to her "new subjects" without giving added offense to her "old subjects" to the southward who were already restive under the economic policies of George Grenville. Finally, the demands for tax relief in the mother country, the depressed condition of the fur trade, and the continued restlessness of the natives in the western areas of Canada, made it obvious that Carleton's position as governor would be a difficult one.

It was unfortunate, moreover, that many of Carleton's earliest recommendations for assuring Canada's military security were ignored, while some of his errors survived to plague him and belatedly bore bitter fruit in the internecine conflict that developed. Concerned with the threat to imperial authority posed by the colonies' hostile reaction to the Stamp Act, Carleton as early as 1767 laid out a prescription for permanently attaching Canada to the empire. Militarily, the defenses of Quebec and Montreal would have to be rebuilt.[2] Since Quebec and New York were the keys to British control over the colonies, the line connecting them would have to be kept strongly fortified. He repeatedly urged restoration of the defenses of Ticonderoga, and his worst fears were realized when the fort became the first British position to fall to the rebels when war broke out.[3]

His political views were much more complex. Although he was supported by some members of the British minority who were well disposed toward the Canadians, his program was a direct challenge to the "English party," which previously had balked at Murray's decision to postpone election of a legislative assembly. Convinced that the colony could not be governed

without the services of the Canadian leaders, Carleton wished
to restore at least French civil law, give legal force to the tithe,
and maintain the seignorial system. Canadians, he believed,
should be appointed to governmental posts of secondary importance. There should be no elected assembly, as no viable government could truly represent the various elements in Canada.
Legislative power should be reposed in the governor and an appointive council. When the substance of this policy was incorporated into the Quebec Act, the principal Canadian leaders—
especially the higher clergy who were the most influential repre-
sentatives of the Canadian community—rallied to Carleton's
support. His benevolent despotism fulfilled their aspirations, although they continued to fear the augmented personal power
placed in his hands.

In contrast to his broad policy views on Canada's future,
Carleton's administrative conduct and exercise of executive
power was arbitrary and narrow. Unwilling to implement his
policies with the generosity that marked their conception, he
needlessly antagonized important persons who experienced the
sting of his whip and learned to fear his methods. Carleton
brought to Quebec in 1766 a preconceived hostility to Murray's
supporters. He had heard only one side of the troubles that had
led to Murray's return and hence had a contempt for the English mercantile minority. Above all, he distrusted them because
of their eagerness to pursue profits at the expense of the welfare
of the Canadians. Furthermore, his autocratic temper led him to
brook no interference with his will, and he soon set out to elimi-
nate from the government those whom he distrusted. At the outset he excluded certain Council members from the regular
meetings of that body, and when challenged struck down his
opponents and misrepresented their action in his reports to
London.[4] In the course of his long administration in Canada
he unjustly managed the virtual political destruction of a lieutenant governor, a chief justice, and a judge of the Court of
Common Pleas; eliminated the Council as a check on his executive authority; and prevented any really free discussion of his

decisions. In the words of one leading authority, "he had a mean temper, and would stop at nothing to cover up his mistakes." [5] A man so sensitive to criticism and exposed to possible censure in case of an unexpected investigation would be extremely vulnerable if agents of sedition from outside the province arrived to foment discontent and encourage rebellion.

Carleton's first administration in Canada was interrupted by his return to England in August, 1770. He was originally granted leave to settle personal affairs, but four years elapsed before he returned to Quebec. During the long interval he had ample opportunity to expound his views on Canadian questions, and though months dragged into years before he finally saw his recommendations safely through Parliament, the Quebec Act, which received the king's assent in June, 1774, embodied most of the essential features he desired. His return to Canada that fall was therefore a happy one.

Carleton had reason to be happy on personal as well as political grounds. On his return, he was accompanied by a newly acquired wife and two children. During his unexpectedly prolonged visit in England he had, at the age of forty-seven, married Lady Maria Howard, the eighteen-year-old daughter of the Earl of Effingham. Her presence in Quebec added a charming new dimension to his social life, and her partiality for things French, a reflection of her education at Versailles, perhaps reinforced Carleton's optimism about Canada's future under the Quebec Act.

But if he hoped to find repose in Quebec he was rudely disappointed. While his ship was still at sea, the first Continental Congress was convening at Philadelphia and the crisis was deepening. General Thomas Gage in Boston, alarmed over Massachusetts' response to the Coercive Acts, penned a letter calling on Carleton for reinforcements from Canada. Less than 24 hours after Carleton set foot in Canada, Gage's letter of September 4, 1774, was handed to him. Transports for the 10th and 52nd regiments, which comprised half the entire Canadian garrison, he learned, had already been dispatched to Quebec. Moreover, he was requested to report on the prospects for raising "a body of Canadians & Indians" for future use in conjunction with the king's forces in Massachusetts should resort to force become necessary.[6]

Carleton's response to Gage was an optimistic one.[7] In fact, during the following winter his reports to both Dartmouth, the American secretary, and Gage, his immediate superior officer until Carleton was placed on independent command in September, 1775, betrayed no real sense of alarm. Even when some months passed and the Americans became more intransigent, Carleton was slow to reappraise his position. His four-year absence soon proved to be a serious handicap. Nursing dubious conceptions of Canadian society from the outset, and out of touch with the events of 1770–74, Carleton obviously was not master of the Canadian situation after his return. He gradually lost the initiative which the Quebec Act should have placed in his hands. His enthusiasm about the future effect of the Quebec Act, strengthened by those in high positions around him, blinded him to immediate conditions and dangerously prolonged the illusions nursed by Dartmouth and Gage concerning the faithfulness of most colonists. Such illusions were the very stuff of the American Revolution.

Knowing that his policy had secured him the support of the clergy and the seigniors, Carleton hoped to make Quebec a secure base from which to launch any attack required against the colonies in rebellion. Encouraged by the response of those who applauded the Quebec Act, he imagined that a Canadian militia manned by docile habitants could secure the province from invasion. He did not recognize, or refused to believe, that the bulk of the habitants sullenly acquiesced in the recent restoration of ancient clerical and seignorial privileges directed against their liberties, and accepted British occupation with a measured loyalty that bordered on passive resistance. Considering the degree to which he was out of touch with the bulk of the population, it was to be expected that Carleton would be disappointed at their response when the American invasion in May, 1775, shattered Quebec's calm. Despite exhortations from the pulpit and the urgings of the seigniors, the habitants simply refused to take up arms. When not merely indifferent, they occasionally joined the invading Americans. Because the Americans had little to offer the habitants, and harbored deep-seated religious prejudices against them, the number of Canadians who openly deserted their leaders was not large. But even their prudent neutrality was fatal to Carleton's plans, and it very nearly enabled the Americans to prevail in the province.

Carleton gradually awakened to the flaws in his earlier assumptions as reports reached him that the Americans were already among his people spreading sedition and threatening waverers who refused to throw in their lot with the insurgents. As a result, he revived a scheme for arming the Canadians that previously had been ignored. As the habitants could not be trusted to throw back an invasion, and even the gentry did not "relish commanding a bare Militia," Carleton renewed his request for the establishment of a "Canadian" regiment. Regular commissions in the army, he hoped, would revive the zeal of the seigniors and bestir them to take up the defense of their country. Creation of a "Canadian" regiment would not only "restore them to a significance they have nearly lost," but it would rectify a wrong done them in 1764 when those who had volunteered for service against Pontiac's warriors were dismissed "without gratuity or recompence . . . tho they all expected half pay." [8] Only by placing a "Canadian" regiment on the establishment could Britain allay the fears of the seigniors that they might again be ignored at the close of the present disorders.

In this instance Carleton had accurately diagnosed the situation and recommended a suitable remedy. But he should have anticipated that his recommendation would be ignored. Placing a new regiment on the establishment would be expensive, and it would jeopardize vested interests throughout the entire British officer corps. The government normally augmented the army by enlarging old regiments—a procedure that minimized the irregularities and abuse of seniority that often attended creation of new ones—and it could hardly be expected to approve a regiment to be officered by French Catholics. Military convention and the prejudices of the ruling officer class had long thwarted similar efforts to organize regular "provincial" regiments even among Britain's "old subjects." Carleton was unrealistic in his hopes of receiving preferential treatment for his supporters from the British establishment.

Additional troubles were just around the corner. At the approach of the first of May, 1775, the day the Quebec Act was to take effect, Carleton returned momentarily to his civil duties. He had to face the rising opposition of the English-speaking mercantile minority who feared the consequences of enforcement of the new act. The North Ministry, anticipating their concern, had already taken steps to protect them against injuries that full restoration of French civil law would inflict. But Carleton decided to ignore the Ministry's recommendations. In flagrant disregard of these orders—which directed him to consult the Council on legislation to preserve the right to habeas corpus and English law for civil suits in which a natural-born subject was a party—Carleton kept his royal instructions secret.[9] The effect on Britons in Canada was disastrous for the security of the province. Disappointed with the home government's apparent callousness and exasperated at their obvious betrayal, dozens of them now sought recourse in rebellion. They welcomed revolutionists from the south and aided in spreading sedition among the credulous habitants. Thus when Canada was invaded, Carleton quickly found himself occupied on two "fronts": fighting agents of revolution from without and engaged in a double game on the political front from within.

The day of reckoning came in mid-May. Hearing of the American capture of the British-held forts at Ticonderoga and Crown Point on Lake Champlain, Carleton took what limited measures he could. When a rebel force under Benedict Arnold appeared at St. Johns a few days after the forts fell, the security of the settlements of the upper St. Lawrence Valley seemed shattered. Carleton sent all the available troops in the province, plus a few Canadian volunteers, to the area. Almost immediately he abandoned Quebec and left for Montreal, which he reached the 26th day of May. St. Johns became the object of all his attention and work on implementing the new government stopped. Troops arriving from distant points took up positions in the fort at St. Johns. Ship carpenters and supplies were also ordered in to begin construction of armed vessels adequate to clear the rebels from the river and the lake above. St. Johns on the Richelieu controlled both the funnel through which rebel troops could pour into the valley and the road west to Montreal just fifteen miles away. Arnold's men had abandoned the fort almost immediately after capturing it, but had taken away with them a sloop and a well-armed schooner which gave them control of the entire waterway from St. Johns to Ticonderoga.[10]

In Montreal, Carleton found himself facing other problems. Although he had all summer to prepare against a full-scale invasion, his efforts came to very little. The English merchants at Montreal offered him almost no support and indulged instead in intrigue and treason. Small bands of American troops reappeared through the woods from time to time and intimidated the inhabitants of the valley who otherwise might have been persuaded to join the king's troops. Carleton simply had too few regulars to defend against an invading force of any significance, and the Canadians would not voluntarily risk their lives in behalf of British sovereignty. In a desperate effort to revive the militia, Carleton proclaimed martial law on June 9, 1775, but he foolishly continued to rely upon the seigniors and old French army officers to rouse the habitants.[11] His proclamation produced meager results; it succeeded only in further irritating the habitants, and stirring up the English merchants who viewed the measure with suspicion as another act of arbitrary government.

There was one major alternative in raising a military force which Carleton refused to consider. He might have been able to rally upwards of 2,000 Indians—a number far greater than that needed to check any invasion the rebels could launch—but he rejected proposals to turn them loose. Curiously enough, how-

ever, his policy of not employing Indians produced some unexpected results. Carleton's ambiguous letters to Dartmouth and
Gage on this matter failed to change the minds of these military
planners about using Indians in future operations. They continued to base their beliefs upon optimistic reports from Indian
Superintendent Guy Johnson, who claimed that redskins could
be hurled against rebel invaders. Carleton, on the other hand,
had refused to state openly his opposition to using the Indians,
choosing instead, somewhat deviously, to complain of their un-
dependability, and to hint that Johnson was unable to mobilize
them at the proper moment.[12] Thus, he left the implication that
Indians might be available for future use. The rub was that officials in England were accurately informed of the Indian forces
available, and instead of preparing to send Carleton reinforcements at once—having swallowed also Carleton's confident predictions of Canadian loyalty—they expected him to reinforce
Gage's army in New England and to make a diversion along
the northern frontier to relieve the pressure on Boston.

With so much confusion swirling about, it was little wonder
that Carleton was left to his own inadequate resources. Few
officials were able to recognize the dimensions of the struggle
that was about to engulf them, and Carleton was no exception.
Furthermore, at the beginning of the American rebellion all
shared the great illusions of their day: the assumed loyalty of
most Americans, the incapacity of the rebels to fight, and the
invincibility of the redcoats. Government by instruction in
America contained the seeds of its own failure. It was left to
chance to determine whether the harvest would yield thirteen or
fourteen provinces.

Fortune finally smiled on Guy Carleton. Although he suffered
many defeats, he was ultimately able to spin out the campaign
until he was saved by the elements. The Americans, novices at
organizing large-scale warfare, were only able to plan a modest
invasion of Canada. Congress wasted valuable time during the
summer before coming to a resolution to invade Canada, and
it was hesitant to launch an offensive that might slam the door

to a peaceful reconciliation. Once the invasion was approved, moreover, Generals Philip Schuyler and Richard Montgomery consumed weeks struggling with shortages of money and supplies, provincial jealousies, and inadequately trained troops, before they were ready for a second assault on St. Johns. Carleton in the meantime returned to the seat of government in Quebec to convene his first Legislative Council under the Quebec Act, trusting the St. Johns garrison to withstand any initial blow the rebels might deliver.[13]

On September 4, Montgomery's men camped on Isle-aux-Noix in the river just twelve miles from St. Johns. Although two initial attempts on the post were beaten off, the fort was finally invested on September 17. Since nearly four-fifths of all regulars in the area were inside the walls—or at Chambly a few miles down river where Major Stopford commanded 80 men—the Americans were now free to roam that triangle of land formed by the St. Lawrence and the Richelieu, exhorting the Canadians to arms in defense of liberty. Carleton learned to his chagrin, upon hurrying back to Montreal on September 7, that several hundred Canadians had joined the rebels. When most of the Indians under Johnson's command, who had been disappointed with months of inactivity, slipped away into the forests after St. Johns was invested, Carleton's last real hope for saving Montreal was virtually extinguished.

Carleton nevertheless had nearly six weeks to play out his hand, and twice during that interval he found cause for hope. The first opportunity given him to check the tide resulted from a foolhardy, poorly planned assault on Montreal—the only one attempted during the period—commanded by the brave but blustering Ethan Allen. Encouraged by several dissident Montreal merchants led by Thomas Walker—who nursed ancient grievances against the governor—Allen became convinced that Montreal could be taken by a *coup de main*. Thus on September 24 he crossed the river at Long Point at the head of 110 men, expecting the city to be delivered to him on command. Having got wind of the scheme, however, Carleton had a force three times the size of Allen's under Major Carden ready to greet them. Within a few hours the British were able to capture 36 of the attacking force, including their embarrassed leader. Taking heart momentarily, Carleton acknowledged with guarded optimism that "our victory has had good effect." [14] Two-thirds of Allen's rebels, he estimated, were Canadians "who expected to march in without opposition." He hoped, no doubt, that the lesson would be taken to heart and that other Canadians who had joined the Americans might recover their senses.

In mid-October, however, a fatal blow was struck that apparently caught Carleton unawares. Disappointed with the progress against St. Johns, Montgomery was persuaded by James Livingston to turn his attention to the fort at Chambly scarcely ten miles down river. The post was defended by fewer than 100 men under the command of Major Stopford and was known to be stocked with a large quantity of valuable stores. Under the cover of darkness a few cannon placed in bateaux were easily floated by St. Johns undetected and brought to bear against the thin stone walls that offered feeble protection to the garrison at Chambly. The result was more satisfying than Montgomery ever could have dreamed. On October 18, Major Stopford surrendered at the first cannonading and delivered up not only his troops but all his supplies, which he neglected to have his men throw over the walls into the river. For their troubles the Americans were paid handsomely with 124 barrels of gunpowder, over 6,000 cartridges, 150 stand of arms, and 238 barrels of provisions. While the major's concern for his men was commendable, his delivery of everything in the fort was patently inexcusable. Carleton apparently knew little about the man's character or judgment and had overlooked an important detail in permitting such a quantity of stores to remain so poorly protected. Although Carleton never censured Stopford, he surely saw that disaster had struck. Perhaps he thought it would be well if the issue could be forgotten without a searching investigation that might cause him some embarrassment.

Although the loss was immediately made known to the St.

Johns garrison because Montgomery hoped to use the victory to undermine the morale of the defenders there, the commander, Major Preston, ignored the incident and continued to hope for relief. Preston noted, however, he "had not a syllable of intelligence from Genl Carleton . . . from the first day of the blockade." [15] Facing mounting criticism from several leading seigniors as Preston's position became progressively more desperate, Carleton finally decided upon making an attack. Lieutenant Colonel Allen Maclean, who had been authorized to raise a regiment of "provincials" from among the Highland Emigrants who had settled in America after the Treaty of Paris, was called up from Quebec for the assault. Carleton, with a few regulars and a mixed force of Canadians and Indians, planned to cross from Montreal and join Maclean as he moved up from Sorel. As matters turned out, however, Seth Warner and his Green Mountain Boys were prepared on the eastern bank of the river and beat off Carleton's boats before they could effect a landing. Maclean, encountering a superior force, turned back to the safety of his boats and wisely decided to make the protection of Quebec his primary object. Finding the French-Canadian militiamen deserting fast and his remaining Indians slinking away, Carleton finally gave up the idea of a relief expedition on October 30. Three days later, Preston reported to Montgomery his readiness to negotiate an end to the 55-day siege. On November 3, the surviving defenders laid down their arms. During the preceding two months more than 700 men had been lost or taken prisoner in the unsuccessful effort to halt the American invasion. The entire region was now devoid of any means of further defense.

On November 5, Carleton reported the surrender of St. Johns to Dartmouth and took advantage of the occasion to analyze the reasons for his inability to check the American advance.[16] At the root of each point he listed lay a common answer—"want of hands." He had lost the race in constructing vessels "to dispute the passage of Lake Champlain" because ship carpenters were not available. Entrenchments adequate to protect Chambly and St. Johns could not be constructed and manned because of "the

corruption and stupid baseness of the Canadian peasantry."
When St. Johns was put under siege the Indians had left and the
militia deserted. He was now prepared to abandon Montreal as
soon as attacked because "the lower orders will not act, and there
are not means to defend the place."

With such a dismal record, Carleton was even apprehensive
about defending Quebec. The military defenses of the capital
were ill-prepared and he now knew that an American force
under Benedict Arnold was marching on Quebec from Maine
via the Chaudière. Carleton, anxious to make his way back to
the government seat, waited only for the loading of his vessels
and a breeze before making off for the capital.

But what ought to have been a routine trip downstream
quickly turned into a perilous adventure. It was to cost him
dearly and exposed his unfortunate tendency to underestimate
the enemy and to overlook ordinary, though vital, details. By
November 10 all the powder and supplies that could be carried
away were loaded on 11 small vessels that had been collected at
Montreal. The following day, with the 130 men and officers
who yet remained under his command, Carleton stepped on
board to catch a fair wind to Quebec. But his force was delayed
first by a sand bar and then by a change of wind before they
reached Sorel. When he reached the mouth of the Richelieu,
Carleton was surprised to find his way blocked by a floating
battery and cannon placed on shore by the resourceful Americans. He had not expected Montgomery to undertake anything
below Montreal until that city had been secured, but by the
time his fleet approached Sorel, troops under James Easton and
John Brown had been working hard there for a week.[17] Barred
from landing by an enemy detachment hurrying down from
Montreal, and finding escape past the American batteries impossible, Carleton was in desperate straits. His pilots were mutinous, and the commander of the powder ship made it known
that he would surrender before risking a fatal bombardment.
Although Carleton himself succeeded in slipping by the American artillery in a whale boat on the night of November 16,

Montgomery had the satisfaction of capturing the entire fleet with the last remnant of redcoats who had been brought up in September to oppose his advance. After having been delayed eleven weeks by Carleton's small force, nothing now lay between Montgomery and Quebec. He had put Carleton to a challenging test and had found him a worthy but far from ingenious opponent.

The next great challenge to Carleton's leadership, which he met more successfully, had already begun when he arrived in Quebec on November 19. Although he had escaped Montgomery's troops, Carleton appeared for a time to have merely exchanged one trap for another. The capital to which he returned was already a beleaguered city. Benedict Arnold had arrived at Quebec two weeks earlier at the head of 600 men after an incredibly difficult march across the northern wilderness from Maine. Within a few days after Carleton's arrival, Arnold was joined by Montgomery. Together the American commanders were able to muster about 1,000 effectives, little more than half the number of men available to Carleton. But the rebels retained the advantages of mobility and surprise and they posed a serious threat to the city.

Carleton's qualities in this trying situation showed to their best advantage. His calm and aristocratic bearing awakened confidence in his subordinates and his tireless energy aroused the fainthearted. Expelling all able-bodied men who refused to bear arms and cracking down hard on malingerers, he appreciably lessened the threat of sedition within the walls and reduced the strain on his supplies. A new fighting spirit, clearly derived from his presence, was aroused among his troops. Within a few days, the work on the fortifications begun by Maclean was almost completed and the defenders were organized for round-the-clock duty. Sleeping fully dressed for nights on end to be ready for an assault, Carleton was well prepared to put the Americans to a stiff test if they elected to defy the elements and attempt to storm his defenses.[18]

As the end of the year approached, Montgomery and Arnold

came to a desperate decision. Facing the dismal prospect of a long winter siege, concerned over an outbreak of smallpox, and worried about the impending expiration of the terms of enlistment of their men, they decided to launch an attack on the first night that there was a storm. To succeed, the Americans were counting on the element of surprise. They needed as well a large measure of luck, for in the game they elected to play they were working against long odds.

When the assault came, in the predawn hours of the last day of the year, Carleton was equal to the occasion. He was certain an attack was pending from reports of deserters and was prepared. Since he expected a diversion against the Lower Town while an attack was delivered against the landward walls—perhaps at Cape Diamond Bastion or St. John's Gate—Carleton maintained a command post at the Récollect monastery where he could be contacted by couriers from his scattered defenders and quickly send men where they were most needed. He was wrong about the details of the plan—for Montgomery and Arnold were personally leading converging columns in a main attack against Lower Town—but his error in this regard made little difference. Montgomery was killed instantly when trying to penetrate the Près-de-Ville barricade, and Arnold took a ball in the leg trying to enter the walls from the opposite direction. Livingston's feint against the landward walls did not distract Carleton long enough to permit Arnold's men—now under Daniel Morgan's command—to carry the second barrier after they entered Lower Town. Montgomery's men, on the other hand, failed to press on after the fall of their leader. Although he was surprised when Maclean reported the breakthrough of Morgan's men, Carleton was able to send Major Caldwell with reinforcements in time to check their advance. As the darkness lifted, Carleton also ordered a detachment out through Palace Gate to take Morgan's men by surprise from the rear. Four hundred exhausted and nearly leaderless rebels were rounded up, and half that number nursing wounds escaped back to the American camp. Carleton buried nearly a hundred of their fallen comrades. He counted fewer than one-tenth as many casualties among his own men, and concluded that the victory was as nearly perfect as could have been desired.[19] Although the siege was maintained until May, 1776, by the remnant of the American force, Carleton's defense against the assault had been an able one.

During the winter of Carleton's confinement in Quebec, the North Ministry began to respond more vigorously to the requirements of the war in America. In comparison to the opening moves of the war that had taken on something of the appearance of a series of "midnight" sieges, 1776 was to see the delivery of a grand offensive. General William Howe replaced Gage in command in Boston, and a determined Lord George Germain was appointed to succeed the gentle Dartmouth in the American Department. Simultaneously a strategy of reconquest had begun to crystallize and was already beginning to take form when Germain took office.[20] Howe was ordered to transfer from Boston to the more useful base at New York in order to prepare for a spring offensive. Reinforcements were readied for Canada. Moreover, seven regiments had been dispatched to Carolina for a winter campaign against the southern colonies. Howe was to have the reinforcements he requested for delivering the main blow at New York, and a 10,000-man striking force was to be sent to the St. Lawrence for an advance from Canada.

Of all this, however, Carleton knew nothing. Cut off from the outside world in early November, he received no word about these preparations until May 10, 1776. Indeed, though he had been established in an independent command when Gage returned to London, he gave little thought to his military role within the over-all perspective of the 1776 campaign.[21] As governor of Quebec he was preoccupied with re-establishing order in his own province, clearing the rebels from the St. Lawrence, implementing the Quebec Act, restoring the Canadians to a sense of duty to their sovereign, and, in general, vindicating his Canadian policy. Carleton only faintly grasped the idea that a sizable force was about to be placed in his hands and that he was expected to deliver a decisive blow to the rebels on the frontiers of New York. Whether he was overconfident that Howe would overwhelm the enemy in New York on his own or underestimated the Americans, he refused generally to concern himself with the larger problems of suppressing the rebellion in the other colonies. His experience of a decade had been that of a provincial governor, and he continued to perform as a provincial governor.

Uninformed of the details of the strategy of reconquest, and conditioned by his civil responsibilities and a winter of confinement to assume that the burden of crushing the revolt would be left to others, Carleton was not quite equal to the challenge placed before him. Yet it was understandable that his response betrayed no real sense of urgency. During the few weeks after reinforcements arrived in the spring it was extremely difficult for him to form an adequate image of the size and capabilities of the army available to him at any particular moment. His reinforcements were dispatched from no fewer than five different points over a period of several weeks and consequently the bulk of them straggled into the St. Lawrence intermittently between early May and the middle of June. Similarly, he had difficulty gauging the strength of the American forces contesting his advance back up river—intelligence reports reached him that the enemy numbered from 5,000 to 25,000 men. Since Carleton had already experienced several bitter failures because of faulty intelligence in 1775, he became inclined toward an uncharacteristic caution. And finally, Carleton was extremely irritated with the appointment of Germain. He believed, because of the court-martial that had pronounced judgment on Germain's conduct at the battle of Minden in 1759, that the new secretary was unfit to hold any important public office. The contempt with which Carleton regarded Germain therefore ruled out the possibility that any genuine understanding might prevail between the governor and the secretary of state. This animus left a bitter legacy and was to cost Britain dearly in 1777.[22]

Despite Carleton's hesitancy, the 1776 campaign opened auspiciously for him. The desperate siege before Quebec that was maintained by the Americans throughout the winter broke up with the appearance of the first British relief ship on May 6. Carleton immediately sent 900 men marching out of Quebec and across the Plains of Abraham, but they found only a disordered abandoned American camp. Since he had received only token reinforcements as yet, Carleton made no further attempt to pursue the retreating Americans. Even after General Burgoyne arrived in Quebec on June 1 with full instructions for the 1776 campaign, Carleton took no energetic action. Instead he paused to supervise elaborate preparations for the advance up the St. Lawrence against Montreal and St. Johns, as day after day additional British transports and warships arrived. Not the least of his concerns was the need to re-establish his communications across the Canadian countryside to learn what he could of the enemy's retreat.

Fearing that the rebels were still strong enough to threaten his exposed moving columns should he drop his guard, Carleton prepared to establish and organize his forces at Three Rivers before advancing upon Sorel and Montreal. His caution apparently was warranted. On June 8, General Sullivan with about 2,000 men dropped down from Sorel, crossed the St. Lawrence, and struck the redcoats collecting at Three Rivers. Ignorant of the British strength and disposition, and delayed from delivering a surprise blow at the critical moment because of the treachery of his guide, Sullivan was completely routed by the vastly superior force he encountered. The American general thus found himself on the north side of the river and all but cut off from his main army by the British forces controlling the waterway. Had Carleton been disposed to give chase, or had he fully realized the predicament the rebels were in, he might have smashed Sullivan's force in short order. But other matters were uppermost in his mind. Lacking precise knowledge of the situation, he permitted his "deluded" foe to escape, hoping the Americans might return home convinced of the benevolence of British rule and of the futility of trying to resist British regulars.[23] His thinking along these lines was perhaps natural when serving as a statesman of the empire, but it was odd conduct for a military commander.

Rather than attempting to follow up his unexpected victory over Sullivan by pressing the pursuit and improvising to meet changing conditions, Carleton chose to proceed with his original plan. Brigadier General Fraser, placed in command of a strong column, was directed to march up the north shore of the St. Lawrence for Montreal to cut off one avenue of retreat. General Burgoyne with 4,000 men was ordered to move against the main body of Americans withdrawing toward St. Johns from Sorel. Carleton himself set off with the remaining troops on board ship for Montreal. He intended to advance from that point on the St. Lawrence overland to cut off the Americans at St. Johns before they could escape southward. To ensure that the enemy would not elude the trap, Burgoyne was cautioned to advance slowly, lest the Americans flee too rapidly. This would enable Carleton to move into position. But Carleton had failed to reckon with two factors—the wind, which delayed his advance up river from Sorel, and the energy of the Americans, who learned of the British approach in time to effect a hasty retreat. Burgoyne, as a result, was denied a deserved victory by a very narrow margin. Just as Burgoyne's advance guard rushed into St. Johns, the last boatloads of Arnold's men rowed out of sight toward Lake Champlain.[24] By moving ponderously and with such measured speed, Carleton had clearly demonstrated that he did not have the instincts of a skilled military commander.

Although St. Johns was his, the governor now found that he had to fight for control of the lakes before he could make the force of his numbers felt against the rebels to the southward. Having foreseen the need of vessels for just this occasion, he had long ago requested that boats, naval stores, and artificers be sent out with his relief. But shortages of materials and skilled labor, coupled with Howe's more urgent need for landing craft at New York, had made it impossible for the government to meet his request.[25] A few small gunboats capable of mounting one gun each and flat-bottomed boats for carrying troops were sent, but they hardly met his requirements.

Carleton had no choice, then, but to set his men to building vessels capable of wresting control of Lake Champlain from the Americans. In the meantime, he returned to Quebec to address himself to the problems of the province. During the long pause in the fighting that followed, he was again plunged into the oft-delayed task of organizing the Canadian government. Simultaneously, however, he had the pleasure of learning that for his successful defense of Quebec he had been knighted by a grateful king.

The task of constructing a fleet dragged on throughout the summer and was pursued with little sense of urgency. The Americans meanwhile were left virtually unmolested, and Carleton did almost nothing to reconnoiter the enemy positions. Although the American situation at Ticonderoga was often desperate and the leading officers there were for a time divided on the wisdom of contesting passage of the lake, Carleton made no significant move to ascertain the enemy's ability to defend the forts at the southern end of Lake Champlain. Early in September, when he learned of the unexpected strength of the rebel armament on the lake, he belatedly decided to have the *Inflexible*—a square-rigged three-master mounting eighteen guns—dismantled, dragged up from Chambly to St. Johns, and reassembled. His decision to do so was correct, for the *Inflexible* provided the margin by which Carleton would dominate the lake, but the project was a herculean one that consumed an additional 28 crucial days.

By the time Carleton sailed from Isle-aux-Noix on October 4 and began to search for the American flotilla under Benedict Arnold which was to dispute his passage, the season for campaigning was drawing rapidly to an end. Proceeding slowly and keeping a sharp watch, Carleton spotted the enemy vessels on the eleventh. They were anchored advantageously between Valcour Island and the west shore of the lake where he would be forced to attack them from the leeward. The battle that fol-

lowed, decisive as it was, was a very unequal match.[26] Although
the Americans fought heroically, Carleton's men performed
skillfully and the British naval force had guns capable of dis-
charging double the weight thrown out by the enemy. Arnold's
flotilla suffered a disastrous defeat. Prolonging the inevitable,
Arnold maneuvered his battered force past the British under
cover of fog and darkness and momentarily escaped southward.
But two days later, Carleton finished off the American fleet
within sight of Crown Point. Watching his advance, the American troops on shore put the Crown Point fort to the torch and
marched off to Ticonderoga, leaving the British to take possession of the smoldering ruins the following morning, undisputed
masters of the lake.

Carleton now faced the most crucial decision of his military
career—whether to attempt to drive the Americans from Ticonderoga at once or withdraw for the winter and resume the attack in the spring. Maintaining a large garrison deep in the
wilderness exposed to enemy harassment during a northern
winter involved risks that even a less careful commander would
have hesitated to take. Considering Carleton's prudence, the
advanced season, and the hazards to which his army would be
exposed in winter quarters on the lake, the decision was perhaps
inevitable. After surveying the outer works of the fortress,
Carleton feared that General Gates, now in command of the
northern army, had done his work too well to attempt a challenge so late in the year. The vigor with which Arnold and
Gates had already moved to slow his advance suggested that Ticonderoga would be difficult to storm, and too little time remained to carry out a protracted siege. Following a cautious
thrust at the American defenses on October 27, Carleton ordered
a more vigorous probe on the twenty-ninth, which confirmed
his worst suspicions. He promptly ordered a withdrawal.[27] A
few hours later, preparations were also underway for the evacuation of Crown Point.

Within two weeks Carleton was back in Quebec immersed in
his work as governor of the province. Although he did not know

it at the time, his days of active campaigning against American armies were at an end. From this point on in his career, he was to be a statesman rather than soldier.

During the winter, Carleton could reflect pleasantly on the changes he had wrought in Quebec's situation, and on the honor bestowed upon him for his tenacious defense of the city—the red ribbon of a Knight of the Bath—but surely little else gave him comfort. He knew he had failed to destroy the American army thrown against him, and the lake forts remained in enemy hands. Moreover, when meetings of the Legislative Council were resumed in the spring he found himself in the unaccustomed presence of men who dared to question his recommendations. Before long he was embroiled in controversy over alleged irregularities in his administration.[28] Thus, when he received letters from Germain questioning his management of the 1776 campaign coupled with news that General John Burgoyne would be given command of the northern army for the 1777 offensive, the implied criticisms were more than Sir Guy could stand. His letters of May 20th and 22nd to Germain, written in whatever passion he permitted himself, were surely two of the most vitriolic ever penned by a British officer to a secretary of state.[29] Even the king took note of them, remarking that "Carleton was highly wrong in permitting his pen to convey such asperity to a Secretary of State." [30]

Although the quarrel between the two men ostensibly flared up as a consequence of Germain's criticism of Carleton's conduct in 1776, the dispute actually arose from an accumulation of disappointments which Sir Guy had encountered since his return to America in 1774.[31] Despite his early confident predictions, the Quebec Act had not won the active support of the Canadians. Neither his military victories nor his humane treatment of prisoners had brought the rebels to their senses. He had been criticized for dividing his army into brigades and ignoring eligible senior officers in filling the new positions he had created. Several of his civil appointments had been questioned or vetoed.[32] And his use of the Council had drawn him into political squabbles which eventually led him to a painful confrontation with the chief justice of Quebec. Germain, no less frustrated by the outcome of the 1776 campaign and already stung by offensive letters from Carleton, had reacted to the withdrawal from Lake Champlain by binding Carleton to inflexible orders—orders which left Carleton little future discretionary control over troops in Canada and which could only be construed as a want of confidence.

Carleton's reaction, intemperate as it was, is not at all surprising. Germain, whipping boy of the Ministry and architect of Britain's aggressive military plans, was an easy mark for his attack. No individual was responsible for all the delays and shortages that had contributed to the failures of British arms in 1776, but the secretary of state was the person most vulnerable to criticism. He was not inclined to be charitable toward his commanders in America. Believing that Carleton had mismanaged the defense of Canada in 1775, he had begrudged him the red ribbon in recognition of his preservation of Quebec. And from the time he received Carleton's first insulting letters in mid-1776 he had intrigued to have him recalled from Canada. Their reaction to one another after 1777 was the struggle of two offended prima donnas. Certainly neither man was entirely free of guilt nor merited the full abuse they heaped upon one another. But since Carleton launched the attack and resorted to false charges and devious accusations, his surely was the greater offense.

Nevertheless, Carleton did not permit the dispute with Germain to hamper preparations for Burgoyne's invasion of New York. Carleton rose momentarily above his pique and contributed importantly, as only he could do, to place the resources of Canada at the disposal of Burgoyne's army. Indeed, the zeal he displayed in behalf of the expedition was later explicitly acknowledged by Burgoyne in a speech before Parliament. Despite the decisive consequences of his failure to capture and retain control of Lake Champlain in 1776, Carleton's conduct in 1777 was clearly not directly responsible for the British defeat at Saratoga.

Yet his usefulness in Canada, he felt, was at an end. In an explosive letter on June 27, 1777, he finally released his remaining pent-up feelings against Germain and formally requested permission to return to England. Since his letter of resignation was written in the aftermath of an unpleasant political encounter with one of the most respected members of his Council, it is probable that he had more than the secretary of state's criticisms on his mind. His shafts were aimed unmistakably at Germain, however, and could not help but have the intended effect. Every line bore the mark of Carleton's bitterness.[33]

> [As] . . . all the marks of your Lordship's displeasure affect not me but the King's service and the tranquillity of his people, I flatter myself I shall obtain his royal permission to return home this fall, the more so that from your first entrance into office, you began to prepare the minds of all men for this event, wisely foreseeing that under your Lordship's administration it must certainly come to pass, and for my own part I do not think it just that the private enmity of the King's servants should add to the disturbances of his reign. For these reasons I shall embark with great satisfaction, still entertaining hopes and ardent wishes that after my departure you may adopt measures tending to promote the safety and tranquillity of this unfortunate Province; at least, that the dignity of the Crown may not appear beneath your Lordship's concern.

Although a successor was immediately named to replace him, Carleton remained in Canada until the summer of 1778. Bad weather intervened to delay the changing of the Canadian command, forcing him to remain yet another winter in Quebec, and extending his term of office in the province to nearly twelve years. He had filled a taxing post, demanding a wide range of talents, during some exceedingly difficult years, and though he was returning under something of a cloud all who knew his record still regarded him as one of Britain's foremost statesmen. Few questioned the results of his command in America at that time, for attention in 1778 was drawn to Saratoga and the entry of France into the war; the grosser details of his conduct of government in Canada were as yet undisclosed.[34]

Within a few months after his return, Carleton had settled down to the leisurely routine of a Hampshire country gentleman. But he was not destined for early retirement. With the passage of time, his name was frequently mentioned in connection with a possible new assignment in America. Yet there were obstacles to be overcome. As long as Germain remained in office, Carleton's appointment was out of the question. And he apparently nursed such a grievance against the commander-in-chief (Jeffrey Amherst) that George III was once led to remark that "Sir Guy Carleton dislikes Ld. Amherst so much that it is not very easy to employ him." [35]

But by the time of the Yorktown disaster, over three years had elapsed since Carleton's departure from Canada, and Britain had nearly exhausted her supply of eligible generals. When Germain was jettisoned in February, 1782, in a last-minute political move to save the North Ministry, the way was cleared for Carleton's selection as Sir Henry Clinton's successor as commander-in-chief in America. All that had to be decided was the precise nature of the powers that were to be conferred upon the new commander. On his part, Sir Guy ardently hoped to negotiate a reconciliation of the American colonies. On March 26, 1782, he was formally notified that in addition to his military appointment he had been designated, along with Admiral Digby, commissioner "for restoring peace and granting pardon to the revolted provinces in America." [36]

Much to his subsequent regret, Carleton had unwittingly stepped back onto the stage of history in the midst of a momentous political crisis.[37] During his last days in England, the Opposition in Parliament had gained momentum, and barely forty-eight hours after he received his appointment the Rockingham Ministry took office. Despite all the king could do—for he kept insisting that he would sanction only "a change in men" —the occasion became one for sweeping changes. The result has been labeled a "political massacre"; and in the aftermath, those in office were "shot by platoons." In order to carry out the wishes of the new Ministry to liquidate the war with America and to make peace, Carleton was pointedly notified, on the eve of his departure, that "the first object of your attention must be to provide for withdrawing the Garrison . . . from New York and its dependencies to Halifax." Similar arrangements were to be made for Charleston, Savannah, and St. Augustine.[38] With a few strokes of the pen, Carleton's dreams of a reconciliation were shattered beyond repair.

The news must have hurt Carleton deeply. As he made the voyage to America, the parallel between the position he was now in and that of the Carlisle Commission in 1778 could not have escaped his attention. If he were to conduct any negotiations at all, it would be from a position of obvious weakness. Although the Ministry had not formally recognized the independence of the colonies, he now believed with others that a giant step had been taken in the headlong plunge toward the dissolution of the whole empire.

Nevertheless, Carleton put on a good face as he stepped ashore at New York in the first week in May, 1782. He was determined to make the best of a bad situation. Within a few days, he was hard at work trying to find out what might yet be done to save his mission from failure. In a play for time, he made polite overtures to Washington while he wrote reports to London that he had reason to believe the colonies might acknowledge allegiance to the king, if they were given control over the management of their internal affairs.[39] He proposed also that he evacuate the southern ports first and bring their garrisons to New York— where their presence might strengthen his hand with Congress— claiming that adequate tonnage was not available for the immediate evacuation of New York. Finally, to complete his scheme, he audaciously diverted to New York reinforcements intended for Halifax.[40] For a time he must honestly have believed that he could so augment the strength of the New York garrison that he might bring the Americans to the bargaining table, despite the drift of the Ministry on another course. Historians, surprisingly enough, have never noted Carleton's interesting attempt to challenge the Ministry's policy at this stage.[41]

It was all in vain. To open the way for serious negotiations with the American commissioners in Paris, the Ministry already had made concessions that Carleton interpreted as tantamount to a recognition of independence. He learned of these concessions on July 31. Two weeks later he decided to request the king's permission to resign, for he had accepted the American command only to promote a reconciliation.[42] Moreover, recent reports from his American informants were less favorable than previous ones. The "rulers of the provinces" had not yet shown the least disposition to take "pacific measures," and it was all too obvious that "every artifice" was being employed to inflame the passions and mislead the understanding of the public.[43] Thwarted in a noble enterprise by misguided leaders bent on sacrificing American interests to France, and feeling victimized by ministers at home once again, he wanted to wash his hands of the whole affair. Only fourteen weeks had passed since his arrival in New York.

But it was not to be. Tedious communications and a late change in British strategy designed to exploit Rodney's stunning naval victory in West Indies waters in April, 1782, delayed acceptance of Carleton's request until January 1, 1783. Ironically enough, the orders directing Carleton to embark for Barbados to take on new duties after he had completed the evacuation of New York were dispatched from London the very day Sir Guy had written for permission to resign.[44] Since the Ministry now planned a new West Indian campaign, it was at first assumed that Carleton would withdraw his request to resign once he received his new instructions. Another exchange of letters was required in October, 1782, before the Ministry learned that he was firm in his intention to leave. Apparently not even the prospect of a new offensive could reconcile Carleton to the government, and General Charles Grey was finally appointed to relieve him.

The change of command, however, never took place, and in

consequence the greatest opportunity of Carleton's career now opened to him. Sent to New York on a difficult mission, and stranded there by a quirk of fate, he soon found a new cause worthy of his commitment—the protection of the refugee American loyalists. New York, the site of some of the most heart-rending scenes during the closing months of the war, provided Carleton a unique vantage point from which to survey the ruins of the Old British Empire and to catch a glimpse of a new one. He helped to evacuate all loyalists who desired to remain under His Majesty's protection, and used every resource at his command to secure them new homes. These refugees, he believed, would form the nucleus of a regenerated empire which Carleton hoped to salvage from the American wreck.

When the last refugees had been evacuated, Carleton sailed for London, where plans were matured to consolidate the remaining North American provinces under a single government.[45] Within a short time, he reluctantly abandoned the idea of retirement for the prospect of returning to Canada as governor-general of British North America. But he failed to secure the broad powers that would have made him an American viceroy. The government, perhaps in response to Carleton's previous authoritarian rule in Quebec, was reluctant to place such authority in the hands of one agent so far removed from direct control. Though created Baron Dorchester in 1786 and returned to Canada as governor and commander-in-chief of several provinces jointly, he was consistently thwarted in his final efforts at imperial consolidation. He later made only minor contributions to the Constitutional Act of 1791, which against his will divided a great imperial domain into Upper and Lower Canada. Characteristically, he ended his days in America wrangling with the United States over British control of the Northwest posts and arguing with Canadian officials whom he could not bend to his decisions. Rebuked by the home government for inflammatory conduct against the United States at a time when John Jay was on his mission to London in 1794 to settle the Anglo-American dispute, Carleton for the third and last time in his life offered his resignation. He returned to England finally in the summer of 1796, and spent the last twelve years of his life in retirement on his country estates.

In the strict sense that he had not achieved what had been expected of him and had made inadequate use of the resources placed at his disposal, Guy Carleton's military command was a failure. But to stop the evaluation of his military career at that point is to miss much of the significance of his role in America. Carleton's generalship can no more be separated from his governorship than one can study the war with the colonies independently from the war between England and France. He must be judged, if judged fairly, in the context of the operation of the British imperial system and eighteenth-century provincial government as well as in the light of his military record.[46]

There was a certain logic in his conduct, which if not always excusable, is certainly explicable. Although a general by profession, he became an active military leader by force of circumstance, and made the transition from peacetime provincial governor to wartime commander with difficulty. His experience of nearly a decade led him at the outset to view the Revolution primarily as a political rather than a military matter, and long after the government had decided to apply a military solution to the problem Carleton was still preoccupied with provincial political issues. The result was to blunt the ministerial program of coercion. He was not, of course, entirely wrong in his assumptions, but at times he arrogated to himself choices that were not his to make.

An autocrat, suspicious of the motives of others and often devious in his methods, Carleton was frequently at odds with his superiors. In part, the conflicts must be charged to ample defects of character. He had a strong tendency to self-righteousness, and too little sense of his fallibility. His self-confidence often betrayed him into arrogance, and his independence of will into insubordination. Yet who could rule Canada for a dozen years, cut off from the outside world six months of each twelve, without developing such defects? Governors of Quebec were expected to exhibit many of Carleton's qualities. His orders almost always reserved to him options that only he could judge at the scene of action. If in the end the empire suffered because of the character of her officials, such abuses were inevitable.

As a military commander, Carleton had obvious shortcomings. His was not an agile mind; he did not respond quickly to changing conditions, and too often seemed content merely to meet the most immediate threat, leaving greater initiative to others. He responded unenthusiastically to Gage's earliest calls for a military diversion on the frontier and consistently looked first to the defense of his own province. When the American command was divided after Gage returned to England, Carleton never quite fully grasped the fact that his responsibilities for checking the rebellion transcended provincial boundaries. Charged with more than any man could handle, busy vindicating his Canadian policies, and forced to grapple with "seditious" merchants and "stupid" habitants, he probably never adequately identified the real enemy.

Yet Canada itself was "saved." Although there were some in Britain who hoped that Carleton might have helped to save the other provinces as well, many believed that he had done enough. He had not, of course, and as a result of this contradiction Carleton will always remain a controversial figure.

Any assessment of Carleton as a military man has similar contradictions. His critics, on the one hand, have argued that he virtually "threw away" resounding victories that were within his grasp, without adequately considering whether *any* defeat administered to an American army within the borders of Canada would have had a decisive effect beyond its boundaries.[47] Carleton's military responsibilities beyond the frontier of the province of Quebec were never clear, but this ambiguity cannot be laid entirely to the governor. His apologists have generally been even less helpful, for too often they have absolved Carleton of almost every failure. Uncritically attributing his defeats simply to incompetence in London,[48] they have ignored much of the reality of eighteenth-century warfare. Moreover, they go much too far in claiming that Carleton was indispensable after Yorktown, and that in this last crisis Britain was forced to seek "the master-hand of Carleton . . . for no government could have done without him."[49]

To numerous loyalist exiles, particularly those "British Canadians" who sought to make a new life for themselves as neighbors of the French already in Canada, Carleton was a statesman without peer. If ever they and the "French Canadians" were to be reconciled to a life together within a single state, their leader had to combine the vision that produced the Quebec Act with the humanity that marked the British treatment of the loyalists. Thus, with the passage of time Carleton easily became a legend. For many he became a hero in Canada comparable perhaps to Parson Weems' Washington, but such myth-making could only be achieved by neglecting critical contemporary accounts. In the popular imagination he was easily contrasted with a bumbling Germain, and serious students, noting the dearth of surviving Carleton manuscripts, shied away from any evaluation of him until the past generation. Perhaps enough never will be known of him to remove the shell of legend from the kernel of truth that lies inside. But those who would understand Carleton's role in the War of American Independence must attempt to see both the man and the legend.

FOOTNOTES

1. The bare details of his early life can be found most conveniently in Arthur G. Bradley, *Sir Guy Carleton (Lord Dorchester)*, (3d ed.; Toronto, 1966); and William Wood, *The Father of British Canada: A Chronicle of Carleton* (Toronto, 1916).

2. Carleton to Shelburne, November 25, 1767. Adam Shortt and Arthur G. Doughty, eds., *Documents Relating to the Constitutional History of Canada, 1759–1791*, 2 vols. (Ottawa, 1907), I, pp. 196–99.

3. Carleton to Gage, February 15, 1767, Gage Papers, Clements Li-

brary, Ann Arbor, Michigan. Hereafter, all Gage Papers cited are in Clements Library.

4. William Smith, "The Struggle over the Laws of Canada, 1763–1783," *Canadian Historical Review*, I (1920), pp. 166–86; and Alfred L. Burt, "Sir Guy Carleton and His First Council," *ibid.*, IV (1923), pp. 321–32.

5. Alfred L. Burt, *Guy Carleton, Lord Dorchester, 1724–1808*, Canadian Historical Association, Historical Booklet No. 5 (Rev. ed.; Ottawa, 1964), p. 3.

6. Gage to Carleton, September 4, 1774, Gage Papers.

7. Carleton to Gage, September 20, 1774, *ibid.*

8. Carleton to Gage, February 4, 1775, "secret," *ibid.*

9. Smith, "The Struggle over the Laws of Canada," pp. 173–76.

10. The fullest accounts of these events and the operations that follow are Justin H. Smith, *Our Struggle for the Fourteenth Colony*, 2 vols. (New York & London, 1907), I, pp. 304–491; and Allen French, *The First Year of the American Revolution* (Boston, 1934), pp. 376–442.

11. Peter Force, ed., *American Archives*, Fourth Series (Washington, 1837–53), II, p. 940; Alfred L. Burt, *The Old Province of Quebec* (Minneapolis & Toronto, 1933), p. 213.

12. The extensive correspondence bearing on this problem is conveniently summarized in "Extracts from records of Indian affairs under Colonel Guy Johnson during 1775," Germain Papers, Clements Library. It can be followed more laboriously through Carleton's correspondence with Dartmouth, "Q" series, Volume XI, pp. 152–271, Public Archives of Canada (O-tawa), and with Gage, in the volumes for February 4, 1775–September 29, 1775, Gage Papers.

13. Carleton to Gage, July 27, 1775, Gage Papers; and Carleton to Dartmouth, August 14, 1775, "Q," XI, pp. 222–25.

14. Carleton to Dartmouth, October 25, 1775, *ibid.*, pp. 268–69.

15. "Papers Relating to the Surrender of Fort St. Johns and Fort Chambly," *Report of the Work of the Public Archives for the years 1914 and 1915*, (Ottawa, 1916), Sessional Paper 29a, App. B, p. 25.

16. Carleton to Dartmouth, November 5, 1775, *Report on Canadian Archives, 1890* (Ottawa, 1890), pp. 65–66.

17. Smith, *Struggle for the Fourteenth Colony*, I, pp. 487–88.

18. *Ibid.*, II, pp. 76–110.

19. In addition to Smith, *ibid.*, pp. 111–47, see also French, *The First Year of the American Revolution*, pp. 595–620; Christopher Ward,

The War of the Revolution, John R. Alden, ed., 2 vols. (New York, 1952), I, pp. 181–95; and Carleton to Germain, May 14, 1776, "Q," XII, pp. 7–10.

20. For an authoritative discussion of the "strategy of reconquest," see Piers Mackesy's splendid work, *The War for America, 1775–1783* (Cambridge, Mass., 1964), pp. 56–61. From our present perspective, the vigor and energy that went into the organization of the 1776 campaign appear as something of an illusion, but no assessment of British strategy can ignore the very real achievements of the North Ministry in this work. No one could have foreseen that neither Howe nor Carleton would be able to strike the rebels a mortal blow with the great armies about to be placed at their command.

21. Since Carleton was the senior officer in America when Gage left Boston, the American command was divided at that time to enable Carleton to remain in Quebec to deal with that province and "the frontiers bordering thereupon," while Howe was left in command of all forces operating in the remaining colonies. Dartmouth to Gage, August 2, 1775, Gage Papers; and Dartmouth to Carleton, August 2, 1775, "Q," XI, pp. 198–99. The fact of Carleton's seniority over Howe was also at the root of another important matter, the appointment of Burgoyne to command the northern army in 1777. It was always assumed that Carleton would supersede Howe should their armies be united, and Burgoyne was eventually given command to avoid this embarrassing possibility. But Carleton by chance failed to learn the reasons for the decision until nearly nine months had elapsed after it had been made, and he preferred to believe that the appointment was a form of censure. The episode therefore contributed importantly to his estrangement from Germain. Germain to Carleton, August 22, 1776, "Q," XII, pp. 88–90, and March 26, 1777, Historical Manuscripts Commission, *Report on the Manuscripts of Mrs. Stopford-Sackville, of Drayton House, Northamptonshire,* 2 vols. (London, 1904–10), II, pp. 60–63; John W. Fortescue, ed., *Correspondence of King George III,* 6 vols. (London, 1927–28), III, Nos. 1630, 1685.

22. Gerald S. Brown, *The American Secretary: The Colonial Policy of Lord George Germain, 1775–1778* (Ann Arbor, 1963), pp. 6–16, 83–85, 89–93, 103; Alfred L. Burt, "The Quarrel between Germain and Carleton: An Inverted Story," *Canadian Historical Review,* XI (September, 1930), pp. 202–22.

23. Similarly, when Carleton later took time to explain to Germain his policy of releasing prisoners, he emphasized the need "to con-

vince all His Majesty's unhappy subjects, that the King's mercy and Benevolence were still open to them." Britain could only "turn the scale," he believed, by exhibiting "valor and good conduct in action, with humanity and friendly treatment to those who are subdued and at our mercy." Carleton to Germain, August 10, 1776, "Q," XII, p. 135. See also his letter to Howe of August 8, 1776, quoted in Bradley, *Sir Guy Carleton*, p. 139.

24. Carleton to Germain, June 20, 1776, "Q," XII, pp. 64–67. For an interesting contemporary picture reflecting a sense of the confusion and disorder that marked the army's activities during the spring and summer of 1776, see the journal of Lt. William Digby, "Some Account of the American War between Great Britain and her Colonies," in James P. Baxter, *The British Invasion from the North* (Albany, 1887), pp. 104–77.

25. Mackesy, *The War for America*, pp. 94–95.

26. There is considerable literature upon the subject, for the control of the lake was rightly considered crucial to the outcome of the War of Independence. See, for example, Alfred T. Mahan, *Major Operations of the Navies in the War of Independence* (Boston, 1913), pp. 13–26; Gardner W. Allen, *A Naval History of the American Revolution*, 2 vols. (Boston, 1913), I, pp. 163–79; and Ward, *The War of the Revolution*, I, chapter 35.

27. The fullest recent account dealing with Carleton's career in 1776 is Perry Eugene Leroy, "Sir Guy Carleton as a Military Leader during the American Invasion and Repulse in Canada, 1775–1776," (unpublished Ph.D. dissertation, Ohio State University, 1960). For the decision to withdraw from Lake Champlain, see pp. 472–81, and for the staggering logistical problems that faced Carleton, pp. 542–47. For a contemporary view of Carleton's "very unaccountable conduct" during this period, see Historical Manuscripts Commission, *Report on the Manuscripts of the Late Reginald Hastings*, 4 vols. (London, 1928–41), III, p. 189.

28. Smith, "The Struggle over the Laws of Canada," pp. 177–78.

29. Germain to Carleton, March 26, 1777, *Manuscripts of Mrs. Stopford-Sackville*, II, pp. 60–63; and Carleton to Germain, May 20 and 22, 1777, "Q," XIII, pp. 111–20, 156–59.

30. *Correspondence of George III*, IV, No. 2202. George III was equally disturbed with Germain's performance during the dispute between the two men, noting "the malevolence of his mind." *Ibid*.

31. The dispute has been treated at length by Alfred L. Burt, "The Quarrel between Germain and Carleton: An Inverted Story." For an interesting discussion of Burgoyne's contribution to the quarrel

and the influence of the dispute on the selection of a commander for the 1777 invasion of New York, see William B. Willcox, *Portrait of a General: Sir Henry Clinton in the War of Independence* (New York, 1964), pp. 133–34.

32. Since Carleton by chance received no fewer than fourteen letters from Germain on May 6, 1777, dated August 22, 1776, March 24 and 26, 1777, an accumulation of Germain's criticisms fell upon him as a single blow. See "Q," XII, pp. 84–93, and "Q," XIII, pp. 73–98.

33. Carleton to Germain, June 27, 1777, *Report on Canadian Archives, 1890*, pp. 88–89.

34. Lord North, for example, believed him to be "so much of a soldier, and so little of a politician, such a resolute, honest man, and such a faithful and dutiful subject," that he wished another command was available for him. North to George III, August 30, 1779, *Correspondence of George III*, IV, No. 2753. And of his professional qualities even Germain retained a high opinion throughout the war. See Germain to William Knox, July 13 and November 11, 1782, Historical Manuscripts Commission, *Report on Manuscripts in Various Collections*, 8 vols. (London, 1901–14), VI, pp. 186, 189.

35. *Correspondence of George III*, IV, No. 2754.

36. Welbore Ellis to Carleton, March 26, 1782, British Headquarters' Papers, No. 4302. New York Public Library. Hereafter N.Y.P.L.

37. Mackesy, *The War for America*, pp. 466–74.

38. Orders of April 4, 1782, Colonial Office Papers, Series 5, vol. 106, pp. 1–13. Library of Congress.

39. Carleton to Shelburne, May 12, 1782, *ibid.*, p. 41. For the place of Carleton's mission in the policy of Secretary of State Shelburne, see Vincent T. Harlow, *The Founding of the Second British Empire, 1763–1793* (London, 1952), pp. 263–68.

40. Carleton to Shelburne, May 24, and June 18, 1782, C.O. 5: 106, pp. 50–51, 267–68. Library of Congress.

41. Though it would be unfair to charge that Carleton upon his arrival deliberately hatched a plan to challenge the Ministry, it is nevertheless clear enough that so long as he thought he still had the chance he seized every opportunity available to play the role of an American viceroy. The day after he decided to resign, he wrote the following explanation of his recent acts. "My intentions were to have assembled here the troops from the southward, with the years' reinforcement from Europe; had this measure taken place, it would have given some security till an evacuation became pos-

sible; *it would have added some weight too to any negotiation here*, had such been thought advisable; in every circumstance *it must have commanded a respect which we have no claim to in our present situation.* Carleton to Shelburne, August 15, 1782, *ibid.*, pp. 332–33. Italics mine.

42. See Carleton to Haldimand, August 3, 1782, British Headquarters' Papers, No. 5203, N.Y.P.L.; and Carleton to Shelburne, August 14, 1782, *ibid.*, No. 5292.

43. Carleton to Shelburne, June 18, 1782, C.O. 5: 106, p. 269. Library of Congress.

44. Townshend to Carleton, August 14, 1782, *ibid.*, pp. 291–306.

45. Leslie F. S. Upton, *The Diary and Selected Papers of Chief Justice William Smith, 1784–1793*, 2 vols. (Toronto, 1963), I, pp. xxxiv–xxxvii.

46. For an analysis of the complex interaction between political and military factors that shaped British policy before the Revolution, see John Shy's admirable recent study, *Toward Lexington: The Role of the British Army in the Coming of the American Revolution* (Princeton, 1965), especially pp. 418–24.

47. Burt, *Guy Carleton, Lord Dorchester, 1724–1808*, p. 9.

48. Bradley, *Sir Guy Carleton (Lord Dorchester)*, pp. 165–70.

49. Wood, *The Father of British Canada*, p. 164.

BIBLIOGRAPHY

Bradley, Arthur G. *Sir Guy Carleton (Lord Dorchester)*. Toronto, 1907. A readable study, first published in the Makers of Canada Series, sympathetically portraying Carleton as one of the greatest proconsuls of the empire, but innocent of any real appreciation of the actualities of his administrations. Should be read only in the revised editions (1926, 1966), for which Alfred L. Burt furnished numerous critical appendices.

Burt, Alfred L. *Guy Carleton, Lord Dorchester, 1724–1808*. Ottawa, 1964. A brief summation by the leading Carleton authority, erring seriously only in his estimate of Carleton's conduct in New York in 1782.

———. *The Old Province of Quebec*. Minneapolis & Toronto, 1933. The indispensable work on the subject of the forces working upon Carleton. Mild reservations to Burt's judgments have been registered in Michel Brunet's brief *French Canada and the Early Decades of British Rule, 1760–1791* (Ottawa, 1963).

French, Allen. *The First Year of the American Revolution*. Boston, 1934. A good detailed account of the American invasion of Canada and the assault on Quebec.

Mackesy, Piers. *The War for America, 1775–1783*. Cambridge, Mass., 1964. The best comprehensive study of the British conduct of the war. Accurately depicts the place of Canada in the opening phases of the war, and shrewdly assesses Carleton's qualities as governor and commander in the field.

Smith, Justin H. *Our Struggle for the Fourteenth Colony*. 2 vols. New York, 1907. An older reliable work containing the most detailed descriptions of military operations in Canada before 1777.

Wood, William. *The Father of British Canada: A Chronicle of Carleton*. Toronto, 1916. A popular survey, drawing heavily upon Bradley's work.

Wrong, George M. *Canada and the American Revolution*. Toronto, 1935. A useful study assessing broadly Carleton's conduct and the impact of the Revolution on the development of Canada.

John Burgoyne:

AMBITIOUS GENERAL

GEORGE ATHAN BILLIAS

Clark University

OF THE British generals in the American Revolution, none has been ridiculed more than John Burgoyne. Perhaps this was so because no other British military leader lent himself so readily to caricature. Certain of his contemporaries pictured Burgoyne as a playboy general—a card-playing, wine-loving *bon vivant* who had a winning way with women in the boudoir but a losing style on the battlefield; a buffoon in uniform who bungled his assignments badly; and a dilettante who pursued three careers— those of soldier, politician, and playwright—and mastered none. Such a conception of Burgoyne was based upon hostile sources of the period—the *Parliamentary Debates* in which Lord George Germain vilified him, the memoirs of Baroness von Riedesel, and the journals of Horace Walpole. The baroness, who accompanied Burgoyne's army to Saratoga, was responsible for one of the brilliant but bitter portraits left for posterity: Burgoyne liked a "jolly time," she wrote, and spent "half the night singing and drinking and amusing himself in the company of the wife of a commissary, who was his mistress, and, like himself, liked champagne." [1] More touches were added by Horace Walpole, the English author, who dubbed him "General Swagger" and "Julius Caesar Burgonius," and complained of his boasts to cross America in "a hop, step and jump." [2] But this characterization of

142

Burgoyne is misleading. While revealing some of his personality traits, it discloses little regarding his military capabilities. To understand Burgoyne's qualities as a general, one must look beyond his moral foibles as a man.

Many military historians and biographers writing about Burgoyne in later years often perpetuated much the same conception of the man as that held by his less friendly contemporaries; hence, the widespread use of the nickname, "Gentleman Johnny." Picturing him as an eighteenth-century gentleman-general, these writers drew conclusions about his military ability based upon this crude stereotype. Even when fighting in the forests of upper New York, they noted, he insisted upon the social amenities of an English drawing room—silver plate, fine wines, and female companions. Burgoyne's need for creature comforts in the wilderness, they went on, caused him to swell the size of his baggage train and slowed down the advance of his invading army. This weakness, coupled with his ignorance of conditions in America and his incompetence as a commander, led to his downfall at Saratoga. Those historians who projected the myth of the Revolutionary War as a struggle between two sets of generals—bumbling British aristocrats versus shrewd American citizen-soldiers—often used Burgoyne as their British example.

Like most stereotypes, this picture of Burgoyne as a gentleman-general had some truth to it. He was, after all, a member of the English ruling class, one accustomed to holding and wielding power throughout most of his life. As a military man, he was the product of a system in which family, "connexions," and wealth played a greater role in securing promotions than did merit. Functioning within this system, Burgoyne became as adept in the politics of the English military establishment as any of his fellow officers. If he differed in this respect from his colleagues, it was only because he was brighter, bolder, and often more open and direct in the manner in which he solicited patronage and position. In his personal as well as professional life, Burgoyne acted out the role of aristocrat; he drank, gambled, and pursued women as did other members of English high society.

But there was much more to Burgoyne than the stereotype suggests. His flamboyant style of life, in fact, concealed a complicated personality; both as a human being and soldier, he presents something of an enigma. He was, on the one hand, an appealing person to many; one with "a thousand good qualities," as Charles Lee put it.[3] Tall, graceful, and handsome, his charm and magnetism attracted men and women alike. Far from being a gay playboy, however, Burgoyne was a bleaker, tougher, and more driven individual than most historians realize. Throughout his life he displayed a ruthless egoism and constant compulsion to prove himself in whatever he attempted. A military man of considerable talent, he was romantic enough to have visions of gaining a great reputation as a general. His towering ambition and passion for fame explain, in large part, his restless energy as an army commander, his tendency to draw attention to himself, and his willingness to take risks on the battlefield.

Burgoyne's ideas on military matters likewise show that he was not the shallow person pictured by many writers. His views regarding the psychological basis for much of the military discipline of his day were striking. Such an understanding of disciplinary psychology helped him to evaluate foreign armies and to formulate his concept of leadership in the British army. His recognition of the role of ideology in the Revolutionary War enabled him to view the conflict in terms different than those of his fellow generals. And he demonstrated some degree of flexibility in changing his tactics to deal with an enemy who resorted to what he considered unorthodox methods of fighting.

Burgoyne, moreover, must be seen in broader perspective than that of a military man. With his extraordinary variety of talents, he was a perceptive critic as well as a participant in the events of the period. As a politician and playwright, Burgoyne showed the ability of standing apart from those English institutions of which he was a member and of viewing them in a critical light. The opinions he expressed in politics and literature did not always square with the stereotyped portrait presented by historians.

The circumstances of Burgoyne's birth—bearing as they do the breath of scandal—provide a possible insight into his aggressive drive for recognition in his military career. Presumably his father was Captain John Burgoyne, a baronet's son who squandered his wife's fortune and died a debtor; his mother, who reportedly gave birth on February 4, 1722, was the daughter of an English merchant.[4] Horace Walpole spread the story, however, that Burgoyne was illegitimate—the bastard offspring of Lord Bingley, chancellor of the Exchequer under Queen Anne and treasurer of the household at the time of his death in 1731. Walpole's remarks might be dismissed as malicious gossip were it not for the terms of Bingley's will. After providing for his wife, legitimate daughter, and an illegitimate daughter, Bingley left an annuity of £400 and two houses to Burgoyne's mother with the stipulation that her husband was to have no claim to the legacy. Bingley stipulated further that, if his legitimate daughter had no children and his illegitimate daughter no male heirs, his remaining property was to pass to John Burgoyne, "(which godson, I desire take [my name] . . . if my estate comes to him) for the rest of his natural life."[5] When a legitimate heir was born, Burgoyne lost his claim to the Bingley fortune. Whether he was illegitimate or merely Bingley's godson will never be known, but reports circulating during his lifetime regarding his parentage may have troubled Burgoyne and accentuated his desire to achieve distinction.

Burgoyne's runaway marriage at the age of twenty suggests not only a headstrong young man but one who was also a social climber. He eloped with Lady Charlotte Stanley—the daughter of the Earl of Derby and sister of his closest friend and former classmate at the Westminster School, Lord Strange. Running off with a woman of means was generally frowned upon in aristocratic circles, but Burgoyne was by no means unique in this respect. The practice became so commonplace that Parliament passed an act in 1753 to prevent such clandestine marriages. The bride's father, disapproving of the match, supposedly cut off the couple from any financial support for several years. Burgoyne's marriage into the great Stanley family, however, provided him with the necessary "connexion" with which to gain entry into the English power structure.

For his career, Burgoyne chose soldiering—one of the paths of preferment open to sons of the nobility. The fact that his father, several relatives, and his own son became army officers indicates that soldiering was in the family tradition. Burgoyne may have held an officer's commission prior to his marriage, but his rapid purchase of commissions after his elopement suggests that his bride brought a dowry with her despite parental objections to the match. The year after his marriage—1744—he was made a cornet in the 1st Royal Dragoons; in 1745 he purchased, in rapid succession, a lieutenant's and then a captain's commission.[6]

Burgoyne's army career, like that of so many British officers, was often interrupted for long periods. Having expensive tastes, he incurred huge debts which forced him to sell his commission in 1751 in order to pay off part of his bills. He fled to France to escape his unsatisfied creditors and lived on the continent for five years in self-imposed exile.[7] Being a man of a lively and inquiring mind, he put his time to good use; he mastered the French language and literature, studied the contemporary political scene, and learned much about conditions in the continental armies. Exactly how he settled his debts so that he might return to England is not known, but there is a strong suspicion that his father-in-law, the Earl of Derby, had become reconciled to the runaway match and changed his mind about helping his married daughter.

Burgoyne re-entered the British army in 1756, but apparently did so only because he was promised rapid promotion. After complaining to a friend about serving under officers he had formerly commanded, Burgoyne hinted that he could not long endure such an experience "had I not good assurances that I should not remain long a captain." [8] These "assurances" coupled with his purchase of a captaincy in the 11th Dragoons provide further evidence that the Derby family influence and fortune were being employed in Burgoyne's behalf. His prospects for a promising military career brightened even more when Britain and France went to war in mid-1756.

In the Seven Years' War, Burgoyne distinguished himself by a series of daring exploits. After participating in the coastal raids against Cherbourg and St. Malo, he was commissioned a lieutenant colonel in 1759 and ordered to raise a regiment of light cavalry. The 16th Dragoons bore so much the imprint of their dashing commander that they became known as "Burgoyne's Light Horse." Placed in command of an Anglo-Portuguese brigade of which his regiment was a part, Burgoyne sailed off to Portugal in the spring of 1762 to fight against the French and Spanish. His bold use of cavalry as an offensive striking arm soon earned him a reputation. Storming the town of Valencia with cavalry alone, Burgoyne surprised and destroyed an entire Spanish regiment in the summer campaign. He distinguished himself a second time by directing a raid of cavalry and grenadiers against the Spanish camp near Villa Velha in the fall. Although this stunning little victory over a superior force was actually carried out by his subordinate, Charles Lee, Burgoyne was given credit for planning the attack. Count William von der Lippe, the brilliant German general commanding the Portuguese army, sent glowing reports of Burgoyne's achievements to the British government and recommended him as an "excellent officer" and one "extremely worthy of his Majesty's remembrance." [9]

During this period, however, Burgoyne did not depend solely upon his military exploits to gain promotions; he resorted also to family influence, powerful friends, and personal effrontery. In a day when place-hunting was common, Burgoyne pushed his claims for higher command more ruthlessly than usual and without regard for the unwritten rules which normally governed politics within the English military establishment. Just how greedy he was in grasping for higher rank and personal privileges may be seen in two episodes. The first took place in 1759 when Burgoyne wrote to Viscount Barrington, the secretary at war, demanding a chaplain and hautboys for his regiment. Barrington refused the request, insinuating that it was an unseemly one from a man "who was [only] a captain a year and a half ago." Burgoyne, he noted, had became one of the youngest lieutenant colonels in the service "after a series of favors of which the army does not furnish a precedent." Barrington took exception also to the insolent tone of Burgoyne's request. It was, he wrote, "the least courtly letter ever written by an officer to a Secretary at War." Angrily, Barrington went on: "You threaten me with the House of Commons. . . . This is not the way to influence me." [10] Burgoyne employed similar strong-arm tactics when he was refused a promotion in the spring of 1762. Writing to Charles Townshend, the new secretary at war, Burgoyne complained that his failure to be promoted was not only a personal disappointment but could be construed as a slight against his patron and brother-in-law, Lord Strange. Such threats apparently proved effective; he was promoted to colonel that fall "out of regard to Lord Strange and your own merit." [11]

On the basis of his combat experience, Burgoyne emerged from the war with some firmly held military ideas. For one thing, he became a confirmed cavalryman—one who tended to look upon his dragoons as mounted light infantry which could be employed either in hard-hitting surprise raids, skirmishing, or reconnaissance. According to Burgoyne, it was the Seven Years' War which demonstrated the tremendous potential of the cavalry; prior to the war this branch of the service had long been neglected because generals neither understood nor were prepared to use it.[12] In retrospect, Burgoyne's experience with the cavalry in this war may have set the pattern for what he was to do in the Revolution. He learned that boldness, swiftness of movement, and surprise attacks could bring military success.[13]

Besides the cavalry, Burgoyne showed a keen appreciation for the uses of artillery. In this matter he may well have been reflecting the views of Count von der Lippe, his remarkable commander-in-chief in the Portuguese campaign. The count, one of the great military minds of the eighteenth century, gained his reputation in part as a teacher of two famed German generals, Gneisenau and Scharnhost, and he may have been Burgoyne's mentor as well. Although both men were about the same age, von der Lippe was already a veteran of almost twenty years of uninterrupted combat. Before being called to command the army in Portugal, the count had served as master general of the artillery under Prince Ferdinand of Brunswick. Thomas Carlyle called von der Lippe "the best artillery officer in the world," and Burgoyne's penchant for employing that branch of the service in America may well be traced back to his European experiences.[14]

Burgoyne also held certain views regarding the common soldier which were hardly typical of the military men of his day. His ideas on the subject may best be seen in two documents: the report he prepared comparing European armies in 1766 after a tour of the continent; and a treatise he wrote for his regimental officers in 1759. His assessment of the Prussian, French, and Austrian military systems showed him to be a shrewd student of disciplinary psychology. To Burgoyne the soldiers in the army of each country reflected faithfully the national character of its people: the Prussian military system being based upon blind obedience; the French upon appeals to love of king and country, and the Austrian representing a composite of the Prussian and French systems. Viewing the troops in terms of such archetypes, Burgoyne believed that the military methods used to recruit and train soldiers in each of these countries should be related to these same elements of national character. Since one-third of the Prussian army was made up of foreigners, appeals could not be made to national spirit or to love of king and country; hence, the Prussian system relied primarily upon rigid discipline, fear of punishment, and impressive appearance while on parade. French soldiers, on the other hand, responded best to sentimentality—appeals to their pride, honor, and glory.[15]

For the British army, Burgoyne recommended a middle-of-the road approach between these two extremes—"the [Prussian] one . . . *of training men like spaniels by stick; the other after the* French, *of substituting the point of honor in place of severity.*" [16] In his regimental treatise, Burgoyne stressed the role of reason in dealing with British troops. The British soldier, according to Burgoyne, was distinguished by education and a concern for his fellow creature which developed in him the faculties of reason and sensitivity. Soldiers should be treated as "thinking beings;" officers should appeal to their reason, spirit of nationalism, and sense of personal loyalty and comradeship. Since British soldiers were drawn from the dregs of society, Burgoyne's view was obviously a highly idealized one. But the impact of Enlightenment ideas on Burgoyne's military thought is striking.

When Burgoyne became an army commander in America he seems to have followed the philosophy he had expressed. He had a genuine affection and respect for his soldiers and was always thoughtful of their needs as his general orders show. As a result, Burgoyne was beloved by his men. William Digby, one of his subalterns in the Saratoga campaign, called him "the soldiers friend" and analyzed the reasons for his success: Burgoyne's winning manner and impressive appearance made him a hero in the eyes of the private soldier and he was "idolized by the army"; his orders seemed to assume subordination rather than to enforce it; and he always made soldier-like conduct appear honorable and worthy of emulation while slackness was characterized as "odious and unmanly." Burgoyne, Digby concluded, was well aware that "the most sanguine expectations a general can have of success, must proceed from the spirit of the troops under his command." [17]

Burgoyne's military ideas represented but a single facet of his broader outlook on the nature of man and society in general. He was, in this sense, a conventional eighteenth-century English gentleman—one who considered himself a citizen of the most enlightened and liberty-loving of all nations. Conditioned by the society in which he lived and the ideas current at the time, Burgoyne believed in an orderly and rational world. In his eyes man's best hope for achieving a reasonable and rational society lay in the British constitution—the greatest instrument of government ever devised. His political and military careers, then, were of a piece and seemingly dedicated to the same common objective—the defense of the British constitution and English liberties as he understood them.

It was not uncommon for military men to serve in Parliament, for the British army was not yet a professional service offering lifetime employment. Officers, once commissioned, remained on the army list (unless they resigned or were discharged for misconduct) even though they were simultaneously engaged in other pursuits. Many men from good families combined a career of soldier and politician, and, more often than not, used their political positions to further their service careers. In Burgoyne's case, his parliamentary career for over 31 years played an important part in his rise within the military hierarchy.

Lacking family political connections by birth, Burgoyne was forced to find some other means of entering Parliament. A friend and fellow officer in his regiment, Sir William Peere Williams, generously came to his support. Williams, having bought a number of burgages at Midhurst in 1760, offered to bring him into the House of Commons in 1761.[18] As a result, Burgoyne was returned unopposed and was the Midhurst M.P. for the next seven years. But in the election of 1768, Burgoyne entered the contest for the Preston borough in the electoral interests of the Derby family. After one of the most fiercely contested elections of the century, he was seated on petition. The following year Burgoyne was brought to trial for attempting to incite violence during the past election and admitted going to the polling place with a military guard and a loaded pistol in each hand.[19] After escaping imprisonment and paying a stiff fine of £1,000, Burgoyne went on to represent Preston from 1768 until the day he died.

Throughout his parliamentary career prior to the Revolutionary War, Burgoyne showed a consuming interest in three major matters—opportunities for military promotions, questions concerning the army, and controversies between the colonies and mother country. His promotions after the Seven Years' War came mainly as the result of family influence, royal favor, and good fortune. Political manipulation by the powerful Derby family, the great expense to which he had gone in the 1768 election, and the fact that his dragoons were among the regiments the king prized most, soon raised Burgoyne to a position as court favorite. In 1769 he was rewarded by being appointed governor of Fort William, a lucrative sinecure rarely granted to an officer below the rank of general. Three years later, he was made a major general. Some measure of his rapid rise may be seen by comparing his military career at this stage with that of Sir William Howe. Although Howe was born into a more prominent family and had seen more combat service, both men were promoted to major general at about the same time.

Burgoyne claimed that his political maxim in Parliament was "to assist [the] government in my general line of conduct," but this aim did not prevent him from showing occasional flashes of political independence when issues arose concerning the army. In at least three episodes between 1768 and 1774, he spoke out or voted against the court when the employment of army units was at stake.[20] One such break with the court came during the East India Company scandal. Burgoyne was appointed chairman of an investigating committee to inquire into the affairs of that organization in 1772 and promptly introduced a resolution to prevent the military forces in India from being used by company officials for private rather than public purposes.[21] Although he was not altogether successful in getting his views accepted, Burgoyne acted independently of the government in this matter; his speeches hint of an ideology quite different from that which one might expect of a military man in Parliament who had to depend upon the king's favor for rewards and advancement.

When it came to questions concerning the American colonies, however, Burgoyne generally supported the government. He favored the Stamp Act, for example, and made a speech in support of the Declaratory Act during the crisis of the mid-1760's. In keeping with his ideas on the British constitution, he could not understand why the Americans were unhappy under the just and orderly government provided by the mother country. His conception of the British empire was that of a family—Britain, as the kind parent, exercising a benevolent authority over her children, the colonies.

Burgoyne believed that Britain had been too lenient and forbearing toward the colonies in the past. Speaking on a motion to repeal the tax on tea in April, 1774, he said: "I look upon America to be our child, which I think we have already spoiled by too much indulgence." On the question of American independence, he declared himself ready "to resist that proposition, and to contend, at any future time, against such independence." But like most Britishers, Burgoyne had a blind spot on this issue: he could not bring himself to believe that the colonists might resort to force to resolve the matter. He relied upon reason to prevail in imperial relations. His April speech made clear his position on the colonial crisis: he "wished," he said, "to see America convinced by persuasion rather than the sword." [22]

When the North Ministry proposed to take military measures in America, however, Burgoyne delivered a speech in support of the government in February, 1775. "Sir, in foreign war, the conscience of the quarrel belongs to the state alone. . . . In civil discord . . . I believe a consideration of the cause will find its way to the breast of every conscientious man. . . . Is there a man in England (I am confident there is not an officer or soldier in the King's service) who does not think the parliamentary rights of Great Britain a cause to fight for, to bleed and die for? . . . The reason of the nation has been long convinced; the trial now only is whether we have spirit to support our conviction." The speech made a great impression and Burgoyne observed: "I spoke from my heart and to that cause I impute its success." [23]

As a general, parliamentarian, and son-in-law of one of England's wealthiest peers, Burgoyne was accustomed to moving in the best social circles. He cut an imposing figure in the glittering high life of London, and his reputation as a wit, man of fashion, and connoisseur of good wines was well known. A member of many London clubs, he numbered among his friends some of the most famous artists of his time—Sir Joshua Reynolds, who painted his portrait, and David Garrick, the Shakespearian actor. His compulsion to shine in whatever company he found himself soon led him to seek recognition in literary circles as a playwright.

Burgoyne showed more than a little talent as a dramatist. In 1774 he wrote a play, *Maid of the Oaks*, in celebration of the marriage of his wife's nephew. The play, a witty commentary on the importance of class and status in English society, was brought out by Garrick at Drury Lane in 1775. After his return to England from America, Burgoyne resumed writing plays and scored his greatest success with *The Heiress* in 1785. Even the hostile Horace Walpole confessed that this play was "the best modern comedy." [24]

In his plays Burgoyne demonstrated a spontaneous wit combined with a lively commentary on English social customs. Although the plots were typical of the elaborate fabrications popular in that day, the dialogue was replete with pointed characterizations that revealed an awareness of the difference between social artifice and reality. His works show that while Burgoyne was a member of English high society, he could view that society from without—criticizing and even mocking it in an effort to reform it.

Certain other aspects of Burgoyne's social life brought to light the same grasping qualities in his make-up that were evidenced in his military career. Along with other members of the aristocracy, he was swept up in the general craze for gambling that seized British society in the mid-eighteenth century. Burgoyne soon proved to be expert; he became known as a "fortunate gamester" who drew a "splendid subsistence" from card playing.[25] But his methods left something to be desired. "Junius," an anonymous essayist who wrote a series of satirical sketches on leading figures of the day, hinted that Burgoyne was not above "taking his stand at gaming-table, and watching with the soberest attention for a fair opportunity of engaging a drunken young Nobleman at Picquet." [26]

"Junius" observed one other outstanding characteristic in Burgoyne's personality: "No man," he noted, "is more tender of his reputation." Terms like "reputation," "honor," and "fame" held a high place in the lexicon of eighteenth-century Englishmen and in their code of social values. To Burgoyne, whose birth was neither celebrated nor free from the suggestion of scandal, such words held an even greater significance. Although he poked fun at English society in his plays, he was more anxious than most men to succeed and to be accepted within it. He had, therefore, an extreme sensitivity to any slights or aspersions cast upon him. "If the wretch, Junius, is now lurking here in any corner of the House," Burgoyne declared in Parliament, "[I] would tell him to his face that he was an assassin, a liar, and a coward." [27]

Burgoyne's appointment to an American command in February, 1775, thrust him abruptly back into active military life. With the crisis deepening in the colonies during the winter, George III decided to dispatch three major generals—Howe, Clinton, and Burgoyne—to Boston to assist Thomas Gage, commander-in-chief of the British army in North America. Burgoyne, curiously enough, did not view his appointment with favor at first. When tendered the offer in January, he seemed unwilling to accept. The reason for his reluctance was obvious: he was the junior general of the three. Burgoyne agreed to go, but only after being told that he had been named by George III himself.[28]

His attitude changed once he realized America would open up new opportunities for advancement. He was soon busily exploring the possibility of becoming governor of New York. Tryon, the incumbent, was in England; Colden, the lieutenant governor, was aged and failing in health; and the British government was planning to send a body of troops to New York City. After politicking furiously, Burgoyne discovered that General Howe had been promised the proposed post. George III confessed later that he felt Burgoyne could "best manage any negotiation" required of a New York commander.[29]

Undaunted by this failure, Burgoyne tried a different tack. Before leaving for America, he solicited the king's permission to return to England by the end of the year. Ostensibly his request was based on two grounds: first, that certain private matters would require his attention; and secondly that there would be value in a personal report to the king about American affairs. His real purpose for returning, however, was to make certain he would figure in any future appointments of importance. The king approved the request, though Burgoyne was not informed at the time.

Burgoyne sailed with Howe and Clinton in what he called "a triumvirate of reputation" on April 20—the day after the Americans drove British troops back to Boston from Lexington and Concord. Arthur Lee, Congress' confidential diplomatic agent in London, wrote a letter at about the same time describing the trio. In Lee's opinion, Burgoyne would be the most dangerous to deal with.

> The first [Howe] is an honorable man, respected in the Army, & trained in the late American War. He goes reluctantly.
> The second [Clinton] is a man of very fair character. He served all the late War in Germany. His abilities, tho not brilliant, are yet respectable.
> General Burgoyne is of a very different character. A man of dark designs deep dissimulations, desperate fortunes, & abandond of principles. He is closely connected with the Bedford Party in this Country. No Banditti were ever bent on blood & spoil, & on more desperate principles than this Bedford Party. . . . They are as ready to sacrifice this Country as America to the arbitrary views of a tory, tyrannical Court. Among the worst of their Party is Gl. Burgoyne. You will see his character well drawn in the Letters of Junius. . . . To finish his character of dissimulation tho an abandond & notorious Gambler & engaged in every scene abhorrent

from true religion & virtue, he has always effected to be exemplary
in religious Worship. . . . You will judge however from what I
have said, that he is a dangerous character; & therefore be on your
guard. If he is solicitous to commune with you, it will be to betray
you.[30]

Burgoyne had barely landed in Boston in late May before he
began complaining about his insignificant role in American affairs. His position, he wrote Lord North on June 14, was "too
humble" to enable him to contribute in a meaningful way "to
his Majesty's service in the military line in America." [31] Even
as a lowly lieutenant colonel, he had led more troops than the
number now under his immediate command. Burgoyne's claim
that his talents were not being used properly was to be a chronic
complaint until he secured a separate command in America.

Ambitious to play a more important part, Burgoyne proposed
a scheme for settling the American crisis by peaceful means. He
requested dismissal from the army and authorization for a rov-
ing commission to visit those colonies where there was no fighting in order to sound out American sentiment for a possible
compromise. Burgoyne asked that he not be charged with any
direct proposal from the British government nor authorized to
treat with the Americans in any official capacity. Instead, he
would deal with the Americans as an individual member of
Parliament, "a friend of human nature," and a "sincere well
wisher to the united interests of the two countries." [32] His proposal was rejected, but it was significant from two points of
view: it showed his self-assurance in proposing a solution after
being in America only a few weeks, and it indicated his conviction that negotiation and compromise were preferable to war
and bloodshed at this stage.

Burgoyne's hope of settling the issue by other than military
means could be seen also in the proclamation he framed in General Gage's name.[33] When the home government suggested that
a proclamation be published indicating the policy Britain proposed to adopt in Massachusetts, Gage, feeling inferior as a pen-
man to Burgoyne, turned to the playwright-soldier for assist-

ance. The proclamation, issued on June 12, imposed martial law on Massachusetts but promised pardons to all who would lay down their arms—except for political leaders like Sam Adams and John Hancock. Its tone, however, was intemperate; Burgoyne denounced the "infatuated multitude" who "with a preposterous parade . . . affected to hold the [British] Army besieged." [34] Because of its bombastic language, the proclamation aroused ridicule rather than alarm. Some Americans jokingly proposed that a counterproclamation be published pardoning certain British generals, admirals, and government officials.

Historians, for the most part, have criticized Burgoyne's proclamation, calling it "foolish," "sounding brass," and a "pompous, high-flown, inaccurate and silly production." [35] But Burgoyne, as a writer, was rarely careless in his use of words—his plays reveal a tight control of language, and his private correspondence shows he resorted to crude verbiage only when such usage seemed necessary for emphasis. Read in its proper context, the language of the proclamation was not at all inappropriate. The document was an attempt at psychological warfare—a propaganda piece aimed at frightening Americans into submission with words rather than bullets. Burgoyne was convinced that if the rebel forces in and around Boston were dispersed, Americans elsewhere were not likely to offer any drawn-out resistance.

Five days after the proclamation appeared, American patriots called Burgoyne's bluff when the British resorted to military force in the battle of Bunker Hill. Although British redcoats captured their main objective, the redoubt on Breed's Hill, they did so at tremendous cost—losing 1,054 killed and wounded out of 2,200 men engaged. Burgoyne did not participate in the fight because, as he wrote, "the inferiority of my station as the youngest Major-General on the staff, left me almost a useless spectator." But what he saw raised his respect for the fighting ability of the Americans. "The defence was well conceived and obstinately maintained," he reported. "[T]he retreat was no flight; it was even covered with bravery and military skill." Burgoyne was shocked, on the other hand, by the behavior of the British soldiers; they showed a lack of discipline and hesitated in the midst of their attack.[36]

Bunker Hill resulted in some changes in Burgoyne's thinking regarding the American rebellion. Evaluating the situation soon after the battle, he viewed the rebellion in broad terms as both a political and military problem. His long letter to Lord Rochford, member of the cabinet, suggested that two long-range alternatives were open to Britain: to make the greatest political concessions possible to America, or to wage an all-out war. If the mother country adopted halfway measures between these two "disagreeable extremes," he predicted they would only produce "much fruitless expense, great loss of blood, and a series of disappointments." [37]

Burgoyne's suggestion that the issue be settled by political means has escaped the attention of most historians. One reason for this was Burgoyne himself. Confessing that his judgment was limited by his army position, Burgoyne confined most of his remarks to military matters. Nevertheless, his comment to Rochford regarding political concessions to the colonies must be taken seriously: "Should it be thought more expedient to the nation, and reconcilable to its honor, to relinquish the claims in question, I doubt not the wisdom of those councils of which your Lordship is so distinguished a part, will propose such relinquishment as will be at once effectual." [38]

If America was to be subdued by force, on the other hand, Burgoyne warned there was little prospect of a speedy victory unless important military steps were undertaken immediately. It was readily apparent to him that the soldiers available from Great Britain and Ireland would be insufficient for the enormous task at hand. Burgoyne recommended, therefore, that three armies be raised to wage war on America: a huge army of foreign mercenaries striking up the Hudson; a second army composed of trained British troops and Canadians invading from the north; and a large levy of Indians and Negroes to cooperate with detachments of British regulars in overawing the southern colonies. With such formidable allies on land and the Royal

Navy patrolling the entire coast, Burgoyne speculated that the British might conquer the Americans in a single campaign.

Since such long-range measures would take time to implement, Burgoyne proposed also a plan for the current campaign. With four regiments of reinforcements reportedly on the way, the British army would be in a position to launch an offensive. Burgoyne saw no sense in attacking the strongly entrenched American posts surrounding Boston with so small an army—a successful assault would only win one line of entrenchments or a hill, leaving more entrenchments and hills to be taken without any substantial gain in military advantage. Instead he suggested two steps: the continued occupation of Boston and a war of expedition to the southward. Placing part of the British army on shipboard, he proposed attacks upon parts of Rhode Island, Connecticut, and New York to test the strength and temper of the rebels in these colonies. Burgoyne was still hopeful of regaining New York for the British if sent to that province with an independent command.

Besides these immediate military moves, Burgoyne pressed for what might be called psychological warfare measures. He was quicker than his colleagues in grasping the implications of the revolutionary idea that the British were fighting a people in arms rather than a professional army. He suggested, for example, that Gage release the prisoners taken at Bunker Hill because such an act of mercy might make a great impression upon the Americans. "You have been deluded," the prisoners should be told. "[R]eturn to your homes in peace; it is your duty to God and your country to undeceive your neighbors." [39] Aware that at bottom the war was a war of ideology, Burgoyne asked also that the most able men in England frame a proclamation urging the Americans to lay down their arms; such a proclamation was to be issued prior to carrying out the military expeditions he had proposed. Few of Burgoyne's ideas regarding long-range policies, plans for a 1775 campaign, or psychological warfare methods were adopted by the government; but the proposals showed his understanding of strategy, comprehension of the magnitude of effort required to reconquer America, and insight into the true nature of the war.

After the battle of Bunker Hill, Burgoyne revealed also just what his relations with his fellow generals would be; he was consistently to undermine those with whom he was competing for higher command. He began criticizing Gage almost from the moment he landed in America. His estimate of the commander-in-chief in the letter to Lord Rochford was clever, indeed; it provided some small measure of praise, but suggested at the same time that Gage's abilities were limited and that a more talented man was needed for the job. "I hope I shall not be thought to disparage my general and my friend in pronouncing him unequal to his situation, when I add that I think it one in which Caesar might have failed." [40] Reading between the lines the implication was clear: since Caesar was unavailable, Burgoyne might do instead. Such backbiting, of course, was common among British senior officers; Howe and Clinton wrote similar letters about Gage. But Burgoyne seems to have handled this technique more effectively than his colleagues and for this reason earned their fear and dislike in some instances.

During the remainder of his stay in Boston in 1775, Burgoyne did little except propose plans and write letters. Much of what he had to say he had said before. In August he advocated two possible courses of action: either remove the army from Boston to New York, or dispatch an expedition to Rhode Island.[41] But his commander-in-chief ignored both plans. Burgoyne thereupon became more critical, calling Gage "an officer totally unsuited for command," and the man responsible for "many of the misfortunes the King's arms have suffered." His estimate of the Americans, on the other hand, remained high: "The rebels though undisciplined are expert in the use of firearms, and led by some very able men." [42]

Throughout this same period, Burgoyne seized every opportunity to use his pen as a propaganda weapon. In June and July he exchanged letters with Charles Lee, his former fellow officer who had been appointed general in the Continental army, hoping to bribe or wean him away from the Americans. When General Washington complained in August about the ill-treatment of American prisoners, Burgoyne carried on an exchange of correspondence in Gage's behalf. Toward the close of the year, he turned to playwriting and prepared a prologue and epilogue for the tragedy of *Zara* that was performed at Faneuil Hall.[43] In his lines, Burgoyne called upon the conquering British to be merciful and the rebellious Americans to return to the fold. By this time, however, the army had gone into winter quarters and he was able to return to England in December in accordance with his agreement with the king.

Burgoyne's foresight in insisting upon a return to England soon became apparent. During the early spring of 1776, the British government was engaged in planning military operations for the coming year and appointing the appropriate army commanders. Burgoyne, a veritable johnny-on-the-spot, was strategically situated for voicing his opinions and pushing his claims for higher command. His presence in England early in 1776 and during the same period in 1777, was partially responsible for his success two years in a row in superseding men who outranked him.

When called upon to submit his views regarding military operations for 1776, Burgoyne, some time in the first three months of the year, produced an interesting paper entitled, "Reflections upon the War in America." His major proposal called for an invasion of New York from Canada. Burgoyne mistakenly believed that Quebec had fallen to the enemy; but he was certain that the navy could push past the city to land a British army that could drive south from the St. Lawrence. He pointed out at the same time the possibility of a joint expedition—one army marching south while another moved north out of New York City—to make a juncture at some central location. Burgoyne, in short, was proposing in broad outline the strategy attempted in the campaigns of 1776 and 1777. He was, however, by no means the only one thinking along such lines.

Burgoyne's paper was equally important for revealing the

flexibility of his military ideas. He arrived in America a confirmed cavalryman, but gradually changed his views because of the geography of the country and its mode of warfare. The Americans, Burgoyne predicted, would not risk a general combat, or a pitched battle, or even stand to fight at all, except in entrenchments such as those found outside of Boston. Accustomed to working with shovels and axes, they would throw up earthworks with surprising speed, and fight behind them with great skill:

> Composed as the American army is, together with the strength of the country, full of woods, swamps, stone walls, and other enclosures and hiding places, it may be said of it that every private man will in action be his own general, who will turn every tree and bush into a temporary fortress, from whence, when he hath fired his shot with all the deliberation, coolness, and certainty which hidden safety inspires, he will skip as it were to the next, and so on for a long time. . . .

What then, was the solution? To dislodge the Americans either with cannon fire or an attack by light infantry. Heavy cannon and howitzers could destroy such defenses. Light infantry units —made up of fast-moving men who carried less equipment— would possess the necessary mobility to outflank entrenched positions. Burgoyne was to stick fast to these ideas: in his paper he proposed that "light infantry in greater numbers than one company per regiment" be added throughout the British army; and in his operations in America he was to rely heavily upon cannon.[44]

When the campaign plan for 1776 was finally adopted and commanders picked for the respective armies, Burgoyne emerged with a key role. The campaign called for a two-pronged invasion of America: the main army landing in New York and pushing north up the Hudson, while a smaller but substantial army was to reinforce Quebec and then sweep south from Canada down through the Lake Champlain-Hudson River corridor. It was hoped this dual offensive would either force Washington's army

to stand and fight or make the Americans abandon the Hudson
River line and thereby expose New England to an attack from
the west. Plans were also made for a small expeditionary force
to sail against the southern colonies, but it was to return north
in time to participate in the invasion of New York. Lord George
Germain, the colonial secretary, had little difficulty in choosing
his top commanders: General Howe, now commander-in-chief
in America, was named to head the main army; and General
Carleton was placed in charge of the one in Canada. Originally,
plans called for Clinton, who outranked Burgoyne, to become
Carleton's second-in-command. But Clinton had already sailed
with the expeditionary force to the south, and Burgoyne was
picked instead.

Burgoyne left for Canada in early April, but he did so with
a heavy heart. His wife was so ill that he despaired of ever seeing
her alive again. After landing in America, he poured out his
grief to Clinton, who was himself a widower. Calling Lady Charlotte "that truest friend, amiable companion, tenderest, best of
women and of wives," Burgoyne declared he had been ready to
sacrifice both ambition and fortune to avoid the coming campaign to remain at her side. But, he went on to say, his sense of
duty to his king, his country, and profession enabled him to
control his private feelings. While asking for Clinton's sympathy,
Burgoyne protested—perhaps too much—that his position as
Carleton's second-in-command had been "unsought for." [45]

In the midst of the campaign, Burgoyne learned of Lady Charlotte's death. Overcome with grief, he described himself as "an
unconnected Cypher in the world—The partner lost which made
prosperity an object of solicitude—Interest, ambition, the anima-
tion of life is over." All that remained, he wrote, was "professional honor"; it was better to be "finished in a professional
grave" than waste away to a slow death of old age.[46] Burgoyne
apparently meant what he said; at the second battle of Saratoga,
a year later, he deliberately courted death at the head of his
troops to retain some semblance of professional honor prior to
his impending surrender.

Burgoyne found himself facing professional as well as personal problems during the campaign. His relations with Carleton followed much the same pattern as those with Gage the year before. Anxious to prove himself and to gain some share of glory, Burgoyne made a series of proposals to his superior only to find them rejected. Disenchantment soon set in. He became restless, increasingly critical of his chief's dilatory tactics, and soon was undermining Carleton's position as he had Gage's earlier.

Carleton, aided by heavy reinforcements of British regulars and German mercenaries, raised the siege of Quebec and launched a counteroffensive during the summer months of 1776. Driving a dispirited American army before him, he advanced south almost to the head of Lake Champlain. Here both armies halted and began constructing fleets to contest for command of the lake—the key to all strategy. Rather than allow the entire British force to remain idle during this period, Burgoyne proposed a bold plan. He would lead a detachment across Lake Ontario and thence move east by way of Oswego, Fort Stanwix, and the Mohawk to meet Carleton at the junction of that river and the Hudson. Such a move, he noted, would raise a "powerful diversion," enabling Carleton's army to move south down the lake and Howe's army north up the Hudson. The plan, though approved in principle, was never put into operation because of a lack of supplies.

The proposal itself, however, was important from two points of view. Burgoyne's idea for a diversion down the Mohawk served as the basis for St. Leger's expedition from that direction in 1777. Of even greater significance was Burgoyne's remark regarding the ultimate destination of Carleton's army: "I cannot suppose any General," he wrote, "would have remained at Ticonderoga, Fort Edward or any other post above the junction of the Mohawk and Hudson Rivers." His reasoning here helps to explain, in part, Burgoyne's determined drive to reach Albany— located near the junction of these two rivers—with an army of his own the following year.[47] His attention was focused not on the enemy's army but upon Albany as a territorial objective.

When Carleton was finally ready to sail down Lake Champlain in early October, Burgoyne came up with a second suggestion. He proposed that a corps of the army accompany the naval force to exploit any military opportunity that might develop. Carleton, after some indecision, rejected this plan too. Instead he proceeded down the lake in command of his naval force, leaving the army behind. Writing of Carleton's rejection to General Clinton, Burgoyne resorted to his usual technique of denigrating his superiors with a combination of praise and blame:

> I should be unjust to General Carleton, if I denied that odd and misplaced as his part may appear at the Head of the naval department only, he has reasons to justify that proceeding. They would carry me too far, nor is the occasion proper to open them to you now.[48]

After Carleton had smashed the American fleet on Lake Champlain, occupied Crown Point, and advanced on Ticonderoga, Burgoyne's ideas regarding a future course of action differed even more sharply with those of his superior. He acquiesced in Carleton's decision not to attack Ticonderoga, but only because he assumed that Crown Point would be held through the winter. Before retreating to Crown Point, however, Burgoyne indicated that he would have surrounded the Americans in Ticonderoga, "felt their pulse" in a probing action, and attempted to cut off their lines of communication to the south. Since none of these ideas were seriously considered and the army was going into winter quarters, Burgoyne felt free to leave the field and to begin his trip back to England.

Shortly after leaving the army, Burgoyne was astonished to learn that Carleton had abandoned Crown Point. "I think this step puts us in danger . . . of losing the fruits of our summer's labor & autumn victory," he wrote bitterly. Burgoyne had suggested that a brigade be left behind to hold the post, and since all the buildings had been burned, that huts be hastily constructed to house the men. But Carleton, guided by the advice of his "dull, formal, methodical fat engineers," had been persuaded that Crown Point could not be held. Commenting on this decision Burgoyne observed:

> I must honor Carleton's abilities & judgement, I have lived with him upon the best terms & bear him friendship—I am therefore doubly hurt that he had taken a step in which I can be no otherwise serviceable to him than by silence.[49]

Burgoyne's "silence" lasted only as long as it took him to cross the Atlantic. Rushing to Germain on December 10—the day after he landed in England—Burgoyne criticized Carleton by emphasizing that he had been strongly opposed to giving up Crown Point. Before leaving Canada, Burgoyne had expressed unhappiness over his status in "a secondary station in a secondary command"; now he proceeded to do everything in his power to correct that situation. Despite his protestations at a later date that he had not intrigued to supplant Carleton, and the false impression given by Burgoyne's biographer of his complete faithfulness to his superior, Burgoyne's actions in writing to Clinton and speaking to Germain belie such an interpretation.[50]

With the Ministry dissatisfied over the disappointing results in the Canadian campaign, Germain at odds with Carleton, and the king expressing the need for a "more enterprizing Commander" for the northern army, Burgoyne loomed as a likely candidate.[51] His ambition was fired further when he learned that Germain had sent a dispatch during the previous summer ordering Carleton back to Quebec and giving Burgoyne command of the army. The order, issued to prevent a clash of jurisdiction between Carleton and Howe in the event of a juncture between the two armies, had never been carried out; the vessel bearing the dispatch had been forced to turn back because of bad weather.

When Burgoyne submitted an important memorandum in February, 1777, containing suggestions for conducting the war, his chances of succeeding Carleton improved markedly. The origins of this memorandum provide additional proof that Burgoyne was angling for the Canadian command. Prior to Burgoyne's departure from Canada, Carleton had discussed his own views regarding the 1777 campaign and set down his thoughts in a letter. When Burgoyne was leaving for England, Carleton instructed him to frame a memorandum incorporating these ideas and to present it to the government. Burgoyne did as instructed and submitted a short and rather sketchy résumé. He then followed it up with a memorandum of his own which was much more impressive, forceful, and complete. In late February, Burgoyne drew up still another document entitled, "Thoughts for Conducting the War from the Side of Canada," elaborating more fully his views regarding the coming campaign. Burgoyne's last memorandum in large part was responsible for his being selected over Carleton and Clinton to command the army in Canada.[52]

His paper contained three possible courses of action for the Canadian army, and the government adopted one. This operational plan revived Burgoyne's proposal of a year before calling for the main army to advance south from Montreal to the upper Hudson at the same time a small diversionary force was working its way east down the Mohawk River Valley to link up at Albany. Historians in the past believed that Burgoyne was solely responsible for the general conception of the 1777 campaign. The scheme, in reality, was an old and familiar one for many of its more important features had already been suggested by others.[53]

The purpose behind Burgoyne's plan has likewise been a matter of historical dispute. Scholars long assumed that the *immediate* objective of the 1777 campaign called for a convergence of not two but three forces at Albany—Burgoyne's northern army at Montreal, St. Leger's expedition down the Mohawk, and Howe's southern army moving north from New York City up the Hudson. It was assumed further that the main aim of the campaign was to seal off New England from the rest of the colonies and therefore that Howe had strict orders to advance up the Hudson to effect a juncture with Burgoyne. Some recent historians have demonstrated, however, that the British may have viewed Burgoyne's northern invasion as an attempt to draw Washington's attention away from Howe's offensive in the south against Philadelphia as well as a move to form a juncture between the northern and southern armies. The two moves—Burgoyne's toward Albany and Howe's against Philadelphia—were not considered incompatible; the British believed confidently that both objectives could be achieved. Although the juncture of Burgoyne and Howe remained an essential part of the plan—it was to be an ultimate, not an immediate, goal of the campaign.[54]

Burgoyne's own ideas in his paper, "Thoughts," regarding the purpose of the campaign were ambiguous. His paper, on the one hand, showed that Burgoyne was well aware at the outset that Howe's main army might turn south rather than proceed north up the Hudson to join him. On the other hand, a key sentence implied that Burgoyne was counting upon Howe's co-operation to some degree: "These ideas are formed upon the supposition, that it be the sole purpose of the Canadian campaign to effect a junction with General Howe," he wrote, "or after cooperating so far as to get possession of Albany and open the communication to New York, to remain upon the Hudson River and thereby enable that general to act with his whole force to the southward."[55] Although this statement can be interpreted several ways, it strongly suggests that Burgoyne believed that even if Howe intended to go to Pennsylvania he was expected to make some move to help the northern army establish itself at Albany. Such an interpretation did not mean, however, that Burgoyne expected Howe to meet him in Albany immediately, or that the entire southern army was to be committed on the Hudson—any detachment of forces or diversionary attack which permitted the northern army to reach Albany would do. The statement implied also that once he reached Albany, Burgoyne expected his army to sustain itself, to keep open the communications to New York, and to act independently while Howe campaigned to the south.[56]

If Burgoyne's views on strategy were vague in his paper, he

was extremely perceptive in anticipating the problems he would encounter on his march toward Albany. He predicted accurately that he would meet no naval opposition on Lake Champlain such as Arnold's fleet had provided in 1776. Nor did he expect to encounter the enemy in great force until he reached Ticonderoga —another assumption in which he was correct. He forecast rightly what the Americans would do to oppose his advance south by either of the two alternate routes, Lake George and Skenesborough—he expected them to maintain a strong naval force on Lake George and to block the trail from Skenesborough to Albany by felling trees and destroying bridges. Finally, he singled out the supply problem as "one of the most important operations of the campaign, because it is upon that which most of the rest will depend." [57] Although he anticipated many of his problems, Burgoyne, as will be seen, underestimated the difficulties he would encounter in trying to overcome them.

To carry out his invasion, Burgoyne requested that the northern army be supplied with a sizable force. At least 8,000 regulars, 2,000 Canadians, and more than 1,000 Indians would be required. With characteristic care, Burgoyne named in great detail the British regiments he wanted and recommended that the German mercenaries assigned him come with their "grenadiers, light infantry, and dragoons complete." He requested also ample artillery because he expected the Americans to fortify strong ground in various places. Because he expected a problem of adequate transportation on both water and land, Burgoyne asked for a corps of watermen, some hatchet men, and other workmen. If such a force were supplied him and adequate preparations made, Burgoyne predicted that Ticonderoga might be taken "early in the summer." [58]

Burgoyne's general conception of the invasion was approved by Germain, but with some changes. For one thing, Burgoyne was told that the total of 8,000 trained troops would be reduced to 7,000. Nothing was said about Howe's coming north to meet him. Most important of all, Burgoyne's orders called for him "to force his way to Albany," and there to place himself and his troops under Howe's command. It was implied, however, that until Burgoyne came under Howe's orders he was to act on his own "as exigencies may require." These two phrases gave rise to a conflict in interpretation. Had Burgoyne been given a narrow peremptory command to proceed to Albany regardless of the costs? Or had he been granted discretionary power that permitted some latitude of action? After his defeat at Saratoga, Burgoyne was to fall back upon a narrow interpretation of his orders. But before the campaign, he did not complain about his orders being inflexible. In fact, he seemed reasonably satisfied with the final outcome of the government's approval of his plan. "Being called upon at home for my opinion of the war on this side," he wrote, "I gave it freely; the material parts of it have been adopted by the Cabinet." [59]

At about the same time that Germain passed upon Burgoyne's plan for invasion, he likewise approved Howe's campaign against Pennsylvania. Howe made it clear in December, 1776, that any move he might make up the Hudson would depend upon two conditions—whether he received reinforcements, and whether he completed his own campaign in time to return north to help Burgoyne. Since Germain did not send the requested reinforcements and yet approved Howe's plan, he has been blamed for agreeing to two seemingly incompatible campaigns. [60] But Burgoyne himself expressed no misgivings on this score at this stage —he too thought that both campaigns could be completed by the close of 1777.

Burgoyne's self-assurance, it should be emphasized, reflected the optimistic outlook of the British government as a whole regarding the outcome of the 1777 campaigns. The king and his ministers at Whitehall were in high hopes that the summer of 1777 would bring the rebellion to an end. Basing their plans upon the presumed weakness of the Americans and the supposed strength of the loyalists in both upper New York and Pennsylvania, British officials confidently prepared two major campaigns against widely separated objectives with the expectation that both would succeed. The result was a lack of careful planning;

relatively little effort was made to co-ordinate the moves of Burgoyne's army in the north with Howe's main force in the south. Despite the fact that Germain sent eight letters to Howe between March 3 and April 19, for example, he neglected to make clear in any of them the strategy upon which Burgoyne's campaign was based.[61]

Burgoyne's confidence that he could carry out his campaign to Albany with relatively little help was revealed again when he saw a letter from Howe to Carleton written in April, 1777—before the northern army had begun its invasion—expressing the limited degree of cooperation that might be expected from the southern army. First, there was the matter of timing: Howe indicated that in all probability he would be in Pennsylvania when the northern army launched its invasion and therefore would be unable "to communicate with . . . [Burgoyne] so soon as I could wish." Secondly, Howe stated that few, if any, troops from his army would be available to support Burgoyne. He could not spare a corps, Howe wrote, to act upon the Hudson at the beginning of Burgyone's campaign. However, he would leave behind sufficient forces in New York City to open the shipping lanes on the lower Hudson which were being obstructed by American forts in the Highlands. After accomplishing this mission, Howe said, such a corps might "afterwards act in favor of the northern army." This halfhearted promise of a few troops was as far as Howe would go. Despite the fact Burgoyne now knew that he could count on very little cooperation from Howe in the initial advance toward Albany, he was determined to press ahead on his invasion plans.[62]

The inherent inadequacies of the British system of command came to light with a major change in plans for the campaign of 1777. In April, Howe wrote Germain that he intended to carry out his invasion of Pennsylvania from New York by sea rather than a march overland. This change meant that the southern army would be on shipboard rather than being situated somewhere between Washington's force and the northern army. By undertaking his campaign so late—Howe's troops did not embark until July 23—and by carrying out his invasion by sea rather than land, Howe made virtually impossible any kind of meaningful cooperation with the northern army at a crucial time. Howe either honestly did not view the campaign of 1777 as a joint operation, or, finding himself unable to help Burgoyne, pretended to be unaware that some kind of cooperation was expected of him.

The reaction to this change in plans revealed the confusion and misunderstanding that existed in both government and military circles. In his reply to Howe, Germain urged, but failed to insist, that Howe complete his Pennsylvania campaign in time to return north to cooperate with Burgoyne.[63] The old story of the "pigeon-holed dispatch" that Germain reputedly failed to send to Howe specifically ordering him to come to the assistance of Burgoyne seems to be unsupported by any evidence. General Clinton, who had just returned from England, argued with Howe that the only chance of success lay in a move by the southern army up the Hudson instead of against Pennsylvania; but his arguments proved to no avail.[64] So far as Burgoyne was concerned, the fact that he learned about Howe's altered plans at a later date made little difference: he remained optimistic about reaching Albany on his own. While it is true that Burgoyne's overconfidence was a contributing factor in his downfall, Germain and Howe must bear part of the burden of defeat for failing to give him proper orders and information based upon their understanding of the 1777 campaign.

Burgoyne's invasion got under way from St. Johns on June 12. Under his command were over 7,000 regular infantry—about half of whom were German mercenaries. Both the British and German troops were of good quality and well led. In keeping with his ideas, Burgoyne brigaded the light infantry companies from the British regiments, some grenadier companies, and one regular British regiment to form his vanguard. He had, in addition, an impressive and powerful train of artillery—more than 138 cannon and about 600 artillerymen. But of the 3,000 Canadians and Indians expected, only 650 Canadians and loyalists and 500 redmen came forward. Nor was Burgoyne provided with adequate transport; only one-third of the horses promised were available and the number of carts for the wagon train fell far short of the estimated requirements. Despite the fact he had not been supplied with precisely the forces and equipment he had requested, Burgoyne issued an order early in the campaign that read: "This army must not retreat." [65]

Although Burgoyne later blamed his failure partly upon the lack of loyalist military support, he gave no indication at the beginning of the invasion that he was counting on any significant assistance from irregulars. His main reliance would be on regulars: provincial troops were to be used for purposes of guerrilla tactics and psychological warfare. "I mean to employ them particularly upon detachments for keeping the country in awe and procuring cattle," he wrote. "Their real use I expect will be great in the preservation of national troops; but the impression which will be caused upon public opinion, should the provincials be seen acting vigorously in the cause of the King, will yet be more advantageous . . ." [66]

Burgoyne made much the same use of proclamations in New York as he had in Boston in 1775. Believing in the power of the written word and that the war was a struggle against a people in arms rather than against an enemy army, he issued one proclamation addressed to the local inhabitants. British military forces had been called forth at first to restore constitutional government, he wrote, but now they were seeking to protect the "general privileges of Mankind." American rebels had set up "the compleatest form of Tyranny that ever God in his displeasure suffered . . . to be exercised over a . . . stubborn generation," and were responsible for "arbitrary imprisonment, confiscation of property, [and] persecution and torture." Burgoyne offered encouragement and employment to all who would participate in "the glorious task of redeeming their Countrymen from Dungeons, and reestablishing the blessings of legal government." But for the rebels, "justice and wrath await them in the field; and devastation, famine, and every concomitant horror." One "horror" Burgoyne had in mind was the Indians in his army. He addressed another proclamation to his redskinned warriors calling upon them to "strike at the common enemies of Great Britain and America—disturbers of public order, peace, and happiness—destroyers of commerce, parricides of the State." [67] Although he forbade the Indians to shed blood except when engaged in combat, events proved that they were sadly averse to any military discipline.

In one important respect, Burgoyne approached the invasion with a different attitude than he had in earlier campaigns: he had sharply revised his high estimate of American military capabilities. When he arrived in Boston in 1775, he modified his expectations of a quick victory after seeing the Americans fight fiercely in the battle of Bunker Hill. In 1776 in his paper, "Reflections Upon the War in America," he continued to hold the enemy in high regard and warned that their militia would prove to be "respectable" opponents. But by 1777 these more realistic observations seemed to give way to the same unwarranted optimism of an imminent victory in that year held by the British government. This attitude was evident in the plans Burgoyne made for the invasion from Canada. When he took Ticonderoga with deceptive ease in early July, 1777, any careful appraisal of American capabilities seemed to vanish completely. "The manner of taking up the ground at Ticonderoga," he wrote, "convinces me that they have no men of military science." [68] He was so cocky at this point and so unconcerned for the safety of his army that he expressed regret his orders would not permit him to turn his troops toward New England so that he might conquer that region instead of continuing south in the direction of Albany.

One reason for Burgoyne's great optimism arose from his assumption that his march in northern New York would be made through a region essentially loyal to the king. He expected to meet little resistance in the countryside because large numbers of loyalists had already been recruited for the British army from that area. But it was soon apparent that Burgoyne had made a major miscalculation; he began encountering local opposition instead of local support. Two months before his surrender, Burgoyne recognized his error and confessed to Germain on August 20: "The great bulk of the country is undoubtedly with the Congress, in principle and zeal; and their measures are executed with secrecy and dispatch that are not to be equalled. Wherever the King's forces point, militia, to the amount of three or four thousand, assemble in twenty-four hours." Although he had begun to realize the depth to which Americans were committed to their cause, he still had faith that his army could overcome such odds.[69]

Despite a series of unexpected setbacks—the Bennington defeat on August 16 which cost him one-tenth of his army, and St. Leger's retreat toward Oswego on August 22 which canceled out any hope of help from that diversionary force—Burgoyne was determined to plunge ahead. He was fully aware of the dangers involved. His army was diminishing in numbers while the size of the enemy force in his front was growing daily; his communications to Canada were vulnerable to attacks from the militia on his flank and would cease to be safe once he crossed the Hudson; and his supply system had broken down to the point where he had to halt almost a month to collect provisions in order to proceed further. Why then did he advance? His explanation at this stage was that he had positive orders to "force a junction with Sir William Howe"; but this was probably an excuse to cover himself in the event he failed.[70]

His real reasons for refusing to retreat were twofold: personal ambition and professional honor. Burgoyne was simply too ambitious to turn back while his army was still intact and there remained some chance of success—no matter how slim that chance might be. Having clawed his way to an independent command, he was not about to let pass this opportunity to gain greater glory. Professional honor, moreover, compelled him to pursue his drive to Albany. What would his countrymen say if he stayed where he was? "My conduct would have been held indefensible," he wrote in a telling letter after his surrender, "by every class and distinction of men in government, in the army, and in the public." [71] Burgoyne, in fact, felt that the honor of the king's army was at stake in his campaign: he considered a retreat under any conditions an ignominious act and a sign of weakness. In a characteristic move, he refused to retreat from the Skenesborough route, where he was experiencing some difficulty moving cross-country, to start over again down the Lake George route because of "the general impressions which a retrograde movement is apt to make upon the minds of enemies and friends." [72]

But even more important in Burgoyne's decision to push ahead was his romantic faith in the superior fighting abilities of British soldiers coupled with a correspondingly low opinion of American troops. His confidence in British regulars was great, indeed. "Had all my troops been British," he declared to Howe after Saratoga, "I, in my conscience, believe I should have made my way through Mr. Gates's army." [73] Easy successes in the early stages of the campaign, on the other hand, had given him a false picture of American capabilities. "The spirit of the enemy in combat against regular British troops, had only been tried at Ticonderoga, at Huberton, at Skenesborough, and Fort Anne," and, he noted, "in all which places it had failed." [74] Remembering that such encounters were his first as an independent army commander, he was, no doubt, overly impressed with these initial experiences.

Only after his army had laid down their arms on October 17 did Burgoyne fully realize how much he had underestimated the Americans. He was allowed to inspect Gates' troops at close range and sent Germain this revealing statement:

> The standing corps which I have seen are disciplined: I do not hazard the term, but apply it to the great fundamental points of military institution, sobriety, subordination, regularity, and courage. The militia are inferior in method and movement, but not a jot less serviceable in woods. *My conjectures were very different after the affair of Ticonderoga; they were delusive, and it is a duty to the state to confess it.*[75]

If Burgoyne was willing to admit he was wrong in his appraisal of his opponents, another letter to Germain on October 20 showed that he had not yet grasped the full implications of the strategic problem. Rather than calling a council of war, he wrote, he had taken it upon himself to make the decision "to force a passage to Albany." Burgoyne in this phrase was revealing, once again, the single fixed idea in his mind. His eyes were set only upon Albany; to reach that objective, in his view, was tantamount to a major victory. But was it? He never seems to have looked beyond Albany—to the questions of what he would do once he got there, how his army would be supplied, or what measures he might take against Gates' army.[76] In leaving such large questions unanswered, Burgoyne showed he had not completely thought through his campaign on a strategic level. By committing his force solely to the idea of reaching Albany, and by being obsessed with the thought of seizing that objective at all costs, Burgoyne perhaps had surrendered his army miles before Saratoga.

Burgoyne capitulated under terms that he considered both honorable to himself and advantageous to England. The Saratoga Convention called for his army to be marched to Boston and shipped back to England with the understanding that the men were not to fight again in the war against the colonies. Since his troops could replace garrison forces abroad, thus releasing other men for service in America, Burgoyne boasted: "I have made a treaty that saves them to the State for the next campaign." Despite his satisfaction at having made the best of a bad situation, Burgoyne was anxious to return home to defend himself against the expected storm of criticism:

> [M]y honor and my life in great measure depends upon my return to England . . . . I think that the persons who are most bound to vindicate me will be the first to attack my reputation, those for whom I cheerfully undertook a forlorn hope, and who would have crushed me had I remained inactive, I expect to find my accusers for rashness.[77]

Having obtained permission to give his parole, he arrived in England in May, 1778, ready to place the blame on anybody but himself. He had not yet decided upon the line of defense he would take, but as he cast about for a scapegoat his fellow general, Howe, seemed to be the most likely victim. Burgoyne quickly discovered, however, that the nature of his defense was destined to be political rather than military and that any hope of restoring his reputation lay in shifting his traditional allegiance from the court party to the Opposition. Thomas Hutchinson, the former governor of Massachusetts, described in his *Diary* why Burgoyne changed his mind: "It is said that when Burg[oyne] arrived, Charles F[ox] asked him his plan?—To charge Howe with leaving him to be sacrificed [Burgoyne answered] 'If that's y[ou]r plan we must forsake you: we are determined to support H[owe].' The next news—that [the] Ministry is chargeable; and his [Burgoyne's] speech in the H[ouse], and his new publication, are conformable to this account." [78] In short, Burgoyne discovered he could not count on Fox's support if he planned to attack one of the generals the Opposition hoped to use to embarrass the Ministry. When in late May Burgoyne demanded a Parliamentary inquiry to defend his conduct in the campaign and was refused, he clearly aligned himself with the Opposition.[79]

The Parliamentary inquiry into Burgoyne's conduct begun in May, 1779, was thoroughly political in nature and shed no new light upon the military reasons for the failure of the 1777 campaign. It was, in fact, part of a much larger political maneuver in which the generals—both Burgoyne and Howe having inquiries in 1779—combined with the Opposition politicians to embarrass the Ministry.[80] Germain, on his part, tried to shift the blame for the campaign to Burgoyne. Burgoyne's defense was, of course, that the disaster resulted from the inflexibility of his orders from Germain, leaving him no choice but to force his way to Albany regardless of the consequences. The findings of the inquiry were inconclusive and Burgoyne became a bitter man.

He persisted in provoking the Ministry and kept asking for a court-martial to review his conduct in the campaign. His request was denied, but political retaliation against him was prompt. In September, 1779, he was told that his failure to return to his army in America was considered by the king "as a neglect of duty, and a disobedience of orders." [81] Burgoyne defended himself in a long letter, closing with a demand for a court-martial to clear his name, and offering to resign his appointments to the American staff, his regiment, and the governorship of Fort William.[82] Such steps would leave him only his pay as lieutenant general, the rank to which he had been promoted in 1777. His resignation was quickly accepted and resulted in a considerable financial sacrifice of about £3500 a year.[83]

Having broken with the court party, Burgoyne began acting more and more in concert with the Opposition. Charles Fox insisted that Burgoyne had been used badly and the general's reputation within the ranks of the Opposition became that of a martyr whose defeat was due to the deficiencies of the Ministry. At the urging of Burke and Rockingham, Burgoyne published in 1780 his account of the campaign in which he repeated his old argument concerning his orders, claimed his army was one-half the size he demanded, and insisted that his force was poorly supported.[84]

With the fall of the North Ministry, Burgoyne's fortunes revived briefly as his friend Rockingham returned to power. In 1782 he was made commander-in-chief in Ireland and secured an appointment as colonel of the 4th Regiment. When the subsequent coalition Ministry fell, however, Burgoyne resigned his post as commander-in-chief in 1784. Denouncing the new Pitt administration as unconstitutional, Burgoyne used a familiar weapon, his pen, to ridicule his political opponents and wrote part of the vicious "Westminster Guide." From this point on, Burgoyne withdrew more and more from politics and devoted himself to literary and social affairs. He died on August 4, 1792, after having fathered four children by Susan Caulfield, an actress whom he had taken as his mistress about 1780.

It might be said of Burgoyne that he has been condemned by historians for allowing himself to be defeated in a situation which admitted of nothing but defeat. Too much has been made of the tactical reasons for the capture of his army—the size of his baggage train, his supposed dawdling after taking Fort Ticonderoga, his choice of the Skenesborough route over that of Lake George, and his move in crossing over to the west bank of the Hudson. The causes of the failure of the Saratoga campaign were strategic rather than tactical; the greatest mistakes were made in the planning in London rather than the fighting in upper New York—though Burgoyne himself participated, of course, in the planning. Given the misunderstanding that existed between Burgoyne, Howe, and Germain, the lack of careful planning and co-ordination, the unwarranted optimism about ending the war in 1777, and the mistaken assumptions concerning loyalist support in America, the collapse of the northern campaign might well have been predicted.

The question of his Saratoga defeat aside, what else might be said about Burgoyne's generalship? One of his outstanding characteristics as a commander was his boldness. As Carleton's second-in-command in 1776, he proved aggressive: he almost trapped the retreating Americans at St. Johns on the Richelieu River, called upon Carleton to test the Ticonderoga defenses, and urged the occupation of Crown Point to provide a suitable jumping-off point for an invasion the following spring. Burgoyne was equally bold as commanding general in 1777 when he continued marching toward Saratoga after his plan had received two major setbacks—St. Leger's retreat and the Bennington defeat. But boldness in war is not always a virtue; indeed, there is reason to believe that the Americans counted on this trait in Burgoyne. A month after the fall of Ticonderoga, Washington's adjutant general commented: "Burgoyne is supposed to have ability, but be too sanguine and precipitate, and puffed up with vanity;

which failings, we hope may lead him into traps that may undo him." [85] Just before the second battle at Saratoga, General Gates shrewdly anticipated Burgoyne's move and sized up his opponent as an "old gamester" whose "despair may dictate him to risque all upon one throw." [86]

Burgoyne also gave evidence of greater understanding of the complexities of the war than some other generals such as Gage and Howe. He quickly came to the conclusion that the Revolutionary War was a different kind of war—a war of ideology and waged against a countryside under arms rather than against a professional army—and hence one which required different methods. Recognizing that the war was a battle for men's minds, Burgoyne insisted initially on seeking a solution by political as well as military means. For similar reasons, he persisted in issuing proclamations to persuade Americans to lay down their arms and looked upon the presence of loyalists within his army as important because they provided tangible evidence that many Americans still sided with the king.

By the same token, Burgoyne was ready to resort to psychological warfare when applying military force. Burgoyne believed that when British troops were employed in battle it should be for psychological as well as tactical reasons: to drive home the lesson that regular troops would always prove superior to untrained men in combat. He discussed the battle of Bunker Hill in precisely these terms:

> [The] event . . . effaces the stain of the 19th of April, and will, I hope, stand a testimony and record in America of the superiority of regular troops over those of any other description. . . .
>
> In this point of view the action is honourable in itself; and whatever measures his Majesty's councils may now pursue, it must be of important assistance by the impression it will make, not only on America, but universally, upon public opinion. It may be wise policy to support this impression to the utmost, both in writing and discourse . . .[87]

This insistence upon maintaining the impression of British military superiority explains why Burgoyne refused to allow his army to retreat except under desperate circumstances.

Burgoyne's use of certain allies and weapons must be viewed within the same context as a form of psychological warfare. He advocated using Indians primarily for the psychological impact they would have upon the enemy. As early as the summer of 1775, he noted, "the rebels are more alarmed at the report of engaging the Indians than at any other measure. And I humbly think this letter alone [General Charles Lee's letter] shows the expediency of diligently preparing and employing that engine." [88] His employment of cannon likewise was based, in part, on the premise that artillery would appear "extremely formidable" to raw American troops who were unused to such weapons.

In his tactics, Burgoyne showed some ability to adapt to American conditions and to the different kind of opposition that he faced in the Continental army and militia. His emphasis upon the use of light infantry was a direct response to the use Americans made of entrenchments and the techniques of guerrilla warfare they employed in wooded country. Even more important was Burgoyne's willingness to learn from the Americans and to adopt their tactics. In his standing orders issued during the Saratoga campaign, Burgoyne called upon his own officers to fortify and entrench their positions wherever possible by "Felling Trees with their Points outward, barricading Churches and Houses, [and] Breastworks of Earth and Timber." Such measures were necessary, Burgoyne noted, because "the Enemy, infinitely inferior to the King's Troops in open space and hardy Combat, is well fitted by disposition and practice for the Stratagems and Enterprises of little War." Burgoyne also paid the Americans the compliment of emulation when he formed a body of sharpshooters in his army similar to Daniel Morgan's corps of riflemen just before the battles at Saratoga. [89]

But if Burgoyne showed considerable boldness, an insight into the true nature of the war, and a certain flexibility in his tactics, one major flaw in his generalship arose from his failure to free himself more completely from the military orthodoxies of his day. Although he perceived dimly that the war might be won or settled by resorting to rather unorthodox military methods, Burgoyne tended to think in traditional terms when he suggested solutions. Most of his suggestions in the first year of the war were predicated on two assumptions: that the American military forces, although able and respectable opponents, were unlikely to offer any long and drawn-out resistance; and that the mass of the population would be duly impressed by a sufficient show of strength on the part of the British army. He continued to cast about, therefore, for some form of political adjustment that would obviate the need for anything more than a show of force. After 1775, however, he seems to have shifted to a more traditional view and called for more men and more material to exert greater military pressure.

Burgoyne remained rather optimistic about Britain's chance for success during the first two and one-half years of the war. His optimism rested mainly on two premises. First, his lifelong belief as a professional soldier that trained troops were inevitably bound to win out over untrained forces. Secondly, his skepticism regarding the strength of the revolutionary movement. Burgoyne initially took the position that the supporters of the American cause were dominated by a few despotic figures, and that these leaders were subject to bribery. "[T]here was hardly a leading man among the rebels, in council, or in the field, but at the proper time, and by proper management, might have been bought," he wrote in 1775.[90] That Burgoyne was deadly serious about this idea was made evident when he suggested that General Charles Lee, a former British officer, might be bribed and persuaded to come over to the cause of the king.[91] Only during the late stages of the Saratoga campaign did Burgoyne begin to recognize the degree to which American soldiers were committed to their cause. "The panic of the rebel troops is confined, and of short duration," he wrote after his surrender, "the enthusiasm is extensive and permanent."[92]

When it came to ideas of strategy, Burgoyne seems to have been similarly hidebound by military orthodoxy. Many of his suggestions on strategy were aimed at seizing a specific geographical objective—such as Albany—rather than capturing one of the American armies. Such ideas, of course, were in keeping with the traditional military thought of the day. Nor did he appear to understand the connection between logistics and sea power. He seems to have been unaware that the lifeline of every British army, including his own, rested upon its communication with the sea.[93] Generally speaking, many of his strategic ideas were shallow and self-centered; he was often angling for the very command he proposed be sent.

Burgoyne showed a similar reluctance to break completely with many of the European methods while fighting in America. Like most officers schooled in the art of European warfare, he tended to place greater reliance upon the bayonet than the bullet and favored the bayonet charge over the close-order volley. During the Saratoga campaign, he exhorted his officers to impress their men with the use of the bayonet:

> Men of half their bodily strength, and even Cowards may be their match in firing; but the onset of Bayonets in the hands of the Valiant is irresistible. The Enemy, convinced of this truth, place their whole dependence in Entrenchments and Rifle pieces. It will be our Glory and preservation to storm where possible.[94]

The purpose of such tactics was obvious: to teach the rebels the superiority of trained troops and show them the military consequences of their defiance of the king.

A second major flaw in his generalship—besides his fear of straying too far from orthodox military practices—was Burgoyne's overpowering ambition. Too much has been made of his tendency to resort to intrigue to gain a higher command; in this he was no different than his fellow generals. It was in allowing his ambition to color his military judgment that Burgoyne showed his greatest weakness. His desire to reap fame resulted in an excessive optimism that often blinded him to a realistic assessment of his chances. Such overconfidence sometimes led directly to miscalculation.

In summary, Burgoyne was hardly the stereotyped figure of the English gentleman-general as usually represented. Living in a transitional period of great military, political, and social changes, he appears to have been acutely aware of contemporary developments and attempted to adjust to them accordingly. Militarily, his recognition of the Revolutionary War as an unorthodox war that could not be settled by the usual means brought forth some suggestions on his part for a political solution, changes in tactics, and a greater emphasis upon a show of force to impress the insurgent population. Politically, Burgoyne showed he was cognizant of the changes underway when he began speaking of the Americans as a "nation" rather than "rebellious subjects" while the war was still going on, and by declaring his support of American independence as early as 1778.[95] Had he been able to curb his ambition, to break more completely with his European past, and to be more innovative and less traditional in his professional outlook, Burgoyne might have made the War of Independence—in a military sense—a truly revolutionary war.

FOOTNOTES

1. Marvin L. Brown, Jr., ed., *Baroness von Riedesel and the American Revolution* (Chapel Hill, 1965), pp. 55–56.
2. Horace Walpole to Countess of Upper Ossory, August 8, 1777; Horace Walpole to same, August 24, 1777; and Horace Walpole to same, November 13, 1777, in W. S. Lewis, *et al.*, ed., *Horace Walpole's Correspondence* (New Haven, 1955), XXXI, pp. 368–71, 372–76, and 397–99; hereafter, *Walpole's Correspondence* since all Walpole letters will be cited from the Yale edition of Walpole's correspondence.
3. Charles Lee to Miss Sidney Lee, [?] 1782, *Lee Papers,* New York Historical Society *Collections,* 1871–74, IV, p. 12; hereafter referred to as *Lee Papers.*
4. Lewis Namier and John Brooke, eds., *History of Parliament: House of Commons 1754–1790* (New York, 1964), II, p. 141; hereafter Namier and Brooke, *History of Parliament.* The discrepancy concerning the date of Burgoyne's birth is discussed in Edward B. de Fonblanque, *Political and Military Episodes . . . Derived from the Life and Correspondence of the Rt. Hon. John Burgoyne* (London, 1876), pp. 4–8.

5. Lord Bingley's Will, June 27, 1729, cited in *Walpole's Correspondence*, XXVIII, p. 336.

6. Namier and Brooke, II, *op. cit.*, p. 142.

7. *Ibid.*

8. Burgoyne to George Warde, November 23, 1757, in Fonblanque, *op. cit.*, p. 11.

9. Fonblanque, *op. cit.*, p. 46.

10. Viscount Barrington to Burgoyne, October 27, 1759, Shute Barrington, *The Political Life of William Wildman, Viscount Barrington* (London, 1815), pp. 55–62.

11. Lord Bute to Burgoyne, November 2, 1762, Fonblanque, *op. cit.*, p. 49.

12. Fonblanque, *op. cit.*, p. 79.

13. *Ibid.*, p. 14.

14. *Ibid.*, p. 32.

15. *Ibid.*, pp. 15–20 and 62–82.

16. George O. Trevelyan, *The American Revolution* (4 vols. London, 1913), IV, p. 75.

17. James Phinney Baxter, ed., *The British Invasion from the North: The Campaigns of Generals Carleton and Burgoyne from Canada, 1776–1777 with the Journal of Lieutenant William Digby* (Albany, 1887), p. 157; hereafter Baxter, *Digby's Journal*.

18. Namier and Brooke, *op. cit.*, II, p. 142 and III, p. 645.

19. *Ibid.*, II, p. 142. To be fair to Burgoyne, it should be noted that the "corporation mob" in Preston was likewise armed.

20. Fonblanque, *op. cit.*, p. 124; John Debrett, *History, Debates, and Proceedings of both Houses of Parliament of Great Britain from the Year 1743 to the Year 1774* (7 vols. London, 1792), VI, pp. 10–13; VI, p. 444; and VII, pp. 175–76.

21. Debrett, *op. cit.*, VI, p. 79.

22. *Ibid.*, VII, p. 175–76. Burgoyne had a reputation as a pompous speaker. In the course of his speech on April 19, 1774, members of the House of Commons became bored and the remark passed that Burgoyne "belonged rather to the heavy than the light horse." Burgoyne, considerably embarrassed, promptly sat down.

23. *The Parliamentary Register* or, *History of the Proceedings and Debates of the House of Commons . . . During the First Session of the Fourteenth Parliament* (London, 1779), I, p. 252; Fonblanque, *op. cit.*, p. 130.

24. Walpole to Lady of Upper Ossory, June 14, 1787, *Walpole's Correspondence*, XXXIII, p. 563.

25. Walpole to Mason, October 5, 1777, *Walpole's Correspondence*,

XXVIII, p. 336; and Nathaniel W. Wraxall, *Historical Memoirs of My Own Time* (2 vols. London, 1815), II, p. 50.

26. Fonblanque, *op. cit.*, p. 90.

27. *Ibid.*, p. 91.

28. *Ibid.*, pp. 120–21.

29. George III to Lord North, April 11, 1775, in John W. Fortescue, ed., *Correspondence of George III*, (6 vols. London, 1927–28) III, p. 202; hereinafter *Correspondence of George III*.

30. [Arthur] Lee to John Dickinson, April 25, 1775, Dickinson Papers, pp. 25–28, Library Company of Philadelphia.

31. Burgoyne to Lord [North], June 14, 1775, Historical Manuscripts Commission, *Tenth Report* (London, 1887) app., pt. VI, p. 8.

32. *Ibid.* Burgoyne proposed his plan for conciliation and requested official leave from America on the very same day, Allen French, *First Year of the Revolution*, p. 204 fn.

33. Lord George Germain to General Irwin, July 26, 1775, in Historical Manuscripts Commission, *Report on the Manuscripts of Mrs. Stopford-Sackville . . .* (London, 1904–10), I, p. 136.

34. Proclamation, June 14, 1775, in Peter Force, ed., *American Archives*, 4th Series, II, pp. 968–69.

35. Fonblanque, *op. cit.*, p. 136; French, *op. cit.*, p. 202; and John Alden, *General Gage in America*, p. 264.

36. Burgoyne to Lord Rochford, June [?], 1775, in Fonblanque, *op. cit.*, pp. 142–54. This may be the letter abstracted in *Correspondence of George III*, III, p. 224 and, if so, is dated June 25.

37. *Ibid.*

38. *Ibid.*

39. *Ibid.*

40. *Ibid.*

41. Fonblanque, *op. cit.*, p. 190.

42. Burgoyne to Germain, August 20, 1775, in Historical Manuscripts Commission, *Report on the Manuscripts of Mrs. Stopford-Sackville*, II, pp. 6–8.

43. French, *op. cit.*, p. 537.

44. "Reflections upon the War in America," 1776 [?], is abstracted in Fonblanque, *op. cit.*, pp. 208–10. The fact that Burgoyne assumed that Quebec had fallen places the date of the paper probably in January or February of that year. Burgoyne in a separate memorandum suggested also that the number of light dragoons in America be increased for purposes of greater mobility. Burgoyne to Germain, January 4, 1776, in Historical Manuscripts Commission, *Report on the Manuscripts of Mrs. Stopford-Sackville*, I, pp. 383–84.

45. Burgoyne to Clinton, July 7, 1776, in Clinton Papers, William L. Clements Library, Ann Arbor, Michigan.

46. Burgoyne to Clinton, November 7, 1776, in Clinton Papers, William L. Clements Library, Ann Arbor, Michigan.

47. *Ibid.*

48. *Ibid.*

49. *Ibid.*

50. Germain to the king, December 10, 1776, *Correspondence of George III*, III, 1936; Burgoyne to Clinton, November 7, 1776, in Clinton Papers, William L. Clements Library, Ann Arbor, Michigan. Fonblanque, *op. cit.*, pp. 225–28.

51. King to Lord North, December 13, 1776, *Correspondence of George III*, III, 1938.

52. General S. Brown: The American Secretary (Ann Arbor, 1963), pp. 92–97.

53. *Ibid.*, p. 99.

54. *Ibid.*, 93–107.

55. See "Thoughts for Conducting the War from the Side of Canada," in Hoffman Nickerson, *Turning Point of the Revolution* (Boston, 1928), pp. 83–89.

56. Piers Mackesy, *The War for America, 1775–1783* (Cambridge, 1964), p. 115; William B. Willcox, *Portrait of a General: Sir Henry Clinton in the War of Independence* (New York, 1964), pp. 146–47.

57. Nickerson, *op. cit.*, p. 85.

58. *Ibid.*, pp. 83–89.

59. Burgoyne to Fraser, May 6, 1777, quoted in Eric Robson, *The American Revolution, 1763–1783* (New York, 1955), p. 139.

60. Brown, *American Secretary*, pp. 107–16.

61. Paul H. Smith, *Loyalists and Redcoats* (Durham, N.C., 1964), p. 51; William B. Willcox, "Too Many Cooks: British Planning Before Saratoga," *Journal of British Studies*, II (November, 1962), p. 66.

62. Howe to Carleton, April 5, 1777, Historical Manuscripts Commission, *Report on the Manuscripts of Mrs. Stopford-Sackville*, II, pp. 65–66.

63. Brown, *American Secretary*, p. 115.

64. Willcox, *Portrait of a General*, pp. 153–68.

65. Fonblanque, *op. cit.*, p. 245.

66. Burgoyne to Germain, July 11, 1777, in John Burgoyne, *State of the Expedition* (London, 1780), app., p. xxxvii.

67. Fonblanque, *op. cit.*, pp. 489–92.

68. Burgoyne to General Harvey, July 11, 1777, Fonblanque, *op. cit.*, p. 247.

69. Burgoyne to Germain, August 20, 1777, Burgoyne, *State of the Expedition*, app., p. xlvi; Smith, *op. cit.*, pp. 51–55.

70. Burgoyne to Germain, October 20, 1777, Burgoyne, *State of the Expedition*, xcvii.

71. *Ibid.*

72. Fonblanque, *op. cit.*, p. 264.

73. Burgoyne to Howe, October 20, 1777, in Historical Manuscripts Commission, *Report on American Manuscripts in the Royal Institution of Great Britain* (London, 1904), I, p. 140.

74. Burgoyne to Germain, October 20, 1777, in Burgoyne, *State of the Expedition*, app., pp. xcvi–xcviii.

75. *Ibid.*, italics are mine.

76. Willcox, *Portrait of a General*, pp. 147 and 153.

77. Burgoyne to Howe, October 20, 1777, Historical Manuscripts Commission, *Report on American Manuscripts in the Royal Institution of Great Britain*, I, p. 140.

78. Peter O. Hutchinson, ed., *Diary and Letters of His Excellency Thomas Hutchinson* (London, 1886), II, p. 210.

79. Namier and Brooke, *History of Parliament*, II, p. 144.

80. Brown, *American Secretary*, pp. 135–36.

81. Jenkinson to Burgoyne, September 24, 1779, *Annual Register*, xxii (1779), pp. 304–05.

82. Burgoyne to Jenkinson, October 9, 1779, *Annual Register*, xxii (1779), pp. 305–08.

83. Namier and Brooke, *History of Parliament*, II, p. 145.

84. This was his *State of the Expedition from Canada.*

85. Timothy Pickering to Mrs. Pickering, August 2, 1777, in Octavius Pickering, *Life of Timothy Pickering* (Boston, 1867), I, p. 150.

86. Horatio Rogers, ed., *Hadden's Journal and Orderly Books* (Albany, 1884), p. lxxxiv.

87. Burgoyne to Lord Rochford, June [?], 1775, in Fonblanque, *op. cit.*, p. 146.

88. Burgoyne to North, June–July [?], 1775, in Fonblanque, *op. cit.*, p. 178; and Burgoyne, *State of the Expedition*, p. 15.

89. E. B. O'Callaghan, ed., *Orderly Book of Lieutenant General John Burgoyne* (Albany, 1890), pp. 2–3, 91.

90. Burgoyne to Lord Rochford, June [?], 1775, in Fonblanque, *op. cit.*, p. 150.

91. Burgoyne to Lord North, [?], 1775, in Fonblanque, *op. cit.*, pp. 176–77.

92. Burgoyne to Germain, October 20, 1777, in Burgoyne, *State of the Expedition*, p. xcviii.

93. Willcox, *Portrait of a General*, p. 45.
94. E. B. O'Callaghan, *op. cit.*, p. 3.
95. *The Parliamentary Register* or, *History of the Proceedings and Debates of the Fourth Session of the House of Commons of the Fourteenth Parliament of Great Britain* (London, 1778), IX, p. 258.

BIBLIOGRAPHY

Brown, Gerald S. *The American Secretary: The Colonial Policy of Lord George Germain, 1775–1778*. Ann Arbor, 1963. The fullest discussion, by far, of the planning of the Saratoga campaign and concludes that Germain gave Burgoyne great latitude in the instructions about whether he should proceed to Albany.

Burgoyne [John], Lieutenant-General. *A State of the Expedition from Canada as Laid Before the House of Commons by Lieutenant-General Burgoyne*. London, 1780. Burgoyne's own defense of his conduct of the Saratoga campaign and indispensable for an understanding of the man.

Clark, Jane. "Responsibility for the Failure of the Burgoyne Campaign," *American Historical Review*, XXXV (April, 1930), pp. 543–559. An important article which inspired a major revision about the purpose of the Saratoga campaign as being an effort to drive a wedge between the New England colonies and those areas further south.

Fonblanque, Edward B. de. *Political and Military Episodes . . . Derived From the Life and Correspondence of the Right Hon. John Burgoyne*. London, 1786. The classic apologia for Burgoyne.

Hudleston, Francis J. *Gentleman Johnny Burgoyne*. Indianapolis, 1927. A popularized biography in the pro-Burgoyne tradition, and one in which the line between history and romance is often a thin one.

Nickerson, Hoffman. *The Turning Point of the Revolution, Or Burgoyne in America*. Boston and New York, 1928. Still the most complete and authoritative treatment of the Saratoga campaign, and quite critical of Burgoyne. Must be supplemented, however, by the recent work of Willcox and Brown about the planning of the campaign.

Stone, William L. *The Campaign of Lieut. Gen. John Burgoyne and the Expedition of Lieut. Col. Barry St. Leger*. Albany, 1877. Contains much material about the campaign that cannot be found elsewhere, but often does not document key points.

Willcox, William B. "Too Many Cooks: British Planning Before Saratoga," *Journal of British Studies*, II (November, 1962), pp. 56–90.

A brilliant article that concludes the most fundamental errors were made not so much in the execution as in the planning of the Saratoga campaign.

————. *Portrait of a General: Sir Henry Clinton in the War of Independence.* New York, 1964. Focuses more on the execution of the Saratoga campaign than the article above and concludes that General Clinton did all that could be expected of him in coming to the assistance of Burgoyne.

Charles Lord Cornwallis:

STUDY IN FRUSTRATION

HUGH F. RANKIN

Tulane University

MEASURED in terms of his military experience, Charles, Earl
Cornwallis, should have been the outstanding British general in
the American Revolution. Educated at Eton, tutored by a Prussian officer, and trained at the military academy in Turin, his
knowledge of strategy and tactics encompassed a far greater
scope than that of the average British officer. His formal education in martial matters was broadened by a lengthy career in
active service. He was not quite eighteen when he secured a
commission in the First, or Grenadier Guards in 1758; he purchased a captaincy in the 85th Foot a year later; was promoted
to lieutenant colonel of the 12th Foot in 1761; and became
colonel of his own regiment, the 33rd, in 1766. As a young
officer he was battle-tested at Minden, Kirch Donkern, Wilhem-
stadt, and Lutterburg. He was commended on several occasions
for his gallant conduct upon the battlefield. But neither training
nor experience guarantees military greatness and Cornwallis was
destined to go down in history as the general whose defeat made
possible American independence.[1]

Cornwallis' rapid rise in military and political circles was as
much the result of a distinguished ancestry as of his inherent
talents. Born into a noble family, he was appointed aide-de-camp
to the king in 1765, lord of the bedchamber that same year,

chief justice of Eye in 1766, and constable of the Tower in 1770. In 1760, he entered the House of Commons as Lord Brome, representing the family borough of Eye. Upon the death of his father and his succession to the earldom in 1762, Cornwallis took his seat in the House of Lords. He was neither particularly active nor original in politics, however, usually voting with the faction controlled by Lord Shelburne. In this latter connection he was alleged to have opposed taxing the American colonies. When Shelburne left office, Cornwallis resigned his positions as lord of the bedchamber and chief justice of Eye. From this time on, he devoted more attention to military affairs than to political activity.

When the rebellion in America broke out in 1775, the earl was in Ireland with his regiment. With his military ambition piqued by rumors of an expedition to the southern colonies, Cornwallis indicated to the Ministry his willingness to serve in America. Lord North was pleased: "his example will give credit & spirit to our proceedings against America. The Ardor of the Nation in this cause has not hitherto arisen to the pitch one could wish, & it certainly should be encouraged whenever it appears." [2] As his reward, Cornwallis was given the command of the force to be dispatched from Ireland to make a junction with Henry Clinton in the Cape Fear River of North Carolina. He was to serve as second-in-command to Clinton, who expressed his pleasure at the prospect of a reunion with "my friend Lord Cornwallis." [3]

The witty, charming and frail Jemima, who married Cornwallis in 1768 and bore him a son and a daughter, protested her husband's eagerness to serve overseas. She enlisted the influence of her husband's uncle, the Archbishop of Canterbury, in a vain effort to have the orders revoked. Yet the earl, who obviously loved his wife, refused to listen to her pleadings and appeared determined to seek those laurels that the American war seemed to promise.

The expedition was beset with delays and disappointments. Not until February 12, 1776, some four months after the campaign had been ordered, did the first transports sail from Cork. Contrary winds and turbulent seas delayed the passage and the fleet did not assemble in the vicinity of Cape Fear until late May. By that time it was too late to be of aid to the North Carolina loyalists who had been decisively defeated in the battle of Moore's Creek Bridge. Rather than leading his command into battle, the earl's first military duty was exercising his troops on the hot sands beneath the towering pines and leading them on several small raids to burn the homes of prominent Carolina rebels.[4]

Cornwallis' first exposure to actual combat in the colonies—the expedition against Charleston in June, 1776—proved to be an equally frustrating experience. In the subsequent attack on that city, he and Clinton could only stand by helplessly, isolated by an inlet too deep for the ground troops to ford, as Parker's fleet received a mauling from the makeshift fort on Sullivan's Island. With the collapse of the southern campaign, Cornwallis sailed north to join the main army in New York.

His arrival under Howe's command clarified his standing among the generals of the army. Earlier, Cornwallis had been promised the post of second-in-command in Carleton's army in Canada. But Burgoyne returned to England at the end of 1775 and managed to secure that position. Both Henry Clinton and Hugh, Earl Percy, were senior to Cornwallis in Howe's army and the earl had to be content with the command of the reserve.

Despite this seemingly minor post, Cornwallis managed to gain a share of the glory at the battle of Long Island on August 22, 1776. His reserve supported Clinton's flanking movement through Jamaica Pass and on August 27 the earl personally led his troops in a spirited charge along the Gowanus Road. Several observers noted that both Clinton and Cornwallis exposed themselves to enemy fire with almost reckless abandon. Victory came so easily that Cornwallis was led to believe the war would soon be over and that he was "bless'd with the Prospect of being soon restored to my Family."[5]

After the action on Long Island, Cornwallis was involved in several engagements around New York—often as Clinton's sub-

ordinate. He was active in the landing at Kip's Bay and maintained a position on the right flank at White Plains. When Fort
Washington was overrun, his astute disposition of troops sealed
the rebel escape route. After White Plains there was a breach
in the seemingly cordial relations between Cornwallis and Clinton when Cornwallis repeated to Howe Clinton's peevish criticisms of the commanding general. In this betrayal of confidence
lay the embers of a smoldering feud that was to break out later
in a heated controversy.[6]

Cornwallis received his first independent command on November 19, 1776, when he was sent across the Hudson to reduce
Fort Lee on the Jersey shore. His mission was accomplished with
ridiculous ease. As the rebels fled before him, Cornwallis took
up pursuit. But he was restrained by Howe's orders and could
move no farther south than the Raritan. Cornwallis was forced
to cool his heels five days while Howe made his leisurely way
down from New York to inspect the situation personally.[7] By
the time pursuit was resumed, Washington had put the Delaware
River between his force and the British army.

With the army going into winter quarters, Howe granted
Cornwallis leave to return to England to be with his ailing wife.
The war, it was felt, was nearly over. Cornwallis was to return
in the spring, if there was need of another campaign. Just as he
was preparing to embark, however, grim news of the Trenton
disaster arrived. His leave canceled, Cornwallis rode 50 miles
through a frigid night to assume command of the Jersey force.
After overcoming some difficulty in gathering scattered troops
and artillery, he arrived at Trenton late in the afternoon of
January 2, 1777, to find Washington encamped on the far side
of Assunpink Creek.

Cornwallis' decision to wait until the following morning to
launch his attack was to be subjected to critical review in later
years. His choice at the time, however, made sense. Although his
troops were superior to the rebels, they were weary, rain-soaked,
and badly in need of rest. The Americans, moreover, wherever
protected by good terrain, had always been able to give a good

account of themselves. Cornwallis in the meantime so posted his force that it was impossible for Washington to recross the Delaware. The earl's greatest mistake was in allowing his intelligence to break down. Sounds of activity and the sight of blazing fires on the far side of the Assunpink lulled him into such a state of complacency that no patrols were ordered out. While the British slept the night away, Washington marched through the darkness to attack the post at Princeton. Despite the tendency of many British officers to praise Washington for his deft maneuver, Cornwallis, in covering his own blunder, dismissed it as a last defiant gasp. In any future move by Washington, he declared, "the march alone will destroy his army." [8]

It was not until the early morning of April 12, 1777, that Cornwallis again took the field against the Americans. He marched out of Brunswick to attack what were termed "the most miserably looking creatures that ever bore the Name of Soldiers, covered with nothing but Rags and Vermin" at Bound Brook under Benjamin Lincoln. Once again, he gained an easy conquest. The rebels, discovering themselves encircled, ran "off in their shirts." Despite the insignificance of the engagement, the affair was blown up out of proportion in dispatches and did much to puff Cornwallis' reputation. His shrewd maneuvers around Quibbletown in enticing Washington out of a strong position in the hills to "act according to circumstances," added additional luster to the earl's fame.[9]

Although his actions in New Jersey were neither large-scale nor brilliant, Cornwallis had demonstrated that he was a field commander of considerable ability. He had lost little prestige as a result of his humiliating experience at Trenton. General Howe, for reasons of his own, may have wished to elevate Cornwallis above Clinton (who was in England at the time) in the minds of those at Whitehall, for he constantly commended the earl's actions. Indeed, Cornwallis was praised so lavishly that Lord George Germain wrote Howe that he was fortunate to have serving under him "an Officer, in whose Zeal, Vigilance, and active Courage you can so safely confide." [10]

An opportunity for additional glory became possible when Cornwallis was selected as second-in-command on Howe's expedition against Philadelphia. When Washington chose to make his stand at Chad's Ford on the Brandywine, and the Hessian general, Knyphausen, directed a feint toward that crossing, Cornwallis led the flanking movement that resulted in ultimate victory. Near Birmingham Meeting House, despite the favorable position of the rebels under John Sullivan, the earl directed the bayonet charge that forced the enemy from their lines. Had he been given a free hand to push his advantage, Cornwallis might well have made Brandywine the long-sought decisive defeat of Washington. But Howe followed his usual dilatory tactics and consolidated his gains very slowly.[11]

Perhaps it was because of his actions in battle that Cornwallis was permitted to assume the role of conquering hero in leading a detachment of the army into Philadelphia on September 26, "amidst the acclamations of some thousands of the inhabitants mostly women and children." [12] Not only did Cornwallis supervise the fortification of the city, but he directed the drive against the Delaware forts that blocked the entry of British vessels into Philadelphia. When Washington attacked Howe at Germantown in October, Cornwallis wisely refused to allow himself to be distracted by the diversionary militia force sent to amuse him and rushed fresh battalions to the scene of the primary action. Cornwallis added to his laurels when he stormed Fort Mercer at Red Bank in November, forcing the Americans to evacuate that post.

Cold weather brought an end to formal campaigning and Cornwallis now reapplied for the leave he had been forced to give up a year earlier. When measured by the yardstick of reputation, the delay had been fortunate; for the most part, fortune had smiled upon his efforts. In his first 18 months in America, the earl had distinguished himself in subordinate roles and proved he was an able and colorful field commander. On December 16, 1777, he sailed for home aboard the *Brilliant*.

England provided few opportunities for relaxation. His wife's health had steadily declined. He kept the political fences mended by an occasional appearance in the House of Lords. The Ministry subjected him to a rather heavy grilling about Howe's operations and attempted to wring from him a statement fixing the responsibility for Burgoyne's defeat at Saratoga on Howe. But Cornwallis appeared reluctant to criticize his commanding officer—especially one who had sought to favor his fortunes.[13]

Moreover, Cornwallis' previous optimism had been tempered by now by the continuing resistance offered by the Americans. His true feelings perhaps were best sensed by Lady Jemima, who wrote, "I am really so bilious as to think our army in America, Fleets everywhere, Possessions in the West Indies, &c., &c., &c., will be frittered away and destroyed in another Twelve months." [14]

Some of his contemporaries suggested that Cornwallis' answers to the questions put to him were too critical of the Ministry and that he was reprimanded accordingly. Horace Walpole, for example, observed that the earl was rather summarily ordered back to America "with little civility." [15] But the facts do not substantiate this assertion. When Howe was relieved of his command and Clinton elevated to commanding general, Cornwallis was issued a dormant commission as commanding "General in Our Army in America only," which was "not to take place, but in case of a contingency in order to secure you in such case the chief Command over the foreign Generals, [and] is not to be made public if this contingency does not happen." [16]

Upon his return, Cornwallis was not at all pleased with the way things were going in America. There was little future in any army that was obviously going on the defensive—or so it seemed on the basis of Clinton's instructions from the Ministry. On the day the British army evacuated Philadelphia, Cornwallis wrote a letter to Germain requesting permission to return to England as quickly as possible. Germain's ultimate refusal was based on the grounds that Cornwallis' dormant commission made it necessary that he remain with Clinton, in the event of the latter's death or incapacity.[17]

Both Clinton and Cornwallis were unhappy with the lack of

discipline and the "indecent, ungovernable impetuosity" among the officers in the army. The situation took on a more serious tone when, on the march from Philadelphia to New York, it became apparent that Washington would seize the first opportunity to strike at the long column winding its way across New Jersey. Clinton posted the earl with 2,000 of the "elite of the army" to cover the rear guard, and supported Cornwallis with another 4,000 troops under his personal command. It was Cornwallis' division that counterattacked under the burning sun on the plains of Monmouth.[18]

The glory of the day—if glory it may be termed—seemed to belong to Clinton, who "appeared at the head of our left wing accompanied by Lord Cornwallis, crying out 'Charge, Grenadiers, never heed forming!' " Cornwallis shared the embarrassment of other officers "at seeing the Commander of an Army galloping like a Newmarket jockey at the head of a wing of Grenadiers." [19] The same criticism, however, might well have been leveled against Cornwallis as Clinton; he reacted much the same way in the course of the battle.

In New York, the earl established himself in a fine country house on Long Island, and, as under Howe, acted as Clinton's field commander. With Clinton's force weakened by orders to dispatch troops to the West Indies, the commander-in-chief confined his army to routine operations. Cornwallis soon grew bored with this duty that seemed to have no other purpose than to protect foragers.[20] As his wife's health grew increasingly worse, Cornwallis became even more restless and was finally permitted to return to England in November, 1778.

For Clinton's aide, Captain William Sutherland, Cornwallis' return occasioned no great sorrow; "Lord Cornwallis is gone home to cock his eye in the House of Lords, insipid good natured Lord & the worst officer (but in personal courage) under the Crown." [21] Nevertheless, Clinton and Cornwallis seemingly enjoyed cordial relations. Cornwallis promised while in England to look in on Clinton's motherless children. Clinton, on his part, seemed willing to stake his reputation on the earl's report to the Ministry, "where his Knowledge of this Country and of our Circumstances may during this Season be as Serviceable as I have found his Experience and Activity during the Campaign." [22]

After his arrival in England, Cornwallis seemed to have second thoughts about remaining in service and resigned his commission. His wife's death in February, 1779, however, led him to change his mind once again and he offered to return to America. But by the time he advanced his services, Germain had already dispatched a dormant commission to General John Vaughan. Perhaps Germain had been piqued by the earl's recent testimony in the House of Commons; certainly he was reluctant to recall Vaughan's commission, stating that "If the King and Lord Amherst like this new arrangement it must be their measure not mine. . . ." But Lord Cornwallis went over Germain's head and carried his offer of service to the Court, and "His Majesty was graciously pleased to accept." [23]

Cornwallis returned to America, in part, because he could no longer tolerate England. To his brother, William, he explained: "I am now returning to America, not with view of conquest & ambition, nothing brilliant can be expected in that quarter; but I find this country quite unsupportable to me. I must shift the scene. I have many friends in the American Army. I love that Army, & flatter myself that I am not quite indifferent to them: I hope Sr. H. Clinton will stay, my returning to him is likely to induce him to do so. If he insists on coming away, of course I cannot decline taking the command, & must make the best of it, & I trust that good intentions & plain dealing will carry me through." [24]

There was more to his returning to America than mere restlessness. Sir Henry was periodically offering his resignation and the path to the post of commander-in-chief seemed clear for Cornwallis. Still he preferred not to show his hand, and played his cards in a disingenuous fashion. On April 4, 1779, he assured Clinton that he would not have offered his services if it meant "consenting to take command in case you should persist in coming home." [25]

When the earl landed in New York on July 21, 1779, Clinton appeared genuinely happy to see him. In fact, Clinton looked upon Cornwallis' return as an opportunity to resign his command. "I flattered myself that every objection to my request of being released from my very arduous and unpleasant situation must now cease," he wrote years later, "since His Majesty had upon the spot an officer of rank and experience upon whom to confer the command of his army." [26] Clinton's request for relief, however, went unanswered for seven months.

During the second Charleston campaign that took place in 1780, Clinton took Cornwallis more into his confidence, discussing every move with him on the grounds that his own strategy should be clear to his successor should the request for resignation be honored. Although on the surface he remained a dutiful subordinate, a tone of arrogance began to creep into the earl's letters. Even Clinton noticed, after the rumors spread that Cornwallis was to succeed him, that the earl was "regarded by a majority of the officers as actually possessed of the command: and so certain did his Lordship himself be of it that he made no scruples to declare he would assume it as soon as my leave should arrive, let the siege of Charleston be ever so advanced at the time." [27] So much had Cornwallis assumed the pose of a commanding general that a denial of Clinton's request for relief could bring only humiliation.

During the initial stages of the siege, Clinton received word that the king had denied his request for relief. Cornwallis immediately seemed to withdraw into a shell of self-pity as a result of his acute embarrassment. His subsequent behavior suggests that he blamed Clinton for his troubles. Within a week he requested that he not be consulted on future planning as, Clinton explained, "he feared he was a clog upon me, that I gave way too much to his opinion." [28] To Sir Henry's credit, he made an attempt to work matters out between himself and his sulking subordinate. Cornwallis merely took the occasion to deny that he was fomenting discord among the officers of the army, although he admitted suggesting to them several irregularities on the part of the commanding general. Cornwallis likewise counterattacked by accusing Clinton of not complying with all of the king's instructions.[29]

The dispute between the two generals abated temporarily when Cornwallis requested a separate command and was dispatched up the Cooper River to block the American escape route from Charleston. Yet Clinton feared to allow his second-in-command to range too far and soon began to "repent that I sent him. He will play me false, I fear; or at least Ross will." [30] Captain Alexander Ross, Cornwallis' friend, aide, and alter ego, was beginning to play a sinister role in widening the breach between the two generals. Despite the growing antagonism, when Clinton considered storming Charleston Cornwallis requested that he be allowed to share the glory of the day, reasoning that "perhaps you may think that on an occasion of this sort you cannot have too many officers," and concluding with "it is my hearty wish to attend you on that occasion." [31] But the city fell before such a massive assault became necessary.

Following the surrender of Charleston, the ill-feeling between the two men continued in churlish silence. Indeed, on the day after the capitulation, Cornwallis wrote Lord Amherst complaining that since Clinton had "now come to a resolution to remain in this country, my services here must necessarily be of less consequence." [32] Cornwallis requested duty in any part of the empire where there was action and Clinton did not command.

Although he seemed to hold Clinton personally responsible for his plight, past prejudices were quickly forgotten when Cornwallis learned that he was to be left in command of the southern army when Clinton returned to New York. In fact, there were even some indications of cordiality toward the commander-in-chief. When Clinton requested that Cornwallis move toward Camden to block the retreat of those troops who had been marching to the relief of Charleston, the maneuver was executed with alacrity. This move resulted in the slaughter of Buford's Virginians and the capture of Andrew Williamson and around 300 rebels. With this success, Cornwallis confidently reported to

Clinton that all resistance in South Carolina had been eliminated.[33] Clinton sailed for New York on June 8, 1780, convinced that "we may have gained the two Carolinas in Charles Town." [34]

With Clinton's departure, Cornwallis seemed intent on making himself popular with the troops, even if it meant a decline in discipline. The affection for him was reflected in the observation that "His army is a family, he is the father. There are no Parties, no Competitiones." [35] Banastre Tarleton was allowed to remount his British Legion on so many South Carolina horses that one loyalist newspaper boasted: "Colonel Tarleton took so great a number of exceeding fine horses, as enabled him to produce 400 as well mounted and well appointed cavalry, as would do him credit *en revue* at Wimbleton." [36] Soldiers were permitted to plunder at will. Looting was so widespread that crusty old Admiral Arbuthnot, no saint himself, had felt compelled earlier to protest "that this province with common prudence will submit & esteem it happiness to enjoy that freedom they once possessed if Lord Cornwallis can restrain their rapacity, etc." [37]

Despite his popularity with the troops, Cornwallis was a lonely man. He began to turn to a quartet of young officers in his quest for companionship: Nisbet Balfour, commandant at Ninety Six; Banastre Tarleton, of the British Legion; Francis, Lord Rawdon, who commanded the Volunteers of Ireland, a provincial unit; and Alexander Ross. To Balfour he issued an invitation to familiarity, "I beg you will continue to mention your opinion freely to me, without the Assistance of my Friends, I could never get through this arduous task. . . ." [38] His letters to this select group held a tone of cordiality that was conspicuously absent in his correspondence with other military men.

There was one officer under his command—Major Patrick Ferguson—whom Cornwallis did not cultivate. Ferguson, probably one of the most brilliant young officers in the British army, had been issued his commission as inspector of militia by Clinton and was charged with organizing loyalists in the back country: a Clinton appointee could hardly hope to find favor in Cornwallis' eyes. The general constantly threw obstacles in the major's path under the pretense that Clinton's instructions were too imprecise. Nisbet Balfour, who had warned Clinton not to appoint Ferguson, did not like the man. Balfour had disparaged the major with "Ferguson and his Militia . . . [have] great matters in view, and I find it impossible to trust him out of my sight, he seems to me, to want, to carry the war into N. Carolina himself at once." [39] In his reply to this observation, Cornwallis confided, "Entre nous, I am afraid of his getting to the frontier of N. Carolina & playing us some cursed trick." [40] Balfour, with the full approval of Cornwallis, kept Ferguson occupied with busy work rather than fully utilizing his talents to counteract the guerrilla raids and plunderings of the loyalists by that bold partisan, Thomas Sumter. And so it was that military politics and petty jealousies cost Cornwallis the services of an officer whose abilities might have eased the problems of the back country.

As early as June 30, Cornwallis was reporting to Clinton that victories in several skirmishes had "put an end to all resistance in South Carolina." Yet when Clinton wanted to detach troops from South Carolina to bolster his own operations, Cornwallis painted a grave and exaggerated picture of local conditions.[41] The more troops he retained, the greater his chance would be of gaining that glory that had eluded him at Charleston.

Despite the activities of guerrilla bands led by Thomas Sumter, Francis Marion, and Andrew Pickens, the British control of South Carolina was not seriously threatened until General Horatio Gates, the hero of Saratoga, commissioned by the Continental Congress to lead an army south to challenge Cornwallis, arrived on the scene. When Gates, with a motley collection of Continentals and militia, began to march against the British outpost at Camden, Cornwallis set out to meet him with about 2,400 men. Attack, Cornwallis felt, was the best defense. With the rebel army encamped only 14 miles away and "seeing little to lose by a defeat, & much to gain by a Victory," Cornwallis set out on the evening of August 15, determined to fall upon

Gates' force in a surprise attack at daybreak. After a chance encounter with the enemy around two o'clock in the morning, the earl was surprised the following morning when the American general "persisted in his resolution to fight." The bravery and discipline of the British regulars, and their effective use of the bayonet in the blue haze of fog and burned powder, burst the "Gates bubble" in less than an hour. With one stroke Cornwallis destroyed the effectiveness of the southern army of the rebels and they, with Gates leading the way, streamed from the field in terror and confusion.[42]

Cornwallis' victory was so overwhelming that he sent word to the North Carolina loyalists to arm themselves immediately, to seize all rebel leaders, military stores, and to pursue the refugees from Gates' shattered army. At the same time, he promised to "march without Loss of time to their Support." So infectious was his confidence that one military surgeon boasted, "We shall in a few days take another Stripe off by reduction of a Neighbouring Province." [43]

Curiously enough, Cornwallis reported his victory to the government and to Clinton in strikingly different terms. His dispatch to Germain was more detailed, more cheerful in outlook, and stressing the possibilities of success in future operations. The report to Clinton, on the other hand, emphasized the large number of sick troops in his command. The latter letter appeared to be written with a view of convincing the commanding general of the necessity of a diversionary expedition into the Chesapeake area to take some of the pressure off of Cornwallis' North Carolina venture.[44]

The Camden victory made Cornwallis overly optimistic and colored his reasoning. Despite the rising tide of partisan activities and hit-and-run raids by Francis Marion, the earl seemed to think that these actions were of little consequence in light of the victory over Gates and Tarleton's overwhelming defeat of Sumter at Fishing Creek. Cornwallis had long suspected certain political leaders of fanning the "flame of Rebellion," but had resisted the temptation of taking them into custody lest the action "might be considered rather as an act of Fear than of Justice." After Camden, or so Cornwallis claimed, evidence that a number of prominent South Carolinians had broken their paroles was discovered among Gates' captured papers. Twenty-nine citizens, among them Lieutenant Governor Christopher Gadsden, were sent to St. Augustine for confinement. To all protests Cornwallis would answer merely that the measures had been adopted from "motives of policy." [45] This stroke, he seemed to feel, restored South Carolina to a state of subjugation.

Cornwallis was anxious to acquire new laurels in North Carolina despite "the Insolence & Perfidy of our Enemys and the Timidity of our Friends" in South Carolina. The victories in South Carolina, he believed, would awe the rebels of North Carolina into submission. Yet he must keep on the move, he told Clinton, for if the army retired behind the fortifications of Charleston both Carolinas would soon be lost. [46] Ambition had colored his reason to the point of recklessness.

His plans called for a detachment under Major James Craig to take Wilmington, giving the British control of the Cape Fear River and a supply route into the interior. Ferguson's militia were to be thrown out on the left flank as protection from attack by the back-country people. Cornwallis still did not trust Ferguson or his "miserable naked Corps" of militia, "whom he says he is sure he can depend on for doing their duty & fighting well, but I am sorry to say his own experience as well as that of every officer is totally against him." [47] On September 8, 1780, despite the obvious growing unrest in South Carolina, Cornwallis began a slow, almost leisurely, march northward. His advance was hampered by the agues and fevers that beset his troops as well as by the harrying activities of rebel partisan bands. On September 25 he bivouacked in Charlotte to rest his men and to investigate the reports that great bodies of militia were turning out to oppose his march. [48]

Out in the west, Ferguson had met with some success in several skirmishes with the "Back Water Plunderers." As the aroused frontiersmen, under Charles McDowell, Isaac Shelby,

Benjamin Cleveland, John Sevier, and William Campbell, began to gather against him, Ferguson's dispatches reflected an increasingly dangerous situation. He requested that Tarleton's Legion be sent out to cover him as he fell back toward the main army, and a note of urgency crept into his "Something must be done soon." [49] Cornwallis refused to take Ferguson seriously, but finally sent out a battalion of the 71st Regiment to make a junction with Ferguson on the banks of the Catawba River. Within three days, alarmed at the reports of rebel militia gathering around him in the neighborhood of Charlotte, Cornwallis recalled this relief force. He explained this move to Ferguson with the statement, "I now consider you Perfectly safe." [50] By the time this dispatch was written, Patrick Ferguson had no need of reinforcements—he had been killed the day before when the backwoodsmen had wiped out his force at King's Mountain.

With his flank exposed and fearful of the enemy militia, anxious for the health of his own troops, and himself abed with a "feverish Cold," Cornwallis pulled back into South Carolina. There were, however, other reasons for this withdrawal. Because of the low spirits of the loyalists after Ferguson's defeat, it was feared that the "Over Mountain Men" would grow bold enough to attack the frontier forts in South Carolina, especially Ninety Six. Moreover, there were persistent rumors that Gates had collected a new army and once again was marching south. In the face of these considerations, Cornwallis weakened his own command by dispatching reinforcements to Ninety Six and Camden.[51]

Clinton had earlier sent Major General Alexander Leslie into the Chesapeake area to act "in favor of Lord Cornwallis." From his camp at Winnsboro between the Broad and Catawba rivers, Cornwallis sent word to Leslie to abandon his operations in Virginia and to sail to South Carolina as reinforcements for his own army. By late November, with both himself and his army healthy again, Cornwallis was almost exuberant as he boasted, "for the numbers there never was so fine an Army. . . ." [52]

Cornwallis now had to match wits with a new rebel general, for Nathanael Greene had been sent south to relieve Gates. Despite the growing activity in back country South Carolina, Cornwallis was impatient to resume his invasion of North Carolina. When Greene split his force and sent Daniel Morgan into the Broad River region, posing a threat to Ninety Six, Cornwallis unsuccessfully attempted to persuade the Indians to divert the attention of the enemy by attacks upon frontier settlements.[53]

Although he was in a situation that could grow dangerous, many of Cornwallis' letters brimmed with confidence. Tarleton was sent to take care of Morgan at about the same time Benedict Arnold was dispatched by Clinton to replace Leslie in the Chesapeake. With this disposition of troops Cornwallis was predicting to Lord Rawdon that "we may make a great change in the Southern Colonies in the next few months." [54] But there was a different cast to his dispatches to Clinton on January 6, 1781; he reported a "constant alarm" in South Carolina. Cornwallis appeared to be of two minds, for in this same letter he declared he was beginning his march into North Carolina. He had no intention of moving, however, until three basic conditions had been met: Leslie's reinforcements had joined him, Tarleton had disposed of Morgan, and a base had been firmly established at Wilmington.[55] In all these plans, Cornwallis left little margin for unexpected developments.

No one anticipated what came to pass at the Cowpens battle. Heavy rains prevented Tarleton's suggestion that the main army be stationed so as to cut off any possible retreat by Morgan. Tarleton's dispatches, written with the flourish of a conqueror, assured his commander that he would crush Morgan just as soon as the rebel force could be made to stand and fight. Cornwallis was encamped at the confluence of Turkey Creek and Broad River, some thirty miles from Winnsboro, when he first received reports of Tarleton's defeat at the Cowpens. Tarleton himself did not come into camp until the following morning, January 18, 1781. A rebel prisoner of war was to write in later years that the general was leaning forward on his sword as Tarleton made his report. In his fury, Cornwallis pressed forward with such strength that the weapon broke beneath him; he swore loudly that he would free Tarleton's men who had been taken prisoner by Morgan, no matter what the cost.[56]

The earl's pride had been hurt at so "extremely unexpected" a defeat that "almost broke my heart." He seemed to take it as a personal affront that Morgan should dare inflict disaster upon one of his young protégés. There was also the possibility that Tarleton's defeat might be interpreted at Whitehall as evidence of the earl's inadequacies. After Leslie arrived on the morning of January 18, and another day was spent collecting the fugitives from Cowpens, Cornwallis set forth in search of Morgan. When intelligence reached him that Morgan had retreated northward the same day of the battle, Cornwallis took up the pursuit. In a note of self-pity, he wrote, "I was never more surrounded with difficulty and distress, but practice in the school of adversity has strengthened me." [57]

By the time he reached Ramsour's Mill in North Carolina, it was reported that Morgan had already crossed the Catawba River. Despite the possibility that Greene might attack the British outposts in South Carolina, and the increasing improbability of catching Morgan, Cornwallis decided to press the pursuit, rationalizing, "I see definite danger in proceeding, but certain ruin in retreating," for to adopt "defensive measures would be the certain ruin to the affairs of Britain in the Southern Colonies." [58] When Greene was reported marching northward to make a junction with Morgan, time became a vital factor. Much of the mobility of Cornwallis' army had been destroyed with the defeat of Tarleton's light troops at Cowpens, but the earl resolved to burn the majority of his wagons and excess baggage to enable his force to move with greater speed.[59]

The pursuit through North Carolina resembled more a game of hare and hounds than a military operation. Greene constantly outwitted Cornwallis, beginning at the Yadkin River where he gathered up all available boats and forced the British to detour upstream to passable fords. Then, too, the earl had a penchant for accepting faulty intelligence. When word was received that the lower fords of the Dan River were impassable, Cornwallis had his men discard their packs and marched swiftly to intercept Greene on the upper reaches of the Dan. Frustration was compounded when he discovered that he had been led away from the main American army by a detachment commanded by Otho Williams and that Greene had safely crossed the lower fords into Virginia. Cornwallis thereupon turned back into North Carolina.[60]

Hillsborough, supposedly a center of loyalist activity, was reached on February 20, 1781. Two days later, the king's standard was raised to the accompaniment of a twenty-one-gun salute. A proclamation invited all friends of government to aid in "the re-establishment of good order and constitutional government." Despite the claims of loyalist newspapers that loyalists were flocking into the village, few actually joined the British force.[61]

Those who came in expressed their resentment that so little had been done to aid them since the beginning of the war. Others had grown wary because of the miscarriage of British plans in the past. Persecutions by the rebels had broken the spirits of some, while still others openly voiced the opinion that the British army was spread too thin to offer effective protection.[62] Inasmuch as relief for the loyalists had been one of the primary objectives of the North Carolina campaign, their poor response lent an air of failure to the enterprise.

Cornwallis was happy to leave Hillsborough. The massacre of a loyalist force under Dr. John Pyle by Henry Lee and Andrew Pickens, coupled with Tarleton's impetuous charge against another group of the king's friends marching in to join the British, dampened all enthusiasm for the forces of the Crown. Greene, meanwhile, had been reinforced in Virginia, and had recrossed the Dan. Although his troops were ragged and nearly barefoot, Cornwallis began to move slowly toward Cross Creek where supplies might be brought up the Cape Fear from Wilmington. After a brief skirmish with Greene's forces at Wetzel's

Mill, he encamped at New Garden Meeting House. There, on March 14, he learned that the American general was moving in his direction. Hoping to revive loyalist interest by an impressive show of British strength, the earl began a move to bring Greene to a decisive action.[63]

It was a foolish decision; the British army simply was in no condition to fight. Although outnumbered by approximately 4,400 to 1,490 troops, Cornwallis himself was inclined to discount the difference between the two forces because the majority of Greene's army was composed of militia. As at Camden, the very fact that he moved against such odds revealed his contempt for the poorly trained and supposedly undisciplined American militiamen. His ego needed a victory at this point, no matter what the odds. Apparently he had decided that a defeat of Greene would cancel the humiliations suffered at Cowpens and during the race to the Dan. Information about the terrain proved inaccurate, and on March 15 he found Greene's army stationed at Guilford Court House in a rather formidable position—three battle lines judiciously positioned on steep and wooded ground. Despite these unfavorable conditions, Cornwallis decided to do battle, relying, perhaps, too much on the use of the bayonet which was to prove ineffective in some of the more thickly wooded areas. It was a grubby, vague kind of combat, the broken terrain leading to gaps in the battle lines and the isolation of some units. Still the earl kept driving his troops ahead and was forced to commit his reserves much earlier than he had planned.[64]

During the battle, Cornwallis was foolhardy in his personal bravery. He was slightly wounded, but refused to allow his name to be placed on the casualty list. Two horses were killed beneath him. When the Guards were thrown into retreat, the general ordered a charge of grape fired through the British ranks at the pursuing enemy—a desperate measure, but an effective one.[65] Cornwallis was to claim a "compleat Victory" at Guilford Court House, but one is inclined to agree with the statement in the *Annual Register* that proclaimed the battle to be "productive of all the consequences of defeat." [66] And one young officer, after boasting of gaining the field of battle, added rather wist-fully, "I must own, without any brilliant advantage arising from it." [67]

After announcing his victory in a pompous declaration, Corn-wallis marched for Cross Creek. Greene pursued him as far as Ramsey's Mill on Deep River before turning back into South Carolina, hoping to lure the British general away from North Carolina and Virginia. Finding the supply situation at Cross Creek impossible, Cornwallis moved down to Wilmington. By this time, his letters had taken on a tone of desperation. They were filled with excuses for past misadventures, explored the possibilities for future action, and complained that he was "quite tired of marching about the Country in Quest of Adventure." [68]

Although he had agreed with Clinton that Charleston should be held at all costs, it was at Wilmington that the earl permitted his imagination to get out of hand. He decided that an offensive war should be carried into Virginia, seeking the ever-elusive decisive victory over the Americans. The main focus of the war, he now decided, should be the Chesapeake, even if it meant abandoning New York.[69] By moving into that area, he seemed to think, he might force Clinton into abandoning some of his own plans.

With his army but a shadow of its former strength, Corn-wallis was in desperate need of reinforcements. Since January 15, he had lost 1,501 men from a total of 3,224.[70] On April 24, 1781, therefore, the earl wrote General Phillips that he was marching to the Chesapeake to assume command of the British troops in that area. He was almost certain, as were a number of other officers, that Greene was returning to South Carolina for another strike at Camden, but Cornwallis felt himself too weak to return to the state.[71] Marching toward Virginia in an almost aimless fashion in late April, Cornwallis allowed his army to plunder so much that he alienated the countryside and the Brit-ish gained a reputation therein for "Cruelty & inhumanity." Somewhere along the way he lost another 300 men from his command.[72]

Cornwallis finally made a junction with Phillips' army on May 20 at Petersburg and discovered that Phillips had died three days earlier of a "teazing indisposition." His small force, added to the troops on the ground and subsequent reinforcements, soon brought Cornwallis' strength up to 7,500 men. Once he assumed the command, however, Cornwallis seemed unable to come up with a definite plan of action. He was worried about a possible junction of the forces of Lafayette and Anthony Wayne, which might well present a formidable obstacle to any operations he might undertake. At the same time, he was apprehensive lest he become the objective of a French fleet reported sailing from Rhode Island.[73]

Clinton was equally concerned for Cornwallis' army. He warned his lordship that "in carrying on operations in the Chesapeake . . . they can be no longer secure than whilst we are superior at Sea." Although there was an air of reproach in Clinton's letter relative to Cornwallis leaving South Carolina, he still allowed the earl a great leeway and freedom of action in his planning of future operations.[74]

Past misfortunes weighed heavily on his mind, yet Cornwallis seemed determined not to accept any blame for them. In dispatches to Clinton he argued that if an offensive war was intended, Virginia was the logical place to wage that war; it was the one region in the south where Americans had so much at stake and the subjection of that state would isolate the areas to the southward.

Most of the remaining days in May were spent in attempting to bring Lafayette to a decisive action. Failing to accomplish this purpose, Cornwallis turned his attention to the destruction of rebel stores. Although his raiding parties met with some success, the earl appeared to feel that such successes were of little consequence. When Lafayette was reinforced, first by Wayne and then by von Steuben, Cornwallis fell back toward the coast and on June 19 established himself at Williamsburg. By late June, with his confidence shattered, the general was writing Clinton requesting that he be allowed to return to South Carolina. Perhaps it was a creeping sense of failure that allowed Cornwallis to let himself be caught up in such an emotional rip tide; he now seemed to harbor an almost overwhelming compulsion to return to South Carolina and Camden, the scene of his greatest triumph.[75]

As the American force gained strength and Clinton requested 2,000 troops to help defend New York against a rumored assault, it appeared as though Cornwallis would have to go on the defensive. But he wanted no part of defensive operations: the idea of returning to Charleston had now become an obsession with him. As a result, the feud between Cornwallis and Clinton fell into the realm of the petty, and their letters became filled with thinly veiled sarcasm and vindictiveness as the two generals argued about future strategy.

In July, Cornwallis finally decided to return to Portsmouth from whence he planned to detach troops to Clinton, throw in the sponge, and, if possible, return to Charleston. It was this move, coupled with the capriciousness of Anthony Wayne, that allowed him to salvage a bit of pride. Wayne attacked the British force as it was preparing to cross the James River at Jamestown. Cornwallis, allowing Wayne to think that he was attacking the rear guard, then attacked with his primary force. Had not darkness fallen, the earl might have inflicted a near disastrous defeat upon the Americans rather than a mere "trimming." [76]

The exultation of having bested the enemy was lessened when Cornwallis learned that General Alexander Leslie had been ordered to South Carolina rather than himself. He grew bitter and morose. Still he felt that he might persuade Clinton to send him back to Charleston and was soon writing friends that "it is not improbable that I shall soon be with you in S. Carolina." [77]

His future moves, however, were determined by the commander-in-chief. Clinton had no intention of allowing Cornwallis to return to Charleston to sulk. Dispatches received from Clinton on July 20 instructed Cornwallis not to detach troops to New York but instead to prepare to hold Old Point Comfort on Hampton Roads "at all Events." Admiral Thomas Graves, commanding the British fleet in North American waters, had concluded that he needed a southern anchorage for the great ships of the fleet during the freezing months. A position on the Chesapeake would likewise provide shelter for ships of the line from which they could protect seaborne commerce between New York and Charleston. In a like manner, French ships would be prevented from using the bay as a base. Then, too, such a stronghold might well become a rallying point for the loyalists of the area, although Clinton never intended that the Chesapeake should become a major operational region at that time. Cornwallis had, in early July, suggested Yorktown as a means of securing Point Comfort from land attack.[78]

The business of going upon the defensive and the possibility of doing garrison duty irritated Cornwallis. He appeared to view these developments almost as a reprimand and as a means of removing him from active duty. Certainly he seemed to leave that impression among the officers; as one wrote, "His Lordship, who has performed Wonders & done more than all the Generals thats been in America. . . ."[79] And to Lord Rawdon, Cornwallis whimpered, "that the C[ommander] is determined to throw all blame on me & to disapprove of all I have done, & that nothing but the consciousness of my going home in apparent disgust would eventually hurt our Affairs in this Country could possibly induce me to remain."[80]

But the responsibility for selecting a defensive position had fallen on Cornwallis' shoulders and duty dictated that he follow the wishes of his commanding officer. Engineers were sent to examine Point Comfort and on July 25, Lieutenant Alexander Sutherland submitted his report, followed by a similar document signed by the "Captains of the Navy." Their conclusion was that a post on Point Comfort "must be attended with many inconveniences." The channel in Hampton Roads was so wide that enemy vessels could sail past beyond artillery range; for those same reasons the post could offer no protection to British naval vessels against a superior enemy fleet. Moreover, the cost of maintaining a post on Point Comfort would be prohibitive. There is the suggestion, however, that these reports reflected opinions previously expressed by Lord Cornwallis. The earl, interpreting instructions originally issued to General Phillips, decided to fortify instead the little village of Yorktown as a protected anchorage for the fleet.[81]

Work on fortifications at Yorktown was underway by the first of August, but there was little sense of urgency. The weather, Cornwallis felt, was too warm for his men to engage in heavy labor and he regarded lightly those rumors that reported that a French fleet would soon be operating in the area. The earl resorted to a labor force of "Hundreds of wretched Negroes, that are dying by scores every day." [82]

Cornwallis, by this time, had assembled a military force of more than 8,400 soldiers to man the works, including about 5,000 British regulars, 1,800 Hessians, and 1,500 loyalists. When Clinton suggested that since he had fortified only the one post, perhaps now he could spare some of his troops for the defense of New York, Cornwallis insisted that he needed every man. Despite the size of the army, however, he did not consider his position a strong one. Now that he had occupied the place, Cornwallis had changed his mind as to the value of Yorktown and concluded the site was "after all I fear not very strong." [83]

By the end of August, rumor became reality and work on the fortifications was pushed with frantic haste. A French ship of the line could be seen lying off the mouth of the York, while reports from Point Comfort stated that between 30 and 40 French vessels were within the Virginia Capes. On September 2, the French began landing troops on Jamestown Island on the far side of the peninsula formed by the James and York rivers.[84]

Intelligence soon reported the combined forces of Washington and Rochambeau marching southward toward Virginia. Matters were further complicated when, on September 5, Comte de Grasse sailed out from the Capes and made contact with the British fleet under Admiral Thomas Graves. In the ensuing battle, the French admiral managed to damage the outnumbered British fleet to the extent that one observer noted that "To explain it to one who was not there requires a considerable explanation." Another officer wrote, "It appears that the English were second Best," and Graves' ships were mauled so badly that his fleet was forced to return to New York for repairs.[85]

Clinton promised aid by sea, but Cornwallis warned that help must come soon or "you must be prepared to hear the worst." Once Admiral Robert Digby's expected naval reinforcements arrived and repairs could be made to Graves' squadron, Clinton promised, the British naval force would sail for Virginia. They would leave New York, he added, no later than October 5th.[86]

Cornwallis' disposition, ironically enough, improved as the military situation worsened. There was an almost exuberant note to his dispatches when the Franco-American forces marched down from Williamsburg to lay siege to Yorktown. As the enemy advanced, the earl pulled in his defenses, abandoning all of his outer redoubts except those located on critical sites. Not only did this allow Washington to begin his siege parallels much nearer the British works, but it massed Cornwallis' men within the town in such numbers as to subject them to saturation bombardment. Nevertheless, his dispatches to Clinton held such confident statements as "I have ventured these last two days to look General Washington's whole force in the position outside my works, & I have the pleasure to assure Your Excellency that there was but one Wish throughout the whole Army, which was, that the Enemy would advance." [87]

The earl's general orders bristled with bravado. His men were assured of their security by exaggerated reports that the enemy were inferior in numbers to the British, that they had no heavy siege artillery, and that the French had come only to procure tobacco and would sail away within two weeks. Cornwallis' soldiers, however, remained unconvinced; a number of them felt they were in "a very bad situation." [88] As enemy batteries began their "awful music," the troops were forced to flee their tents, British ships in the river were set afire by hot shot, and a substantial number of soldiers and sailors deserted. While the houses of Yorktown crumbled into rubble under the intense bombardment, the townspeople crowded down to the river's edge to escape the iron hail. Cornwallis himself was forced to seek shelter in "a kind of grotto . . . where he lives underground." [89] The allied cannonade was so incessant that Captain Samuel Graham of the 77th Regiment complained that the British could scarce fire a shot in return with their "fascines, stockage platforms, and earth, with guns and gun carriages, being pounded together in a mass." [90]

The possibility of ultimate defeat became apparent when word was received on October 10 that Clinton's relief expedition could not possibly sail within the next two days. When the Americans and French, during the nights of October 14th and 15th, overran redoubts nine and ten near the river, allowing them to complete their second parallel, a note of despair crept into Cornwallis' correspondence: "The Safety of this Place is so precarious, that I cannot recommend that the Fleet & Army should run great risque in endeavoring to save us." [91]

Nevertheless, Cornwallis refused to admit defeat until he had exhausted every measure. Early in the morning of October 16, he sent out Major Robert Abercromby in a desperate sally which reached the enemy lines, spiked the guns of a French battery, and ended in savage fighting. The following night he made an attempt to break out of the trap by ferrying his troops across the York to Gloucester Point. Cornwallis had hoped to land within the works commanded there by Tarleton and to fight his way back to New York. A sudden squall frustrated the operation.[92]

On the morning of October 17, 1781, Cornwallis went down into the hornwork, and, after staring at the enemy lines for some time, sent a flag across requesting a 24-hour cessation of hostilities. In the subsequent negotiations, Cornwallis vainly attempted to persuade Washington to grant him the same terms that Burgoyne had wrung from Gates at Saratoga. Washington paid scant heed to such proposals and insisted instead that the conditions be the same as those granted the Americans at Charleston. On October 19, 1781, while Cornwallis pleaded illness, Brigadier General Charles O'Hara led the 6,000 troops out of the town to lay down their arms.[93]

The day after the surrender Cornwallis occupied himself in writing a long dispatch to Clinton, attempting to shift blame from his shoulders. "I never saw this post in a very favourable light . . ." he wrote. "Nothing but the hopes of relief would have induced me to attempt its defence. . . ."[94] His comments assumed the nature of a general accusation, but it dealt in such vague generalities that Clinton was able to demolish most of the arguments by citing specific examples to the contrary.

Allowed his parole, Cornwallis returned to New York in mid-November. His conversations with Clinton began amicably enough, but relations soon grew strained. As each of the two generals sought to absolve himself of the responsibility for Yorktown, they allowed their discussions to lapse into petty quarrels with minor incidents becoming major considerations. Clinton brought up Cornwallis' letter of October 20 in which the earl had vowed that he had never liked Yorktown, that he never would have attempted to hold the place had he not been promised aid, and that the village had not been properly fortified because he had only 400 entrenching tools.

Clinton was quick to seize upon obvious errors, pointing out that the report of Cornwallis' engineer on August 23 had listed as many as 992 entrenching tools and that even then the earl had only requested an additional 500. Because Clinton felt "that some people here suppose there are passages in that letter which Convey an Idea, that you had been compelled by my orders to take the post of York tho' it was not of your preference," he requested "a more formal avowal of your Sentiments. . . ."[95] But Cornwallis was not about to admit anything that might damage him in the future. Although refusing to retract his earlier statements, Cornwallis did admit that his October 20th letter had been written "under great Agitation of mind and in a great hurry, being constantly interrupted by numbers of people coming upon business or ceremony. . . ."[96]

By the time Cornwallis sailed for England in January, 1782,

he had already achieved a distinct advantage over Clinton. At home he was received more as a conquering hero than a defeated general. The government had received and published, without comment, his letter of October 20, thereby adding to the impression that Cornwallis had been made a sacrifice to Clinton's stubbornness. Unsolicited aid to Cornwallis' cause came from Benedict Arnold, who was also writing letters critical of Clinton. As a result there was little resentment against the earl. The king, in fact, went so far as to applaud Cornwallis' patriotism.[97]

Knowing himself to be at a disadvantage, Clinton promptly began publishing pamphlets, inaugurating a controversy that boiled for the next two years. Cornwallis and his supporters remained discreetly quiet, thus creating the impression that there was really little to be explained. When the earl did answer, his arguments were presented with the concise logic of a lawyer's brief. Clinton, on the other hand, seemed compelled to follow the dictates of a sensitive and tortured spirit; the earl became his *bête noire*, a haunting symbol of his own failure in America.

Cornwallis likewise had the advantage of powerful political allies. Lord Shelburne, with whom Cornwallis was "upon a very friendly foot," rose in political influence as the Rockingham Whigs returned to power with the resignation of Lord North. Even prior to the news of the Yorktown defeat, Rockingham had been suggesting that Cornwallis was a victim of circumstance and if, by some miracle, there was a British victory, that victory would only delay "our final Extirpation in America." [98] Then, too, Cornwallis had the advantage of family connection with a naval hero, for his brother William had recently behaved admirably in the action off St. Kitts.[99]

America was the preface and the training ground for the glory that Cornwallis was to gain later in his military exploits in India. In the early stages of the war he performed well in subordinate roles, although he appeared more fond of issuing orders than of receiving them. In fact, he was not above placing a superior officer in an unfavorable light when it suited his purposes or might elevate him in the minds of those who could provide future favors. But in pursuing such practices, Cornwallis was merely adopting traditions already established by other generals in the British army.

Cornwallis, in practice, was a better battlefield commander than a planner of grand strategy. Administrative duties bored him; Alexander Leslie was to note that Cornwallis never "had time to settle anything. . . ." [100] As the commanding general in the south, he attempted to curry too much favor from young subordinates and too often he listened too closely to their opinions without weighing the consequences. And in valuing their prejudiced opinions, Cornwallis allowed himself to distrust Patrick Ferguson before that talented young officer had an opportunity to prove himself in the field. When his young protégés made mistakes, he struggled to find excuses for them. Although the defeat at the Cowpens was largely a result of Tarleton's impetuosity and carelessness, Cornwallis not only salved his subordinate's feelings by placing the blame on the "total misbehaviour of the troops," but recommended him for promotion. [101]

He failed, moreover, to exercise proper discipline over the loyalists. Cornwallis allowed them to plunder friend and foe alike, and, like other British commanders, assigned them to menial roles in the over-all scheme of things. Not only did he permit the loyalists, but his army, to plunder almost at will—a practice that alienated many rebels who might have returned to the royal fold. One of the primary objectives of the campaign in North Carolina had been to arouse the loyalists, yet he marched away and left them at the mercy of the rebels. In fact, he left that state in worse condition than he found it, for loyalism became unpopular after his departure.

Among Cornwallis' failings as a tactician was his impetuosity. His pursuit of Morgan seems to have been dictated more by injured pride than by reason, especially since the British position in South Carolina had not been fully consolidated. His impulsive pursuit of Morgan and Greene through strange terrain in a season when streams were certain to be swollen by winter rains was gallant, but hardly in keeping with sound military tradition. The destruction of his baggage and supplies at Ramsour's Mill at a time of the year when foraging possibilities were not good seemed to lack foresight. Even though he sacrificed supplies for speed, he did not seem to have realized that his pace would be regulated by the presence of a train of artillery. Moreover, he should have sent the large number of camp followers and Negroes accompanying the army back to South Carolina. Not only did they slow the march and complicate the supply situation, but they systematically plundered both loyalists and rebels alike, thereby adding to a growing list of potential enemies.

In the boldness of his pursuit, Cornwallis pushed too far with too little. Like most of the military men of his day he must have been familiar with Frederick the Great's *Instructions,* which ran: "In pushing too far into the enemy's country you weaken yourself . . . it is necessary always to proceed within the rules: to advance, to establish yourself solidly, to advance again . . . always within reach of . . . your resources." [102] His complete disregard of such maxims made his march seem like a boat plowing through the water, pushing aside a bow wave that almost immediately closed in behind the stern. He appeared in great haste, seemingly determined to rush on to one victory after another, as if fearful that the luster of his reputation might fade. Joseph Reed succinctly summed up Cornwallis' North Carolina campaign:

> like a desolating meteor he has passed, carrying destruction and distress to individuals—his army walked through the country, daily adding to the number of its enemies, and leaving their few friends exposed to every punishment for ill-timed and ill-placed confidence.[103]

Following his Pyrrhic victory at Guilford Court House, Cornwallis seemed consumed with a fear of failure. Too often he abandoned caution as he sought to remove the tarnish from his reputation. When he marched into Virginia, he did so without specific orders and against the wishes of his commander-in-chief; he thereby deliberately isolated himself from British strength and the primary British command post at New York.

Perhaps the greatest weakness throughout the southern campaign was Cornwallis' ill-concealed contempt of Sir Henry Clinton. The dispute over Yorktown was, in reality, the climax to an antagonism that had been growing in intensity for several years. When Clinton's request for relief from his American duties was refused by the Ministry, Cornwallis appeared to consider this as a personal affront by his commander-in-chief. From this moment on there was a steadily widening breach between the two men. Cornwallis directed his irritation at Clinton and considered the latter as the source of all his disappointments.

When he was left in command of the southern army, the earl seized upon this as an independent command, virtually free of Clinton's direction. While his dispatches to Germain fairly bubbled with enthusiasm, those to Clinton were drab and too often loaded with complaints. He made elaborate excuses for not honoring Clinton's requests to detach troops, refusing to so weaken his own force as to prohibit extensive operations. Clinton, as commanding general, was often too tolerant of his subordinate. A careful reading of his correspondence could suggest that Cornwallis selected Yorktown as a means of exhibiting his superior military acumen and of embarrassing Clinton. After the fall of Charleston, there is the underlying theme in Cornwallis' letters that Clinton could do nothing right.

The earl's complaints that he had been unable to fortify Yorktown properly cannot be justified. His construction of the works there, up to the time that the French fleet actually appeared, were conducted in an almost leisurely fashion. He seemed to fear that in pushing his men too much, he would lose his popularity with his army. If examined in detail, the major blame for the defeat at Yorktown might be placed upon the navy. Yet, in retrospect, the greatest fault should fall upon the shoulders of Lord Cornwallis; for it was not Yorktown that was the critical factor, but his rash decisions made along the way that led to disaster in the little village on the banks of the York.

Charles, Earl Cornwallis, had seen the American war as an opportunity to achieve greatness, but instead he met constant frustration and his ambitions were unfulfilled. It was this frustration that led him into an inconsistent pattern of behavior. At times, his boldness led to success, while his timidity, such as hastily withdrawing support from Ferguson when there were rumors that the militia were gathering, led to disaster. The blame for King's Mountain, therefore, should be borne by Cornwallis as much as by Ferguson.

Perhaps Cornwallis' major weakness, ironically enough, was his excellent military background. He seemed to feel that his superior abilities were never fully utilized in the field. When he was finally thrust into a position of authority, his frustration was compounded by the relatively untrained American generals, who, with the exception of Horatio Gates, proved to be his equals. Unlike some British generals, his troop dispositions in battle were more in the classic textbook tradition when the situation called for a more fluid arrangement. Not once in the battles in which he commanded an army did he utilize the flanking movements that had proved so successful for Howe, and in which Cornwallis had taken part. He used the same basic battlefield formation at both Camden and at Guilford Court House. At Camden, on an open field, he was successful; at Guilford, in rough and wooded terrain, his losses were so great that his claim of victory was merely academic. In later and more mature years he subordinated his ambition to reason and found in India that success that had so constantly eluded him in America.

FOOTNOTES

1. H. Morse Stevens, "Cornwallis," *Dictionary of National Biography* (London, 1921–22), IV, pp. 1159–66; Charles Ross, ed., *Correspondence of Charles, First Marquis Cornwallis*, (London, 1859), I, pp. 1–43. Hereafter cited as Ross, *Correspondence Cornwallis*.
2. Sir John W. Fortescue, ed., *The Correspondence of King George the Third from 1760 to December 1783*, (London, 1928), III, pp. 294–95.
3. William B. Willcox, *Portrait of a General: Sir Henry Clinton in the War of Independence* (New York, 1964), p. 86.
4. Historical Manuscripts Commission, *Report on the Manuscripts*

of the Late Reginald Rawdon Hastings, Esq., (London, 1934), III, pp. 172–73.

5. Willcox, *Portrait of a General,* p. 108 fn., Cornwallis to Elizabeth, Dowager Cornwallis, September 2, 1776, Admiral Sir William Cornwallis Papers, COR/57, National Maritime Museum, Greenwich, England. Any sympathies that Cornwallis may once have held for the Americans seemed to dissipate in the heat of combat. He wrote his mother that "these unhappy people have been kept in utter darkness by the Tyranny of their wicked leaders & are astonished to hear how little is required of them by Great Britain."

6. Sir Henry Clinton, *The American Rebellion,* William B. Willcox, ed. (New Haven, 1954), p. 65 fn.

7. Archibald Robertson, *His Diaries and Sketches in America, 1762–80,* Harry Miller Lydenberg, ed. (New York, 1930), pp. 113–15.

8. Cornwallis to Germain, January 8, 1777, Germain Papers, William L. Clements Library, University of Michigan, Ann Arbor, Michigan; Thomas Dowdeswell to Rockingham, January 16, 1777, Rockingham Papers, R1–1706, Sheffield City Library, Sheffield, England.

9. New York *Mercury,* April 20, 1777; John Shuttleworth to ———. April 18, 1777, Spencer Stanhope of Cannon Hall (Cannon Hall Muniments, 60578), Sheffield City Library, Sheffield, England.

10. Germain to Howe, March 3, 1777, Secret Dispatch Book, Germain Papers, William L. Clements Library.

11. "Before and After the Battle of Brandywine, Extracts from the Journal of Sergeant Thomas Sullivan of H. M. Forty-Ninth Regiment of Foot," *Pennsylvania Magazine of History and Biography,* XXXI (1907), pp. 413–18.

12. John Montresor, "The Montresor Journals," Gideon D. Scull, ed., in the New York Historical Society *Collections* for 1881 (New York, 1882), p. 464.

13. Remarks on Lord Cornwallis' Evidence, Germain Papers, William L. Clements Library.

14. Lady Jemima Cornwallis to William Cornwallis, September 3, 1778, Admiral Sir William Cornwallis Papers, COR/57, National Maritime Museum.

15. Archibald Francis Steuart, ed., *The Last Journals of Horace Walpole during the Reign of George III from 1771–1783,* II, (New York and London, 1910), p. 161.

16. Germain to Cornwallis, April 12, 1778, Cornwallis Papers, PRO 30/11/60, Public Record Office, London, England.

17. Ross, *Correspondence Cornwallis,* I, pp. 33–34.

18. Clinton, *American Rebellion*, pp. 92–94, 98 fn.

19. Walter H. Wilkins, *Some British Soldiers in America* (London, 1914), pp. 257–61.

20. Lady Jemima Cornwallis to William Cornwallis, September 14, 1778, Admiral Sir William Cornwallis Papers, COR/57, National Maritime Museum; Clinton, *American Rebellion*, p. 104.

21. William Sutherland to Dugald Gilchrist, January 17, 1778, Gilchrist of Opisdale Muniments, Scottish Record Office, Edinburgh, Scotland.

22. Willcox, *Portrait of a General*, p. 255 fn., Clinton to Germain, April 11, 1778, Germain Papers, William L. Clements Library.

23. Historical Manuscripts Commission, *Report on the Manuscripts in Various Collections*, (London, 1901), VI, p. 157. Tradition maintains that the Lady Jemima died of a broken heart occasioned by the absence of her husband. Her death should not suggest such romantic connotations, for although she did love her lord passionately, she had earlier described herself "as yellow as an orange" suggesting a disease of the liver rather than of the heart. Lady Jemima Cornwallis to William Cornwallis, September 14, 1778, Admiral Sir William Cornwallis Papers, COR/57, National Maritime Museum.

24. Cornwallis to William Cornwallis, May 5, 1779, Admiral Sir William Cornwallis Papers, COR/57, National Maritime Museum.

25. Cornwallis to Clinton, April 4, 1779, Sir Henry Clinton Papers, William L. Clements Library.

26. Clinton, *American Rebellion*, p. 138.

27. *Ibid.*, pp. 160, 183; Willcox, *Portrait of a General*, p. 317.

28. Willcox, *Portrait of a General*, p. 318.

29. Clinton, *American Rebellion*, pp. 184–85.

30. *Ibid.*, p. 167 fn.

31. Cornwallis to Clinton, May 7, 1780, Cornwallis Papers, PRO 30/11/73.

32. Cornwallis to Amherst, May 13, 1780, Cornwallis Papers, PRO 30/11/100.

33. Cornwallis to Clinton, May 30, 1780, Cornwallis Papers, PRO 30/11/73.

34. Clinton to Sir Charles Thompson, June 10, 1780, Hotham Collection, DDHO 4/2, East Riding County Record Office, Beverley, Yorkshire, England.

35. James Franklin Jameson, ed., "Letters of Robert Biddulph, 1779–1783," *American Historical Review*, XXIX (October, 1923), pp. 96–97.

36. New York *Royal Gazette*, June 7, 1780.

37. Arbuthnot to Germain, April 20, 1780, Germain Papers, William L. Clements Library. Yet Arbuthnot later expressed the wish to "remain with Lord Cornwallis, who is well qualified." Arbuthnot to Germain, May 31, 1780, Germain Papers, William L. Clements Library.

38. Cornwallis to Balfour, June 11, 1790, Cornwallis Papers, PRO 30/11/87.

39. Balfour to Cornwallis, June 27, 1780, Cornwallis Papers, PRO 30/11/2; Willcox, *Portrait of a General*, p. 321.

40. Cornwallis to Balfour, July 3, 1780, Cornwallis Papers, PRO 30/11/78.

41. Benjamin F. Stevens, ed., *The Campaign in Virginia, 1781: an Exact Reprint of Six Rare Pamphlets on the Clinton-Cornwallis Controversy*, (London, 1888), I, p. 223.

42. Cornwallis to Germain, August 20–21, 1780, Cornwallis Papers, PRO 30/11/76.

43. John McNamara to Charles Mellish, August 22, 1780, Mellish Manuscripts 172–111, University of Nottingham, Nottingham, England.

44. Cornwallis to Clinton, August 23, 1780, Cornwallis Papers, PRO 30/11/79, Cornwallis to Arbuthnot, August 23, 1780, Cornwallis Papers, PRO 30/11/79.

45. Cornwallis to Clinton, September 30, 1780, Cornwallis Papers, PRO 30/11/72; Ross, *Cornwallis Correspondence*, I, p. 56; Mabel L. Weber, ed., "Josiah Smith's Diary, 1780–1781," *The South Carolina Historical and Genealogical Magazine*, XXII (January, 1932), pp. 2–5; David Ramsay, *The History of the American Revolution*, (London, 1793), II, p. 171.

46. Cornwallis to Clinton, August 6, 1780, Clinton Papers, William L. Clements Library; Cornwallis to Alured Clarke, September 5, 1780, Cornwallis Papers, PRO 30/11/80.

47. Cornwallis to Clinton, August 29, 1790, Cornwallis Papers, PRO 30/11/72; Cornwallis to Rawdon, August 29, 1780, Cornwallis Papers, PRO 30/11/79.

48. Cornwallis to Balfour, September 13, 1780, Cornwallis to Archibald MacArthur, September 29, 1780, Cornwallis Papers, PRO 30/11/80.

49. Ferguson to Cornwallis, October 5, 1780, Cornwallis Papers, PRO 30/11/3.

50. Cornwallis to Ferguson, October 8, 1780, Cornwallis Papers, PRO 30/11/81.

51. Cornwallis to Balfour, October 10, 1780, Cornwallis Papers, PRO

30/11/81; Rawdon to Clinton, October 20, 1780, Cornwallis Papers, PRO 30/11/3; Cornwallis to Tarleton, November 8, 1780, Cornwallis Papers, PRO 30/11/82.

52. Cornwallis to Leslie, November 21, 1780, Cornwallis to Balfour, November 29, 1780, Cornwallis Papers, PRO 30/11/82.

53. Cornwallis to Clinton, December 29, 1780, Cornwallis Papers, PRO 30/11/72.

54. Cornwallis to Rawdon, December 30, 1780, Cornwallis Papers, PRO 30/11/83.

55. Cornwallis to Clinton, January 6, 1781, Cornwallis Papers, PRO 30/11/72; Cornwallis to Balfour, January 12, 1781, Cornwallis Papers, PRO 30/11/84.

56. Roderick Mackenzie, *Strictures on Lt. Col. Tarleton's History "Of the Campaigns of 1780 and 1781, in the Southern Provinces of North America,"* (London, 1787), pp. 102–03; "Memoir of Joseph McJunkin of Union," *The Magnolia or Southern Appalachian*, II (January, 1843), pp. 30–40.

57. Cornwallis to Germain, January 18, 1781, Cornwallis Papers, PRO 30/11/76; Cornwallis to Rawdon, January 21, 1781, Cornwallis Papers, PRO 30/11/84.

58. Cornwallis to Rawdon, January 25, 29, 1781, Cornwallis Papers, PRO 30/11/84.

59. Cornwallis to Germain, March 17, 1781, Cornwallis Papers, PRO 30/11/76. A. R. Newsome, ed., "A British Orderly Book," *North Carolina Historical Review*, IX (July, 1932), pp. 284–85.

60. Cornwallis to Germain, March 17, 1781, Cornwallis Papers, PRO 30/11/76.

61. Charleston, S.C. *Royal Gazette*, March 14, 1781.

62. Cornwallis to Germain, March 17, 1781, Cornwallis Papers, PRO 30/11/76; Cornwallis to Sir James Wright and other members of the Board of Agents for the American Loyalists, March 8, 1783, Cornwallis Papers, PRO 30/11/103.

63. Cornwallis to Germain, March 17, 1781, Cornwallis Papers, PRO 30/11/76.

64. *Ibid.*, Field Return of Troops Under the Command of Lieut. General Cornwallis in Action at Guilford, March 15, 1781, Cornwallis Papers, PRO 30/11/103.

65. Ross, *Correspondence Cornwallis*, I, p. 86; *Annual Register for 1781*, p. 69; Banastre Tarleton, *Campaigns of 1780 and 1781 in the Southern Provinces of North America* (Dublin, 1787), p. 275.

66. *Annual Register for 1781*, p. 71.

67. Francis Dundas to Robert Dundas, April 3, 1781, Laing Manuscripts, II, p. 500, University of Edinburgh, Edinburgh, Scotland.
68. Cornwallis to Germain, April 18, 1781, Cornwallis Papers, PRO 30/11/76; Cornwallis to William Phillips, April 10, 1781, Cornwallis to Amherst, April 18, 1781, Cornwallis Papers, PRO 30/11/85.
69. Ibid.
70. State of the Troops that marched with the Army under the Command of Lieut. General Earl Cornwallis, April 1, 1781, Cornwallis Papers, PRO 30/11/5.
71. Cornwallis to Phillips, May 8, 1781, Cornwallis Papers, PRO 30/11/86; James Hadden to Charles Mellish, May 11, 1781, Mellish Manuscripts, pp. 172–211, University of Nottingham.
72. David Mason to Littleberry Mason, May 13, 1781, Cornwallis Papers, PRO 30/11/105; State of the Troops that marched with the Army under the Command of Lieut. Genl. Earl Cornwallis, May 1, 1781, Cornwallis Papers, PRO 30/11/103.
73. Phillips to Cornwallis, May 6, 1781, Cornwallis Papers, PRO 30/11/70; Cornwallis to Clinton, May 20, 1781, Cornwallis to Clinton, May 26, 1781, Cornwallis Papers, PRO 30/11/74.
74. Clinton to Cornwallis, May 29, 1781, Cornwallis Papers, PRO 30/11/68.
75. Stevens, The Campaign in Virginia, 1781, II, p. 37.
76. Cornwallis to Clinton, July 8, 1781, Cornwallis Papers, PRO 30/11/74.
77. Cornwallis to Alexander Stewart, July 16, 1781, Cornwallis Papers, PRO 30/11/88.
78. Clinton to Cornwallis, July 8, 1781, Clinton to Cornwallis, July 11, 1781, Cornwallis Papers, PRO 30/11/68; Graves to Cornwallis, July 12, 1781, Cornwallis Papers, PRO 30/11/88.
79. Ralph Dundas to James Dundas, July 22, 1781, Dundas of Ochtertyre Muniments, No. 57, Scottish Record Office.
80. Cornwallis to Rawdon, July 23, 1781, Cornwallis Papers, PRO 30/11/74.
81. Alexander Sutherland to Cornwallis, July 25, 1781, captains of the navy to Cornwallis, July 26, 1781, Cornwallis Papers, PRO 30/11/74.
82. Charles O'Hara to Cornwallis, August 5, 1781, Cornwallis Papers, PRO 30/11/70.
83. State of the Troops under Lord Cornwallis at Yorktown, August 15, 1781, Cornwallis Papers, PRO 30/11/70; Cornwallis to Clinton, August 16, 1781, Cornwallis Papers, PRO 30/11/74; Corn-

wallis to Leslie, August 27, 1781, Cornwallis Papers, PRO 30/11/89.

84. Cornwallis to Clinton, August 31, 1781, Cornwallis to Clinton, September 2, 1781, Cornwallis Papers, PRO 30/11/74.

85. John Allen to Captain Sherwood, October 20, 1781, Haldimand Papers, British Museum, Additional Manuscripts 21835.

86. Clinton to Cornwallis, September 24, 1781, Cornwallis Papers, PRO 30/11/68.

87. Cornwallis to Clinton, September 29, 1781, Cornwallis Papers, PRO 30/11/74.

88. Stephen Popp, "Journal, 1777–1783," *Pennsylvania Magazine of History and Biography*, XXVI (1902), p. 41.

89. Edward M. Riley, ed., "St. George Tucker's Journal of the Siege of Yorktown, 1781," *William and Mary Quarterly*, 3rd series, V (July, 1948), pp. 386–87.

90. Samuel Graham, "An English Officer's Account of His Services in America, 1779–1781," *Historical Magazine*, IX (August, 1865), p. 248.

91. Cornwallis to Clinton, October 15, 1781, Cornwallis Papers, PRO 30/11/74.

92. Cornwallis to Clinton, October 20, 1781, Cornwallis Papers, PRO 30/11/74.

93. Ralph Dundas to James Dundas, November 6, 1781, Dundas of Ochtertyre Muniments, No. 57, Scottish Record Office; Return of the Killed, Wounded & Missing of the following Corps from the 28th Septr. to the 19th October 1781, Cornwallis Papers, PRO 30/11/103.

94. Cornwallis to Clinton, October 20, 1781, Cornwallis Papers, PRO 30/11/74.

95. Clinton to Cornwallis, November 30, 1781, Cornwallis Papers, PRO 30/11/68.

96. Cornwallis to Clinton, December 2, 1781, Cornwallis Papers, PRO 30/11/74.

97. Willcox, *Portrait of a General*, p. 456; Elizabeth, Dowager Countess Cornwallis, to William Cornwallis, April 2, 1782, Admiral Sir William Cornwallis Papers, COR/58, National Maritime Museum.

98. Rockingham to Portland, November 19, 1781, Rockingham Manuscripts, R1–1767, Sheffield City Library.

99. Cornwallis to William Cornwallis, May 1, 1782, Admiral Sir William Cornwallis Papers, COR/58, National Maritime Museum.

100. Leslie to Earl of Levin, December 6, 1781, Levin and Melville Muniments, Section IX, p. 512, Scottish Record Office.

101. Tarleton, *Campaigns of 1780 and 1781 in the Southern Provinces of North America*, p. 222.

102. [Frederick the Great], *Military Instructions, written by the King of Prussia, for the Generals of his Army; being his Majesty's own Commentaries on his former Campaigns. Together with short Instructions for the use of his light troops. . . . Translated by an Officer* (London, 1762), pp. 12–13.

103. William B. Reed, *Life and Correspondence of Joseph Reed,* (Philadelphia, 1847), II, p. 296.

BIBLIOGRAPHY

Bass, Robert D. *The Green Dragoon: The Lives of Banastre Tarleton and Mary Robinson.* New York, 1957. Contains new materials on Tarleton in America.

Ross, Charles, ed. *The Correspondence of Charles, First Marquis Cornwallis.* 3 vols. London, 1859. Although the emphasis is on Cornwallis' later career, the more significant letters relating to America are included. The introduction contains a useful life of the general.

Smith, Paul H. *Loyalists and Redcoats: A Study in British Revolutionary Policy.* Chapel Hill, 1964. An excellent analysis of the failure of British loyalist policy.

Stevens, Benjamin F., ed. *The Campaign in Virginia, 1781: An Exact Reprint of Six Rare Pamphlets on the Clinton-Cornwallis Controversy.* 2 vols. London, 1888. Contains the more significant of the bitter exchange of charges and countercharges between the two generals.

Tarleton, Banastre. *A History of the Campaigns of 1780 and 1781 in the Southern Provinces of North America.* Dublin, 1787. Portrait of a self-styled hero during his campaigns with Cornwallis in the south.

Willcox, William B., ed. *The American Rebellion: Sir Henry Clinton's Narrative of His Campaigns, 1775–1782, with an Appendix of Original Documents.* New Haven, 1954. Sir Henry Clinton's defense of his American career.

Willcox, William B. *Portrait of a General: Sir Henry Clinton in the War of Independence.* New York, 1964. A brilliant biography of Clinton and an excellent analysis of the dispute with Cornwallis.

Richard Lord Howe:

ADMIRAL AS PEACEMAKER

IRA D. GRUBER

Rice University

WHEN the War of Independence began, Admiral Richard Lord Howe ranked as one of Britain's best-known and most-respected seamen. Although he had never commanded a fleet in wartime, Howe had a reputation for aggressive leadership and professional competence during his thirty-five years in the Royal Navy. One officer serving at Boston in 1775 thought the colonists would soon accept the laws of Parliament if an army of 10,000 men were sent to New York, "accompanied by My Lord Howe or some other Capital man in that Department with a number of Frigates and small ships." Even Howe's opponents acknowledged that he "was certainly a very respectable officer and high in the Opinion of ye publick." [1] Sailors liked to remember how during the Seven Years' War he hunted remnants of a French squadron among the rocks of Quiberon Bay, placed his own ship against the fort on L'Ile d'Aix, and went ashore under fire to direct the evacuation of St. Cas. They were, moreover, fully justified in celebrating his accomplishments as a student of tactics and signaling; by 1778 he would renovate the whole system of managing a fleet in battle, replacing a cumbersome set of fighting instructions with a signal book that admitted far more flexible maneuvering. [2] If not unusually intelligent, Howe was justly respected as a bold commander, who knew his profession and cared for his men. "Give us Black Dick and we fear nothing," echoed from the line at Spithead to the floor of the House of Commons.[3]

Although Howe was proud of his record and ambitious to distinguish himself further, he had no wish to do so by fighting against British subjects in America. He viewed the rebellion as a personal and a national tragedy and wished for nothing more than a chance to promote a lasting reconciliation between the mother country and her colonies. There was, perhaps, more than sentiment and patriotism in his desire to become a peacemaker, for Howe was ambitious enough to think of saving the empire in terms of his personal glory. But, above all, the rebellion reminded him of his family's close ties with Massachusetts Bay. The General Court of that colony had erected a monument to his older brother who was killed at Ticonderoga during the Seven Years' War. Remembering the gesture, Howe had offered to mediate the imperial quarrel as early as Christmas of 1774. He did not propose making significant constitutional concessions to the colonists, but he thought that kind words delivered by the right person would do much to settle the quarrel and suggested that the government send him to America as a peace commissioner. The Ministry, putting its faith in coercive measures, consistently rejected his offers until the autumn of 1775. By that time the government was confident that it could break the revolt by force of arms and agreed to employ him in accepting colonial surrender. Howe, of course, wanted to do more than dictate the terms of peace and immediately began asking for authority to negotiate a settlement.[4]

While he was struggling without much success to increase the scope of his commission, chance seemed to offer an alternative solution. On December 7, 1775, Sir Charles Saunders died, vacating a sinecure worth more than £1200 per year. Lord North, head of the Ministry, had promised this sinecure to Howe but, forgetting his promise, agreed to award it to another officer. When Howe discovered what had happened he threatened to resign from the navy. North certainly had no desire to break with one of Britain's ablest officers and began searching for a suitable way to placate him. After a month of futile negotiations, Howe intimated that he would be willing to go to America as commander-in-chief as well as peace commissioner.[5] In so doing he probably reasoned that being commander-in-chief would strengthen his efforts in any negotiation. The king and all of the ministers, except the first lord of the Admiralty, welcomed Howe's offer. A majority of the Ministry, favoring a military solution to the rebellion, were glad to secure the services of such a distinguished officer and assumed that Howe would not allow his predeliction for peace to interfere with his conduct of the war. A minority, who still hoped for a negotiated settlement (among them Lord North), were delighted to have a commander-in-chief who was well known and popular in the colonies—a man who would do all that he could to preserve lives and restore imperial harmony. Outside the government, Howe's appointment to the American command was equally well received. The *Morning Post*, a newspaper that called for a vigorous repression of the rebels, reported that "no appointment ever gave more general satisfaction"; one of Lord Howe's friends described his nomination as "a most wise and popular measure"; and an inveterate placeman agreed that it was "in all lights a most happy event." [6]

Those ministers who selected Howe solely for his ability as an admiral had no illusions about his views on conciliation. They were, therefore, careful to see that his instructions for carrying on the war and making peace would not permit him to make concessions. Lord George Germain, who as colonial secretary had a large share of the responsibility for managing the war, was especially anxious to see that Howe would be narrowly bound. He tried at first to see if the peace commission might be abandoned altogether. When his efforts failed and when Howe refused to share his commission with someone of sterner views, Germain made sure that the commission would enable the admiral to do no more than receive colonial surrender. Until all congresses had been dissolved, royal officials restored, armed bodies disbanded, fortifications surrendered, and a local assembly had promised to obey the laws of Parliament, Howe could not undertake a negotiation. He might offer pardons, but until the rebels had fully surrendered he was not even to discuss a matter of such fundamental importance as taxation. Although Lord North had given Howe a plan for replacing Parliamentary taxation with colonial contributions for imperial defense, a plan under which the colonies would have granted an equivalent of not less than five or more than ten per cent of the sum voted annually by Parliament for the army, navy, and ordnance, he was to make no mention of the plan until the colonies had surrendered.[7]

Nor did the Ministry in drafting Howe's orders for carrying on the war leave much to his discretion. He was, first of all, to see that the Atlantic seaboard was tightly blockaded, thereby putting economic pressure on the rebels and denying them military supplies from Europe and the West Indies. In order that there might be no mistake about the way he was to deal with the colonists, the Admiralty gave him detailed recommendations for employing the 73 warships and 13,000 seamen that would initially make up the North American squadron. His cruisers were to provide asylum for royal officials and loyalists, retaliate against coastal towns that were in arms against the king, dismantle colonial merchantmen so that they might not be converted to ships of war, destroy all armed American vessels, clear the rivers of floating batteries and sunken obstructions, impress rebel seamen, and, whenever necessary, commandeer supplies. But Howe was not to confine his squadron to enforcing the blockade. He was also to cooperate with the British army in breaking the rebellion.[8] This cooperation promised to put a considerable burden on the fleet, for General William Howe, Lord Howe's brother who commanded the British army at Boston, planned to campaign about New York and in the Hudson River Valley (to isolate and starve New England and, if possible, to bring the Continental army to a decisive action).[9] Whatever Admiral Howe's views on reconciling the colonies, he could not have mistaken the government's desire for a vigorous prosecution of the war.

But when Admiral Howe joined his brother at New York in July of 1776, he promptly deviated from his instructions. Instead of waiting until the rebels had surrendered to open a negotiation, he at once attempted to discuss an end to the war. Although he arrived just after Congress had declared the colonies independent and although his brother doubted that the Americans would retreat before the Continental army had surrendered, Howe was determined to see if the rebels would respond to an offer of reconciliation. He began by issuing a proclamation that announced his appointment as peace commissioner with power to grant pardon and to declare at peace any area where constitutional government had been restored.[10] This done, he attempted to open a negotiation with General Washington. The American commander-in-chief at first refused to receive Admiral Howe's letters, saying they were improperly addressed; and when at last he agreed to meet with General Howe's adjutant, he said he understood the Howes were "only to grant pardons [and] that those who had committed no fault wanted no pardon."[11] For its part, Congress ordered Lord Howe's proclamation published "that the good people of these United States may be informed of what nature are the commissioners, and what the terms, with the expectation of which, the insidious court of Britain has endeavoured to amuse and disarm them."[12] Notwithstanding these rejoinders, the admiral made one last effort to avoid using force. In mid-August he tried to suggest, through an emissary, that he could offer a plan of fixed colonial contributions in place of taxation for revenue. Congress simply refused to reply. As one of Howe's juniors remarked, "It has long been too late for Negotiation, yet it is easy to be perceived, My Lord Howe came out with a different Idea. . . ."[13]

By mid-August, Lord Howe had come to accept the fact that force would have to be applied before the rebels would seriously think of making peace. But even his military decisions seemed to reflect a desire to spare as many lives as possible, to apply the least amount of force necessary to end the fighting. Indeed he had begun gathering a large part of his squadron at New York, leaving Charleston and the Chesapeake unguarded and only one frigate in the Delaware and two off Boston. He would, of course, have to keep a substantial number of ships with the army at New York, at least until the Americans had been driven from Long Island and Manhattan; but he should certainly have been able to spare more than one-tenth of his squadron for the blockade. Yet between mid-August and the first of December he rarely had more than seven or eight cruisers at sea, and none of these seems to have been engaged in retaliating against coastal towns or in dismantling potential warships.[14] The Americans, who were desperately short of military stores, took full advantage of the enormous gaps in the British blockade, importing before Christmas of 1776 more than 80 per cent of all the powder they consumed during the first two and one-half years of the war.[15] Considering Howe's desire for a reconciliation, his efforts to open a negotiation with the rebels, and the fact that he would soon instruct his captains to cultivate friendly relations with the colonists, his failure to establish an adequate blockade seems to have resulted from more than poor judgment.

Howe's arrival also appeared to affect his brother's conduct of the war. Until the admiral reached New York, General Howe had repeatedly declared that he not only desired a decisive encounter with the Continental army but also thought such an encounter essential for breaking the rebellion.[16] After his brother arrived, the general certainly seemed to abandon these views. Although the Continental army was divided between Manhattan and Long Island, and although British and American officers agreed that the British navy could have controlled the East River,[17] General Howe did not attempt to divide or trap his enemy. Instead, he planned to drive the Continental forces from Long Island, so that by placing his artillery on Brooklyn Heights he might also force them to give up New York City: he now preferred occupying territory to seeking a decisive victory. Nor did he deviate from his new design. After landing on Long

Island, he never asked more of the fleet than a diversion, and his brother never offered more. Even after the British army had driven the Americans into their lines at Brooklyn, trapping them against the East River, Lord Howe made no effort to block their line of retreat. When they fled across the river to Manhattan on August 29, at least one of the British captains was thoroughly disappointed: "had our Ships attacked the batteries [at Brooklyn], which we have been in constant Expectation of being ordered to do, not a Man could have escaped from Long Island." [18] General Howe had accomplished his first objective, but he had lost his finest chance for destroying the Continental army.

The Howes' performance during the remainder of the campaign of 1776, like that on Long Island, suggests that they were trying to end the rebellion with as little serious fighting as possible. Lord Howe had apparently convinced his brother that an overwhelming display of force might persuade the rebels to become once more contented and useful British subjects, whereas a series of crushing victories would leave the colonies desolated, hostile, and worthless to Britain.[19] Even before the rebels had fled from Long Island, the admiral was attempting to see if his brother's victory in the battle of Long Island had made the rebels more tractable. To this end he employed a captured American officer to tell Congress that he was empowered to discuss a permanent settlement and that he wished to confer before one side or the other was compelled to sue for peace.[20] Congress, firmly attached to its independence, wished only to discredit Howe and dispatched three delegates to do just that. After meeting with him on Staten Island, the Americans reported that he could only grant pardon and accept colonial surrender.[21] Frustrated once more, he was obliged to see what another application of force would do. When by landing on Manhattan above New York on September 15, the British had forced the rebels to give up the city without bringing on a major engagement, Lord Howe again paused to see if the colonists were ready for peace. Because Congress had demonstrated its unwillingness to negotiate, he now appealed directly to the colonists, inviting them to talk with the commissioners and suggesting that the king was disposed to grant considerable freedom to the colonial assemblies. So unsuccessful was this offer that he made no new overtures until the end of November.[22] By then the British had driven the Continental army away from New York with a succession of flanking maneuvers that were well calculated to win territory and avoid a decisive action. Only when the Americans refused to abandon Fort Washington did the British make a determined assault on the rebels.

Briefly in late November, it seemed that the Howes might have applied just the right amount of pressure to bring down the rebellion and produce a negotiated peace. After taking Fort Washington, the British had struck swiftly into New Jersey. The Continental army, demoralized by endless withdrawals and depleted by expiring enlistments, was no longer able to make a stand. On December 1, Washington decided to retire across the Delaware into Pennsylvania. At New York the British were elated to learn that Congress was losing its popularity, that loyalist strength was increasing, and that the Continental army was beset with internal quarrels. Many a redcoat began to think that the war would soon be over.[23] The Howes, hoping to exploit their advantage, issued a proclamation on November 30 that not only ordered the rebels to put down their arms and disband their congresses but also promised pardon to anyone who within sixty days would pledge his allegiance to King George III. If no important rebels accepted the offer of pardon, nearly 5,000 colonists did.[24] But before half the time for accepting pardon had expired, Washington managed to change the course of the war. On Christmas night he recrossed the Delaware to destroy a detachment of Hessians encamped at Trenton, and a week later fought a second successful action at Princeton. These two victories banished the illusion of British invincibility, restored American morale, and ended the Howes' hopes for a negotiated peace.[25] After Princeton the British army withdrew from western New Jersey to end a campaign that for Lord Howe and his brother had proved a great personal disappointment and for the

British government, a disaster. In their efforts to make the colonies useful and contented members of the empire, the Howes had lost a succession of opportunities to destroy the Continental army and, perhaps, the rebellion. Never again would the British government have so fair a prospect for a military decision.

After the British army had gone into winter quarters at New York and Rhode Island, Lord Howe at last concentrated on establishing a blockade. Although he ordered his ships to enforce the Prohibitory Act of 1775 and to take or destroy all armed colonial vessels, he recommended that his captains be lenient. They were to allow the rebels the "use of their ordinary Fishing-Craft or other means of providing for their daily Subsistence and Support, where the same does not seem liable to any material abuse" and to "encourage and cultivate all amicable correspondence with the said Inhabitants, to gain their good Will and Confidence, whilst they demean themselves in a peaceable and orderly manner. And to grant them every other Indulgence which the Limitations upon their Trade specified in the [Prohibitory] Act . . . will consistently admit: In order to conciliate their friendly Dispositions and to detach them from the Prejudice they have imbibed. . . ." Nor were the cruising ships to raid along the coast, lest such forays instruct the colonists in the art of defensive warfare.[26] In spite of these restrictions and the fact that there were not usually more than 20 cruisers at sea, the British blockade was far more successful during the first six months of 1777 than during any other comparable period of Howe's command. Between January 1 and June 30, 1777, the North American squadron took 277 prizes, an average of over 46 per month. During the first half of 1778, by contrast, the average was 35 per month, even though there were then more cruisers at sea.[27] But the blockade was not to be fully exploited. Lord Howe was unwilling to carry the war to colonial ports, where American ships might most easily have been destroyed; and he was all too willing to sacrifice the blockade whenever he might legitimately keep his fleet in attendance on the army.

While his cruisers spread out along the Atlantic coast from

Rhode Island and the Chesapeake, Howe remained at New York through the winter of 1776–77 searching for ways to reconcile the colonists. American victories at Trenton and Princeton together with adept political maneuvers—publishing accounts of British and Hessian atrocities, distributing supplies captured at Trenton among families that had been plundered by German mercenaries, and commanding all colonists who had accepted British pardon to renounce it or be considered enemies of the United States [28]—ensured the failure of the British proclamation of November 30. But in spite of all his disappointments, Lord Howe still hoped to open a negotiation with Congress. To this end he persuaded General Charles Lee, a high-ranking prisoner, to write to Congress, asking for an interview to discuss something of great consequence to himself and to America. Congress, agreeing that another negotiation could only impede its military efforts (it being "well known the conference with Lord Howe last summer had well nigh ruined our interest at the Court of France"), resolved to do all it could for Lee but refused to send a committee to meet with him.[29] It is little wonder that by April of 1777, Lord Howe declared he knew not "what were best to be done." [30] He had come to America to reunite the empire, but in nine months his efforts had earned him only rebukes from Congress and, as he would soon discover, the displeasure of his own government.

Up to February of 1777, most members of the North Ministry had been pleased with the progress of the war. Although the Howes were not acting with the vigor that the government desired, a succession of victories obscured the opportunities they had lost. But when on February 23 the *Bristol* reached England with news of Trenton and Princeton, the Ministry saw the need for enspiriting its commanders-in-chief. Approving Sir William's plans for invading Pennsylvania in 1777, Lord George Germain urged the Howes to raid the New England coasts, both to destroy rebel cruisers and to interrupt recruiting for the Continental army.[31] Above all, he recommended that they stop being lenient with the enemy: "I fear that you and Lord Howe will find it necessary to adopt such modes of carrying on the War, that the Rebels may be effectually distressed; so that through a lively Experience of Losses and Sufferings, they may be brought as soon as possible to a proper Sense of their Duty." [32] Scarcely had Germain completed his dispatches when on March 4 copies of Lord Howe's instructions for establishing a blockade arrived. What a striking contrast these instructions made with the secretary's recommendations. Both men proposed to end the rebellion: the admiral by cultivating "all amicable correspondence with the said Inhabitants" and granting them every indulgence "in order to conciliate their friendly Dispositions"; the secretary by bringing "a lively Experience of Losses and Sufferings" to the colonists. Yet in spite of Lord Howe's patent disregard for his orders the government was not prepared to do more than encourage him to change his methods. Because this was the first specific violation of his instructions and because he was a celebrated admiral with many powerful friends, Germain and Sandwich, first lord of the Admiralty, merely reproved him for showing too much generosity to the American fishermen and sent a Major Nisbet Balfour to call both the Howes to arms. [33]

Until the Ministry learned the result of Balfour's mission, it took no further measures to influence the Howes' conduct of the war. On July 10, however, Germain discovered that Balfour had failed: Lord Howe not only defended his leniency toward rebel seamen—saying that by allowing them to continue fishing he kept them from enlisting in the Continental army and navy —but he and his brother also refused to undertake raids against New England ports, because such raids would interfere with the "more important Operations of the Campaign." The Howes' arguments might well have stifled further criticism had they not arrived with news of a rebel sortie from New England in which four frigates and 14 smaller vessels had put to sea unopposed from Boston, Salem, and Marblehead on May 21. [34] The government needed no further proof that mistaken generosity was losing the war. Germain, determined to change the commanders-in-chief or their policy, applied irony in dealing with the Howes.

He was happy that the indulgence "shewn to the Inhabitants upon the Coast, in not depriving them of the means of Subsistence has had so good an Affect"; indeed, he continued, Lord Howe's blockade was so effective that American privateers were swarming about the British Isles. He hoped that the Howes might still undertake raids on New England and win the applause of their countrymen, who, if not strategists, would rejoice to see the bases of the privateers destroyed. Sandwich and the lords of the Admiralty, feeling no need for indirection, declared themselves "greatly astonished" that Admiral Howe had neglected to provide an adequate blockade for New England and that he had failed to send them intelligence of rebel preparations.[35]

Germain and Sandwich would have been even more distressed had they known precisely what the Howes were doing with the campaign of 1777. Lord Howe, seeing no prospect for bringing about a reconciliation and having little taste for prosecuting the war, seemed quite content to tie his ships to the British army for the duration of the campaign. General Howe, who intended to invade Pennsylvania by sea, seemed equally content to play out the campaign in elaborate maneuvers. While the fleet waited off Staten Island, the army expended the second half of June in a futile effort to bring Washington to a decisive action in New Jersey. Sir William wasted two weeks in abortive maneuvers and three more in preparing to sail from New York. Thus, the Howes did not reach the mouth of the Delaware until July 30. When the general then decided to go to Pennsylvania by way of the Chesapeake, he condemned his army to an additional three weeks at sea, delayed his arrival in Philadelphia by more than a month, and committed one-fifth of the North American squadron to a two-month cruise with his storeships. Although General Howe's extravagance affected the navy, Lord Howe seems to have been too demoralized to make an effective protest against the voyage to the Chesapeake.[36] Nor did the capture of Philadelphia restore his spirits. Pennsylvania was not, as the general had been told, teeming with loyalists;[37] and the brothers soon

discovered that they would have great difficulty holding Philadelphia if they could not drive the rebels from their forts on
the Delaware.

In fighting to open the Delaware the Howes were, for once,
unencumbered by political aspirations. Yet because they failed
to co-ordinate their efforts and because the Americans resisted
with extraordinary determination, this was one of the least successful of their undertakings. When Lord Howe arrived off
Chester on October 6, he discovered that the rebels were firmly
in control of the passage to Philadelphia. By fortifying Mud
Island at the confluence of the Delaware and Schuylkill rivers,
placing a chain of sunken obstructions in the main channel between Mud Island and the New Jersey shore (where they had
built a fort at Red Bank), and reinforcing the whole with a
variety of floating batteries, fire ships, armed vessels, and galleys,
the rebels effectively closed the river to all craft except boats of
very shallow draft, which might still pass up the secondary
channel between Mud Island and the Pennsylvania shore. To
dislodge the Americans, the Howes planned a concerted attack.
But when on October 22 the general's troops stormed the rebel
fort at Red Bank before the admiral's ships were in position,
the troops were repulsed and several British ships lost.[38] Profit-
ing by this lesson, which they might well have learned at Long
Island when the army attacked before the fleet was able to provide a diversion, the Howes finally took Mud Island by reserving
their troops until gunfire from the fleet had destroyed the American works. All of their efforts had, however, consumed more
than a month, and the Delaware was not open to Philadelphia
until November 23, two months after the city had been captured.[39]

While the Howes struggled for control of the river, their
differences with the government reached a crisis. On October 17,
Lord Howe received Germain's ironic congratulations on the
success of the blockade. He refused, temporarily at least, to be
baited by the colonial secretary, saying he was pleased that his
"conduct with respect to the inhabitants of the Sea Coasts on

this Continent, appear to have met with your Lordships approbation." [40] Sir William, for his part, did not possess such self-
restraint. Knowing that Burgoyne was in trouble, that he would
be blamed for failing to do more to assist him, and that the
capture of Philadelphia had been less decisive than he had hoped
—certainly not of sufficient importance to justify the loss of the
Canadian army—General Howe was ill-prepared to ignore Germain's irony. On October 22 he asked to be recalled, asserting
that as his recommendations were ignored he had lost the confidence of the government. He also went to some trouble to
detach himself from all responsibility for whatever had happened to Burgoyne. [41] A month later, after the Howes had had
an opportunity to discuss the consequences of Burgoyne's surrender, Lord Howe asked the Admiralty to name an officer to
replace him in case poor health should force him to resign. He
did not refer to the ministers' dispatches; nor did he do so until
early December, when he finally replied to the charge that he
had neglected the blockade of New England. The admiral then
admitted that the blockade was inadequate but argued that his
force was too small both to support the army and to contain
American privateers. [42] Although the government might well
have asked why he had waited so long to say that his squadron
was too small, the need for further debate had passed.

Burgoyne's surrender and the Howes' resignations forced the
Ministry to consider changes both in strategy and in commanders-in-chief. The loss of the Canadian army ended all plans
for occupying the Hudson River Valley; it impelled the Ministry
to concentrate on ending the rebellion through a blockade, a
series of raids on colonial ports, and land operations elsewhere.
When Burgoyne's defeat subsequently brought France into the
war, the British government subordinated raids against the
rebels to a retaliatory expedition against the French in the
West Indies. [43] But before this change in plan had taken place,
the British had also decided to change commanders. Although
the Howes' resignations were under consideration early in January, no final action was taken at that time. The brothers had

many powerful friends, including the king, and Germain and Sandwich had to be careful lest in removing the Howes they sacrifice their own political ambitions. By mid-February, however, Sir William had been ordered to give up his command to Sir Henry Clinton and Lord Howe told that he too might resign.[44] Because Clinton was in America, there was no further delay in relieving General Howe. The same was not true of his brother. Lord Howe had to wait for a successor, and while that successor was preparing to sail from England, France entered the war and the Ministry changed Howe's orders. He was told to retain his command until he had mounted an expedition against the French island of St. Lucia, sent troops to the Floridas, directed an evacuation of Philadelphia, destroyed a French squadron under La Motte Picquet that was reportedly bound for America, and sent reinforcements to the Channel fleet.[45]

Nor was the change in Howe's orders the only factor that would determine the length of his stay in America. Although La Motte Picquet promptly returned to Brest, the Ministry had scarcely concluded its secret dispatches of March 21 when it learned of a more powerful French squadron of 12 ships of the line and five frigates that was fitting at Toulon. This squadron, commanded by Count d'Estaing, was reportedly under orders to attack the British somewhere in North America or the West Indies. The king and Lord George Germain were anxious to intercept d'Estaing at Gibraltar but were dissuaded by Sandwich and the commander of the Channel fleet, who argued that such an undertaking would unduly expose the British Isles. Even though this decision made England more secure, it did nothing to protect British forces in America. When subsequent intelligence confirmed the earlier reports that d'Estaing was bound for America, the Ministry ordered Admiral Byron to reinforce Lord Howe with 13 ships of the line. But while contrary winds kept Byron in port, the Ministry, fearing an invasion of England, decided not to let him sail until it received confirmation that d'Estaing had gone to America. As a result of the Ministry's indecision, compounded by bad luck, Byron did not proceed to

New York until June 9, three weeks after d'Estaing had left
the Mediterranean. Lord Howe would soon be able to thank his
own government as well as the French navy for his summer's
employment.[46]

While in London the ministers took counsel in their fears, at
Philadelphia Howe was devoting the late spring of 1778 to preparations for giving up his command. On May 8 he received the
Admiralty's instructions of March 21 together with the news
that Admiral Gambier was appointed to succeed him. By then
he was heartily tired of being commander-in-chief and anxious
to carry out his orders and go home.[47] As he had heard nothing
of La Motte Picquet, he began at once assembling his ships at
Philadelphia to escort the expeditions ordered to St. Lucia and
the Floridas. Unfortunately for his hopes of a speedy departure,
the North American squadron was widely scattered in order to
intercept increasing numbers of armed French blockade runners.
Before he could assemble enough ships for the expedition to
St. Lucia, Sir Henry Clinton decided not to make any detachments from the army until Philadelphia was abandoned.[48] While
Sir Henry was making preparations to go to New York, Lord
Howe learned that La Motte Picquet had returned to Brest;
hence when finally he sailed from Philadelphia on June 18, he
did so with the expectation that he would soon be rid of his command. As Gambier had already reached New York, and as there
no longer seemed any danger of being interrupted by a French
fleet, Howe could expect to resign his command as soon as he
had dispatched the expeditions to St. Lucia and the Floridas and
sent part of his squadron to England.[49]

But Howe's plans for returning home were soon superseded
by the necessity of preserving his fleet from d'Estaing. Delayed
by calms and frequent groundings, his fleet did not reach the
mouth of the Delaware until June 28. On the following day as
he sailed north along the Jersey shore, he first learned of the
Toulon squadron. Germain's dispatches warned Howe of d'Estaing and told him that Admiral Byron was en route to Halifax
with a reinforcement.[50] News of the French squadron forced

Howe to defer the projected expedition to St. Lucia as well as his plans for resigning the American command. Herding the transports and warships to New York and dispatching cruisers to find d'Estaing, he prepared to put to sea with his warships in an effort to join Byron and attack the French.[51] He had scarcely begun the necessary preparations when his cruisers announced d'Estaing's approach: on July 7 he learned that the Toulon squadron had reached Virginia on the fifth; and on July 8, that they had been at the mouth of the Delaware the day before. There was no time to put to sea; indeed the British ships were not in position to defend the channel at Sandy Hook when d'Estaing arrived on the afternoon of July 11.[52] Although Lord Howe had the advantage of position (he promptly arranged all his larger ships so that their guns commanded the bar at Sandy Hook), and although his ships were better manned and in better repair than those of his enemy, the French had a marked superiority in firepower. Two 80's, six 74's, three 64's, and five frigates were more than a match for six 64's, ten frigates, and an assortment of smaller vessels.[53] But at New York position was all-important, and on July 22, d'Estaing, concluding that the channel off Sandy Hook was too shallow and narrow for his heavy ships, took his force to join General John Sullivan in an attack on the British garrison at Rhode Island.[54]

Having parried d'Estaing at New York, Howe was now faced with the problem of preserving the British garrison at Rhode Island. Temporarily, at least, his squadron was so inferior to d'Estaing's that he could do no more than send a warning to Rhode Island, order his cruisers to keep a close watch on the French, and hope that Byron would soon reach New York. While he waited at Sandy Hook, his force grew stronger: one 50-gun frigate arrived from the West Indies, a 64 and a 50 came in from Halifax, and July 30 the first of Admiral Byron's ships, the *Centurion* of 74 guns, anchored at Sandy Hook. Reinforced by two ships of the line and two heavy frigates and having learned from the *Centurion* that Byron was bound for New York, Howe prepared to put to sea at once to relieve Rhode

Island, where his cruisers reported the French had gone.[55] Although he said publicly that he intended to attack d'Estaing, his close friends believed that he would try to lure the French from Rhode Island and avoid an action until he had been reinforced.[56] Whatever his plans, he was ready to sail on August 2 but, detained by contrary winds, did not reach Rhode Island until August 9, by which time the French had begun landing troops in support of a much-delayed American offensive. Even then Howe was in time to relieve the garrison without attacking d'Estaing. When he learned that his arrival had persuaded the French to re-embark their troops, he decided to lie off Block Island, watching d'Estaing and waiting for Byron.[57]

Howe did not have long to wait. On the morning of August 10 the French, having no desire to be caught at anchor by the combined forces of Howe and Byron, took advantage of a northeast wind to sail from Rhode Island. D'Estaing apparently hoped to destroy Howe's squadron before it was reinforced. For his part, Howe had no intention of fighting the French except on the most favorable terms; he had little to gain by engaging d'Estaing before Byron arrived. When, therefore, he saw the French putting to sea, he immediately cut his cables and sailed south, waiting for a change in the wind that would give him the weather gauge and permit him to use his fire ships to offset the enemy's heavy guns.[58] After twenty-four hours, there being little change in the wind or in the relative position of the two squadrons (north and south of each other, eight miles apart), Howe decided to maneuver for a more favorable position. At eight in the morning he brought his line of battle from southeast to south, at ten to southwest, at eleven-thirty to west, and at one-thirty to northwest. Instead of changing course to match the British and thereby keeping their position relative to the wind, the French chose to press after the sternmost of Howe's line, closing rapidly as they did but slipping from the north to the east and then to southeast of the British.[59] By late afternoon Howe had nearly weathered d'Estaing; indeed his adjutant judged that one more change of course would have done so.

But by that time the wind and sea had grown so violent that another change of course was impossible, and as darkness and flying spray enveloped the two squadrons, both admirals turned their attention to the weather.[60]

The storm, which continued unabated until the morning of August 14, damaged and dispersed both squadrons. In its aftermath the French reassembled 75 miles east of Cape May, while the British straggled to their rendezvous at Sandy Hook. Howe and Sir Henry Clinton, assuming that d'Estaing would return to Rhode Island, began planning an expedition to relieve the British garrison. But before Howe could put to sea, he learned that d'Estaing had returned to Rhode Island, gathered several frigates left behind on August 10, and sailed again. Because he knew that several of the largest French ships had been dismasted in the storm, Howe felt sure that d'Estaing had taken his ships to Boston to refit; indeed he was so sure that he sailed directly for Boston in an attempt to intercept the French and to exploit whatever damage the storm had done to their ships.[61] Although he made the passage to Boston in five days, he arrived on August 30, two days behind d'Estaing. Realizing that the enemy was unassailable in Nantasket Road and that they would be detained a considerable time by repairs, he put back to Rhode Island to see if he might help the garrison.[62] But again he was too late. By the time he reached Newport, Clinton had not only secured the town and island but also sent an expeditionary force to Buzzards Bay and Martha's Vineyard. After remaining a few days off Rhode Island, Howe returned to New York, where on September 11 he turned over his command to Admiral Gambier. The arrival of most of Byron's ships had at last given the British naval superiority in North America and provided Howe with an opportunity to resign.[63]

When he was sure that Byron himself was at Newport and that the incompetent Gambier would not be left to face the French alone, Howe sailed for England.

Lord Howe's service in America was, with one exception, disappointing both to the admiral and to the government. The source of their disappointment lay in the incompatibility of their aspirations. Howe went to America to promote a reconciliation, though he was bound by instructions that required colonial surrender. He soon discovered that Congress would not accept his meager terms, no matter how sweetly he entreated them to do so. But he had come to America to save an empire, to make the colonists happy and useful partners with the mother country. Destroying the Continental army, devastating the Atlantic ports, and ravaging the colonies might produce a military victory, but such a policy would never, he thought, render the colonies useful to Britain. Howe resorted, therefore, to the only plan that seemed likely to make the rebels accept his terms without jeopardizing a reconciliation: a show of strength, a limited use of force, and repeated overtures to the colonists. This plan, which often sacrificed military opportunities, might have succeeded had not Washington spoiled the Hessians' Christmas at Trenton. By April of 1777, however, it was clear that the rebels were not to be threatened or coaxed from their independence and that the British government would no longer tolerate Lord Howe's half-measures. Without prospect of negotiating peace or of receiving ministerial support for his efforts, Howe turned listlessly to transporting the British army to Philadelphia. Here his service in America might well have ended, if chance and d'Estaing had not conspired to prolong his stay. His last two months in America were unquestionably his most successful; still, two months of skillful defensive maneuvering were not enough to banish the disappointments and frustrations of two years. For the admiral and the British government, his experiment in peacemaking had been a failure—the least significant portion of his long and illustrious career.

FOOTNOTES

1. Robert Roberts to Sir Charles Thompson, Boston, August 14, 1775, Hotham Papers, HO/4/16, East Riding Record Office, Beverley, Yorkshire; Admiral Keppel to the Marquis of Rockingham,

January 5, 1776, Rockingham MSS, Wentworth Woodhouse Muniments, Sheffield City Library, Sheffield, Yorkshire.

2. Julian S. Corbett, *Signals and Instructions, 1776–94* (Publications of the Navy Records Society, vol. XXXV [London, 1908]), pp. 17, 33.

3. J. Almon, ed., *The Parliamentary Register . . . Proceedings and Debates of the House of Commons*, 83 vols. (London, 1775–1804), XII, p. 166.

4. For a more detailed account both of the ministers' attitudes toward the rebellion and of Lord Howe's relations with the government see Ira D. Gruber, "Lord Howe and Lord George Germain, British Politics and the Winning of American Independence," *William and Mary Quarterly*, 3d ser., XXII (1965), pp. 225–243.

5. Lord Hyde to Lord North, January 10 and 11, 1776, the Clarendon Deposit, Bodleian Library, Oxford University.

6. *The Morning Post and Daily Advertiser* (London), February 6, 1776; Sir Charles Thompson to [the Earl of Huntingdon], February 15, 1776, Hastings MSS, Henry E. Huntington Library, San Marino, California; Hans Stanley to [Andrew S. Hamond], March 27, 1776, Hamond MSS, Alderman Library, University of Virginia.

7. Instructions for the Howes, May 6, 1776, Colonial Office Papers, class 5, vol. 177, Public Record Office, London (cited hereafter as C.O. 5/vol. number); separate instructions for the commissioners, May 7, 1776, Great Britain, Historical Manuscripts Commission, *Sixth Report of the Royal Commission on Historical Manuscripts, Part I* (London, 1877), pp. 400–401.

8. Admiralty's instructions to Howe, May 4, 1776, and to Graves, July 6, 1775, Admiralty Papers, class 2, vol. 1332, Public Record Office, London (hereafter cited as Adm. 2/1332, etc.); Admiralty to Graves, August 31, September 14, October 23, October 15, and September 14, 1775, Adm. 2/100; Admiralty to Howe, May 4, 1776, Adm. 2/101. Abstract of monthly disposition, July 1, 1776, Adm. 8/52.

9. General Howe to the Earl of Dartmouth, October 9, 1775, C.O. 5/92; to Lord George Germain, April 25, 1776, C.O. 5/93; and to Germain, April 26, 1776, private, Hist. MSS Comm., *Report on the Manuscripts of Mrs. Stopford-Sackville . . .*, 2 vols. (London, 1904–10), II, pp. 30–31.

10. Henry Strachey's journal, July 12, 1776, Hist. MSS Comm., *Sixth Report*, p. 402; Howe's proclamation of June 20, 1776, enclosed in Howe to Germain, August 11, 1776, C.O. 5/177; July 14, 1776, Edward H. Tatum, ed., *The American Journal of Ambrose*

Serle, Secretary to Lord Howe, 1776–1778 (San Marino, California, 1941), pp. 31–33.

11. July 14, 1776, Tatum, ed., *Journal of Serle,* pp. 32–33; George Washington to the president of Congress, July 14 and 22, 1776, John C. Fitzpatrick, ed., *The Writings of George Washington . . . 1745–1799,* 39 vols. (Washington, 1931–44), V, pp. 273–74, 321 fn–23 fn.

12. July 19, 1776, W. C. Ford, ed., *Journals of the Continental Congress, 1774–1789,* 34 vols. (Washington, 1904–37), V, p. 592.

13. Thomas, Lord Drummond to Howe, August 12, 1776, and Howe to Drummond, August 15, 1776, enclosed in Washington to the president of Congress, August 18, 1776, Peter Force, ed., *American Archives . . . ,* 5th ser., 3 vols. (Washington, 1848–53), I, pp. 1025–27; August 22, 1776, Ford, ed., *Journals of Congress,* V, p. 696; quoting Andrew S. Hamond to [Hans Stanley], September 24, 1776, Hamond MSS, Alderman Library.

14. Disposition of North American squadron, August 13, 1776, enclosed in Lord Howe to Philip Stephens, August 14, 1776, disposition, September 18, enclosed in Howe to Stephens, September 18, and disposition, November 27, enclosed in Howe to Stephens, November 27, Adm. 1/487.

15. Orlando W. Stephenson, "The Supply of Gunpowder in 1776," *American Historical Review,* XXX (1925), pp. 272–80.

16. General Howe to Germain, April 25 and July 7, 1776, C.O. 5/93.

17. Collier's journal [c. September 1, 1776], 35 MS 0085, National Maritime Museum, Greenwich, England; Washington to the president of Congress, August 31, 1776, Fitzpatrick, ed., *Writings of Washington,* V, pp. 508–09.

18. General Howe to Germain, August 10, 1776, Germain Papers, William L. Clements Library, Ann Arbor, Michigan; to Germain, September 3, 1776, C.O. 5/93; and Lord Howe to Stephens, August 31, 1776, Adm. 1/487. Quoting Collier's journal [c. September 1, 1776], 35 MS 0085, National Maritime Museum.

19. Although General Howe had talked of destroying the Continental army as the best way of ending the rebellion, he was at the same time anxious to promote a reconciliation: Mrs. Howe "flatters herself his [General Howe's] advice will be a little attended to, and she knows he wishes to have a peace that is creditable to both." Lady Sarah Bunbury to Lady Susan O'Brien, August 21, 1775, the Countess of Ilchester and Lord Stavordale, eds., *The Life and Letters of Lady Sarah Lennox, 1745–1826,* 2 vols. (London, 1901), I, p. 244.

20. September 3, 1776, Ford, ed., *Journals of Congress*, V, pp. 730–31.
21. John Adams to Mrs. Adams, September 6, 1776, Edmund C. Burnett, ed., *Letters of Members of the Continental Congress*, 8 vols. (Washington, 1921–36), II, pp. 74–75; September 17, 1776, Ford, ed., *Journals of Congress*, V, pp. 765–66.
22. Proclamation of September 19, 1776, enclosed in the Howes to Germain, September 20, 1776, C.O. 5/177. Because there was no time limit for claiming pardon, the rebels fought until desperate and then asked for pardon. Lisburne to George Jackson, December 22, 1776, Additions to the Manuscripts, 34,187, British Museum.
23. October 1, 24, and 25, November 1, 10, and 11, December 8, Tatum, ed., *Journal of Serle*, pp. 117, 128, 130, 135, 138–39, 155–56; Lord Rawdon to the Earl of Huntingdon, November 28, 1776, Hist. MSS Comm., *Report on the Manuscripts of the Late Reginald Rawdon Hastings* (London, 1928—), III, 188.
24. Proclamation of November 30, 1776, enclosed in the Howes to Germain, November 30, 1776, C.O. 5/177; December 11, 1776, Tatum, ed., *Journal of Serle*, p. 157; the Howes to Germain, March 25, 1777, C.O. 5/177.
25. William Eddis to William Eden, July 23, 1777, C.O. 5/722: "Previous to the unhappy Affair at Trenton the general Disposition of the Colonies tended towards a Reconciliation with Great Britain on almost any terms . . . but the Surprise of the Hessian Post, however trifling it might have been thought in a regular War was attended with the most prejudicial Consequences to His Majesty's Arms. It gave Spirits to the Demagogues, recruited their Forces—and enabled their Leaders to magnify in the most exagerating terms, the amazing Advantages that would arise from this unexpected Incident."
26. Howe to Sir Peter Parker, December 22, to Commodore Hotham, December 23, and to Hotham, secret, December 23, 1776, all enclosed in Howe to Stephens, January 15, 1777, Adm. 1/487.
27. Dispositions, January 15 and March 31, 1777, enclosed in Howe to Stephens, January 15 and March 31, 1777, Adm. 1/487. Lists of prizes in Howe to Stephens, March 31, 1777, Adm. 1/487, and in Howe to Stephens, October 24, 1777, October 23 and 30, 1778, Adm. 1/488. The one list that is now missing from the official correspondence may be found in the *London Chronicle* (London), July 12–15, 1777.
28. January 17, 1777, Tatum, ed., *Journal of Serle*, p. 156; Charles Stuart to the Earl of Bute, February 4, 1777, E. Stuart Wortley, ed., *A Prime Minister and His Son* . . . (London, 1925), p. 99; Wash-

ington's proclamation of January 25, 1777, enclosed in the Howes to Germain, March 25, 1777, C.O. 5/177.

29. February 21, 1777, Ford, ed., *Journals of Congress*, VII, pp. 140–41; Benjamin Rush to Robert Morris, February 22, 1777, Burnett, ed., *Letters of Members*, II, pp. 270–71.

30. April 17, 1777, Tatum, ed., *Journal of Serle*, pp. 212–13.

31. General Howe had been knighted for defeating the rebels on Long Island.

32. Germain to Sir William Howe, Nos. 4 and 5 of March 3, 1777, C.O. 5/94, quoting No. 4.

33. The Earl of Sandwich to Lord Howe, March 10, 1777, G. R. Barnes and J. H. Owen, eds., *The Private Papers of John, Earl of Sandwich, First Lord of the Admiralty, 1771–1782* (Publications of the Navy Records Society, vols. LXIX, LXXI, LXXV, and LXXVIII [London, 1932–38]), I, pp. 288–89; Germain to William Knox, June 11, 1777, Knox Papers, Clements; Lord Howe to Germain, May 31, 1777, Germain Papers, Clements.

34. Lord Howe to Germain, May 31, 1777, Germain Papers, Clements; Sir William Howe to Germain, June 3, 1777, C.O. 5/94; Lord Howe to Stephens, June 8, 1777, and intelligence from Captain Fielding enclosed in Howe to Stephens, June 8, 1777, Adm. 1/487; Stephens to Howe, August 20, 1777, Adm. 2/555.

35. Germain to Lord Howe and Germain to Sir William Howe, August 4, 1777, Germain Papers, Clements; Sandwich to Lord Howe, August 3, 1777, Barnes and Owen, eds., *Papers of Sandwich*, I, pp. 293–95; Stephens to Lord Howe, August 20, 1777, Adm. 2/555.

36. W. H. Moomaw, "The Denouement of General Howe's Campaign of 1777," *English Historical Review*, LXXIX (1964), p. 505.

37. Sir William Howe to Germain, November 30, 1777, C.O. 5/95.

38. Lord Howe to Stephens, October 25, 1777, Adm. 1/488; minutes of courts-martial for loss of *Augusta* and *Merlin*, November 26, 1777, Adm. 1/5308.

39. Lord Howe to Stephens, November 23, 1777, Adm. 1/488; November 23, 1777, Henry Cabot Lodge, ed., *André's Journal . . . June 1777 to November 1778 . . .* , 2 vols., (Boston, 1903), I, p. 121.

40. Lord Howe to Germain, October 18, 1777, Germain Papers, Clements.

41. Sir William Howe to Germain, October 22, 1777, C.O. 5/94.

42. Henry Duncan's journal, October 31, 1777, John Knox Laughton and W. G. Perrin, eds., *The Naval Miscellany* (Publications of the Navy Records Society, vols. XX, XL, LXIII [London, 1902–]),

I, p. 154; Lord Howe to Stephens, November 23 and December 10, 1777, Adm. 1/488.

43. Germain to Sir William Howe, February 18, 1778, and to Sir Henry Clinton, most secret, March 8, 1778; secret instructions to Clinton, March 21, 1778, all in C.O. 5/95. Secret instructions for Lord Howe, March 21, 1778, Adm. 2/1334.

44. Gruber, "Lord Howe and Lord George Germain," 242–43.

45. Secret instructions for Lord Howe, March 21, 1778, Adm. 2/1334.

46. Gerald Saxon Brown, *The American Secretary: the Colonial Policy of Lord George Germain, 1775–1778* (Ann Arbor, 1963), 149–73 gives a full and reliable account of the debate in the cabinet. For the idea that foul winds alone kept Byron from sailing between May 9 and May 13 see the King to Lord North, May 9, 1778, John W. Fortescue, ed., *The Correspondence of King George the Third from 1760 to December 1783*, 6 Vols. (London, 1927–28), IV, 138 and Sir Hugh Palliser to Sandwich, Spithead, May 12, 1778, Barnes and Owen, eds., *Papers of Sandwich*, II, 57–58.

47. Howe to Stephens, April 23 and May 9, 1778, Adm. 1/488.

48. Howe to Stephens, May 9, 1778, and disposition of American squadron, March 9, 1778, enclosed in Howe to Stephens, March 16, 1778, Adm. 1/488. Clinton to Germain May 23, 1778, C.O. 5/96.

49. Howe to Stephens June 10, 1778, Adm. 1/488.

50. Germain to Clinton, May 4, 1778, C.O. 5/95; Howe to Clinton, July 1, 1778 Clinton Papers, Clements; Howe to Stephens, July 6, 1778, Adm. 1/488.

51. Howe to Stephens, July 6, 1778, Adm. 1/488.

52. Howe to Clinton, July 8 and [July 8], 1778, Clinton Papers, Clements; Howe to Byron, July 8, 1778, in Howe to Stephens, July 11, 1778, Adm. 1/488; Duncan's journal, July 11, 1778, Laughton and Perrin, eds., *Naval Miscellany*, I, 159–60; captain's log *Eagle*, July 12, 1778, Adm. 51/293.

53. Captain John Montresor's sketch of Sandy Hook, showing the two fleets on July 22, 1778, G. D. Scull, ed., *The Montresor Journals* (Collections of the New York Historical Society for the Year 1881 [New York, 1882], opposite 505; list of d'Estaing's squadron bound with Admiralty's letter to Byron May 3, 1778, Adm. 2/1335; lists of Howe's and d'Estaing's squadrons in Germain Papers, Clements.

54. Alexander Hamilton to Washington, July 20, 1778, Harold C. Syrett and Jacob E. Cooke, eds., *The Papers of Alexander Hamilton* (New York, 1961-), I, 525–26.

55. Howe to Stephens, July 31, 1778, Adm. 1/488; Howe to Clinton, [July 30, 1778], Clinton Papers, Clements.
56. Sir William Howe to Henry Strachey, September 15, 1778, Strachey MSS, New York Public Library; George Mason, *The Life of Richard Earl Howe* (London, 1803), 43–44.
57. Captain Brisbane to Howe, August 9, 1778, enclosed in Howe to Stephens, August 17, 1778, and Howe to Stephens, August 17, 1778, Adm. 1/488.
58. Howe to Stephens, August 17, 1778, Adm. 1/488; Duncan's journal, August 10, 1778, Laughton and Perrin, eds., *Naval Miscellany,* I, 160.
59. Howe to Stephens, August 17, 1778, Adm. 1/488; Duncan's journal, August 11[–17], 1778, Laughton and Perrin, eds., *Naval Miscellany,* I, 162; captain's log *Nonsuch,* August 11–12, 1778, Adm. 51/64.
60. Duncan's journal, August 11[–17], 1778, Laughton and Perrin, eds., *Naval Miscellany,* I, 162; captain's log *Isis,* August 12, 1778, Adm. 51/484; d'Estaing to the secretary of the marine, November 5, 1778, Henri Doniol, *Histoire de la Participation de la France a l'Éstablissement des États-Unis D'Amérique,* 6 Vols. (Paris, 1884–92), III, 452.
61. Howe to Clinton, August 25, 1778, Clinton Papers, Clements; Howe to Stephens, August 25 and August 17, Howe to Fielding, September 2, 1778, enclosed in Howe to Stephens, October 25, 1778, all in Adm. 1/488.
62. Howe to Stephens, September 12, and Howe to Fielding, September 2, 1778, enclosed in Howe to Stephens, October 25, 1778, Adm. 1/488.
63. Howe to Byron, September 9, and to Gambier, September 11, 1778, enclosed in Howe to Stephens, October 25, 1778, Adm. 1/488.

BIBLIOGRAPHY

Anderson, Troyer Steele. *The Command of the Howe Brothers During the American Revolution.* New York, 1936. An imaginative study that is devoted mainly to Sir William Howe; it suffers, however, because Anderson relied too heavily on official correspondence and political pamphlets.

Barrow, Sir John. *The Life of Richard Earl Howe.* London, 1838. The only full life of Lord Howe. Not of much use to modern students of the Revolutionary War.

Brown, Gerald Saxon. *The American Secretary: The Colonial Policy of Lord George Germain, 1775–1778.* Ann Arbor, 1963. The best study of Germain, useful for following the development of British plans for the campaigns of 1777 and 1778.

Brown, Weldon A. *Empire or Independence, A Study in the Failure of Reconciliation, 1774–1783.* Baton Rouge, 1941. An examination of British peace efforts to 1778 that does little to show the relationship between Lord Howe's work as commissioner and as commander-in-chief.

Gruber, Ira D. "Lord Howe and Lord George Germain, British Politics and the Winning of American Independence," *William and Mary Quarterly,* 3d ser., XXII (1965), pp. 225–243. An attempt to relate British politics and political considerations to the conduct of the war in America.

Mahan, A. T. *The Major Operations of the Navies in the War of American Independence.* Boston, 1913. Still probably the best general study of the naval side of the American Revolution.

Mackesy, Piers. *The War for America, 1775–1783.* Cambridge, Mass., 1964. Puts British strategy in America into the context of a world war.

Willcox, William B. *Portrait of a General: Sir Henry Clinton in the War of Independence.* New York, 1964. The best biography of any British soldier, sailor, or statesman of the Revolutionary War.

Arbuthnot, Gambier, and Graves:

"OLD WOMEN" OF THE NAVY

WILLIAM B. WILLCOX

University of Michigan

THE British navy during the War of Independence, according to a writer of a generation ago, was in adversity.[1] He might with almost equal truth have said that it was in stupidity. The great struggles that came before and after the Seven Years' War and the Wars of the French Revolution, gradually taught the British Admiralty and admirals their business: competent men rose to command, and in the long run sound policies won out over stupid ones. No such progress occurred between 1778 and 1782. The Channel fleet was in the hands of a succession of nonentities. In the West Indies only Rodney and Hood distinguished themselves; one was a hard fighter and poor strategist, and the other seldom had scope for his talents. On the American station, after Lord Howe had returned home in dudgeon from his successful defensive in 1778, his successors were what their harassed colleague in the army, Sir Henry Clinton, called "old women," who strutted and fretted their hour upon the stage and accomplished nothing positive. The first of them, Gambier, had little chance to do harm. But the negative accomplishments of his two successors, Arbuthnot and Graves, were of great value to the American cause. Arbuthnot helped to prepare, and Graves presided over, the defeat of the Royal Navy in the Yorktown campaign.

The question of why Britain was so badly served at sea throughout the war is unanswerable, like most such questions in history; but some factors are clear. One is as simple as it is unscientific: plain bad luck, in men and in events. The navy was in a trough between two periods of energetic leadership; Lord Anson was dead, Lord Hawke superannuated, and the leaders of the future, Cornwallis and Collingwood, Jervis and Nelson, were too young for major commands. The field was left to senior admirals who were for the most part mediocre, and their operations were plagued by mischance—by storms that scattered the reinforcement needed for success, by the capture or delay of crucial dispatches, by sickness that incapacitated a fleet or winds that held it back until a few hours after the enemy had escaped. "There is a great deal due to us from fortune," wrote Lord George Germain in the summer of 1778; "and I hope our luck will turn before we are quite ruined." [2] Three years later he was still waiting for the turn.

But luck turns, it may be argued, only for those who deserve it; Germain was ignoring Bacon's maxim that "the mould of a man's fortune is in his own hands." The administration of which Lord George was a part had its deserts, according to this argument, because it did not know how to mould the fortunes of war. The king had the will to win, and some flashes of strategic common sense, but little influence upon military policy. Lord North had neither the will nor the acumen to be a war leader, and knew that he was not one. Neither was Lord Amherst, who after 1778 was commander-in-chief of the army at home and a member of the cabinet; he buried himself in the details of his office, particularly of patronage, and left the war largely to his colleagues.[3] The chief responsibility, in consequence, devolved upon two men in the cabinet, and neither one was fitted to bear it.

Lord George Germain, the secretary of state for the American colonies, was as determined upon victory as his royal master, and was the chief architect of military policy. He was therefore concerned perforce with naval affairs, because without the navy no British army could function overseas. He had an intelligent grasp of how sea power should be used, and did what he could to make his views prevail; but for all his forcefulness he could not impose them upon the Admiralty. There Lord Sandwich was autonomous. He and his service chiefs ruled the navy as their own preserve, and the first lord could vitiate even policies upon which the rest of the cabinet agreed. On Sandwich, more than on any other single man, depended the use to which British sea power was put throughout the war. The first lord did not deserve all the bad things said about him, at the time and since; nobody could. He was an experienced and competent administrator, much more competent than his enemies admitted. But he had two fatal flaws: he could not pick a winning strategy or a fighting admiral.[4]

As a strategist Sandwich was the chief designer of a policy at once defensive and supine, which almost lost the American war in the spring of 1778, and was a main factor in losing it three and a half years later. The crux of this strategy was detachment. The Bourbon fleets were not contained by a blockade in home waters, but left free to attack overseas wherever and whenever they pleased; and their attacks were parried by detaching squadrons from the home fleet. Such a policy tempted fortune because it rested upon hope—hope that the Admiralty could divine in advance where the blow would fall, that the squadron detached to follow would be equivalent in strength to the enemy, and that it would reach the threatened point in time to be of use. This was the way to lose a war, not to win it; and nowhere was the danger of losing more apparent than in American waters. It appeared in the first campaign against France in 1778, when Byron's detachment from England did not arrive in time; it appeared in 1779, when d'Estaing came north from the West Indies with no covering British fleet; it appeared in 1780, when Graves did not get out of Plymouth in time to join Arbuthnot and intercept the French armament bound for Rhode Island. Still the government did not learn. In the spring of 1781 it permitted de Grasse to sail from Brest for the West Indies with twenty ships of the line, sent no equivalent British force to the Caribbean, and thereby set the stage for Yorktown.

The Admiralty failed not only to provide the naval strength needed at the points of danger, but also to ensure the efficiency of ships already there. A program for sheathing hulls with copper to prevent their fouling was begun in 1778; it more than doubled the length of time that men-of-war stayed in service between cleanings and greatly increased their speed, but was not pressed hard enough to be effective on any large scale. A proposal made in 1778 to improve the New York dockyard fell by the wayside, and every commandant in that port was hounded by the problem of refitting damaged ships. "Choice of difficulties," was Gambier's wail, "and scarcity of means!" [5]

Sandwich cannot be held accountable for all the mistakes of his department, but for the choice of flag officers he can be. All he asked of an admiral, apparently, was that he should not make trouble for the administration; ability to make trouble for the enemy seems to have been less important. During the years of the French war, while the first lord was entrusting the home fleet to a succession of timid old men, command on the American station passed from one incompetent to another. Lord Howe's replacement was Admiral Byron, who lived up to his nickname of "Foul Weather Jack" by arriving too late to help in the campaign of 1778, and then departed after a few months. The command devolved upon the senior officer on the station until the late summer of 1779, when Arbuthnot appeared as Byron's successor. Two years later, on Arbuthnot's recall, the same thing happened: the luckless Graves was left in charge during the worst crisis of the war because Arbuthnot's replacement, Admiral Digby, had not yet arrived; and when Digby did arrive he declined to serve until the crisis was over. After Howe, in other words, the three titular commanders-in-chief were Byron, Arbuthnot, and Digby, a sorry lot; and their delays in taking up the post left it for long periods to officers for whom Whitehall had never intended it. This was hardly what might be called an enlightened personnel policy.

The policy should have been discredited by the first experience of how it worked. When Byron finally reached New York in the autumn of 1778, he was authorized to pursue the French fleet if it sailed for the West Indies, as it did. He followed, and left the American station to the man who had been Howe's second in command, Rear Admiral James Gambier. This outcome was precisely what the government had tried to avoid by appointing Byron in the first place. Whitehall was convinced, with good reason, that Gambier was unfit for the command. He had botched his former job as commissioner of the Portsmouth Navy Yard, and had then been sent to America only because he was too well connected to be forced into retirement. The king, Germain, and North all had a low opinion of him. The prime minister was blunt: "I have seldom heard any seaman speak of Gambier as a good naval officer or as one who deserved to be trusted with any important command." [6] Sandwich gave no sign of disagreeing with this opinion, yet he expected Gambier to take over Howe's position both as commander-in-chief and as a member of the Carlisle Commission for negotiating peace; the first lord apparently considered American affairs subordinate to political convenience. Perhaps because of his resistance, it was November before Whitehall tried to redeem its error by ordering Gambier home; and the order did not take effect until the following April.[7]

From the moment he arrived at New York in the summer of 1778, Gambier was slighted. He had such a cold welcome from Lord Howe that he complained of being in Siberia. When his chief sailed off to rescue the British garrison on Rhode Island, leaving him to co-operate on Manhattan with the army commander, Sir Henry Clinton, Gambier had an attack of convulsions that alarmed the doctors, and an attack of nerves that must have alarmed Clinton even more. The admiral oscillated wildly between fright and determination. "Crippled and dying as I am," he wrote Sir Henry, "do you want aught in my power, say

but the word and you shall [have] it, even was it my last shirt."
"For God's sake tell me what I am to do about the Halifax and
Quebec applications. . . . Pray tell me what you wish to have
done." "What in God's name shall I do about transports, should
you find occasion to send for reinforcements? They tell me it's
impossible to procure them. I tell them at this time even impos-
sibility must be overcome. I will try at least." [8] The crisis passed,
Howe left, and Gambier continued to be slighted. He was not
named to the Carlisle Commission, and Clinton and the other
commissioners ignored him; he fumed at being "a mere laborious
fitting admiral, or rather superintendent of a port, . . . uncon-
sulted and in a manner uncommuned with in aught material."
But almost in the same breath he declared that Clinton "is spirited, liberal, and communicative, and has the service much at
heart. We have two good months more to operate in, and much
may be done and probably will." [9] Nothing was.

What the admiral had in mind were coastal raids to cripple
American trade. Clinton never had much enthusiasm for a policy
of "conflagration," as he called it; and the last trace of enthusiasm disappeared when he discovered how clumsy Gambier was
in handling the transportation of troops. Friction between the
services, which had been at a minimum in the days of the Howe
brothers, was generated by this issue and continued to plague
the war effort until the end. Sir Henry had a simple solution,
which was to give him control over all amphibious operations on
the coast. "After five campaigns in this country," he burst out
after a frustrating experience with Gambier, "commanding at
every embarcation, do or ought I not to know more than this
same Admiral, who is . . . in every respect a horrid performer?"
"*Entre nous* he is the most impracticable man I ever met with." [10]

Gambier seems to have been widely unpopular. The loyalist
chief justice of New York, William Smith, shared Clinton's
opinion of him for different reasons. Smith always observed what
was going on with a censorious eye, and he concluded that Gambier was an aging fop. "The Admiral is sixty-four [he was in
his mid-fifties] and affects the gaiety of thirty. He is the con-

tempt of the town, the army, and the navy, and the companion of . . . another old coxcomb, who appears in this season (as well as the Admiral) at church in a satin waistcoat. They do not respect their own years." "Gambier is a fool, who will sacrifice a good service to his vanity." Another observer commented, when the admiral finally left for home in the spring of 1779, that his departure aroused "the universal joy of all ranks and conditions. I believe no person was ever more generally detested by navy, army, and citizen than this penurious old reptile." [11]

Gambier arrived in England to find that his career was over. Even though Sandwich continued to express his support, the hapless admiral was denied the promotion that had been promised him, and was ordered to strike his flag while junior colleagues were still flying theirs. He concluded, understandably enough, that the cabinet disapproved his conduct in America; and his only answer was "I could do no more!" "My reward," he wrote Germain, "for every unremitting exertion of zeal, fidelity, and disinterested conduct [is] painful and heartfelt neglect and ostensibility of reprehension." He was not at home as a letter-writer, as this bombast suggests; and he urged Lord George to excuse inaccuracies "from an officer whose ship has been the only university he has been permitted to study at for upwards of forty years." [12] The tone of his letter is fussy, pompous, self-justifying, and also pitiable. He was a failure in the eyes of his contemporaries, and he seems to have struggled hard to keep from agreeing with them.

For a few months after Gambier's departure the American command devolved upon Sir George Collier, one of the rare naval officers who had a gift for collaborating with the army; and in those months something approaching harmony reigned between the services. Collier carried out a raid in the Chesapeake, and then thwarted an attack from Massachusetts against the loyalist colony on the Penobscot River in Maine. But these were the sum of his achievements, because in August Vice Admiral Marriot Arbuthnot arrived to supersede him. Clinton was disgruntled. He would have preferred Collier, or any one of a

number of names that he had suggested to friends in England
and that the Admiralty had ignored; he concluded that Sandwich neither knew nor cared about America. "I heartily wish
Lord Howe was at the head of the Admiralty. He knows how
the navy on this station and in this war ought to be conducted,
and he would direct accordingly." [13]

Sandwich's direction, as represented by the choice of Arbuthnot, was far worse than Sir Henry yet realized. The appointment
was a major blunder. It seems to have been made with almost no
discussion, and its very casualness suggests the first lord's indifference to "how the navy on this station and in this war ought to
be conducted." The American command had taxed Lord Howe's
resources to the utmost in the campaign of 1778, and it did not
belong in the hands of a man whose long career had brought
him almost to seventy without revealing any outstanding talent.
Arbuthnot had been commandant at Halifax in the early years
of the war, and had recently acted as a judge in the court-martial
of Admiral Keppel. Neither of these services qualified him for a
post that required both tact and vigor—tact to get on with
Clinton, who was by this time notorious as a difficult colleague,
and vigor to meet the perennial threat of French sea power. Any
government that knew its business would have subjected the
admiral's record to searching examination, and would then have
immured him in some harmless sinecure.

Arbuthnot had no tact at all. When he tried to be friendly,
it was in a wayward, blundering fashion that could not stand re-
buff; and when annoyed he either was waspish or wrapped himself in stiff punctilio. His vigor was never sustained: outbursts of
activity, often misdirected, were sandwiched between periods of
somnolence. He could fight the enemy when he had to, but his
tactical ideas resembled those of General Howe at Bunker Hill.
His strategic ideas were, to use the most kindly adjective, dim;
and his sense of the need to collaborate with the army was even
dimmer. Throughout his tenure of command he insisted that
the navy must retain its freedom of action, and nine times out
of ten he refused to act; then, instead of accepting responsibility,

he devoted much time and attention to shifting the blame for inaction onto others. He fawned on his superiors, Germain and Sandwich; he quarreled with his equals; he bullied his subordinates while he was being manipulated by them. He was a timid man, in short, who covered his timidity with blustering.

At first all went reasonably well between him and Clinton. The campaign of 1779 had been abortive, largely because the admiral had arrived late and with troops afflicted by a raging fever. But Arbuthnot and Sir Henry were at once plunged into a flurry of activity. First came news that d'Estaing, who had attacked New York and Rhode Island in 1778, was again in American waters. He was thought to be bound once more for Newport, and the British commanders-in-chief agreed to evacuate the garrison there. But Arbuthnot blew hot, then cold, and could not make up his mind to carry through the evacuation; instead he talked of taking his squadron to Halifax, in case that turned out to be the French objective. He did not understand Clinton's reasoning, or Clinton his; and misunderstanding bred suspicion. The two colleagues communicated for the most part through an intermediary, to whom each poured out helpless profanity about the other. Fortunately for them, d'Estaing did not appear; he had chosen to attack Georgia instead of Rhode Island, and was repulsed before Savannah. As the crisis waned at New York, and the evacuation of Newport was finally completed, relative calm returned to headquarters, and Clinton and Arbuthnot gradually and tentatively mended their relationship. But the first test of their ability to work together had not been heartening.

A much larger test came soon. During the winter the British moved to the south with a large fleet and army, and in the spring of 1780 started a major operation with the siege of Charleston. Clinton had chief responsibility for the siege, and Arbuthnot only a supporting role. But the admiral confirmed his colleague's distrust of him by refusing assistance when needed, by hanging back when he had promised to go ahead, and by hiding behind a smoke screen of words and friendly overtures.

Clinton, now thoroughly on his guard, chilled the overtures with icy politeness. "In appearance we were the best of friends," he wrote in his diary; "but I am sure he is false as hell, and shall behave in consequence." Arbuthnot gave up hope of thawing him, and was hard put to it to maintain a semblance of cordiality. "So many circumstances occur in the course of business that I submit to only for peace, that keeps my command of temper so continually upon the stretch," he confided to Germain, "that I am apprehensive I shall not be able much longer to possess philosophy sufficient." [14]

The summer of 1780 stretched the admiral's philosophy to the breaking point. In June, just after the surrender of Charleston, he and Clinton left for New York, because they had received word that a French army under the Comte de Rochambeau, convoyed by a fleet commanded by the Chevalier de Ternay, was bound for the New England coast. The French intended to establish for the first time a base of operations in America by seizing Rhode Island, as Clinton soon learned from his American correspondent, General Benedict Arnold. The British had three possible ways to frustrate this intention. Clinton might reoccupy Rhode Island before the enemy arrived; Arbuthnot might intercept and destroy de Ternay's armament at sea, while it was encumbered with transports; or the army and navy together might attack after Rochambeau's troops were ashore and before they had time to refortify the old British works around Newport. Either a naval battle or a *coup de main* while the French were landing offered hope of a signal victory. But both depended on getting accurate and prompt intelligence of the enemy's whereabouts, and responding with equal promptness; the all-important factor was timing.

Clinton proposed seizing Rhode Island ahead of the French. Arbuthnot refused. He was skeptical of Arnold's information (he had reason to be, considering its source) and preferred to wait for reinforcements that had been promised him. The Admiralty was using the same policy of detachment that had miscarried with Byron two years before. This time Rear Admiral

Graves, with six ships of the line, was racing de Ternay across the ocean, and was expected to arrive first because his vessels were copper-bottomed and therefore faster sailers than the enemy. If Graves appeared in time, and could be promptly refitted at New York, Arbuthnot would have such force that he would need only to find the French at sea in order to destroy them. He had good cause to wait.

His chance of victory was much better on his own than in conjunction with the army, because he could not work with Clinton and knew it. "The fellow," he said of Sir Henry, "is a vain, jealous fool!" [15] But the admiral could not act alone unless he found the enemy, and this he failed to do. On July 7 he heard that his scouting frigates had encountered de Ternay off Virginia two days before, only to lose him again. No watch whatever, apparently, was kept off Rhode Island. Eleven precious days passed before word arrived on the 18th, through army intelligence, that the enemy had landed there on the 10th. They were presumably busy entrenching themselves. The first and second possibilities, of anticipating the French and of intercepting them at sea, were now foreclosed; the only chance left was to strike before their position became impregnable.

Graves, meanwhile, had reached Sandy Hook on the 13th. Although he was subsequently accused of having delayed en route, he had in fact made one of the fastest crossings on record; and his squadron, except for having seven hundred men down with scurvy, was in fighting trim. Arbuthnot realized that every minute counted, and he showed the energy of which he was sporadically capable. He had prepared to refit Graves' ships outside the Hook, to save the delay of getting them across the bar and into the New York dockyard. The job was done in short order, and volunteers replaced the sick. On the 19th—a mere six days after Graves' arrival—the combined squadron sailed to reconnoiter the enemy. It was a remarkable performance.

It was also the last sign of vigor in Arbuthnot during the campaign. His initiative was never of long duration, and in this case it may have evaporated because he feared to cooperate with the "vain, jealous fool." But he certainly had the means of doing so. His fleet, one 98-gun ship of the line, four 74's, four 64's, two 50's, and a heavy frigate, was substantially superior to de Ternay's one 84, two 74's, four 64's, and five frigates; the old admiral should at least have been able to contain the enemy squadron while British troops landed, and so Clinton thought. He bombarded his colleague with detailed plans. They seem merely to have antagonized Arbuthnot, who was not given to systematic analysis and could not be forced into it. He paid scant attention to Sir Henry's ideas.

They came by letter, for the general was far away, waiting with his army on the Long Island coast. The admiral, cruising off Rhode Island, had to make whatever decisions were going to be made. Would he choose between Clinton's plans or advance an alternative suggestion? Would he determine the enemy's position and strength? Above all would he commit the navy to assist the landing? The answers to all these questions turned out to be no. Arbuthnot did not say a word about how the attack should be made. He disparaged the reports of officers whom Clinton sent to reconnoiter, and obtained no information himself; after more than a fortnight within sight of the French he protested that he had no idea of their dispositions, or of "pretending officially to know their strength." [16] The fleet could take care of de Ternay but render no other help, the admiral concluded; and the army should not come unless it were ready to attack on its own. He was washing his hands of responsibility, in short, and dumping the dirty water on his colleague.

The fleet thereupon withdrew for refitting to Gardiners Bay, some fifty miles from Newport on the eastern end of Long Island. Clinton's troops returned to New York, and the episode seemed to be over. But no. The admiral may have been uneasy about the supine role he had played, or been afflicted with one of his unpredictable attacks of optimism; in any case he proposed that Sir Henry meet him at Gardiners Bay to concert immediate action. Clinton at once agreed. He made the difficult journey overland, and arrived to find the anchorage deserted.

A casual note from Arbuthnot, dated the same morning, informed him that the French were reportedly putting to sea and that he had sailed to intercept them. Not so much as a boat had been left behind to keep communications open.

This incident reveals more than the admiral's flair for discourtesy; it also shows his strategic muddleheadedness. A few minutes of lucid thinking would have told him that if the French were leaving Newport (as in fact they were not) he had no reason to rush off in pursuit but had, on the contrary, every reason to wait for a discussion with his colleague. What were the enemy up to? If they were evacuating Rhode Island entirely, they must presumably mean to attack somewhere else; and measures to counter the blow ought to be arranged at once. If they were leaving their troops and taking only their fleet, they were offering a golden opportunity for a combined assault on their base. In either case a conference between the British commanders was of the first importance, but this idea does not seem to have crossed Arbuthnot's mind. All he saw was what was immediately before his eyes, a chance for the navy to act alone.

His departure on this wild-goose chase ended the last hope of collaboration between the two commanders-in-chief. Clinton sent an ultimatum to the cabinet: either he or his colleague must go. In deciding between them the government delayed unconscionably. Sandwich, loyal to his appointee, found one difficulty after another in removing him. Germain was ambivalent, torn between the desire to replace Clinton with a more energetic general and the fear that the commander-in-chief's resignation would have serious political repercussions.[17] Almost eleven months passed between the contretemps at Gardiners Bay and Arbuthnot's departure, and in that time cooperation between the two services reached its lowest point of the war.

The navy maintained a blockade of the French at Newport, but in the age of sail no blockade was proof against accidents of wind and weather. At any moment the blockaded ships might escape and disappear at sea. In the background there always lurked the danger that they might be released by, and added to, an enemy fleet from Europe or the West Indies. Arbuthnot's naval superiority had always been precarious, and now that he had failed to crush de Ternay it was more so. The army, to make matters worse, was more dependent upon the navy than ever. The British now had two widely separated bases, New York and Charleston, that were connected and supplied entirely by water; Clinton, moreover, was about to make a move that would further disperse his troops and place a contingent of them within striking range of de Ternay, so that its only protection would be Arbuthnot's guard on Narragansett Bay.

In the late summer of 1780, Lord Cornwallis, whom Clinton had left to command in the south, was about to advance into North Carolina. He asked Sir Henry to establish a post on the Chesapeake, to keep the Virginians occupied at home and to impede the movement of enemy troops and supplies southward, through the narrow corridor between the Alleghenies and the bay. In December, after an earlier attempt had failed, Clinton sent an expedition to occupy Portsmouth, Virginia. As commander he selected his new brigadier general, Benedict Arnold, who three months earlier had failed to deliver West Point and had fled to New York. Arnold showed his usual energy, but Portsmouth was a dangerous position. His fortifications were weak, and he was within reach of both Washington's army and the French squadron. Even if the Americans had not been thirsting for Arnold's blood, he would have been a tempting target. In January, 1781, the enemy began to concert an attack upon him from land and sea. The first effort failed because the Chevalier Destouches, who had succeeded to the naval command at Newport on de Ternay's death, sent only one ship of the line. The failure intoxicated Arbuthnot, even though he was in wretched health at the time. He began to plan euphorically, quite on his own, for moving troops to Virginia, conquering it, and perhaps forcing a junction with Cornwallis. When Clinton, baffled and alarmed, inquired what he had in mind, he abruptly dropped the whole idea.

At the beginning of March, the enemy's combined operation

against Arnold began in earnest. Destouches escaped from Narragansett Bay with his entire squadron and headed for the Capes of Virginia, and Arbuthnot set off in pursuit. The situation resembled, on a smaller scale, that which recurred six months later at the climax of the Yorktown campaign: an American army and a French fleet were bound for the Chesapeake to bottle up a British force; Clinton dared not send reinforcements from New York by the best route open to him, the sea, until he knew that the way was clear; and his naval colleague was trying to clear it by finding and defeating the French fleet. Arnold's life, and the existence of his corps, depended on the engagement that Arbuthnot was seeking.

The British line had recently been reduced, through damage wrought by a great storm, to one 98, three 74's, three 64's, and a 50, a force approximately equal to the French. Arbuthnot's ships, being copper-bottomed, were faster; and when the two fleets encountered each other off Cape Charles on March 16 the British were in the lead. They immediately went about to pursue the enemy, who put out to sea. After a time Destouches doubled back, and the two lines engaged. The French were to leeward, where they could use their lower batteries; the British, heeling before a heavy wind, could not use theirs without letting in the sea through the open gunports. The two vans battered each other and then drew apart, but Destouches brought the rest of his line past the damaged British ships and battered them again. The French then disappeared out to sea, having inflicted more harm than they had received. Arbuthnot's squadron was in no state to pursue, and he expected his opponent to return to the Chesapeake. He therefore made for the bay himself, and settled down in Lynnhaven Roads to nurse his battle wounds.

He had certainly not achieved a tactical victory. His method of engaging, line to line, had been the orthodox one to which the Royal Navy had adhered since the Duke of York's Fighting Instructions in the second Dutch War. A battle on this pattern was rarely conclusive when the two fleets were of equivalent strength and competently handled, because their cannonading usually did as much damage to one as to the other. In this case the French had inflicted more, partly because of their final maneuver and partly because, being to leeward, they had had greater firepower. Their behavior, according to a British observer, had been most unsporting: they had first put Arbuthnot's van to the disadvantage of having to close with them in order to make them fight, and had then mauled it, "the French having in this as well as in all other actions during this war constantly persisted in avoiding an engagement." [18] Destouches did not avoid one; he courted it in his own way, and Arbuthnot obliged.

But for once, whatever his tactical shortcomings, the British admiral showed strategic common sense. The point of overriding importance was to save Arnold, and this he did by anchoring in Lynnhaven Roads. When Destouches took to his heels, he threw away the advantage that he had gained by his tactical skill; for he did not have the force to dislodge the British once they were in the bay. His hope of a combined operation evaporated, and he sailed back to Newport with nothing to show for his sortie. D'Estaing and now Destouches: for three years Bourbon sea power had been ineffectual, and the promise that it had once held for the Americans seemed like a will-o'-the-wisp. *Dis aliter visum.* On the other side of the Atlantic, six days after the action off the Chesapeake, Admiral de Grasse put to sea from Brest with twenty sail of the line.

The crisis that de Grasse soon precipitated in North America might have fallen upon Arbuthnot, if he had performed better in the action of March 16. But the reports of the battle that reached London seem to have overcome even Sandwich's loyalty to him, and he was finally recalled. By the time this order reached New York at the end of June, his quarrel with Clinton had reached the point where no combined operations were possible. The two men could not act alone and would not act together, but all Sir Henry saw was that the navy would not act. "Our old Admiral has at last left us," he reported. "It was cruel to keep him here nine months after they had promised to remove him, and that at a time when the most active exertion of the

fleet was necessary." [19] What would have happened if the two
men had continued to be yoked for a few more weeks, while
the campaign against Cornwallis was beginning to unroll, is an
interesting speculation.

Arbuthnot was not at best an agreeable man or a talented
admiral, but the situation into which he was thrown brought
out the worst in him. William Smith, who knew him well, believed that "he may be humored into any useful service." [20] No
one was on hand to humor him. He tried to make a confidant
out of General Robertson, the governor of New York, and to
use him as a go-between in dealing with Clinton (which only
incensed Sir Henry the more); but Robertson was an aging,
catty intriguer, who had no oil to pour on troubled waters.
Neither had Clinton. Sir Henry was coldly suspicious of whatever suggestions Arbuthnot made, and confused and annoyed
the old man by his own almost febrile planning. The admiral was
forced, willy-nilly, to play a lone hand. He played it according
to the rule book and to the best of his ability; but his best was
inadequate.

The same was true of his successor, Thomas Graves, upon
whom the command devolved on July 4. He had served well
under Arbuthnot, and had had the good fortune to be rarely in
his presence; his chief had left him in charge of the blockade and
had chosen for himself the comforts of New York. Graves was
courteous and hard-working, with none of his predecessor's iras-
cibility and none of Gambier's flights of fancy. Although his
letters give the impression of a colorless plodder, the new commander-in-chief won and retained Clinton's respect as few other
admirals did. Whether he deserved it is another question.

Graves was as uninspired a tactician as Arbuthnot, and lacked
the strategic foresight that his situation demanded. Perhaps he
sensed his own shortcomings; certainly he gave no sign of wel-
coming the command. The Admiralty had not intended him to
have it; although he was a relative and friend of Lord North, he
was passed over for Admiral Digby, his junior and a protégé of
Sandwich. Dut Digby was delayed in England till July, and did

not arrive until late September.[21] In the months that Graves held his post he seemed to discharge its responsibilities with unruffled calm. Under his smooth surface, however, was a vein of timidity as strong as Arbuthnot's, although he showed it in different ways. He did not alternate between optimism and gloom, unconsidered action and lethargy; as a planner he was almost as systematic as Clinton. But he found one reason after another for not putting the important plans to the test. He acted twice, once by going on a cruise for which he had insufficient justification, once by attacking the French after his best chance of victory had passed. The rest of his brief command he spent in preparing for moves that were never made, while the British cause went down to defeat.

By the time Graves took charge at the beginning of July, British headquarters knew that Rochambeau's army had marched from Rhode Island to join Washington near New York. A new naval commandant, the Comte de Barras, who had arrived from France in May to supersede Destouches, had expected to retire to Boston as soon as the army left him; but he had not done so, and this the British also knew. The French ships were riding at anchor, protected by only a corporal's guard of regulars and militia, and farther up the bay at Providence was Rochambeau's siege train. The chance of attacking the enemy was brighter than it had been since their first landing a year before, and the incentive to attack was greater than ever. For Clinton and Graves had information that Admiral de Grasse, from the West Indies, planned to visit the American coast during the summer. Although they assumed that he would be followed by an equivalent British detachment, there was every likelihood that he would be able to lift the blockade of de Barras and add those ships to his fleet. The importance of destroying them before de Grasse arrived was self-evident.

But Graves behaved as if no threat from the West Indies existed. In mid-July, just after he had told the Admiralty that he would take shelter from de Grasse, he put to sea to hunt off

Boston Bay for a convoy of enemy supplies from France. This decision is hard to account for. It wasted precious weeks in which Newport might have been attacked. It removed Graves from his favorable position between de Barras and de Grasse, where he could get timely intelligence of what was happening and make his plans accordingly, and put him far to the east of the crucial area. It inflicted further strain on his ships, still suffering from their engagement off the Chesapeake, and put two of them out of action when, a few weeks later, he needed them the most. Apparently none of these considerations occurred to him. All he said about the effect of his cruise was that it would immobilize the enemy, "as they would be unable to guess at the intention of the squadron." [22] A more ridiculous argument is hard to imagine.

He continued, even after his return to New York on August 16, to belittle the menace from de Grasse. Three weeks earlier a sloop had brought the first definite word from Admiral Rodney, in the West Indies, that the French were coming and that a British fleet under Rear Admiral Sir Samuel Hood would follow them. By the 16th, Graves and Clinton had strong indications of what Rodney had not known; that de Grasse was bringing his entire line of battle. This was a formidable threat, regardless of what help Hood might bring; and even Arbuthnot had realized two months before that the help might not arrive in time. On August 19 the Franco-American army left the Hudson and began marching toward the Chesapeake, and in the next few days British intelligence agents bombarded headquarters with reports that a great French fleet was approaching the coast. Graves might have been expected to run for cover. Instead he pooh-poohed the danger, and went on calmly planning with Clinton an attack on de Barras' squadron. If the reports he was receiving had any truth in them, such an attack would be madness; for de Grasse might catch and overwhelm the attackers.

Graves may conceivably have understood the danger better than his letters suggest, and have had no real intention of implementing his plans. But in any case the Rhode Island scheme blinded him to another possibility, which was as obvious as it was promising. The naval problem that faced him had four elements: his own and de Barras' squadrons, of approximately equal strength, and the two great fleets under de Grasse and Hood, which supposedly would also be equal. The question was which two of these four, the French or the British, would join forces first. If the British did, they would have the choice of attacking one or the other of the separated enemy fleets; speed was what mattered, and the speediest junction could be achieved where Graves knew that Hood had been instructed to make his first landfall, the Capes of Virginia. Common sense might have dictated taking the New York squadron there immediately.[23] Instead Graves placidly whiled away his time in port.

On August 28 placidity ended. Hood arrived, and the same evening came word that de Barras had put to sea. Admiral Hood looked and behaved, said William Smith, like a stiff Yankee colonel. But he injected into the calm musings of the commanders-in-chief a new sense of urgency and pugnacity, a single-minded desire to be at the enemy. If he had not been junior and therefore subordinate to Graves, the whole campaign might have gone differently. Yet Hood did succeed in galvanizing his superior, and three days after his arrival the combined fleet set sail for the Chesapeake. The story of the previous spring was apparently being repeated. But this time the British admirals, although they did not know it, faced far heavier odds than Arbuthnot had.

De Grasse had brought twenty-eight ships of the line. He had left French commerce and possessions in the West Indies unprotected, a bold gamble that succeeded because Admiral Rodney did not dream that the enemy would dare take it. Hood brought fourteen of the line, and only five at New York were serviceable; Graves consequently sailed with nineteen. De Barras was at sea with eight.[24] He was convoying Rochambeau's siege grain from Providence and was bound for the Chesapeake, where de Grasse had arrived on August 31. The moment the two French contingents joined, they would outnumber Graves' fleet by almost two to one—odds to give pause to any British admiral.

Graves was happily ignorant of what faced him, for he had accepted Hood's assurance that their combined strength would be a match for whatever the enemy might bring. On September 5, when the British fleet raised the mouth of the Chesapeake, its commanders began to discover their error. French ships came out of the bay in staggering numbers; one by one the sails appeared, until twenty-four of the line were in sight. De Grasse had left four to guard his anchorage; with the remainder he intended to lure the British out to sea and away from de Barras, who would thus be able to enter the Chesapeake unmolested.

The battle of the Virginia Capes that followed—probably more important in its results than any other naval engagement of the eighteenth century—was a pedestrian affair. The two fleets approached each other as usual in parallel lines, the French to leeward; fighting opened between the two vans, and as soon as it became intense the French bore away. Graves did what he could to produce close action all along the line, but his signal flags betrayed him. Most of his captains, fresh from Rodney's quite different school of tactics in the West Indies, did not know their new commander's mind; and he had either not had the time or not taken the trouble to tell them how to interpret his flags. When he signaled to close, and also flew intermittently the signal to keep the line ahead, the result was confusion. Hood did not bring his rear division into the fight at all, and he was subsequently criticized as bitterly as he himself criticized his chief.[25] Who was to blame is not clear, but the result is. The engagement was tactically indecisive and therefore a defeat for Graves, because he needed to win and the French did not. All de Grasse needed was to be left in possession of the Chesapeake.

The battle in itself did not determine who would have possession. During the next week, while the two fleets were maneuvering at sea, Graves had the opportunity to slip by his opponent and enter the bay. Hood and others have censured him for not doing so, in order to paralyze the operations against Cornwallis as Arbuthnot had paralyzed those against Arnold. But the comparison, when examined, breaks down. If Graves had taken this gamble he might have destroyed de Barras' squadron, which slipped into the bay on September 10 carrying Rochambeau's precious siege train; the British would also have disrupted the water communications upon which the approaching enemy army was dependent. But Graves and Hood had left New York before that army had given proof that it was bound for the Chesapeake. Against the likelihood that it was, and that Cornwallis was consequently in grave jeopardy, Graves had to balance the risk to his fleet, upon which the whole British position in North America and Caribbean rested. Only a bold man, perhaps only a foolhardy one, would have dared to bottle up his ships while a superior French force was in the offing. Graves made for New York.

When he arrived there, on September 19, some hope still remained. He had established that there had been twenty-eight French sail of the line in the Chesapeake on the 5th, and assumed that de Barras' squadron had already joined and was included in this total. Graves had had to destroy one of his own ships after the action; but two that had been incapacitated by his cruise and left at New York were in service again, two more were expected from Jamaica, and Admiral Digby was bringing three from England. These increments would bring the British line to twenty-five, which would have a chance against the supposed twenty-eight of the French. On the 23rd, however, arrived crushing news: de Barras had joined *after* the battle, Cornwallis reported, and de Grasse now had thirty-six.

In the weeks that followed, the naval commanders at New York squirmed and twisted to get around the stark arithmetic of reality. They promised Cornwallis to try to rescue him, but postponed the date of sailing over and over again. The dockyard, they said, was to blame; and certainly the government's failure to improve its facilities three years before was one factor in the delay. Another, just as certainly, was the admirals themselves. They faced a staggering problem. To rescue Cornwallis they would have to enter the Chesapeake in the face of a superior fleet that was presumably ready and waiting, would have to fight their way past it to the vicinity of Yorktown, embark the army, and then somehow fight their way out again. Could this be done? Clinton for one knew his *Macbeth;* perhaps the others did.

> If we should fail,—
>
> > We fail!
>
> But screw your courage to the sticking place,
> And we'll not fail.

Yet Macbeth, in failing, had lost only his life; the anxious members of the councils of war stood to lose more than that. If they sacrificed the one and only British fleet on that side of the Atlantic, Britain might lose Halifax, New York, Charleston, the West Indies, her whole position in the western hemisphere. Against the possibility of saving Cornwallis' army, in other words, had to be balanced the probability of imperial catastrophe.

Digby had arrived on September 24. Instead of assuming the command for which he had been commissioned he left it to Graves, perhaps understandably, and remained in the background throughout the crisis. Such influence as he had was negative, for he considered rescue as a desperate undertaking. The only admiral who pressed for action at any cost was Hood, who fumed at the delays and did all he could to overcome them. "He detest[s] the want of exertion he discovers now, and fears the fleet will get to the Chesapeake too late." [26] But Graves seemed to be in no hurry, and on him the chief responsibility rested. He was acting, said General Robertson, as if he thought of himself as already ruined; and as late as October 11 he reopened the question of whether to go at all. "You have engaged under your hand to go before," Hood answered, "and tomorrow is the day." [27] But tomorrow was not: still another week elapsed before the ships were ready. The very day that the fleet sailed from Sandy Hook, October 19, Cornwallis surrendered.

On that day a lot of naval chickens came home to roost. Graves had blundered through the summer, blundered in his one battle, and then taken a month to refit his ships. Digby had remained a spectator while events ran their course. Rodney had made fatal miscalculations in the West Indies and had then sailed for home. Arbuthnot had failed to dislodge the French from Rhode Island. Only Gambier, for lack of opportunity, had contributed little or nothing to the long chain of events that led to Yorktown. All the others had some measure of responsibility, whether their sins were of omission or commission.

But in a larger sense they were sinned against as well as sinning, for they were victims of a government that did not know how to prosecute a war. Lord North's administration never came to grips with the question that faced it from the spring of 1778 on, of how Britain should allocate her resources between the various theaters of operation. Trying to hold onto everything, once France and Spain intervened, was a recipe for failure, as the king realized at the start. "If we are to be carrying on a land war against the rebels and against those two powers, it must be feeble in all parts and consequently unsuccessful." [28] Yet for the next three and a half years Britain attempted not only to suppress the rebellion and protect all that she had elsewhere, but to make new conquests from the Bourbon powers. On the wisdom of this strategy North's colleagues were divided; and the division was particularly marked between the two ministers, Germain and Sandwich, who were most concerned with the war in America. After an abortive attempt at disengagement there, through the Carlisle Peace Commission, military operations were renewed and extended when Germain, intent on victory, encouraged Clinton to attack the south. But the prerequisite for victory was naval predominance, and Sandwich continued to treat the American theater as subsidiary. "Let not thy right hand know what thy left hand doeth."

Sandwich's attitude was revealed in the men he chose or permitted to command on the American station. About Gambier he presumably had no more illusions than any one else, or he would not have cold-shouldered him on his recall; yet the order of recall was not sent until months after it should have been.

By then selecting Arbuthnot, the first lord showed either his indifference to what happened on the station or a desire to put Clinton in his place, or conceivably both; no admiral could have been better calculated to rouse Sir Henry's hackles, and rousing them paralyzed the war effort. Graves was scant improvement as a commander-in-chief, but here Sandwich had no responsibility except as he may have contributed to the delay in Digby's appointment. As for Digby himself, he had only the negative distinction of refusing to exercise command. When all is said and done, the first lord bears a heavy share of blame for the quality of the flag officers who held the American post after Lord Howe relinquished it. Not one of them knew how to plan a campaign or win a battle.

Sandwich, and his underlings at the Admiralty, had an even heavier share of blame for the way in which the policy of detachment worked. Whether the policy itself was necessary because Britain was weak, or whether she could have done more than she did to blockade the Bourbon powers at home, is a question that has long been debated and can never be settled. But, assuming that blockade was not feasible, detachments could succeed only if they were sent at the right moment. A reinforcement that left too late, like Byron's in 1778 or Digby's in 1781, was doubly wasted: it weakened the home fleet and did not affect the outcome of the crisis overseas. Some delays were of course inevitable; the eighteenth-century bureaucratic machine was cumbersome and slow, and no amount of energy at home could avail against unfavorable winds in the Atlantic. In most cases, however, energy would have helped; and the place where it was most needed was at the top. If Germain had had the authority and prestige of Pitt in the Seven Years' War, officials and dockyards might not have made their preparations at such a dilatory pace. But Lord George had little influence over the closed preserve of the navy, and Sandwich did not have his heart in America.

The first lord was obsessed with the defense of the British Isles. This obsession, even more than the shortcomings of the administrative machinery, weakened the whole policy of detachment, which required daring quite as much as efficiency. Every ship detached from the Channel fleet to meet a danger abroad increased the danger of invasion at home, and the second danger was what Sandwich consistently emphasized. His stress upon it appeared as early as the spring of 1778, when d'Estaing sailed from Toulon, and reappeared throughout the war. Germain took the opposite position, that victory overseas would justify some insecurity in the Channel; here again, however, he had no control over the navy. "I think we have little to fear at home," he complained in the spring of 1780, "but Lord Sandwich will not risk this country upon any account, so that I apprehend we shall have some misfortunes abroad. . . ." [29] Refusal of all risk at home precluded, as Lord George implied, effective support abroad.

The ingredients of Britain's naval disaster off the Chesapeake, in summary, had long been present. One was a lamentable choice of men for the command. Another was the habit of sending reinforcements that were too little and too late. A third, and the most important, was the strategy of trying to hold onto everything while reaching for new gains. At the start of the international war in 1778 the government decided that Britain did not have the naval strength to assume the offensive; hence the policy of concentration in home waters. But this policy was not consistently implemented, and became as the years went by no policy at all. Clinton was permitted to scatter his armies along the American seaboard, relying on a naval superiority that by the summer of 1781 no longer existed; for by then British power in the Caribbean, which had risen and fallen erratically, was no longer adequate for the defense of North America. Planning at the Admiralty had become a patchwork of expedients. The enemy concerted one brilliant blow, and the patchwork fell apart.

FOOTNOTES

1. William M. James, *The British Navy in Adversity: a Study of the War of Independence* (New York, 1926). This book is more descriptive than analytical; the best critical evaluation of the factors in Britain's naval defeat is still, in my opinion, the final chapter of

Alfred T. Mahan's classic, *The Influence of Sea Power upon History, 1660–1783* (24th ed., Boston, 1914), pp. 505–41.

2. Historical Manuscripts Commission, *Report on Manuscripts in Various Collections* (8 vols., London, 1901–14), VI, p. 145. This section of the report is a calendar of the papers of William Knox, Germain's secretary; the originals are in the Clements Library of the University of Michigan.

3. See Piers Mackesy, *The War for America, 1775–1783* (Cambridge, Mass., 1964), pp. 20–24, 180–81.

4. A recent biography of Sandwich attempts to defend him in the teeth of historical opinion: George Martelli, *Jemmy Twitcher: a Life of the Fourth Earl of Sandwich, 1718–1792* (London, 1962). The author treats incompetent admirals as a cross that the first lord had to bear, rather than one for which he was responsible, and claims that his calamitous strategy succeeded. For a more balanced view see Mackesy, *op. cit.*, especially pp. 165–68, 175–76, 204. 308–09, 442.

5. Gambier to Clinton, November 13, 1778, Clinton Papers, Clements Library. See also William B. Willcox, *Portrait of a General: Sir Henry Clinton in the War of Independence* (New York, 1964), p. 214 fn. 3; Willcox, "British Strategy in America, 1778," *Journal of Modern History*, XIX (June, 1947), p. 104 and fns. 13–14; Mackesy, *op. cit.*, pp. 156, 285, 356, 400. Much of the material that follows is drawn from my *Portrait of a General*, which I cite only to document direct quotations.

6. G. R. Barnes and J. H. Owen, eds., *The Private Papers of John, Earl of Sandwich, First Lord of the Admiralty, 1771–1782* (4 vols., [London], 1932–38; Navy Records Society Publications, LXIX, LXXI, LXXV, LXXVIII), II, p. 39; see also pp. 40–41.

7. *Ibid.*, II, pp. 292–93; Willcox, *Portrait of a General*, pp. 229, 254 fn. 2; Mackesy, *op. cit.*, p. 219, fn. 1.

8. To Clinton, Nos. 1 and 2, August 27, 1778, largely printed in Willcox, *Portrait of a General*, pp. 249–50.

9. Barnes and Owen, *op. cit.*, II, pp. 318, 314; see also pp. 293–301, 304–06, 308–10, 312–13, 315–19, and Gambier [to William Eden], December 24, 1778, Benjamin F. Stevens, ed., *Facsimiles of Manuscripts in European Archives Relating to America, 1773–1783* (25 vols., London, 1889–98), XII, No. 1232. Gambier's complaints flowed across the Atlantic in an endless stream: his force did not deserve the name; he was reduced to flying his flag in a storeship; he was desperately short of frigates, the whole fleet was in a shocking state, and the dockyards were bare of supplies for

refitting; the Americans had a formidable naval force at Boston and were building in every harbor and inlet. If reinforcements did not come by spring, in short, disaster threatened.

10. Willcox, *Portrait of a General*, pp. 271–72.

11. New York Public Library: William Smith, MS. Diary, entries of February 4 and 9, 1779; Isaac Ogden to Joseph Galloway, March 8, 1779, Balch's Loyalist Letters, Bancroft Transcripts. For the Ogden reference I am indebted to my fellow contributor, Mr. Ira Gruber.

12. September 29, 1779, Public Record Office, C.O. 5/130/469–71, partly printed in Willcox, *Portrait of a General*, p. 274 fn. 6.

13. To the Duke of Newcastle, July 3, 1779, Clinton Papers, Clements Library. Howe was at the time under serious consideration for the Admiralty: Mackesy, *op. cit.*, pp. 244, 246.

14. Willcox, *Portrait of a General*, pp. 311, 319.

15. *Ibid.*, p. 325; see also pp. 308–09, 323–37.

16. *Ibid.*, p. 333 and the reference there to Clinton's memoirs (n. 8, *AR*). A year later the ineffable Commodore Johnstone behaved in the same way at the Cape of Good Hope; see Mackesy, *op. cit.*, p. 390.

17. Arbuthnot considered Germain his friend and benefactor, and according to rumor in New York, Lord George encouraged him to hold onto his post in order to force Sir Henry's resignation. Willcox, *Portrait of a General*, p. 400 and fn. 7; see also pp. 360–70.

18. G[eorge] Damer to Germain, March 26, 1781, Germain Papers, Clements Library, partly printed in Historical Manuscripts Commission, *Report on the Manuscripts of Mrs. Stopford-Sackville, of Drayton House, Northamptonshire* (2 vols., London, 1904–10), II, p. 207. See also Arbuthnot to Germain, March 21, 1781, Germain Papers, and Willcox, *Portrait of a General*, p. 376 and fn. 8.

19. Clinton [to William Eden], filed under July 4, 1781, Clinton Papers, Clements Library.

20. William Smith Diary, New York Public Library, entry of December 17, 1780.

21. Mackesy, *op. cit.*, pp. 421, 452.

22. Willcox, *Portrait of a General*, p. 415.

23. Rodney later claimed, quite erroneously, that he had urged Graves to meet the reinforcement in the Chesapeake. *Ibid.*, p. 412; French E. Chadwick, ed., *The Graves Papers and Other Documents Relating to the Naval Operations of the Yorktown Campaign, July to October, 1781* (Navy History Society Publications, VII; New York, 1916), p. 136, fn.

24. In March the French had captured the *Romulus,* a heavy British frigate, which they pressed into service in their line.

25. Graves expected the signal for close action to take precedence over that for line ahead, according to a recent writer, and was trying to order a slanting attack in line of bearing; his captains, however, had learned in the West Indies that the signal for line ahead overrode the other. He generously put no blame upon them, and explained to Clinton and to Sandwich that the indecisive result had been due to the signal book. But he never explained why he had not clarified his purpose in advance, as Nelson did before the battle of the Nile with captains whom he knew far better. See Richard W. Hale, Jr., "New Light on the Naval Side of Yorktown," Massachusetts Historical Society *Proceedings,* LXXI (for 1953–57; Boston, 1959), pp. 123–32; Willcox, *Portrait of a General,* p. 424, fn. 4; Mackesy, *op. cit.,* pp. 423–24.

26. William Smith Diary, New York Public Library, entry of October 10, 1781.

27. *Ibid.,* entry of October 13, 1781; see also Willcox, *Portrait of a General,* pp. 434, 436.

28. February, 1778, *ibid.,* p. 207. Sandwich said much the same thing. "We are upon the point of a war with France, and perhaps with Spain," he wrote in April, 1778; "an American war added thereto is, I fear, more than we are equal to." Barnes and Owen, *op. cit.,* II, p. 293.

29. Willcox, *Portrait of a General,* p. 214; for Sandwich's role in the naval crisis in the spring of 1778 see Gerald S. Brown, *The American Secretary: the Colonial Policy of Lord George Germain, 1775– 1778* (Ann Arbor, 1963), pp. 154–70. "This country, with such numerous enemies, must be ruined unless what we want of strength is made up in activity and resolution," the king wrote Sandwich in 1781. "Caution has certainly made this war less brilliant than the former; and if that alone is to direct our operations . . . it is easy to tell we must be great losers." (Quoted by Mackesy, *op. cit.,* p. 399; see also his quotation of Middleton's views, p. 448.) The danger of a full-scale French invasion of England was real to contemporaries, particularly during the great scare of 1779; but by hindsight their fears seem wildly exaggerated. Vergennes had no such idea. The logistical problem alone would have been gargantuan; and the Franco-Spanish fleet, even if the Royal Navy had not existed, was in no condition to hold the Channel for the time that would have been required. See Mackesy, *op. cit.,* pp. 194, 279–97, 307–09, 514.

BIBLIOGRAPHY

Barnes, G. R., and Owen, J. H., eds. *The Private Papers of John, Earl of Sandwich, First Lord of the Admiralty, 1771–1782*, 4 vols., Navy Records Society Publications, LXIX, LXXI, LXXV, LXXVIII. London, 1932–38. The principal collection of source material on the making of naval policy during the war. The papers are arranged chronologically, and the later volumes contain a large number of letters to Sandwich from Gambier, Arbuthnot, and Graves.

Beatson, Robert. *Naval and Military Memoirs of Great Britain, from 1727–1783*, 2nd ed., 6 vols. London, 1804. A work published so soon after the War of Independence that it is almost a primary source. It contains a great deal of useful material, particularly about naval operations.

Chadwick, French E., ed. *The Graves Papers and Other Documents Relating to the Naval Operations of the Yorktown Campaign, July to October, 1781,* Navy History Society Publications, VII. New York, 1916. This and the Sandwich Papers are the two major collections of printed source material on the British side of the naval campaign of 1781, and the editor's introduction is extremely valuable for an understanding of Graves.

Clinton, Henry. *The American Rebellion: Sir Henry Clinton's Narrative of His Campaigns, 1775–1782, with an Appendix of Original Documents,* William B. Willcox, ed., Yale historical publications, manuscripts and edited texts, XXI. New Haven, 1954. The appendix contains some letters from Gambier and Graves and a large number from Arbuthnot, though often merely excerpts. In the text Sir Henry describes at length his quarrel with Arbuthnot, and the formal language only partly veils his bias and bitterness.

Clowes, William L., ed. *The Royal Navy: a History from the Earliest Times to the Present,* 7 vols. London, 1897–1903. Still the standard large-scale naval history. The chapters on the War of Independence are by Alfred T. Mahan, and are much more detailed than his *Influence of Sea Power.*

James, William M. *The British Navy in Adversity: A Study of the War of Independence.* New York, 1926. The only book specifically on the subject, and valuable as a survey of the campaigns rather than for its judgments upon them.

Mackesy, Piers. *The War for America, 1775–1783.* Cambridge, Mass., 1964. An excellent discussion of the British war effort in all its aspects, the product of thorough research and balanced judgment. The author is particularly skillful in relating broad governmental policies to specific operations, and in bringing out the administrative difficulties and the paucity of resources that underlay Britain's clumsy war-making.

Mahan, Alfred T. *The Influence of Sea Power upon History, 1660–1783.* 24th ed., Boston, 1914. Chapters IX through XIV deal with the War of Independence in various theaters. Much of the presentation has been rendered obsolete by later research, but the final chapter is still a stimulating critique of the strategy employed by both sides.

Willcox, William B. *Portrait of a General: Sir Henry Clinton in the War of Independence.* New York, 1964. A survey, with Clinton for its focus, of the whole American war, from which the bulk of the material for this article is drawn.

Sir Samuel Hood:

SUPERIOR SUBORDINATE

DANIEL A. BAUGH

Princeton University

FEW British admirals involved in the Revolutionary War managed to survive without a loss of reputation. Samuel Hood was one of the few. Not that he became a naval hero: the fortunes of war failed to favor him with a great victory. But his decisions and actions in combat revealed the mind and spirit of a great admiral. When Hood retired from active service, Horatio Nelson judged him "the best officer, take him altogether, that England has to boast of; equally great in all situations which an admiral can be placed in." [1]

By temperament Hood was a man of action: "I never knew good to come from procrastination." [2] His decisiveness arose from a justifiable confidence he had in his professional knowledge and the great care with which he analyzed every strategic situation. Hood always understood that the enemy's difficulties might be greater than his own; this assumption freed him from the fears that often paralyze a commander and render him powerless to take bold action.

The vigor and clarity of Hood's thought were matched by his plain, blunt manner of speaking. This behavior frequently led to rough encounters with his superiors, but at the same time inspired loyalty in his subordinates. Hood was also esteemed by his colleagues because of an unselfish attitude toward his own career. To a degree quite rare in the Royal Navy, Hood refused to allow self-interest to interfere with his country's interest. This dedication was so unusual at the time that one is led to wonder from whence it came.

Like Horatio Nelson, Samuel Hood was a clergyman's son. He was born on December 12, 1724, at Butleigh, Somersetshire. Although his father was the village vicar and the family respectable, Hood possessed neither the connections nor the wealth necessary for a promising naval career. Most officers who wound up at the top in the eighteenth-century navy—and Nelson was no exception—were closely related to some person of influence; the upper ranks were filled with sons and nephews of admirals, captains, leading politicians, naval officials, and, of course, landed aristocrats. Hood began his career in 1741 at the age of sixteen, when he and his brother, Alexander, went on board the *Romney* to serve under Captain Thomas Smith. Tradition has it that the Hood brothers were introduced accidentally to Captain Smith when he stayed the night at Butleigh vicarage while en route to Plymouth. But it is almost certain that the introduction came through the Grenville family instead. Smith knew the Grenvilles well; Thomas Grenville was his first lieutenant at the time, and James Grenville had recently become the chief landowner in Butleigh parish.[3]

Like hundreds of other aspiring young candidates who had had a remote introduction to a leading political family, Hood received negligible support from his connection. Although the Grenvilles were influential and immersed in the factional struggles within Parliament, they had other more important protégés to look after. Later on, when Hood had acquired some status in the service, the Grenville family might have welcomed him. But he was never destined to come within the family's orbit or to acquire the attitudes that such a move would have implied. That he did not do so must be credited, in part, to the influence of Captain Smith, his superior.

Smith, the illegitimate son of Sir Thomas Lyttelton, was in many ways an unusual officer. Well-educated, unaffected, generous, and honest, he made scarcely any enemies. Although Smith understood the importance of powerful friends and political connections, he rarely allowed such considerations to guide his behavior. He relied, instead, upon performing good and faithful service. Staying clear of factions, he managed, nevertheless, to find friends everywhere and eventually to rise to flag rank. This lesson was not lost on Samuel Hood. Although Hood was not endowed with the easy manner and personal charm that had made Smith's course so easy, he followed a similar pattern in his own career.

At the outset, Hood needed help in the service. Unlike young men who could count on well-placed friends ashore to gain promotions for them, Hood was dependent on his mentor at sea. Under these circumstances, it was assumed that if Smith valued Hood, he would do his best to advance the young officer. And indeed, after serving out his required six years of apprenticeship at sea under Captains Smith, Thomas Grenville, and George Rodney, Hood was assigned to a squadron commanded by Smith and promptly promoted to lieutenant. His promotion came in 1746 and was not difficult to arrange because Britain was at war. Once peace came in 1748, however, Hood's prospects dimmed. The navy reverted to a peacetime footing and officers were discharged in droves.

Hood soon was cast ashore. In 1749 he married Susannah Linzee, the daughter of an important figure in Portsmouth politics. Married, and in his late twenties, he was understandably concerned about his future. Unless he could gain a promotion to captain and thus take post on the seniority list, a naval career would hardly prove worthwhile. There was no regular path of advancement from lieutenant to captain. To rise he would have to secure a command, and such an appointment would have to be made either by the Admiralty or by a commander-in-chief at sea (who had the power to fill vacancies). But in peacetime any employment was hard to get, let alone a post that would bring promotion.

Hood, however, was better off than most lieutenants. His education and manners were a cut above the average. More important, he had Smith's valuable support, and Smith, now an admiral, considered Hood "one of the foremost" of his protégés. Hood, in addition, was helped by his intimate connection with the Linzees of Portsmouth, who, though not to be ranked with the great families, could claim a modest measure of influence in the navy. Hood, therefore, did not remain unemployed for long. In 1753 he was assigned aboard a guardship in Portsmouth harbor. Although the post enabled him to be with his family and to serve with full instead of half pay, it was hardly a step toward professional advancement. He still yearned for a command and promotion.[4]

Hood thought for a time he might be assigned to the East Indies, but his first opportunity came from the other side of the world. The captain of the sloop *Jamaica* stationed at Charleston, South Carolina, was reported to be near death's door early in 1754. All in all there were enough possibilities for Hood to feel that at last he had "some chance of being a captain." Both his father-in-law and Smith were working hard in his behalf, and to strengthen his hand further Hood asked Sir Richard Lyttelton, who was very close to Lord Anson, the first lord, to "throw in a word." Despite the help of influential friends, Hood remained anxious. He feared, above all, that his connection with Portsmouth politics might do more harm than good and wrote to Smith: "All my friends here (as well as myself) are afraid his Lordship wants to put me off till after the election, and then will not do it unless Mr. Linzee will do everything he wants in regard to making aldermen. If so all will be over with me."[5] Political influence, Hood knew, could be a sword that cut two ways.

Whether Anson would have helped Hood will never be known. When Henry Pelham, the kingpin of the Ministry, died in the spring of 1754, Hood predicted that the resulting confusion might bring Smith's relations "more in play"; indeed, within three years the Pitts, Grenvilles, and Lytteltons were scattered throughout the top echelons of government.[6] One consequence of Pelham's death was the elevation of George Grenville to the treasurership of the navy, and shortly thereafter Hood received command of the *Jamaica*. Before the end of June, he said good-by to his wife ("my Susy") and sailed for America. "The parting was very severe," he wrote to Smith, "I did not think it would have affected me so much, but I find I love my sweet wench better than I thought for." [7]

Command of the *Jamaica* gave Hood the rank of master and commander, and he remained with the vessel for two years. In Charleston he was treated with great "civility and respect by all the best of the people" and admitted that if the assignment did not prove happy, it would be his own fault. Had peace continued, Hood hoped to bring his wife over, and wrote he would "then be happy indeed." But a war was brewing between the British and French in America, and Hood welcomed the coming conflict with enthusiasm and optimism.[8] Soon after war was officially declared, he received his promotion to captain. He took post on July 22, 1756, one month after his brother. Considering that peace had interrupted his career, Samuel had done quite well to rise to the rank of captain at the age of thirty-one.

Returning to England later in the year, Hood was eager for action. He wrote to Richard Grenville, now Lord Temple and head of the Admiralty Board, saying he was "no ways inclined to be idle" if a good command could be had. All he received at first, however, were temporary assignments. In the spring of 1757, he commanded three ships in rapid succession. In the third, the *Antelope*, he had an opportunity to demonstrate his ability. With considerable skill he drove the French frigate *Aquilon* ashore off the coast of Brittany, leaving her a total wreck. On this cruise, he also captured a small prize and a privateer. He fought so well that the Admiralty gave him a permanent command of the *Bideford*. Subsequently, he was promoted to the *Vestal*, a frigate of 32 guns. Once again he had occasion to distinguish himself. While en route to America in early 1759 the *Vestal* overtook a French frigate, the *Bellona*, also 32 guns, off Cape Finisterre, and after a three-hour battle forced her to surrender. Hood stayed with the *Vestal* for the rest of the war. After earning Rodney's praise for his conduct at the bombardment of Le Havre, he requested duty in the Mediterranean and spent three rather inactive years there.[9]

Although his benefactor, Admiral Thomas Smith, died in 1762, Samuel Hood hardly needed his help any more. He was well established, both socially and professionally. The same could be said of his brother. In 1758, Alexander married Maria West, a woman of position and wealth. It might be assumed that the 31-year-old Alexander took a 54-year-old bride for advancement rather than for love, but apparently such was not the case. Two years after the wedding, Lord Lyttelton reported: ". . . they live together like Celadon and Astraea in the first week of their marriage. He told me yesterday in a rapture that she was a *glorious girl*. Is not this a glorious proof of the power of Cupid? If a girl of fifty-six be loved at this rate, think what the charms of forty may do."

Alexander's marriage proved to be professionally valuable to Samuel. Maria West was intimate with the Lytteltons and also close to Hester (Grenville) Pitt, wife of the great William Pitt. The Pitts often stayed at Alexander Hood's house in London, and when their youngest son, James, chose a career at sea, he served part of his apprenticeship under Samuel.[10]

Samuel Hood was made commander-in-chief of the naval force in North American waters in 1767—an assignment that many captains had coveted. Although his base originally was to have been Halifax, rioting New Englanders forced him to spend a good bit of time at Boston in 1768 and 1769. His small force, ordinarily employed against smugglers, soon was called upon to transport troops to Boston. Hood himself was in favor of such coercive measures. In view of the colonial reaction to Parliament's revenue acts, he thought it "prudent and necessary" to be strong. Indeed, after the spirit of resistance spread to other colonies, he concluded that it had been a great error not to have shown more firmness in Boston right from the start. He abhorred the "rancorous and dangerous" revolutionary principles that were rapidly spreading among the Americans.[11]

The Admiralty's policy was to relieve commanders in time of peace every three years, and in 1770 Hood was replaced by Gambier. Before he relinquished his command, however, he raised one of his wife's brothers, John Linzee, to the rank of master and commander, and another, Robert Linzee, to captain.[12] Preferment for his relatives was about the only reward that Hood received from this tour of duty in American waters.

Returning to England, Hood enjoyed, once again, the comforts of guardship duty for a time. He established his household at Catherington, near Horndean, Hampshire, and traveled ten miles to work at Portsmouth. But in 1776 the years of inactivity came to an end. The Admiralty, in November, ordered the mobilization of all guardships, and Hood received orders to raise his ship, the *Courageux*, to full complement and to prepare for sea. Throughout most of the following year, he cruised in the Channel, protecting British merchantmen and trying to prevent French ships from carrying supplies to America. It was not an appropriate assignment for a 74-gun ship like the *Courageux*, but most of the frigates and sloops were employed elsewhere and the Admiralty had no other choice.[13]

By early 1778 it was fairly clear that war with France was imminent. Hood must have been aware of the possibility of a coming conflict and to have realized the great opportunities that war would bring to an officer of his rank. Nevertheless, on February 10, he discharged himself from the *Courageux*, resigned from sea service, and took up civilian employment as resident commissioner of the Royal Navy at Portsmouth Dockyard.[14]

Why did Hood leave the service at such a critical time? He later said he took the step not "from inclination," but "from a desire of giving accommodation to Government" in general and to Lord Sandwich in particular.[15] However, he probably had other personal reasons. His choice was between ambition and risk, on one hand, and ease and security, on the other. For the moment, he chose the latter. He was fifty-three, had fears for his health, and needed money. Moreover, the location of his civilian assignment was ideal. It is important to realize that Hood did not think he had irrevocably given up a career at sea; otherwise he might not have accepted the commissionership. Many officers in the past had taken up civilian employment in the navy and subsequently returned to active service without losing rank. Admittedly, it was risky to seek such employment in wartime, but Hood had not solicited the post he held. Moreover, although hostilities with the American colonists were underway, a major war involving European powers had not yet begun.[16]

As Britain prepared for such a war, Hood's thinking changed. The first months on his new job were marked by feverish activity as the navy plunged into full-scale mobilization. In May, the king himself visited Portsmouth Dockyard. "On quitting the carriage," George III wrote to his sons, "I instantly took every step necessary to quicken the sailing part of the fleet, and trust my directions will expedite the service." [17] The king's visit, no doubt, complicated Hood's administrative duties, but it carried also a reward. George III concluded that Hood was an officer who knew his business and granted him a baronetcy.

Hood now could not help looking at his career from a new perspective. He was Sir Samuel, an officer who was favorably noticed by the king. With a major war brewing, he indicated he was still available for sea service. "I think my Lord," he wrote to Lord North in June, 1778, "I may . . . say, that as an *officer* I stand fair & have good pretensions." At the same time, he took pains to avoid identifying himself with the Pitts and Grenvilles, who were members of the Opposition, and told North that not only in public business, but also "as a *private man*" he had "given great support" to the Ministry.[18]

Despite his change of heart, Hood was forced to stay on in the dockyard for the next two years. In the spring of 1780, he made another determined effort to get back to sea. The war had speeded up promotions, and Hood's name on the seniority list was reaching those who were close to being considered as rear admirals. Hood said he had "the mortification of seeing . . .

juniors placed in the road to glory and preferred to distinguished appointments." Writing to Lord Sandwich, he expressed his "very great desire of hoisting [his] flag and serving in the military line." [19] When his pleas got no results, Hood became impatient. He was irritated by the way he was being ignored by the first lord, but a friend told him that the king had good intentions toward him and advised Hood to be calm and to await further developments.[20] On September 16, 1780, a letter finally arrived from the Admiralty asking him whether—if there was a promotion of admirals—he would take his flag and go to the West Indies.[21] It was the chance of a lifetime, but surprisingly enough Hood turned it down.

Hood's excuse was ill health. His "stomack & Bowels" had given him some "very ugly" and alarming pains, and he claimed he had only a "short time" to live. Two days later, however, he wrote to Lord Sandwich that he was feeling much better, was eager to accept his flag, and hoped his offer had not come too late. And two days after that, on September 20, he reported that he was as "stout and well" as could be expected. All in all it had been a rather miraculous recovery.[22] In truth, to plead ill health was the conventional means by which officers refused assignments which they did not want or which were offered under circumstances they considered distasteful. To refuse on any other ground was to risk losing one's rank and half pay.

Why did Hood initially turn down an offer he plainly wanted? The evidence suggests that he was upset by Sandwich's handling of the Keppel-Palliser affair. The prejudiced manner in which the first lord dealt with the court-martial arising from Keppel's actions in the battle of Ushant cost the Royal Navy a number of fine officers who refused to serve. Samuel Hood came close to being one of them.

Unlike most of the discontented officers, who were shocked by the manner in which Sandwich used his powers as first lord to support Admiral Palliser, Hood was apparently upset by Sandwich's treatment of his brother. Alexander Hood had commanded the *Robust* in the battle of Ushant. Even before the court-martial, it was widely known that Alexander was partial to Palliser and "very adverse" to Admiral Keppel. When testimony revealed that Alexander Hood had altered his ship's log in such a way as to favor Palliser's case, the reaction was intense,[23] and he was *"sent to Coventry"* by his fellow officers.[24] He found himself, as his wife later remarked, "absolutely without support from any person whatever." [25] Even Sandwich abandoned him. The first lord had gone too far, and, eventually finding his position threatened, chose to wreck Palliser's career to save himself; it is not surprising, therefore, that he also turned his back on the unpopular Alexander Hood.[26]

Of Samuel Hood's private thoughts concerning his brother's conduct there is no record. It appears, however, that in his own deliberate way Samuel kept trying to help Alexander—even though his efforts were not always appreciated. Alexander in his bitterness over being denied preferment wanted Samuel to throw his influence at Portsmouth against the Admiralty and the government in the event of an election. But Samuel was not a man to plunge recklessly into opposition. There must be "some degree of consistency," he told his brother; Samuel had supported the Ministry in the past and must continue to do so. He agreed, nevertheless, to be "very strong and pointed" in discussing Alexander's position with those in power.[27]

Samuel's efforts in this regard were the most likely reason for his sudden change of mind in September, 1780. Alexander's name was slightly above Samuel's on the seniority list, and Samuel may have refused his flag on the assumption that his brother had been passed over for promotion. Either his assumption was incorrect or his letter did the trick, for the two brothers were promoted to rear admiral on the same date. Shortly thereafter Samuel hoisted his flag in the *Barfleur,* and by January, 1781, was in the West Indies with Admiral Sir George Rodney.

Because Hood was a junior flag officer during the American war, he performed nearly all his service as second-in-command. Like many other energetic men placed in a similar situation, he had trouble getting along with his superiors. His first com-

mander-in-chief, however, would have been a challenge to anyone. Rodney, ambitious and temperamental, inspired little loyalty
and was quick to suspect infidelity or hostility in others. Sandwich promised Rodney that he would not send him a "factious
person" as second-in-command. The immediate cause of Hood's
assignment, in fact, arose from the inability of the Admiralty
to find a suitable replacement for Rodney's previous second-in-
command, Hyde Parker, who had resigned in anger when Rodney blamed the poor conduct of the battle of Martinique on his
subordinates.[28] Hood was not factious and, indeed, had known
Rodney since 1744 when he served under him as a midshipman.
But the two men never were able to work out a compatible relationship.

For one thing, they were of an entirely different temperament.
Hood had an orderly mind; it was his habit to think things
through and anticipate difficulties. He felt that a man in a position
of responsibility should act according to some "rational well di-
gested plan"; men with "no method" were useless. "What a
misfortune it is," he wrote to his close friend, Sir Charles Middleton, "to have anything to do with men who are guided by whim
and caprice, instead of common sense!" [29] In sizing up Rodney,
Hood saw a man who admittedly had brilliance and imagination, but no taste for orderly planning. His superior, Hood
wrote, was a man whose manner of talking was "very extrava-
gant and extraordinary, but without much meaning," and whose
"unsteadiness" was such that he appeared to change his mind
every hour. Rodney appeared to be "governed by whim and
caprice, even in matters of the highest importance to the welfare
of the State." "[He] requires a monitor constantly at his elbow,
as much as a froward child." [30] Hood felt also that Rodney was
vain and more concerned with the impression he was making
than with winning the war.

One naval historian has claimed that Hood detested and hated
Rodney.[31] This impression is not quite correct. It was rather
that he mistrusted Rodney, and in this matter he was not alone.[32]
Whatever Hood thought of Rodney, however, he was never in-

subordinate; he argued and grumbled, but did as he was ordered. Rodney, on his part, acknowledged that Hood was as competent to command a squadron as himself.[33]

In February, 1781, within a month after his arrival in the West Indies, Hood was in command of a squadron and charged with a major responsibility. His task was to intercept a French squadron that had been spotted in the Bay of Biscay and was presumed to be bound for Martinique with urgently needed supplies under convoy. Both Hood and Rodney realized the possible consequences of failure to intercept these ships: the approaching French squadron, when joined with the six vessels already at Martinique, might outnumber the British force. If so, the initiative in the Caribbean would pass to the enemy.

Hood felt that every available ship should immediately be pressed into service. Therefore, he urged Rodney to take over the command off Martinique and to bring together all the ships in the area. But Rodney was too busy counting the riches recently captured at St. Eustatius. Because, as Hood commented, "The Lures of St. Eustatius were so bewitching as not to be withstood by flesh and blood," [34] he held operational command off Martinique from February to April. But Hood held it without liberty to station his ships as he chose.

The prevailing wind blows toward the Lesser Antilles from the east or northeast with great consistency, and its effect is reinforced by a current which moves from east to west at one to two knots. Thus the line of approach of any fleet destined for Martinique was fairly predictable: the French could vary their landfall in order to avoid interception, but not to any great extent. What Hood could not predict with much confidence was the size of the French force and the time it would arrive. Weighing the situation, he decided that the best place for his fleet was to windward of Martinique. Initially he cruised about forty miles northeast of the island with his frigates spread out still farther to windward. By mid-March, however, it appeared that the original intelligence reports were false. Rodney thereupon ordered Hood to bring his squadron to leeward into the channel between Martinique and St. Lucia, and Hood reluctantly obeyed.

Rodney's change of plan was influenced by a number of considerations. He wanted to keep the six French warships at Martinique bottled up so that they could not threaten the rich convoy he was planning to send home from St. Eustatius. At the same time he wanted to blockade the island, which was known to be desperately in need of supplies. Moreover, when the arrival of the French squadron no longer seemed imminent, the problem of refreshing Hood's men and supplying his ships with water, victuals, and stores had to be faced; if his squadron cruised to leeward of Martinique the ships could be refreshed at St. Lucia one by one.

Hood tried hard to reverse his chief's decision. He considered the interception of the French squadron and its convoy to be of overwhelming importance. For this reason, he believed that the only sensible British station was to the windward side of the island. Against Rodney's view that the interception could be made from leeward, Hood argued: "Should an enemy's fleet attempt to get into Martinique, and the commander of it inclines to avoid a battle, nothing but a *skirmish* will probably happen, which, in its *consequences* may operate as a defeat to the British squadron, though not a ship is lost and the enemy suffer most." Hood, like Rodney, assumed that the original intelligence reports had been wrong, but he was sure that the French squadron would appear ultimately. His plan was to refresh his squadron at St. Lucia in a body—running the risk that the French would arrive in the interim—and then to return to the windward station. The French squadron, he estimated, would be "numerous, probably twenty," and he urged Rodney to send from St. Eustatius any ships that could be spared. But Rodney held Hood to leeward and refused to reinforce him.[35]

Hood's predictions turned out to be correct. Blockading Martinique exhausted his ships, for it proved impossible to refresh them adequately one by one. Scurvy increased alarmingly, and victuals and stores ran low. When the French squadron of 21 ships of the line, accompanying a large convoy, was sighted off the southeastern tip of the island, Hood's force was by no means in the best condition for combat.

Admiral de Grasse, who commanded the French force, cautiously anchored on the windward side of the island. Hood, having been alerted by his frigates, spent the night working his fleet up against the wind. On the morning of the 29th, the French squadron, formed in a line of battle, came around the southern end of the island, and shielded the merchant vessels, which kept near the shore. Hood took his 18 ships southward on a port tack, sailing as close to the wind as possible. The French rounded Diamond Rock heading north, while Hood tacked back and forth in a fruitless effort to close the distance. With the two fleets cannonading one another at long range, the French store-ships gained the safety of Fort Royal harbor. At noon Hood gave up trying to move closer by tacking and brought his squadron to a standstill; as he wrote later: ". . . finding it impossible to get up to the enemy's fleet, I invited it to come to me." But de Grasse kept his distance.

When the contest was renewed the next day, the terms were no longer the same. Some of the British ships had been damaged and the French line now numbered 24 as the ships at Fort Royal joined de Grasse's fleet. Hood had to be wary. He attempted to take advantage of some capricious breezes to bring a portion of the French squadron to action, but at length decided the risks were too great and ran away to leeward. The French for a time gave chase, but in sailing before the wind they could not keep up with Hood's copper-bottomed ships.[36]

Hearing news of the French arrival, Rodney raced to join Hood, but it was too late. The initiative had passed to the French. While the British made repairs, took on supplies, and tried to refresh their crews at Antigua, the French launched expeditions against St. Lucia and Tobago. St. Lucia was saved by the fortunate arrival of three ships that had been cruising independently in the area. But Tobago was lost—largely because most of the

British squadron had to retire to Barbados to restore the health of the men who had cruised so long under Hood's command.[37]

At the end of May, with the hurricane season approaching, both sides began to prepare for the annual move to North American waters. De Grasse refitted at Martinique, went to Cap Français for a time, and then sailed on to North America. Rodney was directed by his orders to follow the French north with an equivalent force and to leave behind enough ships to defend the islands. Since Rodney had been told not to expect any reinforcements, he faced an impossible task. He correctly decided to leave the islands exposed; assigned two ships to convoy the homeward-bound trade; sent another to Jamaica for repairs; and selected a fourth to carry him home to England. The rest of the force, 14 of the line, he handed over to Hood with orders to proceed to North American waters. There was reason to think this diminished squadron, when joined with the ships at New York, would be sufficient to deal with de Grasse, for it was assumed that he would detach a substantial force to convoy home the French merchant vessels. But de Grasse left the French merchantmen sitting at Cap Français and took his full force, 28 ships of the line, to the American mainland.[38]

Hood sailed from the West Indies on August 10. His task was to locate de Grasse and, if possible, join with Admiral Graves in hopes of giving battle to one of the French squadrons—either de Grasse's or the one commanded by de Barras which lay in Narragansett Bay—before they managed to link forces. He made a good passage, and though he did not know it, beat de Grasse to the American coast. After looking into the Chesapeake and finding no sign of the French, he hurried on to New York, where he found Admiral Thomas Graves on August 28. Graves sent pilots to guide Hood's ships into the harbor for replenishing, but Hood was appalled at the thought of any such delay. He refused to enter the harbor, took a boat ashore, and in a conference persuaded his new commander-in-chief to put to sea immediately in search of the French.[39] Three days later, a British squadron of 19 ships of the line sailed for the Chesapeake, where on the morning of September 5 they found de Grasse coming out of the bay to meet them with 24. It was Hood's sense of urgency that brought the British squadron to the right place at the right time. The stage was set for the battle of the Virginia Capes.

The British had fewer ships, and most of their officers were not accustomed to working under Graves. Nevertheless, at the start of the battle the British enjoyed certain advantages. The wind was NNE on the starboard quarter as they bore down in line toward the bay entrance. They were coming upon an enemy hurriedly getting underway and struggling to form a line of battle. In fact, the van of the emerging French fleet was well ahead and to windward of the rest. It was this tactical situation that led Hood to comment after the battle that "the British fleet had a rich and most delightful harvest of glory presented to it, but omitted to gather it in more instances than one." Hood thought that at least three opportunities presented themselves for concentrating the full force of the squadron upon the exposed French van.[40] But such a thought never seems to have entered Graves' mind. As Graves neared the enemy van, instead of attacking he waited. In fact, Graves "brought to [stopped] in order to let the centre of the enemy's ships come abreast." [41]

What Graves had in mind was the standard form of eighteenth-century naval engagement: an exchange of broadsides with two lines of ships sailing parallel on the same course. His problem was a long-standing one for an attacking fleet—how to bring ships down close to the enemy without disordering the line or exposing the fleet to serious damage. There were two standard methods of attack. His line could slant down in column and each ship, upon reaching the proper distance for close engagement, could bear up parallel to the enemy. This method had the advantage of keeping the line tight and in good order; it was safer, moreover, because it afforded more certain mutual support. But this method had certain inherent disadvantages: the slowness with which the whole force was brought into action; and the possibility that the line might jam up if the leading ships lost speed and maneuverability as a result of damage to their upper-works, thus interrupting or halting the attack underway. The other method was to signal a close engagement—that is to order all ships to bear down simultaneously on the enemy line, each seeking its opposite number. The advantage here was speed and the certainty of bringing the whole force into action; the dis-advantage being the possible confusion and disorder which might lead to separation and losses.[42] Graves decided to attack in col-umn. By 3:45 in the afternoon, however, it seemed that the dis-tance was closing too slowly and he gave the signal for close en-gagement. In response to this signal the whole squadron should have turned toward the enemy, but it did not. The reason was that the signal for maintaining the line also continued to fly on the flagship.

For the ships in the van, the simultaneous signaling of the line of battle and close engagement caused no confusion. These ves-sels were close enough to the enemy to answer both signals, and, by means of some minor maneuvering, they were soon hotly engaged and taking considerable punishment. But for the ships in the rear, under Hood's command, it was a different matter. Their opposite numbers in the enemy fleet were at a great dis-tance and it was almost impossible to single them out. Moreover, the ships in the rear could not possibly come to close engagement without temporarily disrupting the line of battle; for them, the signals were contradictory. What should they do? Hood watched the movements of Graves' flagship, the *London*, in the center of the British line. Perhaps she would make clear, through man-euvering, the intentions which her ambiguous signals failed to convey. But the *London*'s movements failed to provide him with an answer. At first, she turned downwind to attack; but then she bore up and opened fire at a range that could hardly be con-strued as close engagement. The *London* thereupon gave signals for dressing up the line. These signals resulted from Graves' anxiety to keep his van in good order, for it was under heavy fire and beginning to bunch up. But Hood, who was in the rear, assumed that the commander-in-chief was much more concerned with the integrity of his line of battle than with close engagement. According to Hood, the signal for the line continued to fly on the *London* until 5:25. When he saw it hauled down, he moved his division closer and fired a few inconsequential shots at long range. The French force at this point fell away to leeward and Hood did not pursue; he found his division was already to leeward of the *London,* which was apparently making little effort to carry out her own signal to engage. At 6:30 both fleets ceased firing and the battle was over.[43]

The fiasco of September 5, insofar as it was a matter of poor execution rather than missed opportunities, arose from the failure of Hood's division to take part in the action. The British were outnumbered, their van had taken a beating, and yet seven ships in the rear had scarcely fired a shot. For this failure, Graves, Hood, and the inadequacies of the signaling system and fighting instructions have all been blamed. The fighting instructions, it is said, placed a fatal overemphasis on maintaining the line, and therefore so did Graves and Hood. In all these criticisms, the assumption has been that nothing should have stood in the way of bringing the entire squadron into a general engagement.

Hood's critics imply that he should have disobeyed the signal to remain in line.[44] Hood, however, valued the power and safety afforded by the line and thought that the battle could have been fought effectively without disrupting it. Certainly he realized that his division should get into action. The question was: Should it get into action at all costs? [45] As he saw it, the best plan of attack for the inferior British force was to concentrate a tightly formed line upon the French van. Being in the rear, Hood had no way of encouraging such a plan through independent action. His only option—aside from staying in line as he did—was to take his division down into the midst of the enemy main body. But a decision to risk a showdown on such terms—involving as it did the over-all strategic situation—was one which a subordinate officer had no right to make. It could only be made by the commander-in-chief, and Graves gave no indication of any desire to risk everything in order to come to grips with the enemy; both the signals and the maneuverings of his flagship revealed caution and uncertainty.[46]

Naval historians, in retrospect, have felt that the risks should have been taken. The safety of Cornwallis' army depended on control of the Chesapeake; such control was bound to be contested by de Grasse; therefore, de Grasse should have been defeated before he was joined by de Barras. But these matters which seem obvious in hindsight, were not obvious to Hood and Graves. In fact, so far as de Barras was concerned, both admirals misunderstood the situation; they thought that de Barras had already joined de Grasse. The idea that de Grasse might bring all his ships to North America seemed so incredible that the British admirals were unable to realize he had done so even while fighting such a force. They did not learn the staggering truth until September 23, when word came from Cornwallis that the French fleet, then united in the Chesapeake, numbered 32 of the line.[47]

In respect to the other points, Hood showed himself to be far more perceptive than his superior. He understood the crucial necessity of controlling the Chesapeake. On September 10, when the British squadron lost touch with the French, Hood urged Graves to hurry back to the bay. But it was too late; de Grasse was already anchored there. Later, while the British squadron was refitting at New York, Hood was furious at the lack of any sense of urgency on the part of either Graves or General Clinton. Hood insisted that a rescue mission should be attempted at once. "*Desparate* cases require *bold* remedies," he wrote. But the refitting dragged on and his superiors decided to await the reinforcements coming out with Admiral Digby. The British relief expedition did not leave New York until October 17 and it arrived too late to be of any help. Cornwallis had already surrendered.[48]

With the close of the Yorktown campaign, Hood turned his attention to the coming operations in the West Indies. Realizing that the French squadron would initially outnumber the British, he pressed Admiral Digby, the new commander-in-chief in

North American waters, to lend him all of his ships of the line for the winter. Digby was reluctant. He probably feared he might not get the ships back in the spring, and thus lose some opportunities for prize money. Hood offered to share equally any prizes that he took while the ships remained with him. This generous offer—which reveals Hood's unusual readiness to place the national interest above his own—apparently worked, for Digby gave him the ships.[49]

Hood sailed for Barbados, surmising that the French would attack there first. He correctly anticipated the enemy's intentions, but the French were twice rebuffed by high winds. Hood realized that in order to defend Barbados he must expose the less valuable Leeward Islands. Thus, on January 14, when he learned that the French had been sighted off St. Kitts, he hurried to leeward. But by the time he arrived off St. Kitts, the only pocket of resistance left was the stronghold on Brimstone Hill on the northwest side of the island.

Hood had hoped to surprise the French squadron in the early morning at its anchorage in Basseterre Road. Unfortunately, two of his ships collided during the night and the resulting delay gave de Grasse time to weigh anchor and form a line of battle to leeward. Hood then decided to occupy Basseterre Road himself. As he told Middleton, "I thought I had a fair prospect of gaining the anchorage he left, and well knowing it was the only chance I had of saving the island, if it was to be saved, I pushed for it." [50] Perhaps his mind was still on what he thought might have been done for Cornwallis at Yorktown. Coming up from the south, he steered his line, which numbered 22 as opposed to 25 of the French, close to the lee shore of Nevis and St. Kitts. He gave every indication of preparing to engage, but when his leading ship was opposite Basseterre Road, he gave the signal to anchor. Each ship turned upwind and anchored in succession. It was a daring maneuver—since it involved deliberately masking part of his firepower and also exposing his ships to a raking from astern as they turned up to anchor—but Hood's execution was perfect and his move a brilliant success.

De Grasse was furious at being outwitted and the next day attempted to drive the British from their position. But the anchored ships were in tight formation and had springs out to their anchor cables which enabled them to aim their broadsides. De Grasse's superior force was driven off and suffered heavier losses than the British sustained.

Hood's flawless maneuvering, however, could not save St. Kitts. The besieged British garrison was ten miles from the fleet. The only hope was that Rodney—whom Hood had been "impatiently" expecting since mid-January—would arrive from England with enough reinforcements to drive off the French fleet and leave the enemy army high and dry.[51] With his victuals running low and his men falling ill, Hood held on, but his hopes were dashed on February 12 when the garrison on Brimstone Hill surrendered. Hood knew that it would only be a matter of time before the French army dragged its guns to a nearby shore, making the roadstead untenable. Yet waiting for him off shore was a French squadron now numbering 29 of the line. On the afternoon of the 14th, therefore, he assembled the captains of his squadron and outlined a plan. All the officers synchronized their watches and at eleven that night, without signal, the ships cut their cables and silently slipped away.[52] Thus the British fleet was saved to fight another day.

The effort at St. Kitts had not been entirely fruitless. Hood's presence detained the French and limited their conquests to St. Kitts and the neighboring islands of Nevis and Montserrat. By the end of February, 1782, the period of French supremacy was over as Rodney joined Hood and took over command. Rodney brought with him 12 ships of the line from England and five more were soon to arrive. De Grasse was also expecting reinforcements, but of the five ships sent to him, only two arrived.[53]

Despite the superior size of their force, things did not go well for the British at first. De Grasse, who was at Martinique, lay anxiously awaiting a convoy from France. Without it he could not carry out the projected Franco-Spanish assault on Jamaica. Hood and Rodney knew about the convoy and were bent on intercepting it. But they disagreed—as they had in a similar situation the previous year—on the best method for doing so. Once again, Hood's estimate of the situation proved to be the correct one.

Hood's plan was to divide the British fleet, which now numbered 36 ships of the line, sending half to cruise to windward of Point Salines, and the other half north, to windward of Guadeloupe. His reasoning was that even if the French escort numbered as many as 14 warships—which was highly unlikely—each British force would be sufficiently powerful to overcome the enemy. As for de Grasse, Hood doubted that the French admiral would venture out. If he did, the two British fleets, being to windward, could easily join in time to meet him. Rodney, on the other hand, was convinced that the French would make for Point Salines and refused to let Hood go further north. Hood argued: ". . . the commander of the French squadron must be a madman to think of coming in sight of St. Lucia, knowing, as he must, the force of the British fleet, which would naturally be upon the look out." [54] But Hood's arguments were to no avail.

The French convoy, with only three escorting warships, did in fact steer clear to the northward, made its landfall at Désirade (just to windward of Guadeloupe), and ran down safely between Marie Galante and Dominica to Martinique. Hood was beside himself when he learned the news: "How Sir George Rodney could bring himself to keep his whole force to guard one path, when half of it was fully equal to the service, and to leave another . . . without any guard at all, is matter of the utmost astonishment to me." [55]

De Grasse finally came out of Fort Royal on April 8 with the Jamaica expedition under convoy. His plan was to proceed to Cap Français along the islands, and, in the event of an attack, to send his transports into a friendly harbor. But the British caught up with him off Dominica. Both fleets were slowed down by calms in the lee of Dominica's mountains; this meant that as their vans worked clear to the north and picked up the sea breezes they became separated from the main forces. As a result, the

British van, Hood's division, was subjected to an assault by a superior French force on April 9. Hood might have been in serious trouble if de Grasse had thrown more ships against his force, for the becalmed British main body could not have come to his aid. But de Grasse's tactics were, for the moment, entirely defensive. After sending his transports into harbor at Guadeloupe, he tried to work up to windward and escape through the Saints passage. When, on the night of the 11th, a collision disabled one of his ships, de Grasse fell back to leeward in an attempt to shield the straggler, and that brought him within reach of the British.[56]

The fleets met at eight the next morning. While they were exchanging broadsides on opposite courses with the wind from the east, the breezes suddenly veered southward. De Grasse's ships, already sailing close to the wind, were forced to fall off toward the enemy; the French line became confused and gaps soon appeared in the formation. For the British, the situation was quite different; the wind had veered aft and they were thus given the choice of maintaining their line on its northerly heading or turning to starboard and knifing through the French line. As a gap opened in the French line opposite the *Formidable*, Rodney's flagship, he steered for it. In spite of the fact that the signal to engage from leeward flew from the *Formidable*'s mast throughout the maneuver, she was followed by the ships in her wake.[57] Not only did these vessels follow, but the *Duke*, the next ship in front, cut through the French line, and Commodore Edmund Affleck in the *Bedford*, the sixth ship aft of the *Formidable*, seeing the flagship's maneuver, also cut through the French line. He was followed by Hood's entire division.

The consequences were staggering to the French. Their fleet was now divided into three ill-formed segments. The ships in the center segment, which contained de Grasse's flagship, the *Ville de Paris*, were unable to maneuver and wound up in a cluster. On each side the British sailed by in column, firing furiously. They could hardly miss.

When the British had passed through to windward, Rodney

signaled close engagement. Hood, like the others, worked fever-
ishly to get back into the thick of the fight, but his division lay
nearest the lee of Dominica and could scarcely maneuver. Not
until late afternoon, when the battle was nearly over, did Hood
again approach the French. He saw the *Ville de Paris* give some
indications of challenging him. Having observed the punishment
she had been taking all afternoon, he guessed correctly that de
Grasse might be looking for a flag officer to whom to surrender,
so Hood steered his ship, the *Barfleur,* toward the French admiral.
The *Barfleur* was virtually undamaged, and her crew was fresh.
After ten minutes of withering fire, honor was satisfied and de
Grasse struck.[58] More men were killed on the *Ville de Paris* alone
than in the entire British fleet. The remaining French ships fled
in disorder downwind and five were captured.

Although Hood acknowledged the battle of April 12 to be a
great victory, he was by no means satisfied with the results.
Since the French were shattered and the British had many good
ships left after the clash, why had Rodney not led a vigorous
chase? Why was no attempt made to maintain contact with the
enemy during the night? The day after the battle Hood went
aboard the *Formidable* and begged Rodney to pursue the enemy.
Rodney said that he would, but did nothing. Hood was disgusted
and in a rage wrote to his friends:

> Sir George Rodney seems to be satisfied with having done enough
> as probably to save Jamaica and keep his popularity alive; but,
> good God! not to avail himself of the manifest advantage his most
> complete victory gave him is not to be thought of with any degree
> of temper. We might as easily have taken the whole of the French
> fleet . . . I find all this wasting of time here is to take the Ville de
> Paris to Jamaica with him. Such is the vanity of the man, he can
> talk of nothing else, and says he will hoist his flag on board her.
> Would to God she had sunk the instant she had yielded to the arms
> of his Majesty! We should then have had ten better ships in lieu of
> her.[59]

In the weeks that followed, Hood was like a man possessed; he
could not dismiss from his mind the golden opportunity that

had been lost and avidly collected every scrap of evidence that showed the vulnerability of the fleeing enemy squadron.[60]

The British fleet eventually went into Port Royal, Jamaica, to refit. Rodney pleaded illness and left to Hood the task of supervising the refitting. While Hood labored in the yard day and night, his disrespect for Rodney became greater than ever ("he is undoubtedly as well as I am"). Indeed, Hood took perverse pleasure in the fact that a broken leg excused him from attending a banquet given in Rodney's honor by the people of Jamaica. How could people celebrate—above all how could the commander-in-chief celebrate—as if Britain had won the war! Obviously, Hood was weary and sick at heart. The misfortunes of his country and the endless months of frustration he had suffered as second-in-command were eating away at his spirit.

Hood guessed that Rodney soon would be relieved by a senior admiral, and he pretended he did not care who it was. "[I] shall not repine if I am relieved also," he wrote Middleton.[61] In reality, he hungered for the West Indies command himself, but would not admit it. As matters turned out, he had to endure the additional frustration of serving under Rodney's replacement, Admiral Hugh Pigot.

The task of Pigot's squadron in the summer of 1782 was to search for a French squadron under the Marquis of Vaudreuil which was thought to have gone to the American mainland. Hood outlined for his new chief an imaginative plan of action, but to no avail.[62] While Hood worried over the possible courses of action open to Vaudreuil, Pigot calmly bore toward New York with some prizes in tow and refused to make any detachments to gather intelligence. "If he will risk nothing," Hood lamented, "and suffer himself to remain in ignorance of what is very material for him to know, he will do nothing but from the chapter of accidents." [63] Fortunately, Vaudreuil was also inactive: he was undertaking an extensive refit in Boston.

When Pigot sailed from New York in October for Barbados, he left Hood behind with 12 ships. Because the French and Spanish were thought to be planning an assault on Jamaica,

Hood's assignment was to intercept any squadrons—particularly Vaudreuil's—that might be bound for Cap Français or Havana. At last he was on his own. "If I am so fortunate as to get hold of Vaudreuil," he told Middleton, "I shall be satisfied of having lived to a good purpose." [64]

Hood laid his plans carefully. In December, 1782, he cruised off Hispaniola between Old Cape (Cabo Frances Viejo) and Monte Christi, with his frigates guarding the Bahamas passages. Too late he learned that Vaudreuil had been sighted off Puerto Rico, and Vaudreuil got through the Mona Passage before Hood could work upwind. Thinking that the Frenchman might run along the south coast of Hispaniola and either put into one of its western ports or try for Havana, Hood turned around and hurried downwind along the north coast in hopes of beating him to Cape Tiburon. By then it was February, and Hood had been at sea ten weeks; his water and victuals were running low; after a few days off Cape Tiburon, with no sign of Vaudreuil, he gave up and went to Port Royal. [65]

He could not help thinking that if Pigot had followed his suggestion and cruised off Puerto Rico, Vaudreuil would have been caught. But at the same time his own disappointment at failing to catch the Frenchman had mellowed him, and Hood acknowledged that his chief might have had "substantial reason" for doing what he did. Hood was obviously reflecting on his own conduct as much as Pigot's when he wrote: "When an officer does that which human prudence as well as sound judgment suggests, he ought to submit with becoming fortitude. There is no guarding against misfortune." [66] He did not know until later that he had tried to intercept an antagonist who was more interested in avoiding a fight than in gaining a strategic objective. Vaudreuil, judging his ships in no condition for battle, had gone south to Puerto Cabello. [67]

Although he sensed that peace was near, Hood would not quit. He hurried the refitting of his squadron, and the exhaustion of Port Royal's stores did not stop him: he cannibalized the worst of his ships to refit the rest. Early in March, 1783, he was at sea again. On the 21st he heard that the Spanish fleet had sailed from Havana, and "in high spirits" sought it out, envisioning "a glorious finish to the war." But before the Spanish were sighted the news reached him that the peace preliminaries had been signed.[68] The war was over before Hood could contribute a significant victory of his own.

Hood's reputation was destined to rest mainly upon his performance in the Revolutionary War. Because he had taken part in the great victory of the Saints, he became famous and was showered with honors. Popularity and honors of this sort may be the gift of fortune, but lasting fame must have a more enduring basis. Hood's reputation, in fact, was based upon his proven abilities and attitude toward service rather than his actions in any given battle. Appropriately enough, the Irish peerage he received was given to him not because of his slender role in the battle of the Saints but because of his consistently fine performance. George III insisted that if Rodney was to be rewarded, Hood should not go unnoticed. Some mark of approbation, the king thought, should be given a man who "has for the second time the misfortune of being superseded in the Command of a Fleet with which he has thrice proved victorious." [69]

What abilities had Hood demonstrated? Had he excelled in tactical maneuver? The king's phrase, "thrice proved victorious," obviously exaggerates Hood's achievements; he had little opportunity to show what sort of tactician he was. At the Virginia Capes and the Saints he was second-in-command and by no means in the thick of the fight. Off Martinique in April, 1781, when he had command, he was unable to draw the French into close engagement. Only at St. Kitts did he have the chance to act decisively, and there he moved with boldness and imagination. But aside from this there is little evidence that Hood was a brilliant tactician, unless one relies on the accounts he wrote— after the battles—of what his intentions had been.

As a strategist, however, Hood was unquestionably brilliant. Time and again he grasped the situation, or guessed correctly the enemy's intentions. He realized fully the necessity of concentrating every ship against de Grasse's squadron; of controlling the Chesapeake to protect Cornwallis; and of awaiting French convoys from Europe on the windward side of Martinique. Twice he suggested to Rodney what proved to be the correct procedures for intercepting the Martinique convoys. After the battle of the Saints he urged Rodney to pursue the defeated enemy, but Rodney demurred, arguing that the French had probably reassembled the bulk of their squadron. In fact, the French were scattered. When Hood was finally detached, after five days' delay, to go after them, he learned that a remnant of the French squadron had preceded him through the Mona Passage only the day before; even so he managed to capture four stragglers.[70] Evidence of these strategic insights lies in Hood's dispatches. There is no question of second guessing here. These dispatches contain analyses and plans that were either acted on at the time or urgently pressed on reluctant commanders-in-chief.

Hood's greatness as a strategist stemmed not only from his intelligence, but also from his character. If there was an enemy to defeat, he could think of nothing else, and fretted over every detail and contingency. Recognizing this trait in himself, he accepted it. Some men's minds, he wrote, "are full of anxiety, impatience, and apprehension, while others, under similar circumstances, are perfectly cool, tranquil, and indifferent. Mine is of the former cast." [71] It led him to argue violently with his superiors; he criticized them without reserve, and sometimes attributed their behavior to the worst of motives. When his advice was ignored, he poured his frustrations into letters to his friends. There was nothing furtive about his criticism: his superiors all knew his thoughts because he expressed them; in fact, he set down every important criticism in his official letters to the Admiralty.[72] When his friends advised him to quiet down, he answered that his views were already known throughout the fleet.[73] "My mind often tells me I express my thoughts too freely," he commented, "but I cannot help it." [74] His tactlessness arose not from a backbiting disposition but from intense dedication and a deep sense of responsibility.

Obviously the will to win was deeply ingrained in Hood—yet Britain was losing and all about him he saw officers who did not seem to care. Toward the end of the war he wrote: "If officers cannot be found that will make the glory of their King and country to take place of every other consideration, there is no salvation for us." [75] Hood himself lived by this dictum. He did all he could to prevent prize money from influencing strategic decisions. Believing that politics and commanding a fleet were incompatible professions, he refused to become identified with any faction. In 1782 the ministers in office, without his knowledge, nominated him for Westminster, the seat vacated by Rodney, but some friends withdrew his name. He considered this a "lucky escape," and remarked: "I shall ever . . . steer clear, as far as I am able, of all suspicion of being a party man; for if once I show myself of that frame of mind . . . I must from that moment expect to lose every degree of consideration in the line of my profession. . . . I am vain enough to think that I am in some small degree qualified . . . to fight the battles of my country upon my own element, but acknowledge myself totally unfit to fight the battles of a minister in a house of parliament; and even if I had abilities equal to the task, I think it an employment derogatory to the true character of a sea officer." [76] Hood's attitude was thoroughly professional; in his day it was admired by many, but adopted by few.

In his later years Hood never abandoned his courageous and energetic approach toward the service. He served on the Admiralty Board for seven years. After war broke out in 1793, he was given the Mediterranean command and had the difficult task of supervising the occupation of Toulon. Characteristically, he quarreled in 1795 with the new first lord over the number of ships he was to have, and was ordered to strike his flag; it was the end of his career.[77] With retirement came a viscountcy in 1796. In 1805, at the age of eighty, Hood was seriously considered as a candidate for first lord of the Admiralty in Pitt's last

Ministry.[78] At eighty-five he still rode every day and had "no complaint but deafness." [79] At ninety he was "in good spirits, and full voice." [80] He died January 27, 1816, at ninety-one, and was buried in the old cemetery of Greenwich Hospital.[81]

FOOTNOTES

1. Quoted in Sir John K. Laughton, ed., *From Howard to Nelson: Twelve Sailors* (London, 1899), p. 394.

2. Sir John K. Laughton, ed., *Letters and Papers of Charles, Lord Barham* (Publications of the Navy Records Society, 3 vols., [London, 1907–11]), I, p. 228. Hereafter N.R.S.

3. The article on Hood in the *Dictionary of National Biography* (London, 1891), XXVII, pp. 263–79. Maud Wyndham, *Chronicles of the Eighteenth Century* (London, 1924), II, p. 84. I am grateful to the Rev. E. F. Synge, Vicar of Butleigh, for showing me the old parish rate book that makes James Grenville's standing in the parish clear.

4. On Hood's apprenticeship and relations with Thomas Smith see Wyndham, *Chronicles,* I, pp. 144–49, 166–72; II, pp. 60–65, 84–94, 96. See also Dorothy Hood, *The Admirals Hood* (London, 1942), pp. 11–14; Sir Richard Vesey Hamilton's biography of Hood in Laughton, *From Howard to Nelson,* pp. 361–64; and the articles on Hood and Smith in the *D.N.B.*

5. Wyndham, *Chronicles,* II, pp. 94–101.

6. *Ibid.,* II, p. 102. Thomas Smith, though of illegitimate birth, was fully accepted by his father's family, the Lytteltons; important in their own right, the Lytteltons were also intermarried with the Grenvilles, Temples, Wests, and Pitts.

7. *Ibid.,* II, pp. 102, 108.

8. *Ibid.,* II, pp. 103–06.

9. *D.N.B.,* "Hood"; *The Naval Chronicle,* II (1799), pp. 5–6.

10. Hood, *Admirals Hood,* pp. 24–25, 35–38; William S. Taylor and John H. Pringle, eds., *Correspondence of William Pitt, Earl of Chatham* (London, 1840), IV, pp. 233–36.

11. P.R.O. Adm. 1/483, March 28, November 22, 1768, February 27, June 4, July 10, 1769; Adm. 1/313, November 13, 1782; William J. Smith, ed., *The Grenville Papers* (London, 1852–53), IV, pp. 333–34, 377.

12. P.R.O. Adm. 1/483, May 5, September 17, September 18, 1768, April 8, April 28, 1769, May 27, August 22, November 6, 1770.

13. Hood, *Admirals Hood,* p. 33; P.R.O. Adm. 1/1902, Hood, November 28, 1776; Adm. 1/1903, Hood, February 5, February 22, March 15, July 27, August 10, September 25, December 20, 1777; G. R. Barnes and John H. Owen, eds., *The Private Papers of John, Earl of Sandwich* (N.R.S. [London, 1932–38]), I, pp. 201–05, 219–20, 242–44, 263–64, 334.

14. P.R.O. Adm. 1/1904, Hood, February 12, 1778.

15. *Sandwich Papers,* III, pp. 161–62; Hood, *Admirals Hood,* p. 46. Miss Hood has surmised that Sandwich was interested in putting Hood's professional knowledge and administrative ability to good use, but it is probable that Sandwich was also interested in gaining Hood's allegiance and that Hood was referring to "accommodation" of this sort. Any dockyard commissioner at Portsmouth was bound to have considerable influence in the town, and of course the appointment of Hood meant, in addition, the support of the Linzees for the Admiralty interest.

16. For the distinction between taking civil employment in peacetime and taking it in wartime, see the correspondence of Commissioner Laforey in *Barham Papers,* II, pp. 139–46. Laforey, searching for precedents, claimed that Hood had taken civil employment after the war "had spread to Europe," which, if one reckons from the actual declaration, was incorrect. The first lord of the Admiralty, ignoring the preliminary hostilities, ruled that Hood had taken civil employment in peacetime.

17. Arthur Aspinall, ed., *Correspondence of George, Prince of Wales 1770–1812* (London, 1963–67), I, p. 25.

18. Sir John W. Fortescue, ed., *The Correspondence of King George the Third* (London, 1927–28), IV, pp. 133, 170.

19. *Sandwich Papers,* III, p. 161.

20. See Fortescue, *Correspondence,* V, p. 52.

21. *Sandwich Papers,* III, p. 161.

22. *Ibid.,* III, p. 228; P.R.O. Adm. 1/1898, February 13, September 2, 1764. It is clear that Hood did not consider his physical defects to be as serious as he made them sound in his first letter; in his letter of the 20th he referred to his first letter as a "hasty reply" which he was anxious to revoke.

23. See Thomas Keppel, *The Life of Augustus Viscount Keppel* (London, 1842), II, pp. 112–15, 171–76; Fortescue, *Correspondence,* IV, pp. 225, 255.

24. Countess of Ilchester and Lord Stavordale, eds., *The Life and Letters*

of Lady Sarah Lennox, 1745–1826 (London, 1902), p. 290. This was Lady Lennox's impression; she sympathized with him and thought him an honest man.

25. *Sandwich Papers*, II, p. 199.
26. See Fortescue, *Correspondence*, IV, pp. 283–84; *Sandwich Papers*, II, pp. 193, 216, 274–76; J. H. Broomfield, "The Keppel-Palliser Affair, 1778–1779," *Mariner's Mirror*, XLVII (1961), pp. 202–03; William M. James, *The British Navy in Adversity* (London, 1926), pp. 139–40.
27. *Sandwich Papers*, II, pp. 237–41, 243–45; III, p. 60. Hood, *Admirals Hood*, pp. 48–49, 51, 54.
28. See Godfrey B. Mundy, *The Life and Correspondence of the late Admiral Lord Rodney* (London, 1830), I, p. 403; Alfred T. Mahan, *Major Operations of the Navies in the War of American Independence* (Boston, 1913), pp. 131–37; *Barham Papers*, I, pp. xlvii–xlviii, 53–55, 101–07.
29. David Hannay, ed., *Letters Written by Sir Samuel Hood* (N.R.S. [London, 1895]), p. 97; *Barham Papers*, I, pp. 198, 261.
30. *Ibid.*, I, pp. 157, 163; *Hood Letters*, pp. 18, 107.
31. It is possible that the rather extreme views put forward by David Hannay in his introduction to the *Hood Letters* (pp. x–xv) arose from his having recently completed a biography of Rodney.
32. See *Barham Papers*, I, pp. 62, 65; see also Rodney M. S. Pasley, *Private Sea Journals kept by Admiral Sir Thomas Pasley* (London, 1931), p. 259.
33. Mundy, *Rodney*, II, p. 163.
34. *Hood Letters*, pp. 21–23. Hannay transcribed "Lares" for what appears to be "Lures" in the original manuscript.
35. The letters exchanged by Hood and Rodney on this matter may be found in *Sandwich Papers*, IV, pp. 129, 155–61; *Hood Letters*, p. 15; Mundy, *Rodney*, II, pp. 55–70, 81–88. The fact that Mundy printed Hood's letter of April 1, in which Hood seemed satisfied with the number of ships he had, but not the letter of April 6, in which Hood wished for more, suggests that Mundy's editing may not be entirely trustworthy.
36. *Barham Papers*, I, pp. 109–16; James, *British Navy in Adversity*, pp. 258–61; Charles L. Lewis, *Admiral de Grasse* (Annapolis, 1945), pp. 106–10; Mahan, *Major Operations*, pp. 162–66.
37. *Barham Papers*, I, pp. 117–19; Mundy, *Rodney*, II, pp. 101–03, 120–37; James, *British Navy in Adversity*, pp. 261–62.
38. *Sandwich Papers*, IV, pp. 133–38; Piers Mackesy, *The War for America, 1775–1783* (London, 1964), pp. 418–20.

39. Mundy, *Rodney*, II, pp. 145–49; *Barham Papers*, I, pp. 121–22, 129–30; *Hood Letters*, p. 26.

40. *Sandwich Papers*, IV, pp. 189–91. It may be, as Prof. Charles L. Lewis has suggested (*Admiral de Grasse*, p. 162), that Hood "was exaggerating the possibilities of such an attack," but every account of the battle, including Lewis', indicates that it was probably the best thing to try.

41. *Sandwich Papers*, IV, p. 184. The words are from Graves' own log.

42. There was a third method, involving what was called "lasking." It was really a variation of the attack in column. Each ship, instead of aligning its heading with the line-of-battle axis, steered slightly upwind, thus allowing its broadside to fire with effect while permitting the wind to carry the ship down to closer range. Richard W. Hale, Jr., has suggested that the "lasking" approach was what Graves had in mind ("New Light on the Naval Side of Yorktown," Massachusetts Historical Society, *Proceedings*, LXXI [1959], pp. 124–32), but if it was, his failure to acquaint his subordinates with the manner in which he would signal seems, in view of its unusual nature, incredible.

43. *Sandwich Papers*, IV, pp. 181–91; Harold A. Larrabee, *Decision at the Chesapeake* (New York, 1964), pp. 184–210. How long the signal for maintaining the line continued to fly from the flagship was a disputed point after the battle.

44. French E. Chadwick, editor of the *Graves Papers*, Naval Hist. Soc. (New York, 1916), judged that Hood "did not do his duty," (VIII, p. lxxiii). Julian S. Corbett, in *Signals and Instructions , 1776–1794*, N.R.S. (London, 1908), suggested that if Hood had "acted with one-half of the spirit that Nelson showed at St. Vincent," the outcome would have been very different (p. 56). Admiral Robison (quoted by Larrabee, *Decision*, p. 276) wrote that Hood should have been court-martialed and would have been, like Palliser and Richard Lestock, had he not been a man of influence. This wild charge overlooks *inter alia* the facts that initially Palliser was not court-martialed, and that Lestock was *acquitted* in spite of the fact that Admiral Mathews (Battle of Toulon, 1744) had made clear his intentions by throwing his flagship into close engagement.

45. On this question see Mackesy, *War for America*, pp. 424, 456.

46. When Nelson performed his magnificent independent action at Cape St. Vincent in 1797 his commander-in-chief had already given every indication of throwing caution to the winds.

47. Larrabee, *Decision*, pp. 227–28.

48. *Ibid.*, pp. 211–35; *Sandwich Papers*, IV, pp. 191–93; *Hood Letters*, pp. 36–38.

49. *Sandwich Papers*, IV, pp. 195–204; *Hood Letters*, pp. 39–40, 48–54; *Barham Papers*, I, p. 126; Fortescue, *Correspondence*, V, p. 315.

50. *Barham Papers*, I, p. 143.

51. *Ibid.*, I, p. 147.

52. A full account of the St. Kitts operation may be found in Alfred T. Mahan, *Influence of Sea Power upon History* (New York, 1957), pp. 418–27.

53. See Mackesy, *War for America*, pp. 446–51, 457.

54. *Barham Papers*, I, pp. 149, 151–56; *Sandwich Papers*, IV, pp. 243–49.

55. *Barham Papers*, I, pp. 151–54.

56. Mahan, *Major Operations*, pp. 206–13; *Influence of Sea Power*, p. 433.

57. David Hannay, *Rodney* (London, 1903), p. 205.

58. *Barham Papers*, I, pp. 160–61.

59. *Ibid.*, I, pp. 161–65.

60. *Ibid.*, I, pp. 178, 181, 186–88, 207; *Hood Letters*, pp. 129–34.

61. *Barham Papers*, I, pp. 174–77, 184, 189–90, 194–200.

62. *Hood Letters*, pp. 140, 148; *Barham Papers*, I, pp. 203–05, 219.

63. *Hood Letters*, pp. 138–50; *Barham Papers*, I, p. 205.

64. *Ibid.*, I, pp. 214, 228–29.

65. *Ibid.*, I, pp. 230–49.

66. *Ibid.*, I, p. 247.

67. *Ibid.*, I, pp. 253, 262, 405–06.

68. *Ibid.*, I, pp. 252–55.

69. Fortescue, *Correspondence*, VI, pp. 33–36.

70. *Hood Letters*, pp. 133–34.

71. *Ibid.*, p. 145.

72. Hood's letters to Lord Sandwich (in *Sandwich Papers*) and those among the Admiralty in-letters at the Public Record Office (Adm. 1/313) contain most of the criticisms that are found in his private letters, printed in *Hood Letters* and *Barham Papers*.

73. Fortescue, *Correspondence*, VI, p. 210.

74. *Hood Letters*, pp. 149, 157.

75. *Ibid.*, pp. 142–43.

76. *Barham Papers*, I, pp. 249–50. See also Paget Toynbee, ed., *Letters of Horace Walpole* (Oxford, 1903–05), XII, p. 263. Hood's decision to stand for Westminster in 1784 may seem wholly inconsistent with this. In reality it was only partly so, for in 1782 he had been nominated by "the old gang" of politicians, whereas in 1784 he stood—he thought, and many others with him—as an opponent of

factions and parties and a supporter of the king and the reform ministry of young William Pitt.

77. Laughton, *From Howard to Nelson*, pp. 388–95.
78. *D.N.B.*, "Hood"; Historical Manuscripts Commission, *Fortescue (Dropmore) MSS.*, VII, pp. 256–57.
79. Francis Bickley, ed., *The Diaries of Sylvester Douglas* (London, 1928), II, p. 34.
80. H.M.C., *Fortescue (Dropmore) MSS.*, X, p. 350.
81. Hood, *Admirals Hood*, pp. 227–28.

BIBLIOGRAPHY

Barnes, G. R. and Owen, John H., eds. *The Private Papers of John, Earl of Sandwich, First Lord of the Admiralty, 1771–1782*, 4 vols., Navy Records Society Publications, LXIX, LXXI, LXXV, LXXVIII (London, 1932–38). The most important printed collection of letters concerning the British navy in the American Revolutionary War.

Hannay, David, ed. *Letters Written by Sir Samuel Hood (Viscount Hood) in 1781–2–3*. Navy Records Society Publications (London, 1895). Contains Hood's letters to George Jackson (Brit. Mus. Add. MS. 9343) plus some official letters to the Admiralty. The introduction is unsympathetic to Hood.

Hood, Dorothy. *The Admirals Hood*. London, 1942. This work contains the only reasonably full biography of Hood. Although it provides much information on the man and is a good guide to the important sources, it is not well organized.

James, William M. *The British Navy in Adversity*. London, 1926. A reliable account of the naval operations of the Revolutionary War.

Laughton, Sir John K., ed. *Letters and Papers of Charles, Lord Barham, . . . 1758–1813*. 3 vols., Navy Records Society Publications, XXXII, XXXVIII, XXXIX (London, 1907–11). The first volume contains Hood's letters to Sir Charles Middleton. It supplements the collection edited by Hannay and is, on the whole, more valuable.

Mackesy, Piers. *The War for America, 1775–1783*. Cambridge, Mass., 1964. A first-rate study of the war; strong where James is weakest—on strategic and logistical problems.

Mahan, Alfred T. *The Influence of Sea Power upon History*. New York, 1957 edn. *The Major Operations of the Navies in the War of American Independence*. Boston, 1913. Mahan's insights into strategy and tactics are still valuable. Hood's style and conduct obviously gained Mahan's admiration.

Wyndham, Maud. *Chronicles of the Eighteenth Century, Founded on the Correspondence of Sir Thomas Lyttelton and his Family.* 2 vols. London, 1924. The best printed source for Hood's early career.

A note on manuscripts.

Except for the Bridport Papers in the Additional Manuscripts of the British Museum, there do not seem to be any important unpublished collections of Hood's letters dealing with the American Revolutionary War. His letters to the Admiralty (in the Public Record Office) are, for this period, virtually all printed, though with minor variations, in the volumes mentioned above.

Sir George Rodney:

LUCKY ADMIRAL

CHRISTOPHER LLOYD

Royal Naval College, Greenwich, England

ADMIRAL GEORGE RODNEY was not a popular figure among his fellow officers. During the Revolutionary War many of his subordinates disliked the attempts he made to impose a stricter discipline upon them. Others pointed to his rapacity for prize money, which was dictated by the circumstances of his private life and at times robbed his victories of their full military impact. Some colleagues ascribed his successes to luck rather than ability, and many of his social inferiors rather resented his aristocratic airs. But during the last years of the war the British public accorded Rodney a welcome which was unrivaled until the days of Nelson, when, after a long sequence of defeats and mishaps, he twice returned victorious from the West Indies. He was certainly no ordinary naval officer. Many of his faults were common to others at this time, but the paradoxes of his public career can only be explained in the perspective of his private life and by a consideration of his personal problems. We shall find much to excuse in the man, but also much to admire.

The Royal Navy of his day attracted many officers of high birth, but none who embodied greater pride of ancestry than George Brydges Rodney. His arrogance might repel, but his conduct was sanctioned by custom and justified by his lineage. A Rodney had served as a crusader under Richard I. The Shropshire estates of Stoke Rodney had belonged to his family for six centuries before passing to Sir Thomas Brydges, who married one of the female line. From him they were inherited by James Brydges, Duke of Chandos, one of the wealthiest magnates in eighteenth-century England. It was not until a barony was conferred upon the admiral toward the end of his life, as a reward for his services during the Revolutionary War, that the estates were restored to the Rodney family.

Born on February 19, 1718, Rodney clearly owed much of his early advancement in the navy to family influence and interest. He inherited his first name from the king, who was his godfather, and his second from the Duke of Chandos. At the age of twelve he was sent to sea as a king's letter boy, a mode of entry instituted by Samuel Pepys by which boys entered under royal patronage which assured them a rapid rise in their profession. It is worth noting that Rodney was the last to enter the navy by this means. In later life he took a somewhat regal view of patronage when he made his son a captain at the age of sixteen and created a totally new post for his personal physician by appointing him physician of the fleet.

Rodney himself became a captain at the age of twenty-four and distinguished himself in the War of the Austrian Succession under Hawke and Anson. His part in the victory off Cape Finisterre was so important that Lord Anson, when he presented him at Court, remarked that "Young Rodney has been six years a captain in your Majesty's navy and I most heartily wish your Majesty had one hundred such captains, to the terror of your Majesty's enemies." [1]

At the end of the war, he was a successful and wealthy man and married Jane Compton, niece of the Earl of Northampton. Moreover, he was in high favor with the government of the day, particularly with Lord Sandwich, whose long connection with the Admiralty began at this time, and who thirty years later found in Rodney the man who might have retrieved the fortunes of an administration staggering under the weight of the reverses of the Revolutionary War. A political career was inevitable for a man of Rodney's standing in society. As he once wrote, "A man in our country is nothing without being in Parliament." [2] But that is not to say that he ever evinced any political views beyond a strong sense of loyalty to the king. Like so many placemen (for he always regarded the navy as his chosen profession), he attached himself to whatever patron he felt might further his interests. To such a man, a seat in Parliament was something to be bought or conferred for public services, as indeed a grateful government realized when they had him elected free of charge for the city of Westminster in 1780.

He entered the House of Commons in 1751 as the Admiralty nominee for the borough of Saltash. When he was dropped from the list at the next election, he transferred himself to the Duke of Newcastle, who got him in at Okehampton on the assurance that "a steady aherence to your Grace's commands shall distinguish me while I have a seat in the House." [3] In the end, however, Rodney ruined himself financially by contesting one of the most expensive elections on record. This was at Northampton in 1768. Total expenses are said to have amounted to £160,000, of which Rodney paid £30,000 and his principal supporters had to flee the country to escape their creditors.

Such folly had important consequences on his naval career. His debts, whether due to his political career or to his passion for gambling in the clubs of St. James', became so considerable that he was forced to put financial considerations first in almost everything that he did. On the other hand, he was not swayed by party prejudices which compelled men like Howe and Keppel to resign from the service and which went far to ruin the navy during the Revolutionary War. As he said in 1780, "There were officers of high rank and unquestionable courage who nevertheless bore so inveterate an animosity to the administration then existing, particularly to the First Lord of the Admiralty, the Earl of Sandwich, as almost to wish for defeat if it would produce the dismission of ministers." [4] Rodney was never a man of that stamp and any assessment of his career must take into consideration the violence of party politics, even in the fleet, during his day.

Rodney the naval officer was a very different person from Rodney the political placeman or the man about town. The Seven Years' War gave him the opportunity to rise to the top of his profession. In 1759 he was promoted rear admiral and put in charge of the bombardment of Le Havre. Two years later he was given the command of the Leeward Islands station, the most sought-after of all appointments on account of the opportunities for winning prize money in the West Indies.

His first experience on that station was a happy one because Britain's maritime strategy was to blockade the French and Spanish fleets in their European ports to prevent them from sending reinforcements to their valuable Sugar Islands. Guadeloupe had fallen to British arms by the time Rodney arrived in 1761, so he turned his attention to the conquest of Martinique in an admirably executed amphibious operation. With the subsequent conquests of St. Lucia and Grenada, he swept the board. Unfortunately, all save Grenada were restored to France by the peace treaty. During the Revolutionary War, Rodney found that all these islands had to be retaken, but under much more adverse circumstances. The same was true of the biggest amphibious operation of the war—the capture of Havana by Sir George Pocock—a campaign in which Rodney could not take part because of an attack of malaria, a disease from which he suffered at intervals for the rest of his life.

During the period between the highly successful Seven Years' War and the disasters of the Revolutionary War, Rodney reverted to his old life of man about town. The result was that his debts assumed staggering proportions. His friend, Sir Nathaniel Wraxall, has left a candid picture of him at this time—

> His person was more elegant than seemed to become his rough profession. There was even something that approached to delicacy and effeminacy in his figure: but no man manifested a more temperate and steady courage in action. I had the honour to live in great personal intimacy with him, and have often heard him declare

that superiority to fear was not in him a physical effect of constitution; on the contrary, no man was more sensible by nature to that passion than himself; but that he surmounted it from the considerations of honour and public duty. Like the famous Marshal Villars, he justly incurred the reputation of being *glorieux et bavard;* making himself frequently the theme of his own discourse. He talked much and freely upon every subject; concealed nothing in the course of conversation, regardless of who was present; and dealt his censures, as well as his praises, with imprudent liberality; qualities which necessarily procured him many enemies, particularly in his own profession. Throughout his whole life, two passions, both highly injurious to his repose, women and play, carried him into many excesses.[5]

Little is known about his love affairs, though we do know that both his marriages, first to the niece of Lord Northampton and on her death to Henrietta Clies, the daughter of a rich Lisbon merchant, were entirely happy. The frank and charming letters which he wrote in his sprawling hand to his "dear Henny" prove the depth of his family affections, and are in sharp contrast to the arrogance of the figure he played in public. Unfortunately a collation between the holographs of these letters and the printed version in the family biography shows that many endearing familiarities have been omitted, together with many parts dealing with financial matters.[6]

Rodney had been well rewarded for his services during the Seven Years' War. He had the honor of being appointed governor of Greenwich Hospital, where he took a more serious interest in the welfare of the pensioners than had his predecessors. Another distinction was the command of the Jamaica station when it looked as if war might again break out with Spain. He also held the ceremonial post of rear admiral of England, but because he ran up some debts with the Navy Board was never paid the salary.

The cost of his political career, his passion for gambling, and the dissolution of Parliament which put an end to immunity from his creditors, finally forced him to flee the country.[7] Paris was the asylum for absconding debtors and he was compelled to live there under straitened circumstances. When the American rebellion was under way, it became obvious to him that France would intervene, not so much out of sympathy with the colonists as for the chance of revenge against England. His conclusions on this score were set forth in a letter, *Observations by an Officer on the Armament making at Brest,* written toward the end of 1776, which he sent to Lord Shelburne.[8] From his own experience at Le Havre during the preceding war, he warned of the dangers of a surprise landing at Plymouth, an operation which was actually intended by the French eighteen months later. The Channel fleet was seriously under strength because of the ships deployed to American waters, and he pointed out how easily the British defense force might find itself windbound in an emergency. In his view, the danger was acute because France was already shipping arms to America.

He was anxious, of course, to be employed once more, but he dared not set foot in England. His wife and son were sent over to raise funds and to persuade the government to help him. Among the unpublished Sandwich papers there is a petition from Lady Rodney "humbly to represent to his Lordship the distressful situation of Sir George, herself and four children, who must be in danger of literally starving if his Lordship is not induced to restore him that countenance and friendship with which he has formerly been honoured." Sandwich replied in October, 1776: "If Sir George will consider things impartially, he will see that, though his merit as an officer is undeniable, there are reasons which make it impossible for me to prevail on his Majesty to appoint him to the command of a foreign station. . . . [By his debts] your husband had deprived me of the power of being useful to him." [9] Rodney continued to bombard Sandwich with letters, both on his own account and on behalf of other "hard cases," until in December, 1777, he extracted a vague promise of money; but nothing came of it.

The military situation meanwhile was steadily deteriorating. Rodney heard of American privateers being fitted out at Nantes. He knew also that the French were receiving Franklin as an unofficial ambassador and was among the first to get wind of the secret treaty of alliance between France and America. Help came with his own problem finally from an unexpected and embarrassing quarter. The Marshal de Biron, one of the grand old men of France, told Lady Rodney that his purse was at her disposal. Rodney twice declined the kind offer. But nothing was forthcoming from England, and France was on the verge of declaring war; so Rodney changed his mind in May, 1778. The children were sent home by way of Calais, but he himself chose a more obscure route to avoid any annoyance on the part of his creditors. It is satisfying to learn that he later repaid his debt and to read Biron's acknowledgment: "I was really delighted to have the opportunity to oblige so distinguished a gentleman as you, whose reputation is known throughout Europe." [10] When the storms of revolution broke over France to ruin the Biron family, Parliament recollected its indebtedness and voted an annuity to the marshal's daughter which continued to be paid until her death nearly a hundred years later.

Since all the senior naval commands had been filled on the outbreak of war—many of them with opponents of the North-Sandwich administration in order to satisfy the disaffected—there was no vacancy for Rodney at the time. He was, however, promoted admiral of the white, the highest rank on the active list, and was invited by Sandwich to advise on problems of strategy. As junior admirals continued to make mistakes, Rodney remained waiting in the wings until, by the fall of 1779, his recall became imperative. The accumulation of failures such as the battle of Ushant, d'Orvilliers' appearance in the Channel, as well as the increasing acerbity of the political faction which resulted in the refusal of many naval leaders to serve under the government of the day, compelled Sandwich to recall a man who was now sixty-one years old, in indifferent health and financially embarrassed. It is possible that Germain, a firm admirer of the admiral, may have had a hand in the matter.[11]

In October, 1779, Rodney was appointed once more to command of the Leeward Islands station—now a key position because the French had decided to make the Caribbean the center of their naval operations. The Franco-Spanish grand strategy for the following year was to include the siege of Gibraltar, the maintenance of a token force in America and in the Indian Ocean, and an offensive by the Brest fleet against British possessions in the Caribbean.[12]

The appointment was a gamble for Lord Sandwich, in part because the decision was made in the face of opposition by the West Indian merchants. Rodney encountered considerable slackness in Plymouth; fitting out his ships and the continuance of contrary winds prevented him from sailing until December 29, in spite of Sandwich's urgent demand that he go to sea immediately. He did so as soon as circumstances permitted and one of his last letters forecast his future line of conduct:

> It is astonishing—the neglect and slowness of the officers, both civil and military. The whole town of Plymouth . . . declare that more work has been done here since my arrival than had been for two months before. Such is the effect of fear. They knew there was no trifling with me and my eyes, though myself confined by the gout, were always upon them.[13]

His first duty was to escort the West Indies convoy until it was clear of the danger area, and then to take a number of supply ships to relieve the siege of Gibraltar. Luck was with him. He ran into an enemy convoy on its way to Cadiz and then followed up a report of the presence of the Spanish fleet off Cape St. Vincent. On the evening of January 16, 1780, he surprised Don Juan de Langara, whose fleet was supposed to be guarding the Straits. The ensuing clash, called the "Moonlight Battle," was the only night engagement in the war, and the conditions under which it was fought were such that only a gambler would have taken the risk: a high sea running, the darkness of a winter's night, a lee shore and an admiral who himself was confined to bed by gout.

Despite what Rodney's detractors said later, it was his decision to engage and order a general chase which made the victory possible. Tactics in warfare under sail by this date had become so stereotyped that the leading theoretician, Bigot de Morogues, was of the opinion that decisive sea actions were no longer probable. Rodney, as Hawke had done before him at Quiberon Bay, proved de Morogues wrong. De Langara's lack of reconnaissance resulted in his being overpowered by a superior force under a resolute commander. Five of eleven Spanish ships (including the flagship) surrendered during the course of the night, another blew up, and a seventh was driven ashore. The prizes were incorporated into Rodney's fleet—"as fine ships as ever swam, now completely refitted, manned and put in the line of battle," he reported. Sandwich gleefully reminded him that he had taken more ships than had been captured in any one battle during the Seven Years' War.[14] As if this were not enough, on its way home the squadron under Vice Admiral Digby, which had formed part of the fleet, overtook an outward bound convoy from French ports and took 36 merchantmen.

In his dispatch Rodney paid the conventional tribute to his officers, notably to his flag captain, Walter Young, whom he called "an excellent brave, good officer, enbued with every quality necessary to assist a commander-in chief." [15] He did not know that Young was writing to Sir Charles Middleton (later Lord Barham, but then comptroller of the navy) to claim the credit of the victory, because he urged "the ailing and irresolute admiral to make the signal." [16] That Rodney was aware that all was not well among his subordinates is shown by the covering letter, in which he wrote: "It is with concern that I must tell your Lordship that my brother officers still continue their absurd and illiberal custom of arraigning each other's conduct. My ears have been tempted to listen to their scandal; I have treated it with the contempt it deserved. In my opinion, every officer did his duty to his king and country. I have reported it so." Nevertheless, he continued, "the unhappy difference between Mr. Keppel and Sir Hugh Palliser has almost ruined the navy." [17] This sentiment was repeated in a letter to his wife in which he went even further: "Without a thorough change in naval affairs, the discipline of our marine will be lost. I could say much, but will not. You will hear of it from themselves. I have done them all like honour, but it was because I would not have the world believe that there were officers slack in their duty. Keep this to yourself." [18]

As Rodney continued across the Atlantic with the ships he was taking out to reinforce the fleet in the West Indies, he must have wondered about the state of morale he was to encounter on the other side. He could, however, take comfort that he now enjoyed the confidence of the government, since Sandwich told him, "The worst of my enemies now allow that I have pitched upon a man who knows his duty, and is a brave, honest and able officer." [19]

His arrival at Barbados on March 17 could not have been more opportune. His predecessor, Hyde Parker, who according to Rodney was a dangerous man because of his political bias and professional incompetence, had failed to inform him that the French Admiral de Guichen was daily expected from Brest with 23 sail of the line. Fortunately Rodney had, contrary to orders, retained one of Digby's ships, in addition to his own four prizes, so that the British fleet amounted to 21 of the line. His force, however, was too late to intercept the French, who arrived at St. Lucia on March 20; Rodney reached the same island a week later. The French then took refuge in their base at Port Royal, Martinique, and two of the most able tacticians of the age now faced each other across 45 miles of water.

De Guichen had a slight superiority in numbers and a much greater advantage in the highly trained corps of officers under his command. But he had a number of factors working against him. For one thing, his orders were ambiguous: "to keep the sea as much as the English forces maintained in the Windward Islands might allow him, without too much compromising his own forces." [20] For another, French tactical training encouraged skillful maneuvers aiming at immobilizing rather than destroying the enemy in action; French officers were taught to fire on the up roll in order to damage sails and rigging, and then to bear away before the wind, in contrast to the British tradition of close in-fighting. Rodney, on his part, realized that a knock-out blow could only be delivered when he had maneuvered his fleet into an advantageous position to windward, from which he could concentrate a superior force against part of the enemy's line. Such a maneuver required an efficient signal system and a well-trained body of officers who knew what he intended to do. Neither of these prerequisites was available when he challenged de Guichen off Martinique on April 17, 1780. The result was a classic example of the consequences of bad communications and lack of a common doctrine.

The day before the battle, while both fleets were maneuvering for position, Rodney gave notice that he intended to concentrate all his ships against the enemy's center and rear. When the signal was acknowledged by every captain, Rodney assumed they had understood his instructions. But on the morning of the battle, every captain interpreted the signal "for every ship to bear down and steer for her opposite in the enemy's line, agreeable to the 21st article of the Additional Fighting Instructions" in his own way. Some thought the word "opposite" signified (as Rodney intended) those ships actually opposite them. Others, confused by the ambiguity of the wording of the article, particularly the phrase "the ship which it must be their lot to engage" thought it meant the ship which would be opposite them if the two lines of ships were coterminous. Rodney's own comment, in a note scribbled in the margin of a treatise on naval tactics many years later, was that he had created "an opportunity of bringing the whole British fleet against part of the enemy and had his orders been obeyed, the whole of the enemy's centre and rear divisions had been disabled before their van could have made a motion to assist them. But his rear tacked without his orders and his van disobeyed and stood to windward of the enemy's van at a distance and scarce within random shot." [21]

While the admiral slowly turned his flagship towards the enemy, he saw Captain Carkett in the leading ship racing ahead to place himself opposite the French leader; Captain Bateman was doing nothing at all; and only three ships of Hyde Parker's squadron in the van were carrying out his plan. "Courage, mon général!" shouted someone on de Guichen's quarterdeck. "The English desert their commander!" Fortunately Rodney's defensive-minded opponent preferred to break off the action by bearing before the wind.

Rodney's fury at missing such a fine opportunity was expressed in such violent language that the Admiralty suppressed his most outspoken comments: "It is with concern inexpressible, mixed with indignation, that the duty I owe to my sovereign and my country obliges me to acquaint your Lordships that during the action the British flag was not properly supported." He wanted Bateman court-martialed and Hyde Parker recalled. On his own account he wrote blistering letters to Admiral Rowley and Captain Carkett, informing them that all he required was obedience to his orders: "the painful task of thinking belongs to me." [22]

During the next few weeks, he did his best to discipline his officers. "My eye on them," Rodney told his wife, "had more dread than the enemy's fire and they knew it would be fatal; no regard was paid to rank; admirals as well as captains, if out of their station, were instantly reprimanded by signals or messages sent by frigate—in spite of themselves I learnt them to be what they had never been before, *officers*." [23] By keeping his force constantly at sea, he drilled his men until the advent of the hurricane season made it advisable for both fleets to vacate the Caribbean. De Guichen returned to Europe instead of moving up to the American coast, as Washington had hoped. In case he had gone there, Rodney decided to sail to New York to deal with him and, if he was not there, to suppress the "piratical rebels" as he called the privateers who endangered communications along the Atlantic seaboard.

Rodney's fleet left the West Indies in a comparatively satisfactory state of health, which in those days was nothing short of a miracle. The station had an evil reputation in that era. If ships were kept at sea for any length of time, scurvy developed; if they stayed in port there was the ever-present danger of yellow fever. During his stay there was fortunately no yellow-fever epidemic as had decimated so many fleets there in the past. But the chief reason for the improved standard of health was the energy of Rodney's personal physician, Gilbert Blane, whom he had appointed to a new post of physician of the fleet without warrant from the Navy Board. This typical example of favoritism had beneficial consequences. Upon his arrival Blane discovered that the annual death rate was 1 in 7, not from combat injuries but from avoidable causes—lack of hospital accommodations, shortage of medical supplies, poor ventilation in ships and too easy an access to fiery Jamaican rum; drunken sailors lay about the streets being bitten by mosquitoes. Of course it was not yet known that these insects were the carriers of the disease, but Blane's insistence, with Rodney's support, on better hygiene saved many lives.

Blane began printing medical instructions for the use of officers, based upon the writings of Dr. James Lind, father of nautical medicine, and the more recent experiences of Captain James Cook.[24] These he distributed, with Rodney's approval, throughout the fleet. Blane pointed out that "though the most laudable pains" were taken to husband and preserve from decay all manner of stores, such as ropes, blocks, spars, gunpowder and arms, little effort had been made to preserve the most valuable commodity of all—the health of the seamen. As a result of such measures, the mortality rate was reduced during the two years of Rodney's command from 1 in 7 to 1 in 29, and when the supreme test of his fleet came on April 12, 1782, "there was less sickness in this month than any of the former 23 months in which I kept a record." [25]

It was normal practice for the big British fleets to clear the Caribbean waters during the hurricane season. Rodney took his fleet to Sandy Hook, where he was welcomed by Sir Henry Clinton, the commander-in-chief of the army. Rodney always got on well with soldiers and had considerable experience in collaborating with them in amphibious operations. Such was not the case with Vice Admiral Arbuthnot, the naval commander in the area, who was junior in rank to Rodney. Arbuthnot and Clinton were on bad terms and the former resented Rodney's incursion into what he regarded as his preserve. In particular he distrusted Rodney's threat to potential prize money. Whether it was Arbuthnot's avarice, as the king thought, or Rodney's, one cannot say; but in the course of a bitter exchange of letters Arbuthnot told his senior in rank that "your partial interference in the conduct of the American war is certainly incompatible with principle of reason and precedents of service." [26]

Rodney's reply was astonishingly moderate in tone. He pointed out that he was the senior officer present and that Arbuthnot's own sphere of operations around Rhode Island remained untouched; but that since no attempt had been made to suppress the privateers to the southward, he would employ all available frigates to clear the seas between New York and the Chesapeake. "I came, indeed, so far to intervene in the American war as to command by sea in it and to do my best endeavours to put an end thereto." [27] In his view, the seas were one and the war must be viewed as a whole, now that France and Spain were engaged. He was bound to come north at this time of year, though he had no specific orders to do so, and he had expected to find de Guichen in the area. In those days commanders-in-chief on foreign stations were given far more independence of action than they are today, and their responsibility was therefore greater. Sandwich agreed with Rodney: "Unless our commanders-in-chief take the great line as you do, and consider the king's whole dominion as under their care, our enemies must find us unprepared somewhere and carry their point against us." [28]

Rodney proceeded to clear the lines of communication southward, so that Clinton was able to send General Leslie's small expedition to Virginia.[29] It is conceivable that the larger plans discussed between the two men might have changed the course of the war. Had a man of Rodney's caliber and grasp of strategic essentials remained on the coast for a longer period, the use of sea power in providing mobility for a striking force might have been more apparent. But such plans never achieved definite shape and Rodney returned south with a warning to Sandwich of the inertia which characterized the war on the American mainland:

> I must freely confess that there appears to me a slackness inconceivable in every branch of it, and that briskness and activity which is so necessary, and ought to animate the whole, to bring it to a speedy conclusion, has entirely forsaken it. It is now turned to a war of posts; and unhappily for England, when they have taken posts of infinite advantage and which, if maintained, would have brought the rebels to reason, they have unaccountably evacuated them; the evacuating Rhode Island was the most fatal measure that could possibly be adopted.[30]

The absence of the bigger ships from the Caribbean between August and December was justified, if for no other reason than the fact that they escaped the worst hurricane of the century. Rodney found the bases at Barbados and St. Lucia devastated and most of the ships which he had left behind him so crippled as to be unseaworthy. His impressive fleet of 23 ships had been thereby reduced to 9, and they were without stores. Everything depended on the arrival of a new second-in-command with a convoy from home before the French fleet made its annual appearance in those seas.

Sandwich found some difficulty in replacing "Vinegar" Parker because, as he complained, so many senior officers were "unfit by their factious connections, others from inferiority or insufficiency." [31] After juggling with the list of sea officers, he chose Sir Samuel Hood, whom Rodney welcomed as an old friend and about whom he invariably spoke in terms of the highest personal and professional approval. But Hood did not return the compliment. As soon as he arrived with the much desired convoy in January, 1781, Hood wrote private letters highly critical of his chief to his superiors in England. It is not easy to explain why Hood took up this attitude so soon after his arrival. Perhaps Rodney's run of luck had gone to his head and his aristocratic arrogance was affecting the morale of his subordinates and the fleet. At any rate, Hood and Young complained of Rodney's irresolution and frequent changes of plan. In a situation where plans had to be altered with each rumor of an invasion, however, this might equally have been called flexibility. However, there seems no doubt that his ill-health made his manner more abrupt than before, even if there is a distinct flavor of jealousy in the letters of his critics.

The turning point in Rodney's career came with the capture of the Dutch island of St. Eustatius. Although the island was supposedly neutral, it had for long been the entrepôt through which essential supplies had passed to the enemy. The Americans used it as a privateering base and obtained most of their gunpowder there in the early years of the war. The French and Spanish fleets had been supplied from it. Holland had given Britain every reason to attack the island and when the government decided to declare war Rodney and General Vaughan moved swiftly. Orders to capture St. Eustatius were dated December 20 and by February 3, 1781, the island was in British hands.[32]

Rodney was astonished at the immense amount of booty. The waterfront was lined with warehouses and the beach littered with hogsheads of sugar and tobacco. In the harbor were 130 merchant vessels, some 50 of them American, five of which were privateers. A convoy of 30 merchantmen which had just sailed for Europe with a Dutch warship as escort was overtaken and the Dutch admiral killed. There were even twelve British vessels which had come out under Hood's protection. It was these traitors who aroused Rodney's anger most: "I have seized all their effects, most of which are calculated to enable the public enemy to continue the ruinous war."[33] A hitherto unpublished letter expresses both his anger and pleasure with the prizes taken which he estimated at £3,000,000:[34]

What terms did perjury, treason, rebels and traitors deserve? None, and none they had. France as well as America feels the blow through their vitals. . . . Since we took the island, it has proved a trap for the Americans; no less than fifty have been taken with tobacco, and every night, though the island has been in our possession two months, they still arrive. We have taken at least £200,000 sterling from them; and I will tell you a secret: they shall cross the Atlantic for Europe. Remember their breach of the Treaty of Saratoga.

Rodney's actions were highly imprudent and on dubious legal grounds in some cases. It was pointed out to him that crews of unarmed vessels ought to be released and that an act of Parliament had legalized trade with the Dutch. For years to come, British West Indian merchants, who had opposed him from the start, plagued him with insurance claims and expensive lawsuits. He and Vaughan had seized everything in the king's name, though they were well aware that a princely share would be handed back to them in the form of prize money. As he wrote his wife, in a sentence typically deleted from the family biography, "If the capture is given to the Army and Navy, every man will make his fortune." [35]

Hood's absence from the scene prevented him from sharing in the plunder and his howl of protest was among the first of many: "They will find it very difficult to convince the world that they have not proved themselves wickedly rapacious." [36] The tale was naturally taken up by the Opposition at home. Nearly a year later, when Rodney was home on sick leave, Edmund Burke moved to appoint a committee to inquire into the affair. Burke was an interested party because of his connection with West Indian property, but to do him justice, Burke declared after the battle of the Saints, that if Rodney had a bald patch on his head he would willingly crown it with laurel.[37] When he moved his motion on December 4, 1781, he had strong political support. His charges are so similar to those advanced in Hood's letters that it may be suggested that Sir Charles Middleton, comptroller of the Navy Board, furnished Burke with some of the material. Rodney defended himself from his seat in the Commons and published the official correspondence to clear his

name and Burke's motion was lost. But the irony of the whole
story is that Rodney never benefited from this grand opportunity to retrieve his fortunes: most of the ships carrying the loot
back to England were captured by the enemy on the high seas.[38]

The public attack on Rodney's professional reputation depended on three complaints originally made by Hood. First,
that he was so busy plundering St. Eustatius that Hood's expedition to Curaçao was canceled. Rodney's reply to this charge was
that rumors of de Grasse's impending arrival compelled him
to keep his ships together. Second, that Tobago was lost because
Rodney failed to defend it. The admiral's answer was that he
was engaged in protecting a much more important base at Barbados and that he had given the inhabitants of Tobago ample
means of defending themselves. The same story was to be repeated when the French recaptured St. Eustatius and it probably
would have occurred at Jamaica, had that island been attacked.
The inhabitants neglected to take proper measures for their defense and Rodney complained that the planters did not seem to
realize there was a war on.

The third complaint by Hood was that he was given an insufficient force and the wrong orders to intercept de Grasse's
arrival at Martinique in the spring of 1781. In Rodney's view,
the 18 ships of the line which he had allocated for the task were
sufficient, as long as Port Royal was closely blockaded, as he
insisted more than once. Rodney never blamed Hood for finding
himself too far to leeward when the French arrived with 20
ships and compelled him to withdraw to St. Lucia. Whether
Hood could have persisted in a close blockade is doubtful. Hood
may well have been right in saying that he should have been
ordered to cruise to windward of the island, not to leeward. All
that is clear was that the first opportunity to defeat the French
was lost.

Rodney hastened to join forces as soon as he heard that De
Grasse had arrived, but neither admiral was anxious to join battle.
At one point the enemy were caught on a lee shore, but Rodney
refrained from attacking because of navigational hazards. As
the months passed, it became clear that de Grasse intended to

move north. Rodney decided to take advantage of the sick leave promised him earlier in the year to return home. Blane had assured him that neither his gout nor the painful stricture from which he was suffering could be cured at sea. Leaving his fleet in Hood's hands, Rodney sailed for home in August with these words: "I am so tired that I have desired leave to go home with the convoy." [39]

Before he departed, Rodney disposed of his forces in such a way as he thought would counter any moves on the part of the enemy. His orders to Hood of July 25 indicate his grasp of the situation. Hood was to take 14 of the line and 7 frigates north to counteract an anticipated junction between the French, now off Haiti, with those at Rhode Island. He also sent two warnings to Graves (neither of which reached that admiral in time) that de Grasse might be coming north and that Rodney himself or his deputy "would endeavour to make the capes of the Chesapeake, then those of Delaware, and so to Sandy Hook." Thus, he assured Germain, the combined British forces "will be superior on the coast and prevent the enemy's designs, provided the officers who command will do their duty." [40]

Rodney's assumption in making these arrangements was that de Grasse would leave part of his fleet behind him in the Caribbean. He assumed also that Sir Peter Parker would send four ships from the Jamaican station, as he had been asked to do. Events proved him wrong. But the fleet of 19 ships of the line which encountered de Grasse's 24 should have proved a match for the enemy when they met in the Chesapeake had they been properly fought. Even if Rodney had sent two of the three ships of the line which he took home with him on escort duty, it is doubtful that their presence would have made any difference to the tactical handling of the battle.

On his way north, Hood missed de Grasse off the Chesapeake by the narrow margin of five days. Having joined Graves, their combined fleets sailed south again for the disastrous battle of the Virginia Capes. Even Hood declared that Rodney would have done better than Graves on that fateful day which sealed the doom of Cornwallis' army at Yorktown.

News of the disaster reached Rodney at Bath, where he was recuperating from an operation for bladder trouble. Once more Sandwich turned to him as his only hope: "The fate of this empire is in your hands." The old and ailing admiral responded to an appeal to go to sea again directly, though his gout was so bad that he could not write a letter and, according to his doctor, "debility and unequal spirits rendered him less equal to the fatiguing and anxious duties inseparable from such high responsibility." [41] Just as he sailed he was heartened by the news of Kempenfelt's success off Brest in destroying de Grasse's reinforcements on their way west, which enabled him to take a strong force of 15 ships across the Atlantic. [42]

By the time Rodney rejoined Hood at Antigua in February, 1782, the situation had deteriorated to a point where it looked as if the West Indies would go the same way as the American colonies. In his absence St. Kitts, Nevis, Montserrat, Demerara, and St. Eustatius had been taken by the French. Jamaica was being threatened by the Spanish from the north. Only a decisive fleet action could save the island and restore Britain's bargaining position in the peace negotiations about to begin in Paris. Fortunately Rodney was in a position to strike such a blow: he had a slight superiority in numbers, many copper-bottomed ships straight out from England, and healthy crews and better gunnery, thanks to the efforts of Sir Charles Douglas, the captain of the fleet.

The two fleets which confronted each other in the Caribbean were the largest ever seen in those waters. Rodney had 36 of the line, de Grasse 33, the French having recently been reinforced by a convoy as a result of a faulty disposition of his forces by Rodney. "Nothing short of a miracle can now retrieve the king's affairs in this country," wrote Hood. [43] That miracle was to occur at the battle of the Saints on April 12, 1782.

De Grasse sailed from Martinique on April 9 with a large convoy of transports and troops to join the Spanish fleet off Cuba for the conquest of Jamaica. Encumbered by his convoy, the French admiral failed to attack when he had an opportunity to cut off Hood in the van. Though some of his ships were disabled de Grasse succeeded in detaching his convoy in safety. Then, on April 11, the accidental collision of two French ships gave Rodney his chance. De Grasse made the mistake of altering course to save the damaged *Zélé* from falling into enemy hands. "I give you joy, Sir George," said Douglas as the morning of April 12th dawned. "Providence has given you your enemy broad on the lee bow." The French could be seen in disorder south of the island of Dominica and east of a group of rocks called Les Saintes.[44]

Two tactical points about the action which followed aroused controversy for years to come. The first was the extent to which Rodney was personally responsible for the innovation of breaking the enemy line—a maneuver which by Nelson's time became the formula for victory. If Rodney's reactions were slower on that day than those of his fleet captain Douglas, it should be kept in mind that he was a sick man who had not slept for four nights while chasing the French fleet. What happened was that the French line was so close-hauled that the third and fourth ships astern of the flagship *Ville de Paris*, which had been badly damaged at the first encounter with the British fleet, were taken aback when the wind veered four points to the south. A fatal gap appeared in the French line. Douglas was the first to notice it as he peered through the smoke. He sent to fetch the admiral, whom he congratulated upon a victory. "The day is not half won yet," replied Rodney. "Break the line, Sir George, the day is your own and I will insure you victory!" "No," said the admiral, "I will not break my line." Or did he say "any line"? As the argument developed, Rodney seems to have realized what Douglas meant. "Well, well—do as you like," he told Douglas. Similar permission was granted to Commodore Affleck aboard the *Bedford* to pass through a second gap which had appeared in the enemy's line.[45]

The second controversial point arose from Hood's charge that Rodney failed to follow up his victory immediately and lost a golden opportunity to deliver an even greater blow against the enemy. Hood, whose squadron in the rear had not been badly damaged, was eager to go after the greater part of the French fleet which had escaped. Rodney refused to order pursuit and made the signal to lie to during the night. Hood claimed that, had he been in command, twenty of the enemy's ships would have been taken, not just five. This comment was from the man to whom Rodney wrote on the evening of the battle: "Many thanks, my dear friend, for your kind congratulations; 'tis with sincerest truth that I must with great justice acknowledge that I am indebted to your very gallant behaviour that we have been so successful." [46]

Next morning, when Hood came aboard the flagship, he vehemently demanded that the chase be continued; but it was not until four days later that Rodney gave him permission. Hood then succeeded in capturing three more French ships, but the main body had passed through Mona Passage to safety twenty-four hours earlier. Rodney later made some notes to justify himself on this score.[47] He claimed that he did not pursue immediately because having himself experienced a night action he realized the danger of friendly ships firing into one another by mistake in the dark. Moreover, some 26 enemy vessels had escaped and he was anxious to keep his damaged fleet together to counter any possible French threat. As he noted in his first dispatch "both fleets have greatly suffered." In a later dispatch, he added that his fleet was becalmed for three days after the action, but the moment a breeze sprang up Hood's division was sent away.[48] If we accept his statement, and not Hood's, he seems to have had substantial reasons for delay.

"You may now despise all your enemies," he wrote to Sandwich. "The French have been given such a blow as they will not recover." [49] Certainly Jamaica was saved and the enemy never again attempted to dispute British superiority at sea in the war. But victory came too late to save either Sandwich or Rodney, or, of course, the situation in America. North's government fell on March 20, 1782. One of the first actions of the new administration was to dismiss Rodney. When the news of victory arrived in May, Keppel, first lord of the Admiralty, sent a messenger down to Plymouth to try to stop Admiral Sir Hugh Pigot from sailing to replace Rodney, but the message arrived too late. The first Rodney knew of these events was when he received orders on July 10 to strike his flag and return home.[50]

There, to the embarrassment of the Ministry, he received a hero's welcome. "Only the enthusiasm roused by Nelson at the Nile exceeded it," says Wraxall, who witnessed both celebrations. Rodney's victory "constituted a sort of compensation to Great Britain for so many years of disgrace, for so great an expenditure of blood and treasure and even for the loss of America itself. The country, exhausted and humiliated, seemed to revive in its own estimation, and to resume once more its dignity among nations." [51] The victorious admiral was given the barony of Stoke Rodney, the property of his ancestors, and a pension of £2000 a year. Only the West Indian merchants continued to plague him with their claims until the day of his death on May 23, 1792.

Rodney's victory in the battle of the Saints had a profound impact on the outcome of the peace negotiations of the Revolutionary War. Shelburne had already begun talks with the French two days after the battle was fought. When the news of victory arrived on May 18, Oswald, the British representative in Paris, was able to persuade Franklin to negotiate separate terms for the United States. Having failed to capture Gibraltar, Spain was equally anxious for peace. Vergennes, with the defeat of the main French fleet, and with bankruptcy staring the nation in the face, was forced to reconsider the Carthaginian terms which he had intended to force Britain to accept in Canada, India, and the West Indies. Besides Rodney's victory, Shelburne was able also to point to Howe's relief of Gibraltar and Hughes' stubborn resistance to Suffren in the Bay of Bengal. He could safely strike the attitude which he expressed: "It is enough to lose one world; it is not necessary to lose a second." [52] On the firm position guaranteed him by his admirals, Shelburne was able to conclude a satisfactory draft of the Treaty of Paris in January, 1783.

"Sea officers in general are apt to be censorious," Rodney told the head of the Admiralty in his old age. "It is their misfortune to know little of the world, and to be bred in seaport towns, where they keep company with few but themselves. This makes them so violent in party, so partial to those who have sailed with them, and so grossly unjust to others. Do them justice, and make them do their duty." [53] The tone of his remark is typically detached. It was this aristocratic hauteur which made him unpopular with so many of his colleagues. His philosophy of command expressed in the last sentence caused the inefficient to fear and dislike him. Whatever his defects of character—and there admittedly were many—Rodney became an outstanding commander-in-chief. He saw the war as a whole, imposed order on his fleet, and proved to be a fine tactician. He was not blinded by party passion. He won the admiration of his countrymen by his victories. He may have been a lucky admiral, but he earned much of the good fortune which attended him at the end of his long career at sea.

FOOTNOTES

1. Donald Macintyre, *Admiral Rodney* (New York, 1962), p. 29.
2. Godfrey B. Mundy, *Life and Correspondence of Lord Rodney* (2 vols. London, 1830), I, p. 298.
3. Lewis B. Namier, *Structure of Politics at the Accession of George III* (New York, 1957), pp. 307, 314, 339.
4. Nathaniel W. Wraxall, *Historical Memoirs of My Own Time* (London, 1904), p. 464.
5. *Ibid.*, p. 190.
6. A comparison between holographs of the letters and the printed version in the family biography shows that many of the endearing familiarities were omitted. For example, Mundy, who prints most of the letters now in the British Museum (Add. Mss. 39, 779), omits this sentence written after the victory in February, 1780: "If, my dear, they think me worthy of reward, I hope it will not

be the empty one of honours, but the more substantial provision for myself and family."

7. Piers Mackesy, *The War for America, 1775–1783* (Cambridge, Mass., 1964), p. 319.

8. William B. Willcox, "Admiral Rodney Warns of Invasion, 1776–1777," *American Neptune*, IV, p. 194.

9. G. R. Barnes and J. H. Owen, eds., *The Private Papers of John, Earl of Sandwich, First Lord of the Admiralty* (4 vols., [London] 1932–38; Navy Records Society Publications, LXIX, LXXI, LXXV, LXXVIII), III, p. 155; and unpublished transcripts in National Maritime Museum, Greenwich, England.

10. Rodney Papers, G.D. 30/20/6, Public Record Office.

11. Mackesy, *op. cit.*, p. 320.

12. William L. Clowes, ed., *The Royal Navy: A History from the Earliest Times to the Present* (7 vols., London, 1897–1903), III, pp. 447–48.

13. Mundy, *op. cit.*, I, p. 215.

14. Barnes and Owen, *op. cit.*, III, p. 199.

15. *Ibid.*, p. 195.

16. John K. Laughton, ed., *Letters and Papers of Charles, Lord Barham* (3 vols., [London] 1904–11; Navy Records Society Publications XXXIII, XXXVIII, XXIX), I, p. 65.

17. Barnes and Owen, *op. cit.*, III, p. 201.

18. Mundy, *op. cit.*, I, p. 229.

19. Barnes and Owen, *op. cit.*, III, p. 206.

20. Edouard Chevalier, *Histoire de la Marine Française pendant la guerre de l'independence Américaine* (Paris, 1877), p. 185.

21. Note to John Clerk's "Essay on Naval Tactics," in appendix to Howard Douglas *Naval Evolutions* (London, 1832).

22. Barnes and Owen, *op. cit.*, III, pp. 217, 233.

23. Rodney Mss., Add. Mss., 39, 779, British Museum.

24. Gilbert Blane, *A Short Account of the Most Effectual Means of Preserving the Health of Seamen, particularly in the Royal Navy* (London? 1781?). This pamphlet was expanded with a medical history of Rodney's fleet in Blane's *Observations on the Diseases Incident to Seamen* (London, 1785).

25. Gilbert Blane, *Observations on the Diseases Incident to Seamen* (London, 1785), p. 88.

26. Barnes and Owen, *op. cit.*, III, pp. 259 and 264; Laughton, *op. cit.*, I, p. 80.

27. Dorothy C. Barck, ed., *Letter-Books and Order-Book of Admiral*

Lord Rodney 1780–1782, New York Historical Society, *Collections,* (1932), pp. 43 and 59; Mundy, *op. cit.,* I, p. 392.

28. Mundy, *op. cit.,* I, p. 402; Barnes and Owen, *op. cit.,* III, p. 231; Mackesy, *op. cit.,* p. 352 criticizes Rodney as having "no good reason for staying" in the north and merely plundering Arbuthnot's supplies.
29. William B. Willcox, "Rhode Island in British Strategy, 1780–1781," *Journal of Modern History,* XVII (December, 1945) describes the discussions with Clinton. See also Barck, *op. cit.,* p. 25.
30. Barnes and Owen, *op. cit.,* III, p. 262.
31. *Ibid.,* p. 232.
32. *Ibid.,* IV, p. 128.
33. Quoted in Macintyre, *op. cit.,* p. 163.
34. From the Clinton Papers, in the Clements Library, Ann Arbor, Michigan.
35. Rodney Mss., Add. Mss. 39, 779, British Museum.
36. David Hannay, ed., *Letters Written by Sir Samuel Hood* ([London, 1895], Naval Records Society Publications) III, p. 18.
37. Philip M. Magnus, *Edmund Burke: A Life* (London, 1939), p. 113.
38. *The Parliamentary Register* (London, 1782), V, p. 92; Barnes and Owen, *op. cit.,* IV, p. 158.
39. Macintyre, *op. cit.,* p. 171.
40. Mackesy, *op. cit.,* p. 420; Mundy, *op. cit.,* II, p. 148. For a criticism of Rodney's dispositions, see William B. Willcox, "The British Road to Yorktown: A Study of Divided Command," *American Historical Review,* LII, (October, 1946), p. 22.
41. Blane quoted in Douglas, *op. cit.,* appendix XIV.
42. For Rodney's fleet, see Mackesy, *op. cit.,* pp. 453, 457.
43. Hannay, *op. cit.,* p. 98.
44. The earliest English plans call them The Saints, but the French spelling persists in the naming of British warships. Rodney called the battle that of April 12th, while the French refer to it as the battle of Dominique.
45. Narrative of Sir Charles Dashwood, Rodney's aide-de-camp. This narrative was printed by Howard Douglas in his *Naval Evolutions,* which also prints the evidence of Sir Gilbert Blane, who first published an account of what passed at breakfast that morning in his *Select Dissertations on Several Subjects of Medical Science* (London, 1822). In the 1804, or third edition, of his *Essay on Naval Tactics* (Edinburgh, 1804), John Clerk of Eldin claimed to have inspired Rodney's tactics, since he suggested the maneuver of breaking the line in the first edition of his book which was privately

printed in 1782. There is no evidence that Rodney ever saw this
edition, but he owned and annotated the second edition of 1790;
however, it is only in the third edition of 1804 that Clerk claims
credit for the battle of the Saints. Douglas was at pains to rebut
this claim. See also Wraxall, *op. cit.*, p. 466.

46. Laughton, *op. cit.*, I, pp. 159, 163, 179; Barnes and Owen, *op. cit.*,
 IV, p. 261; Hannay, *op. cit.*, pp. 104, 112; and Douglas, *op. cit.*,
 p. 95.
47. Mundy, *op. cit.*, II, p. 248.
48. Barck, *op. cit.*, pp. 358, 366.
49. Barnes and Owen, *op. cit.*, IV, p. 257.
50. Barck, *op. cit.*, p. 488.
51. Wraxall, *op. cit.*, pp. 462, 470.
52. Vincent T. Harlow, *The Founding of the Second British Empire,
 1763–1793* (London, 1952), pp. 256, 281, 312.
53. Mundy, *op. cit.*, II, p. 358.

BIBLIOGRAPHY

Barck, Dorothy C., ed. *Letter-Books and Order-Book of Admiral Lord
 Rodney, 1780–1782.* New York Historical Society, *Collections*, LXV
 and LXVI. 2 vols. New York, 1932–33. Contains a wealth of information.
Hannay, David. *Rodney.* London and New York, 1891. A very brief
 biography.
Macintyre, Donald. *Admiral Rodney.* London, 1962. The most recent
 Rodney biography, but undistinguished.
Mackesy, Piers. *The War for America, 1775–1783.* Cambridge, Mass.,
 1964. Quite critical of Rodney and considers his victory at the Saints
 in 1782 more a matter of luck than skill. To Mackesy Rodney was
 a competent but standard eighteenth-century admiral.
Mundy, Godfrey B. *The Life and Correspondence of the Late Admiral
 Lord Rodney.* 2 vols. London, 1830. This typical nineteenth-century
 biography of Rodney by his son-in-law is both uncritical and incomplete.
[Rodney, George Brydges]. London, 1789. *Letters from Sir George
 Brydges Now Lord Rodney to His Majesty's Ministers . . . Together
 with a Continuation of His Lordship's Correspondence with the
 Governors and Admirals in the West Indies and America, during the
 Year 1781, until the Time of His Leaving the Command and Sailing
 for England.* A valuable collection of letters whose major purpose was

to vindicate Rodney and to defend him against the charges of British merchants whose goods had been confiscated at St. Eustatius.

White, Thomas. *Naval Researches; or a Candid Inquiry into the Conduct of Admirals Byron, Graves, Hood and Rodney in the Actions off Grenada, Chesapeake, St. Christopher's, and of the Ninth and Twelfth of April, 1782.* London, 1830. Still a very useful account.

Willcox, William B. "The British Road to Yorktown: A Study of Divided Command," *American Historical Review,* LII (October, 1946), pp. 1–35. Is critical of Rodney's disposition of British naval forces in the West Indies and North American waters prior to Yorktown.

INDEX

A Note About the Author

George Athan Billias was born in Lynn, Massachusetts in 1919. After attending Bates College, he received his M.A. and Ph.D. from Columbia University. He was the recipient of a Guggenheim Fellowship in 1961, and an American Council of Learned Societies post-doctoral fellowship in 1968. Professor Billias' previous books as author and editor are *George Washington's Generals, General John Glover and His Marblehead Mariners, Massachusetts Land Bankers of 1740, Law and Authority in Colonial America, The American Revolution: How Revolutionary Was It?*, and *Interpretations of American History*, Volumes I and II (co-editor). Professor Billias directs Clark University's doctoral program in America colonial history. He lives in Worcester, Massachusetts, with his wife and three children.